POPULISM AND COURTS IN AN AGE OF CONSTITUTIONAL IMPATIENCE

This book addresses one of the most pressing issues of our time: the rise of populism and its implications, particularly for courts and other legal institutions. It questions and ultimately challenges the prevailing view in comparative constitutional law that courts can act as bulwarks against authoritarian, self-aggrandising populists in power. In doing so, it offers both a novel theoretical framework and a fresh contextual inquiry.

Theoretically, the book uses the lens of spatiotemporality – the conjunction of space and time – to analyse populism as a constitutional project. It argues that contemporary populism is marked by *constitutional impatience*: a drive for temporal efficiency and spatial proximity that reshapes and reconfigures law's institutional and normative order.

Contextually, the book focuses primarily on one key institution of liberal constitutional democracy: the judiciary. It offers a contextual analysis of three case studies: Armenia, Ecuador and the United Kingdom. In doing so, it not only highlights populism's reach beyond established democracies but also brings fresh insights from understudied jurisdictions at the periphery or in the Global South.

Overall, the book suggests that populism's relationship with constitutionalism is complex and context-dependent. Instead of yielding uniform outcomes, it produces divergent tensions and impacts, thereby challenging assumptions about both the institutional role of courts and the nature of constitutionalism itself.

Hart Studies in Constitutional Theory: Volume 11

Hart Studies in Constitutional Theory

Series Editors
Charles Barzun, University of Virginia, USA
Maartje De Visser, Singapore Management University
Matthias Klatt, University of Graz, Austria

Authors writing for this series cover a wide range of perspectives, methods, and regions, to enhance our understanding of constitutions as central institutions of modern public life. Taken together, the books in this series aim to challenge established wisdom and advance original ideas.

This series is a natural home for books interrogating the concepts and structures of constitutions on the national, the supranational and the international level. Its guiding philosophy is that the task of constitutional theory is not only to delineate the basic structures of government and to protect human rights, but also more broadly to offer methods for grappling with the social, political, and economic problems societies face today.

The series is open to theoretical, normative, analytical, empirical and comparative approaches, stemming from legal studies as well as from political philosophy and political science. In its ambition to become a global forum for debate about constitutional theory, the series editors welcome submissions for monographs as well as edited volumes from all parts of the world.

Recent titles in this series:

Proportionality and Facts in Constitutional Adjudication
Anne Carter

The Methodology of Constitutional Theory
Edited by Dimitrios Kyritsis and Stuart Lakin

A Constitutionalist Approach to the European Convention on Human Rights: The Legitimacy of Evolutive and Static Interpretation
Lisa Sonnleitner

Judicial Avoidance: Balancing Competences in Constitutional Adjudication
Carolina Alves das Chagas

Constitutionally Conforming Interpretation – Comparative Perspectives: Volume 1: National Reports
Edited by Matthias Klatt

Equality Before the Law: Equal Dignity, Wrongful Discrimination, and the Rule of Law
Michael P Foran

Constitutional Courts and Judicial Review: Between Law and Politics
Dieter Grimm

Essays on Freedom and Proportionality
Edited by Dimitrios Kyritsis

The Distorting Lens of Convergent Constitutional Theory
Peter Cane

Constitutionally Conforming Interpretation – Comparative Perspectives: Volume 2: Connections and Analysis
Edited by Matthias Klatt

Populism and Courts in an Age of Constitutional Impatience

Judges vs the People

Raphaël Girard

• HART •
OXFORD • LONDON • NEW YORK • NEW DELHI • SYDNEY

HART PUBLISHING

Bloomsbury Publishing Plc

Kemp House, Chawley Park, Cumnor Hill, Oxford, OX2 9PH, UK

1385 Broadway, New York, NY 10018, USA

Bloomsbury Publishing Ireland Limited, 29 Earlsfort Terrace, Dublin 2, D02 AY28, Ireland

HART PUBLISHING, the Hart/Stag logo, BLOOMSBURY and the Diana logo are trademarks of Bloomsbury Publishing Plc

First published in Great Britain 2026

A catalogue record for this book is available from the British Library.

A catalogue record for this book is available from the Library of Congress.

Library of Congress Control Number: 2026933373

ISBN: HB: 978-1-50998-754-2
ePDF: 978-1-50998-756-6
ePub: 978-1-50998-755-9

Typeset by Compuscript Ltd, Shannon

For product safety related questions contact productsafety@bloomsbury.com

To find out more about our authors and books visit www.hartpublishing.co.uk. Here you will find extracts, author information, details of forthcoming events and the option to sign up for our newsletters.

To my parents:

to my father, André

and in loving memory of my mother, Francine (1959–2015)

FOREWORD

There is a complex, and often contentious, relationship between populism and the judiciary within liberal-democratic systems. Populist movements and their leaders, emphasising the 'will of the people' and opposition to perceived elite-driven institutions, frequently view courts as obstacles to majoritarian rule. Consequently, populist leaders may seek to undermine judicial independence by politicising judicial appointments, disregarding court rulings, or framing judges as unelected elites detached from popular sentiment. Yet from an institutional and constitutional perspective, courts serve as an important counter-majoritarian mechanism designed to uphold constitutional norms, protect minority rights, and enforce the rule of law – functions that directly challenge populist narratives centred on unmediated popular sovereignty. The rise of populism in a growing number of jurisdictions makes these risks real and serious, demanding careful scholarly attention to better understand the nature of the threat as well as to explore whether and how judicial institutions can respond in ways that safeguard their role and position.

In this monograph, Girard sets out to tackle these issues head-on. He does so by first dissecting the modern populist constitutional project with a view to identifying its core features and relationship to constitutional notions. He uses a novel perspective by employing a spatiotemporal lens, thereby adding to our theoretical toolbox. Having thus laid the groundwork, Girard then draws on three fascinating and well-chosen case studies – Armenia, Ecuador and the United Kingdom – to illustrate how courts can, and do, respond to populism.

Earlier books in this series have explored the nature of courts and assessed methods of judicial decision making. Girard's book complements those volumes by focusing on a phenomenon that complicates the working environment of courts, reminding us of the need to ensure that theory does not stray too far from the practical challenges courts face today when trying to make constitutions more than words on paper.

Maartje De Visser
Charles Barzun
Matthias Klatt
Singapore/Charlottesville/Graz, October 2025

ACKNOWLEDGEMENTS

This book is the product of several years of research and writing. It began as a doctoral thesis at the London School of Economics and Political Science (LSE). First and foremost, I wish to thank my LSE supervisors, Jo Eric Khushal Murkens and Jacco Bomhoff, for their invaluable guidance, time, patience and support throughout the PhD – and beyond. They were always available for me and remain extremely supportive. I also owe special thanks to my examiners, Kim Lane Scheppele and Martin Loughlin, whose generous and insightful feedback, comments, suggestions and criticisms played a crucial role in transforming my dissertation into a monograph. I also gratefully acknowledge the generous doctrinal funding provided by the LSE Law School and the *Fonds de recherche du Québec – Société et culture* (FRQSC), without which this book would not have been possible.

I am, moreover, deeply grateful to my current colleagues at the University of Exeter Law School, including Stephen Skinner, Catherine Dupré, Kubo Mačák, David Barrett and David Yuratich, who have read key parts of this book and provided invaluable feedback at critical times. I have also benefited enormously from my interactions with Exeter students over the past few years, especially those in my *LAW2153 Law, Democracy and Populism: The Rise and Fall of Constitutional Democracy* module, whose curiosity and thoughtful engagement with the ideas explored in this book have been a continuing source of inspiration. The Exeter Law School and the Human Rights and Democracy Forum provided both rich intellectual engagement and practical resources to complete the book, including funding for a research trip to Armenia in April-May 2024 and a six-month research leave in January-July 2025.

In addition, I am indebted to many other colleagues and friends who have provided feedback on parts of this monograph over the years, at different stages and in different forms. The list is too long to be included in full here, but it includes Maria Cahill, Tom Daly, Conor Gearty (whose passing in September 2025, shortly after I submitted this manuscript, was deeply felt), Nicola Lacey, Armen Mazmanyan, Thomas Poole, Wojciech Sadurski, Julian Scholtes, Ioanna Tourkochoriti, Jacob van de Beeten, David Vitale, Winluck Wahiu and anonymous reviewers. I am also profoundly grateful to the former Vice-President of the Constitutional Court of Armenia, Justice Vahe Grigoryan, for agreeing to be interviewed in Yerevan in April 2024 and for his generosity with his time. I also thank Lusine Sargsyan for kindly facilitating the introduction, without which this invaluable conversation would not have been possible. I would also like to thank Kate Whetter, Sasha Jawed and Verity Stuart at Hart Publishing for their enthusiasm about this project, their trust and their support, as well as Chris Harrison for his careful editing.

Finally, I wish to express my gratitude to my friends, family and, above all, my partner, Salli, for her patience, support and understanding over the last six years.

London, 29 October 2025

CONTENTS

Foreword ... *ix*
Acknowledgements ... *xi*
Table of Cases (Including Advisory Opinions and Quasi-Judicial Decisions) ... *xvii*
Table of Legislation (and International Treaties) ... *xxiii*
Table of Constitutions ... *xxvii*

Introduction – *Mapping* Populism: Contemporary Populism and the Spatiotemporal Contours of (Liberal Constitutional) Democracy ... 1
I. Background and Context ... 1
II. Inquiry and Monograph Outline ... 4
III. Situating the Book's Contribution ... 6
IV. Notes on the Case Study Selection ... 13
V. Scope and Limitations ... 17
VI. Conceptual Clarifications ... 21
A. Populism ... 21
B. (Liberal Constitutional) Democracy ... 24
C. Space, Time and Chronotope ... 25
VII. Social Acceleration, Separation of Powers and the Spatiotemporal Contours of (Liberal Constitutional) Democracy ... 27
A. Distant, Slow-Paced, Deliberative and Future-Oriented Legislatures ... 30
B. Omnipresent, Fast-Paced, Expeditious and Present-Oriented Executives ... 34
C. Detached, Slow-Paced and Past-Oriented Judiciaries? ... 36

PART I
UNDERSTANDING POPULISM: TOWARDS A CONSTITUTIONAL THEORY OF POPULISM

1. *Identifying* Populism: Law, Popular Sovereignty and 'the People' ... 43
I. Introduction ... 43
II. Who are 'the People'? ... 44
A. The Ambiguous Nature of 'the People' ... 44
B. 'The People' as Unity: Populism as Monism ... 48
C. The 'Other' as Constitutive of the Identity of 'the People' ... 52

III. The Sovereign People (or the Nation) as the Ultimate Source of Authority ... 57
  A. The Populist Conception of Sovereignty ... 57
  B. Populism, Rousseau, Schmitt and the 'General Will' ... 59
  C. Can 'the People' be Institutionalised as a Sovereign in a Legal Sense? ... 61
IV. Conclusion ... 64

2. *Implementing* Populism: Constitutions, Constitutionalism and 'Constitutional Timelessness' ... 66
I. Introduction ... 66
II. Populism, Plebiscitarianism (Referendums) and the Expression of the Popular Will ... 68
III. The Populist 'Constitutional Timelessness': A Rejection of Liberal Constraints on Popular Sovereignty ... 72
  A. The Primacy of Politics Over Law ... 74
  B. The Populist Conception of Constituent Power ... 75
IV. Practical Implications: Constitutions, Constitutionalism and the Courts ... 77
  A. Constitutions under Populism ... 77
  B. Courts under Populism: Populist, Popular and (or) Political Constitutionalism? ... 80
  C. Populism Outside and within the Courts: Penal and Judicial Populism ... 84
  D. Populism and the Idea and Practice of Constitutionalism ... 88
V. Conclusion ... 90

3. *Characterising* Populism: Space, Time and 'Constitutional Impatience' ... 92
I. Introduction ... 92
II. Space: From Distance to Proximity, Immediacy and Authenticity ... 94
  A. The Populist Critique of Liberal-Democratic Distance ... 94
  B. The Populist Reorganisation of Space: Proximity, Immediacy and Authenticity ... 100
III. Time: From Acceleration to Urgency, Expeditiousness and Instantaneity ... 110
  A. The Temporal Horizons of Populism: Urgency and Expeditiousness ... 111
  B. Populism and the Politics of Instantaneity ... 115
IV. The Populist Chronotope: From Proximity and Urgency to 'Constitutional Impatience'? ... 121
  A. From Proximity, Immediacy and Authenticity to Occupation and Expulsion or Othering ... 122

B. 'Constitutional Impatience', Space-Time Compression and the Oversimplification of Constitutional Democracy? 129
V. Conclusion 133

PART II
RESPONDING TO POPULISM: QUESTIONING THE ROLE OF THE JUDICIARY AGAINST THE 'CONSTITUTIONAL IMPATIENCE' OF POPULISM

4. Revolution, Democratisation and Judicial Obstruction in Armenia 137
I. Introduction 137
II. Background: The 2018 'Velvet Revolution' 138
III. Pashinyan's 'Constitutional Impatience' 141
A. Populist Impatience While in Opposition 142
B. Populist Impatience While in Power 145
IV. Judicial Reform: The Populist against *Ancien Régime* Judges 147
A. From Judicial Intervention to Judicial Vetting and Transitional Justice 148
B. From Judicial Vetting and Transitional Justice to 'Early Retirement Incentives' 150
C. From 'Early Retirement Incentives' to Mass Removal 152
D. The Replacement of the Chairperson and the End of the Clash with the Constitutional Court 154
V. Judicial Deceleration … Or Obstruction? 156
A. Distinguishing Revolutionary or Democratic Populism from Authoritarian Populism 159
B. The 'Final Stage' of the Revolution: Democratisation in the Long Term? 169
VI. Conclusion 173

5. 'Constitutional Impatience', Judicial Capture and Executive Aggrandisement in Ecuador 179
I. Introduction 179
II. Constitutions, 'Constitutional Impatience' and Legal Symbolism: Rafael Correa's Citizens' Revolution 181
A. The Citizens' Revolution and the Enactment of the 2008 Constitution 181
B. Space, Time and Legal Symbolism 185
III. From 'Constitutional Impatience' to Judicial (and Institutional) Capture 187
A. First and Second Steps: Court-Packing and Judicial Reform 188
B. Third and Fourth Steps: *Error Inexcusable* and Judicial Discipline 190
C. Outcome: Judicial and Institutional Capture 192

IV. The Constitutional Court and the Refusal of Institutional Deceleration: Captured Courts as Active Agents of Executive Consolidation? 194
A. The 2011 Judgment on the 'Qualification of the Referendum Questions' 195
B. The 2011 'State of Exception in the Judicial Branch' Judgment....198
C. The 2014 'Term Limits' Judgment 200
D. Judicial Review in Ecuador: From Revolutionary Populism to Authoritarian Legalism?....204
V. Judicial Capture as Part of a Project of Executive Aggrandisement? 206
VI. Conclusion....208

6. Executive Power(s), 'Constitutional Impatience' and the Role of Courts as Institutional Stabilisers in the United Kingdom.... 212
I. Introduction 212
II. UK Courts as Institutional *Stabilisers* 215
A. The Brexit Referendum, the Royal Prerogative and the *Miller (no 1)* Case....217
B. The Prorogation of Parliament and the *Miller (no 2)/Cherry* Case 225
III. The Limits of Institutional Stabilisation (in the UK Context) 233
A. The Public (and Political) Reception of Judgments 234
B. The Forces of Politics or Political Pressure....237
C. Institutional Independence 242
D. Courts as 'Democratic Educators'? 243
IV. Conclusion....245

Conclusion.... 248
I. Recapitulation: Synthesis and Structure 248
A. Part I – *Understanding* Populism: Towards a Constitutional Theory of Populism 248
B. Part II – *Responding* to Populism: Questioning the Role of the Judiciary against the 'Constitutional Impatience' of Populism 251
II. Key Findings of the Monograph 254
III. Ramifications for Future Research 259

Bibliography....263
Index 279

TABLE OF CASES (INCLUDING ADVISORY OPINIONS AND QUASI-JUDICIAL DECISIONS)

Domestic (National) Courts

Armenia

On the Case of Conformity of Clause 4.2 of Part 2 of Articles 5, Parts 2 and 7 of Article 86 of the Constitutional Law Rules of Procedure of the National Assembly on the Basis of the Application of a least One Fifth of the Total Number of the Deputies of the National Assembly of the Republic of Armenia (DCC-1590, 13 April 2021) 156

On the Case of Conformity of Article 300.1 of the Criminal Code of the Republic of Armenia with the Constitution on the Basis of the Applications of Robert Kocharyan and the First Instance Court of General Jurisdiction of Yerevan (DCC-1586, 26 March 2021) 166

On the Case of Conformity of Part 3 of Article 40 of the Law on Military Service and the Status of a Serviceman with the Constitution on the Basis of the Application of the President of the Republic (DCC-1616, 2 November 2021) 168

On the Case of Conformity of Clauses 2 and 3 of Part 6 of Article 50 Prescribed by Part 1 of Article 2 of the Constitutional Law Adopted by the National [Assembly] on Making Supplements and Amendments to the RA Constitutional Law on Rules of Procedure of the National Assembly with the Constitution of the Republic of Armenia on the Basis of the Application of the President of the Republic (DCC-1454, 19 April 2019) 164

On the Case of Conformity of Article 35 and Part 2 of Article 135 of the Criminal Procedure Code of the Republic of Armenia with the Constitution on the Basis of the Application of Robert Kocharyan (DCC-1476, 4 September 2019) 148

Bolivia

Plurinational Constitutional Tribunal of Bolivia (*Tribunal Constitucional Plurinacional de Bolivia*), Decision No 84 of 2017 (28 November 2017) 194, 203

Canada

R v Lippé, [1991] 2 SCR 114 255
Schachter v Canada, [1992] 2 SCR 679 197
Trial Lawyers Association of British Columbia v British Columbia (AG), [2014] 3 SCR 31 197

Colombia

Sentencia C-141/2010, No 09 Comunicado 26 de febrero de 2010 (26 February 2010) 9

Ecuador

Decision (*Dictamen*) No 001-11-DRC-CC, Case (*Caso*) No 0001-11-RC (15 February 2011) 195
Decision (*Dictamen*) No 001-14-DRC-CC, Case (*Caso*) no 0001-14-RC (31 October 2014) 195
Decision (*Dictamen*) No 008-11-DEE-CC, Case (*Caso*) No 0000-10-EE (29 September 2011) 195
Ruling (*Sentencia*) No 3-19-CN/20 (29 July 2020) 190

El Salvador

Constitutional Chamber of the Supreme Court of Justice (*Sala de lo Consitiucional de la Corte Suprema de Justicia*), Habeas corpus (*Ac. Hábeas corpus*) 148-2020 (16 April 2020) 158
Constitutional Chamber of the Supreme Court of Justice (*Sala de lo Consitiucional de la Corte Suprema de Justicia*), Judicial Review (*Mandamiento judicial de inconstitucionalidad*) 1-2021 (1 May 2021) 158

India

Kesavananda Bharati v State of Kerala (1973) 4 SCC 225 10
Minerva Mills Ltd v India (1980) 3 SCC 625 10

Israel

Movement for Quality Government v Knesset, HCJ 5658/23 (1 January 2024) (Isr SC) 1, 10
SHIN Israeli Movement for Equal Representation of Women v Council for Cable TV and Satellite Broadcasting, HCJ 5432/03 [2004] IsrLR 20 88

Kenya

Independent Electoral and Boundaries Commission v Ndii and others (2021), Civil Appeal No E291 of 2021 (Court of Appeal at Nairobi) 234

Attorney General and others v Ndii and others (2022), SC Petition No 12 of 2021 (consolidated with petitions Nos 11 & 13 of 2021 (Supreme Court of Kenya) 234
Ndii and others v Attorney General and others (2020) [2021 eKLR], Petition No E282 of 2020 (High Court of Kenya at Nairobi) 233

Philippines

Republic of the Philippines v Sereno (2018) G R No 237428 (Phil SC) 54

Romania

Ruling No 2 of 5 October 2024 on the Challenge of the Registration of Mrs Diana Iovanovici-Șoșoacă's candidacy in the 2024 elections for President of Romania (Official Gazette No 1050, 21 October 2024) 261
Ruling No 7 of 11 March on the Appeals filed against the Decision of the Central Electoral Bureau no 18D of 9 March 2025 concerning the rejection of the registration of Mr Călin Georgescu's independent candidacy for the 2025 Romanian Presidential elections, as well as the electoral symbol (Official Gazette No 229, 14 March 2025) 261
Ruling No 32 of 6 December 2024 on the Annulment of the Electoral Process for the Election of the President of Romania (Official Gazette No 1231, 6 December 2024) 260

Slovakia

Pl ÚS 3/2024-76 (Constitutional Court of Slovakia) 242

South Africa

Economic Freedom Fighters v Speaker of the National Assembly and Others [2016] ZACC 11 10

Taiwan

Interpretation No 499 of the Council of Grand Justices of Taiwan (24 March 2000) 10

Uganda

Mabiziri v Attorney General (Uganda SC, 2018) 10

Ukraine

Constitutional Court of Ukraine, Decision 13-r/2020 (29 October 2020) 258

United Kingdom

Case of Proclamations [1610] EWHC KB J22; 77 ER 1352; 12 Co Rep 74 228
Cherry v Advocate General for Scotland [2019] CSIH 49 227
Cherry v Advocate General for Scotland [2019] CSOH 68 .... 216, 226
Cherry v Advocate General for Scotland [2019] CSOH 70 .... 216, 226
Dr Bonham's Case [*Bonham v College of Physicians*] [1610] 8 Co Rep 107 246
Ghaidan v Godin-Mendoza [2004] UKHL 30 197
Jackson v Attorney General [2005] UKHL 56 218
R (AAA) v Secretary of State for the Home Department [2023] UKSC 42 239
R (Evans) v Attorney General [2015] UKSC 21 239
R (Miller) v Secretary of State for Exiting the European Union [2017] UKSC 5 .... 214, 223
R (Miller) v The Prime Minister [2019] EWHC 2381 (QB) 216, 226
R (Miller) v The Prime Minister /Cherry v Advocate General for Scotland [2019] UKSC 41 .... 214, 216, 225–28, 231
R (Miller) v The Secretary of State for Exiting the European Union [2016] EWHC 2768 223
R (Nicklinson) v Ministry of Justice [2014] UKSC 38 256
R (Privacy International) v Investigatory Powers Tribunal [2019] UKSC 22 239–40
R (SC) v Secretary of State for Work and Pensions [2021] UKSC 26 240
R (UNISON) v Lord Chancellor [2017] UKSC 51 239–40
R v Adams (Northern Ireland) [2020] UKSC 19 239
Re Allister and others [2023] UKSC 5 240
Reference by the Attorney General and the Advocate General for Scotland – United Nations Convention on the Rights of the Child (Incorporation) (Scotland) Bill; Reference by the Attorney General and the Advocate General for Scotland – European Charter of Local Self-Government (Incorporation) (Scotland) Bill [2021] UKSC 42 240
Thoburn v Sunderland City Council [2002] EWHC 195 (Admin) 218

United States of America

Chisholm v Georgia 2 US (2 Dall) 419 (1793) 44
Trump v CASA, Inc, 606 US 831 (2025) 257
Trump v JGG, 604 US 670 (2025) 49

Supranational Courts and Institutions

East African Court of Justice

Mabirizi v Attorney General (E Afr Ct J, 2019)........10

European Commission for Democracy Through Law (Venice Commission)

First Opinion on the Draft Amendments to the Constitution (Chapters 1 to 7 and 10) of the Republic of Armenia (Opinion No 757/2014, 29 October 2015) CDL-AD(2015)037........138
Second Opinion on the Draft Amendments to the Constitution (In Particular to Chapters 8, 9, 11 to 16) of the Republic of Armenia (Opinion No 757/2014, 28 October 2015) CDL-AD(2015)038........138
Joint Opinion of the Venice Commission and the Directorate General Human Rights and Rule of Law on European Standards Regulating the Status of Judges (Opinion 1206/2024, 14 October 14 2024) CDL-AD(2024)029........176
Joint Opinion of the Venice Commission and the Directorate General of Human Rights and Rule of Law (DGI) of the Council of Europe on the draft laws on making amendments to the Constitutional Law on the Judicial Code and to the Constitutional Law on the Constitutional Court (Opinion No 1074/2021, 21 March 2022) CDL-AD(2022)002........149
Joint Opinion of the Venice Commission and the Directorate of Human Rights (DHR) of the Directorate General of Human Rights and Rule of Law (DGI) of the Council of Europe on the Amendments to the Judicial Code and Some Other Laws (Opinion No 963/2019, 14 October 2019) CDL-AD(2019)024........151
Opinion on Act CLXII of 2011 on the Legal Status and Remuneration of Judges and Act CLXI of 2011 on the Organisation and Administration of Courts of Hungary (Opinion No 663/2012, 19 March 2012) CDL-AD(2012)001........152
Opinion on the Draft Act amending the Act on the National Council of the Judiciary; on the Draft Act amending the Act on the Supreme Court, proposed by the President of Poland, and on the Act on the Organisation of Ordinary Courts (Opinion No 904/2017, 11 December 2017) CDL-AD(2017)031........152
Opinion on the Draft Constitutional Amendments Concerning the Constitutional Tribunal and Two Draft Laws on the Constitutional Tribunal (Opinion No 1293/2024, 7 December 2024) CDL-AD(2024)035........176
Opinion on Three Legal Questions in the Context of Draft Constitutional Amendments Concerning the Mandate of the Judges of the

Constitutional Court (Opinion No 988/2020, 22 June 2020) CDL-AD(2020)016 .... 155, 167

Urgent Joint Opinion of the Venice Commission and the Directorate General of Human Rights and Rule of Law (DGI) of the Council of Europe on the Legislative Situation regarding Anti-Corruption Mechanisms (Opinion No 1012/2020, 11 December 2020) CDL-AD(2020)038........259

Urgent Opinion on the Reform of the Constitutional Court of Ukraine (Opinion No 1012/2020, 11 December 2020) CDL-AD(2020)039........259

European Court of Human Rights

Gyulumyan and Others v Armenia App no 25240/20 (ECtHR, 8 July 2020) 155

Gyulumyan and Others v Armenia App no 25240/20 (ECtHR, 21 November 2023) 155

Organization for Security and Co-operation in Europe (OSCE) – Office for Democratic Institutions and Human Rights (ODIHR)

Opinion on Two Bills of the Republic of Poland on the Constitutional Tribunal (Sejm Prints No 253 and 254, as of 24 July 2024) (JUD-OIK/592/2024 [TN], 24 August 2024) 176

TABLE OF LEGISLATION (AND INTERNATIONAL TREATIES)

Domestic (National) Legislation, Bills, Regulations, Decrees and Executive Orders

Armenia

Amendment to the Constitution of the Republic of Armenia (adopted 22 June 2020)....154
Code of Criminal Procedure of the Republic of Armenia, AL-248 adopted by the National Assembly (Parliament) on 1 July 1998 and signed by the President of the Republic of Armenia on 1 September 1998....166
Constitutional Law on the Judicial Code of the Republic of Armenia, adopted on 7 February 2018....149
Law on Making Amendments and Addenda to the RA Constitutional Law Rules of Procedure of the National Assembly, adopted by the National Assembly on 2 October 2018 (but not signed by the President of the Republic of Armenia)....164
Law on the Constitutional Court, adopted by the National Assembly on 9 December 1997, signed by President Levon Ter-Petrossian on 30 December 1997....151
Prime Ministerial Executive Order No 1986 of 30 December 2019 (Armenia), establishing a new Expert Commission on Constitutional Reform....150

Ecuador

Executive Decree (*Decreto ejecutivo*) No 872 (No T6102-SNJ-11-1124) (5 September 2011)....198
Organic Code of the Judicial Function (*Código Orgánico de la Función Judicial*), Law 0 (*Ley* 0); Official Register Supplement 544 (*Registro Oficial Suplemento* 544) (9 March 2009)....190
Organic Law Amending the Organic Code of the Judiciary (*Ley Orgánica Reformatoria del Código Orgánico de la Función Judicial)*, Law w/n (*Ley s/n*), Official Register, RO 345-S (8 December 2020)....190

El Salvador

Legislative Branch, Decree No 2 (*Organo Legislativo, Decreto No 2*) *Official Gazette*, vol 431, no 81 (*Diario Oficial, Tomo No 431, Numero 81*) (1 May 2021) 158
Legislative Branch, Decree No 4 (*Organo Legislativo, Decreto No 4*), *Official Gazette*, vol 431, no 81 (*Diario Oficial, Tomo No 431, Numero 81*) (1 May 2021) 158

Ireland

Constitution of the Irish Free State (Saorstát Éireann) Act 1922 (No 1 of 1922) 66

Kenya

Constitution of Kenya (Amendment) Bill 2020 234

New Zealand

Sentencing Act 2002 85

Poland

Law amending the Law relating to the organisation of the ordinary courts, the Law on the Supreme Court and certain other laws (*Ustawa o zmianie ustawy – Prawo o ustroju sądów powszechnych, ustawy o Sądzie Najwyższym oraz niektórych innych ustaw*) U of 2020, item 190 (20 December 2019) 193

Ukraine

Verkhovna Rada, Draft Law No 4288 'On the Restoration of Public Trust in Constitutional Justice' (29 October 2020) 258

United Kingdom

Administration of Justice Act 1969 (c 58) 216
Bill of Rights Bill 238
Border Security, Asylum and Immigration Act 2025 239
Coronavirus Act 2020 (c 7) 232
Dissolution and Calling of Parliament Act (c 11) 241
Draft Fixed-term Parliaments Act 2011 (Repeal) Bill (now known as the Dissolution and Calling of Parliament Bill) 241
European Union (Withdrawal) (No 2) Act 2019 (c 26) 225–26
European Union (Withdrawal) Act 2018 (c 16) 225

European Union (Withdrawal) Act 2018 (Exit Day) (Amendment No 2) Regulations 2019 (SI 2019/859) 225
European Union Referendum Act 2015 (c 36) 219
Fixed-term Parliaments Act 2011 (c 14) 240
Human Rights Act 1998 (c 42) 197
Parliamentary Voting System and Constituencies Act 2011 (c 1) 217
Political Parties, Elections and Referendums Act 2000 (c 41) 217
Retained EU Law (Revocation and Reform) Act 2023 (c 28) 232
Safety of Rwanda (Asylum and Immigration) Act 2024 (c 8) 238

United States

Alien Enemies Act 1798, ch 66, 1 Stat 577 49
'Declaring a National Energy Emergency' (Executive Order 14156, 20 January 2025) 90 Fed Reg 8327 118
'Declaring a National Emergency Concerning the Southern Border of the United States' (Proclamation 9844, 15 February 2019) 84 Fed Reg 4949 117
'Declaring a National Emergency at the Southern Border of the United States' (Proclamation 10886, 20 January 2025) 90 Fed Reg 8327 118
'Ensuring Accountability for All Agencies' (Executive Order 14215, 18 February 2025) 90 Fed Reg 10447 118
'Protecting the Meaning and Value of American Citizenship' (Executive Order 14160, 29 January 2025) 90 Fed Reg 8449 257

International Treaties

Treaty on European Union, Consolidated Version [2008] OJ C115/13 .... 222, 225

TABLE OF CONSTITUTIONS

Armenia (Republic of), Constitution of 1995 .... 153–54, 166–67
Bolivia (Plurinational State of), Constitution of 2009...53
Ecuador (Republic of), Constitution of 1979 202
Ecuador (Republic of), Constitution of 1998 202
Ecuador (Republic of), Constitution of 2008 .... 184–89, 195–202, 208–09
El Salvador (Republic of), Constitution of 1983 .... 158, 203
France, Constitution of 1958 (Constitution of the Fifth Republic) 105
German Reich (Weimar), Constitution of 1919..105
Germany, Basic Law for the Federal Republic of (1949).......................................105
Hungary, Constitution of 1949 78
Hungary, Fundamental Law of 2011 ....69, 78–79, 127
Ireland (Republic of), Constitution of 1937 .... 66, 70
Ireland, Constitution of the Irish Free State (Saorstát Éireann) Act, 1922..66
Italy (Italian Republic), Constitution of 1947..105
Spain, Constitution of 1978...105
Venezuela (Bolivarian Republic of), Constitution of 1999................53, 76, 78, 127

Introduction – *Mapping* Populism: Contemporary Populism and the Spatiotemporal Contours of (Liberal Constitutional) Democracy

> Il faut que les affaires [politiques] aillent, et qu'elles aillent un certain mouvement qui ne soit ni trop lent ni trop vite. Mais le peuple a toujours trop d'action, ou trop peu. Quelquefois avec cent mille bras il renverse tout ; quelquefois avec cent mille pieds il ne va que comme les insectes.[1]

I. Background and Context

Nearly ten years after the cataclysmic shock caused by the 2016 Brexit referendum in the UK and the election of Donald Trump as President of the United States (US), populism is very much alive and well. Recep Tayyip Erdoğan (Justice and Development Party, *Adalet ve Kalkınma Partisi* or AKP), Viktor Orbán (Fidesz) and Narendra Modi (Bharatiya Janata Party, 'Indian's People Party' or BJP), to name a few, remain in power in Türkiye, Hungary and India, respectively. Other populists have also recently managed to gain power, including Javier Milei in Argentina, Andrej Babiš in Czechia, Robert Fico in Slovakia and Giorgia Meloni in Italy. While Trump lost power in 2020, he has since then made a dramatic comeback, winning the 2024 US presidential election, securing a Republican majority in Congress and swiftly implementing an assertive agenda, marked by a series of executive orders – many of which aimed at various public institutions. Moreover, the implications of populism on the judiciary more specifically now appear more significant and relevant than ever, as evidenced by the recent attempt by Prime Minister Netanyahu's coalition government to overhaul the judiciary in Israel and curb its powers,[2] which was ultimately blocked by the Supreme Court in January 2024.[3] In many instances, these populist-led attempts to weaken the

[1] Baron de Montesquieu, *De l'Esprit des lois* (Geneva, Barillot & Fils, 1748) vol I, bk II, ch II.
[2] Basic Law: The Judiciary (Amendment No 5) (Reasonableness Standard) Bill 2023 (Israel, Knesset).
[3] *Movement for Quality Government v Knesset*, HCJ 5658/23 (1 January 2024) (Isr SC).

institutional role of the courts have been made in the name of 'the people' and (or) 'democracy', while judicial resistance or intervention has often led to the characterisation of judges as 'anti-democratic' or even as 'enemies of the people'.

This institutional dynamic has generated significant academic interest in recent years: an ever-growing number of scholars from a wide range of disciplines have attempted to analyse, conceptualise and, in many instances, criticise the rise of populism as well as its institutional implications. The interest in populism is, however, not entirely new. In May 1967, scholars from across the world – including Isaiah Berlin, Ghiţa Ionescu and Ernest Gellner – gathered at the first-ever conference on populism at the London School of Economics and Political Science (LSE).[4] In the six decades that followed, countless studies of the concept emerged, mainly in political science and political theory. Given that populism is often perceived as a political phenomenon, it is unsurprising that the bulk of the academic debate on the subject has thus far taken place in political science and political theory. Yet, populism is also undoubtedly a legal phenomenon, or at least one that has significant legal and constitutional[5] ramifications. In fact, Neil Walker has even contended that 'the constitutional dimension of populism's engagement, contrary to certain expectations, is one of its central features'.[6] Some of these legal and constitutional implications, as will be discussed in this book, relate to popular sovereignty, the concept of constituent power, the constitution and the authority of public law in general.

In addition, populism has seldom been analysed through the specific lens of space and time – or what some social and legal theorists call 'spatiotemporality'.[7] Yet, I suggest in this monograph that key considerations of space and time are, in fact, central to the contemporary populist constitutional narrative and imaginary. Indeed, implicit in the ideal-typical populist discourse is the claim that present-day liberal-democratic representation is spatiotemporally distant and slow-paced.[8] In response to these perceived shortcomings of the liberal component of constitutional democracy, and operating in a context of 'social acceleration',[9] contemporary populism puts forward an alternative conception of

[4] For a précis of the conference, see I Berlin, R Hofstadter, D McRae et al, 'To Define Populism' (1968) 3 *Government and Opposition* 137. For an edited collection based on the papers presented at the conference, see G Ionescu and E Gellner (eds), *Populism: Its Meaning and National Characteristics* (London, Macmillan, 1969).

[5] Here, and throughout the book, I mean 'constitutional' in a descriptive sense, ie, in relation to the use of constitutions and other legal instruments, rather than in a more normative and (or) ideological sense (eg, 'constitutionalist').

[6] N Walker, 'Populism and Constitutional Tension' (2019) 17(2) *International Journal of Constitutional Law* 515, 519.

[7] See, eg, M Valverde, *Chronotopes of Law: Jurisdiction, Scale and Governance* (London, Routledge, 2015).

[8] This depiction of courts as 'slow-paced' goes far back in time. For example, in the 1940s, Charles H McIlwain – despite his principled defence of an independent judiciary as a rampart against arbitrary will – referred to judicial processes are 'far too slow and cumbersome'. See CH McIlwain, *Constitutionalism Ancient and Modern* (Ithaca, Cornell University Press, 1947) 132.

[9] See, eg, H Rosa, 'Airports Built on Shifting Grounds? Social Acceleration and the Temporal Dimension of Law' in L Corrias and L Francot (eds), *Temporal Boundaries of Law and Politics: Time*

democratic representation, one that is based on spatial proximity, authenticity and temporal efficiency.

This emphasis on proximity and speed, I contend in this monograph, has important constitutional ramifications – notably on the separation of powers and the main institutions of liberal-constitutional democracy. Legislatures and courts, in particular, are often depicted in populist discourses as distant, elite-driven, opaque, inefficient and slow-paced. As such, they appear ill-suited to social acceleration and the new exigencies of temporal efficiency. However, contemporary populism is not, I suggest, a mere critique of liberal democracy; it also comes with its own constitutional project, one to be taken seriously and on its own terms. Through its promise to re-establish a new form of democratic representation based on spatial proximity, authenticity and temporal efficiency, contemporary populism attempts to reorganise and redraw the spatiotemporal contours of liberal democracy. The aim of contemporary populism, as I understand it, is to offer a new form of democratic representation: one that not only aims to reduce the distance between 'the people' and their representatives, or between *gouvernants* (rulers) and *gouvernés* (ruled), but that is also better suited to the contemporary imperatives of temporal efficiency and rapidity. Contemporary populists are often sceptical – perhaps even distrustful – of intermediaries of various sorts. Apex courts, in particular – viewed by some populists as 'the most serious competitor in their struggle for recognition as the true representative of "the people"' – are frequently the target of populist attacks.[10] It is in this context of distrust that contemporary populists have sometimes attempted to circumvent or simply ignore the lengthy and time-consuming liberal-democratic procedures that are perceived or depicted as illegitimately thwarting the direct expression of the authentic 'will of the people'.

Liberal-democratic institutions such as legislatures and courts, for their part, have often openly rejected this populist constitutional project – and have responded to it in a myriad of ways, from strategic avoidance to head-on confrontation. From a more normative perspective, certain constitutional scholars have stressed the institutional role courts can play in a context of populism. For instance, in an acclaimed article[11] published in 2019, Ming-Sung Kuo contended that courts can play the role of 'institutional decelerators' in response to the 'instantaneous' conception of democracy put forward and

Out of Joint (London, Routledge, 2018); H Rosa, *Social Acceleration: A New Theory of Modernity* (New York, Columbia University Press, 2013); R Prandini, 'The Future of Societal Constitutionalism in the Age of Acceleration' (2013) 20 *Indiana Journal of Global Legal Studies* 731; P Virilio, *Speed and Politics* (trans Mark Polizzotti) (Los Angeles, Semiotext(e), 2006 [1977]); P Virilio, *Le Futurisme de l'instant: Stop-Eject* (Paris, Galilée, 2009); WE Scheuerman, *Liberal Democracy and the Social Acceleration of Time* (Baltimore, Johns Hopkins University Press, 2004); H Rosa, 'Social Acceleration: Ethical and Political Consequences of a Desynchronized High-Speed Society' (2003) 10 *Constellations* 3.

[10] UK Preuß, 'Judicial Power in Processes of Transformation' in C Landfried (ed), *Judicial Power: How Constitutional Courts Affect Political Transformations* (Cambridge, Cambridge University Press, 2019) 364.

[11] It notably won the 2020 I·CON Best Paper Prize.

defended by populists.[12] He observed, in the same vein, that judicial proceedings have been noted – and criticised – for their slow pace. Yet, this ingrained slowness, Kuo argues, 'can be a structural asset of the multistage process of constitutional governance in its pushback against new populism'.[13] Other scholars, however, have expressed their scepticism vis-à-vis the role of courts against authoritarian populism and, more broadly, democratic backsliding or decay.[14]

II. Inquiry and Monograph Outline

It is against this backdrop that I have chosen to inquire, in this monograph, into: (1) the character and discourse of contemporary populism, as well as the content of the populist constitutional project, using a specific spatiotemporal lens; and (2) the institutional reaction or response, by judicial actors, to this very project – including the view that courts can act as democracy-enhancing institutional decelerators.

The book is divided into two parts containing a total of six core chapters, in addition to this introductory chapter and the conclusion. In Part I, my aim is to analyse, theorise and conceptualise populism, from a legal-constitutional perspective, using a spatiotemporal lens. To do so, I begin by identifying the key elements of the ideal-typical populist legal discourse, particularly as they relate to popular sovereignty and the concept of 'the people' (chapter one). Second, I analyse the relationship of populism vis-à-vis constitutions, constitutionalism and what I call 'constitutional timelessness' (chapter two). Third, I investigate populism through the prism of space and time, focusing more specifically on the spatiotemporal claims of the populist critique of liberal democracy, as well as on the content of the populist constitutional project (chapter three).

In Part II of this monograph, my aim is to analyse the institutional reaction or response by judicial actors to the populist constitutional project. More specifically, I test, question and ultimately challenge the widely shared view in the comparative constitutional law literature that generally affirms the power of

[12] MS Kuo, 'Against Instantaneous Democracy' (2019) 17(2) *International Journal of Constitutional Law* 554. In this article, Kuo notably argues that 'new populism, which is characterized by instantaneousness and simultaneity made possible by social media and other communications technologies, betrays a pathology of instantaneous democracy in its pursuit of unmediated politics at the expense of democratic representation and deliberation'.

[13] ibid 571.

[14] See, eg, M Tushnet, *Taking Back the Constitution: Activist Judges and the Next Age of American Law* (New Haven, Yale University Press, 2020); TG Daly, *The Alchemists: Questioning Our Faith in Courts as Democracy-Builders* (Cambridge, Cambridge University Press, 2017); TG Daly, 'The Alchemists: Courts as Democracy-Builders in Contemporary Thought' (2017) 6 *Global Constitutionalism* 101; S Gardbaum, 'Are Strong Constitutional Courts Always a Good Thing for New Democracies?' (2015) 53 *Columbia Journal of Transnational Law* 285, 320; M Tushnet, *Taking the Constitution Away from the Courts* (Princeton, Princeton University Press, 2000).

constitutional and apex courts to effectively act as bulwarks against authoritarian, self-aggrandising populists, broadly speaking, including the more specific view[15] that courts can act as 'effective'[16] institutional decelerators in the context of populist-driven instantaneous democracy. To do so, I dedicate three chapters to three case studies, respectively chapters four, five and six. These three case studies, I suggest, can be seen as illustrative of the differential impact of the tensions between populism and constitutionalism.[17] Far from yielding uniform outcomes, populism's complex and context-dependent relationship with constitutionalism produces divergent impacts, thereby challenging assumptions about both the institutional role of courts and the nature of constitutionalism itself.

In the first case study, which focuses on the aftermath of the 2018 'Velvet Revolution' in Armenia, I discuss the possibility that courts can in fact, in certain circumstances, become institutional obstructors, in this case by blocking the implementation of the reforms of a newly elected, populist-led democratic government replacing a semi-authoritarian regime (chapter four). In such conditions, the populist confrontation with the judiciary may be indicative of a more positive relationship between populism and constitutionalism than standard narratives suggest. By contrast, the second case study, on Ecuador under the presidency of Rafael Correa (2007–2017), highlights the possibility of a more negative relationship between populism and constitutionalism. More specifically, it discusses how courts can even accelerate (rather than decelerate) the populist flow of time by becoming active agents of executive consolidation (chapter five). The third and final case study, which focuses on the United Kingdom in the period that followed the Brexit referendum, suggests a rather mixed relationship between populism and constitutionalism and offers a slightly more positive picture for institutional deceleration. It reveals that the UK Supreme Court has indeed, in at least two high-profile cases, acted as an institutional stabiliser in the face of an impatient and unrestrained executive (chapter six). Nonetheless, and as I argue at the end of that chapter, the more substantive virtues of judicial (or institutional) deceleration – including its alleged contributions to democratic learning as part of the multistage process of constitutional-democratic governance[18] – are grounded in empirical

[15] See, eg, Kuo (n 12).

[16] Kuo uses this term in a theoretical way, despite its empirical connotations. See ibid 573.

[17] Here, and throughout this monograph, I refer to Charles Howard McIlwain's essential understanding of constitutionalism, namely the limitation of government by law: '[I]n all its successive phases, constitutionalism has one essential quality: it is a legal limitation on government; it is the antithesis of arbitrary rule; its opposite is despotic government, the government of will instead of law'. McIlwain (n 8) 21. That said, I also acknowledge that constitutionalism can also be empowering (ie, not just restraining). This is discussed in more depth in ch 2.

[18] Kuo (n 12) 564. On the contribution of courts to the 'learning function' of this multistage process of constitutional-democratic governance, see ibid 556, 571–574. On the idea that courts can act as 'public educators' on the ideals of constitutional-democratic governance, see, eg, IP Stotzky 'The Tradition of Constitutional Adjudication' in IP Stotzky (ed), *Transition to Democracy in Latin America: The Role*

claims that remain, ultimately, difficult to verify. Finally, the conclusion summarises the findings of the monograph and suggests avenues for future research.

III. Situating the Book's Contribution

This monograph makes two principal contributions to the fields of constitutional theory and comparative constitutional law, more specifically: (1) through the development of a theoretical framework that helps re-conceptualise contemporary populism as a serious and at least somewhat coherent constitutional theory, and more specifically through the prism of spatiotemporality; and (2) through a detailed, contextual analysis of the role (and response) of courts in the context of contemporary populism.

First, my theoretical framework, especially in the first part of the monograph, contributes to a re-conceptualisation of populism as a serious and relatively coherent constitutional theory. To do so, I propose to analyse populism from a legal perspective, using the particular interpretative lens of spatiotemporality. Indeed, legal and constitutional phenomena have seldom been analysed through the lens of space *and* time. While scholars like Mariana Valverde have contributed to the literature on law, time and space, they have most often done so in the legal subfield of social theory.[19] With a few exceptions,[20] the implications of legal phenomena (in general) on time and space remain understudied in the literature on constitutional theory, democratic theory and comparative constitutional law. Moreover, even in the broad, multidisciplinary literature on populism, the populist phenomenon has rarely been analysed through the lens of time and space. And when it has, it has most often been through the lens of time *or* space, not both conjointly.[21]

Second, the existing literature in comparative constitutional law on the role (or response) of courts in the context of contemporary populism generally does not make a clear distinction between democracy-enhancing (or -safeguarding) institutional responses to populism (including judicial deceleration, discussed

of the Judiciary (Boulder, Westview, 1993) 348–349 and J Goldstein (1993), 'The Opinion-Writing Function of the Judiciary of Latin American Governments in Transition to Democracy: *Martinez v. Provincia de Mendoza*' in Stotzky (ed), *Transition to Democracy* 301, also mentioned in Daly, *The Alchemists* (n 14) 291.

[19] See, eg, Valverde (n 7).

[20] See, eg, N Walker, 'Out of Place and Out of Time: Law's Fading Co-ordinates' (2010) 14 *Edinburgh Law Review* 13. Philipp Dann also recognises the links between time and space, but his focus is often more on time and temporality than space per se. See, eg, P Dann, 'Temporality and Liberal Constitutionalism' in TA Börzel, J Gerschewski and M Zürn (eds), *The Liberal Script at the Beginning of the 21st Century* (Oxford, Oxford University Press, 2024).

[21] See, eg, M Tushnet, 'After the Heroes Have Left the Scene: Temporality in the Study of Constitutional Court Judges' in Landfried (ed) (n 10).

later in this monograph), on the one hand, and illegitimate and/or anti-democratic judicial obstruction, on the other. My analysis of the three case studies discussed in the second part of this monograph reveals, in my view, the relative incompleteness in the existing literature on populism, law and the courts.

The recent literature on the judicial roles against populism, but also illiberalism,[22] one-partyism,[23] constitutional capture[24] or retrogression,[25] executive aggrandisement,[26] as well as democratic dysfunction,[27] erosion,[28] degradation,[29] degeneration,[30] deconsolidation,[31] backsliding,[32] decline,[33] recession,[34] rot[35]

[22] See, eg, F Zakaria, 'The Rise of Illiberal Democracy' (1996) 76 *Foreign Affairs* 22; F Zakaria, *The Future of Freedom: Illiberal Democracy at Home and Abroad* [2004] (New York, Norton, 2007); Y Mounk, *The People vs. Democracy: Why Our Freedom Is in Danger and How to Save it* (Cambridge, Harvard University Press, 2018); I Krastev and S Holmes, *The Light that Failed: A Reckoning* (London, Penguin, 2019).

[23] Namely, 'the effort to centralize power so as to undermine democratic accountability'. See S Issacharoff, 'Constitutional Courts and Democratic Hedging' (2011) 99 *Georgetown Law Journal* 961, 965.

[24] Namely, 'a process which results in a systemic undermining of the key components of the rule of law such as independent and impartial courts'. See L Pech and KL Scheppele, 'Illiberalism Within: Rule of Law Backsliding in the EU' (2017) 19 *Cambridge Yearbook of European Legal Studies* 3, 9.

[25] A Huq and T Ginsburg, 'How to Lose a Constitutional Democracy' (2018) 65 *UCLA Law Review* 96, 118.

[26] N Bermeo, 'On Democratic Backsliding' (2016) 27 *Journal of Democracy* 5, 10–13; T Khaitan, 'Executive Aggrandizement in Established Democracies: A Crisis of Liberal Democratic Constitutionalism' (2019) 17 *International Journal of Constitutional Law* 342.

[27] R Dixon, *Responsive Judicial Review: Democracy and Dysfunction in the Modern Age* (Oxford, Oxford University Press, 2023).

[28] S Levitsky and D Ziblatt. *How Democracies Die: What History Reveals About Our Future* (London, Penguin, 2018).

[29] M Loughlin, 'The Contemporary Crisis of Constitutional Democracy' (2019) 39 *OJLS* 435.

[30] R Albert, 'Constitutional Amendment and Dismemberment' (2018) 43 *Yale Journal of International Law* 1, 60–66.

[31] A broader and more all-encompassing concept, referring more to substance (or norms) than structures (or institutions). See Y Mounk and RS Foa, 'The Signs of Deconsolidation' (2017) 28 *Journal of Democracy* 5.

[32] See, eg, Bermeo (n 26); W Sadurski, 'How Democracy Dies (in Poland): A Case Study of Anti-Constitutional Populist Backsliding' (2018) Sydney Law School Research Paper No 18/01; T Ginsburg, AH Huq and M Versteeg, 'The Coming Demise of Liberal Constitutionalism?' (2018) 65 *University of Chicago Law Review* 239, 244: 'Democratic backsliding [consists in] neutraliz[ing] the judiciary, dismantl[ing] respect for the rule of law, and restrict[ing] electoral competition'; D Adamski, 'The Social Contract of Democratic Backsliding in the "New EU" Countries' (2019) 56 *CML Rev* 623.

[33] KL Scheppele, 'Autocratic Legalism' (2018) 85 *University of Chicago Law Review* 545.

[34] T Ginsburg and AH Huq, *How to Save a Constitutional Democracy* (Chicago, University of Chicago Press, 2018).

[35] By 'constitutional rot', Jack Balkin means 'decay in the features of [the American] system that maintain it as a healthy republic'. See JM Balkin, 'Constitutional Rot' in CR Sunstein (ed), *Can It Happen Here? Authoritarianism in America* (New York, Dey St, 2018) 147–160, more specifically 151; JM Balkin, 'Constitutional Crisis and Constitutional Rot' (2017) 77 *Maryland Law Review* 147.

or decay[36] can, broadly speaking, be divided into two legal camps that have opposing stances on the role of the courts in such a context. The first camp generally takes the view that courts (especially constitutional courts[37]) often (although not always) have the power, ability, capacity and, in some cases, the duty (sometimes based on militant democracy[38]) to perform democracy-enhancing (or protective) functions, notably by constraining the executive and by acting as bulwarks against populist and (or) authoritarian threats.[39] This applies not only to established democracies, but also to less consolidated ones, such as 'new', 'emergent' or 'third wave' democracies.[40] This includes the work of Kim Lane Scheppele,[41] Tom Ginsburg (and Aziz Huq),[42] Rosalind Dixon,[43] Samuel Issacharoff,[44] Wojciech

[36] TG Daly, 'Democratic Decay: Conceptualising an Emerging Research Field' (2019) 11 *Hague Journal on the Rule of Law* 9.

[37] By 'constitutional court', I refer, here and throughout the rest of this monograph, to apex courts broadly speaking, from specialist courts (with or without constitutional review powers, that is to say the power to invalidate legislative acts or executive decisions) specialised in constitutional adjudication – generally known as constitutional courts – to non-specialist apex courts or courts of final instance or final jurisdiction (with or without judicial review powers), often known as 'supreme courts'.

[38] See, eg, P Castillo-Ortiz and Y Roznai. 'The Democratic Self-Defence of Constitutional Courts' (2024) 18 *ICL Journal: Vienna Journal on International Constitutional Law* 1.

[39] This is not to say, of course, that these scholars all claim that courts *alone* can save democracy. Their role may depend on a myriad of factors and on the combined effect of the actions of other institutions. In the same way, most (if not all) of these scholars acknowledge that courts have failed at preventing democratic erosion or backsliding in some (contemporary) instances, including, most famously, in Hungary, Poland, Türkiye and Venezuela. See, eg, A Huq, 'Democratic Erosion and the Courts: Comparative Perspectives' (2018) 93 *NYU Law Review* 21, 26–27.

[40] See, eg, T Ginsburg, *Judicial Review in New Democracies: Constitutional Courts in Asian Cases* (Cambridge, Cambridge University Press, 2003) 7–8. On 'third wave' democracies, see SP Huntington, *The Third Wave: Democratization in the Late Twentieth Century* (Norman, University of Oklahoma Press, 1991).

[41] See, eg, KL Scheppele, 'Democracy by Judiciary. Or Why Courts Can Be More Democratic than Parliaments' in A Czarnota, M Krygier and W Sadurski (eds), *Rethinking the Rule of Law After Communism* (Budapest, CEU Press, 2005) 25–26, 44, arguing that in some circumstances, 'strong constitutional courts' can be 'more democratic than elected parliaments and elected executives'.

[42] See, eg, T Ginsburg, 'The Jurisprudence of Anti-Erosion' (2018) 66 *Duke Law Review* 823, in which Ginsburg provides examples in recent history where courts intervened to stop democratic erosion or backsliding. That said, Ginsburg adds a caveat at p 840, namely that 'courts are not great heroes here. Their role in saving democracy is a limited one. The view of the role of courts in this account is essentially an informational one. Courts operate by providing high-quality information to publics and elites. But the action taken to protect democracy from erosion is taken by other actors, not courts themselves. What judges can do is speak truth to power, allowing other actors to step up'. See also Ginsburg and Huq (n 34) 186–191, especially 186: 'When properly functioning, the courts can stand in the way of autocratic attempts to curtail liberal rights of speech and association, and can prevent charismatic populists from dismantling other checks on their authority'. That said, Ginsburg and Huq also recognise, at p 190, that in some instances, as observed in Sri Lanka and Hungary, 'courts, once created, can [also] become a kind of *instrument* of erosion'. In an earlier book, Ginsburg also argues that courts in early stages of democratic liberalisation can facilitate transition towards democracy by providing, through judicial review, a certain 'insurance' to prospective electoral losers. See Ginsburg (n 40) 21–33.

[43] See, eg, Dixon (n 27).

[44] With, at times, certain temporary compromises. See, eg, Issacharoff (n 23).

Sadurski,[45] Gábor Halmai,[46] Andrew Arato,[47] Yaniv Roznai,[48] Susanne Baer[49] and others.[50]

A common example referred to by some of these scholars is *Sentencia C-141/2010*,[51] in which the Constitutional Court of Colombia struck down a second constitutional amendment that would have allowed, if approved by referendum, the populist (and popular) President Álvaro Uribe to run for a third term.[52] In this decision, the Court not only held that the proposed referendum was unconstitutional on procedural grounds; it also held that the amendment itself was substantively unconstitutional, as it would alter the essential structure of the 1991 Constitution. As a result of the judgment, President Uribe withdrew his candidacy and left presidential office at the end of his second term. Commenting on the case, Issacharoff wrote that 'the constitutional court emerged as the sole check on the prospect of increasingly unilateral executive power'.[53] Similarly, Tom Ginsburg and Aziz Huq wrote that the 'only institution able to stop [Uribe] was the Constitutional Court – and in this case it proved

[45] See, eg, W Sadurski, 'Judicial Review Versus Populist Authoritarianism' (2025) 3 *Comparative Constitutional Studies* 81.

[46] See, eg, G Halmai, 'Is There Such Thing As "Populist Constitutionalism"? The Case of Hungary' (2018) 11 *Fudan Journal of Humanities and Social Sciences* 323. Halmai, who acted as the chief advisor to Justice László Sólyom during the first six years of his term as the founding President of the Hungarian Constitutional Court, is also well aware of the precarious position of courts in populist regimes. In this article, he argues that populism and constitutionalism are, in essence, antithetical.

[47] With the help of civil society initiatives. See, eg, A Arato and JL Cohen, *Populism and Civil Society: The Challenge to Constitutional Democracy* (Oxford, Oxford University Press, 2022); A Arato, 'Populism, Constitutional Courts, and Civil Society' in Landfried (ed) (n 10) 338–339: 'Populism is a pathology of civil society, or of Rosanvallon's counter-democracy. [...] When representation through elections fails, courts yield a second democratic channel that becomes all the more important under a populist government. It is an important task, therefore, to organize on behalf of judicial independence and to engage in forms of discourse to which courts can positively respond'.

[48] See, eg, Y Roznai, 'Who Will Save the Redheads? Anti-Bully Theory of Judicial Review and Protection of Democracy' (2020) 29 *William & Mary Bill of Rights Journal* 327; Y Roznai, *Unconstitutional Constitutional Amendments* (Oxford, Oxford University Press, 2017).

[49] See, eg, S Baer, 'The Rule of – and Not By – Law. On the Need to Explain and Defend Constitutionalism Today' (2019) 71 *Current Legal Problems* 335.

[50] See, eg, Castillo-Ortiz and Roznai (n 38); A Sethi, 'Towards a Pluralistic Conception of Judicial Role' (2021) 90 *University of Missouri-Kansas City Law Review* 69; AS Katz, 'Taming the Prince: Bringing Presidential Emergency Powers Under Law in Colombia' (2020) 18 *International Journal of Constitutional Law* 1201; D Prendergast, 'The Judicial Role in Protecting Democracy from Populism' (2019) 20 *German Law Journal* 245.

[51] Constitutional Court of Colombia (*Corte Constitucional de Colombia*), Sentencia C-141/2010, No 09 Comunicado 26 de febrero de 2010 (26 February 2010).

[52] See, eg, Ginsburg and Huq (n 34) 187–189; Ginsburg (n 42) 841–842; Huq (n 39) 23; S Issacharoff, *Fragile Democracies: Contested Power in the Era of Constitutional Courts* (Cambridge, Cambridge University Press, 2015) 147–149; D Landau, 'A Dynamic Theory of Judicial Role' (2014) 55 *Boston College Law Review* 1501, 1522–1524; D Landau, 'Abusive Constitutionalism' (2013) 47 *University of California Davis Law Review* 189, 203.

[53] Issacharoff (n 52) 148. That said, Issacharoff criticises at p 151 the lack of justification, in the judgment, for striking down – on seemingly substantive grounds – the constitutional amendment, particularly given the 'freighted political environment'.

up to the task'.[54] Another example that a number of these scholars commonly refer to is the famous case of *Minerva Mills Ltd. v India*,[55] in which the Supreme Court of India – following another high-profile judgment, *Kesavananda Bharati v State of Kerala*[56] – struck down constitutional amendments that aimed to limit the courts' judicial review powers.[57] A similar but more recent example would be the 2024 case *Movement for Quality Government v Knesset*,[58] in which a majority of the Supreme Court of Israel held that the Court has the authority to review and nullify amendments to the country's Basic Laws in exceptional cases when the legislature, the Knesset, deviates from its constituent authority.[59] In these instances, and in others,[60] courts have been seen as (and lauded for) safeguarding constitutional democracy by constraining the executive and stopping what some have called 'executive aggrandisement'.[61]

Legal scholars in this first camp do not necessarily believe that courts are the only barrier against democratic erosion, nor that they are always successful in that regard. However, they believe that courts, particularly constitutional courts, can – and indeed should – play a key role against democratic erosion and backsliding. For instance, in the case of Colombia, mentioned above, the Constitutional Court has even been lauded by Tom Ginsburg and Aziz Huq for 'almost single-handedly saving constitutional democracy'.[62] It is in this context, and building upon the literature in this first camp, that Ming-Sung Kuo put forward his claim, briefly mentioned above, that courts can act as institutional decelerators against forms of populist 'instantaneous democracy'.[63] Others, like David Prendergast, have also made somewhat similar claims, for instance, that '[i]n addressing the populist challenge, courts can, in principle, try to be a few steps ahead in anticipating and, where they can, slowing democratic degradation', thereby protecting democracy from populism.[64] In the same vein, Yaniv Roznai has argued that 'courts can

[54] Ginsburg and Huq (n 34) 189.

[55] *Minerva Mills Ltd v Union of India* (1980) 3 SCC 625.

[56] *Kesavananda Bharati v State of Kerala* (1973) 4 SCC 225.

[57] See, eg, Issacharoff (n 52) 163. See also, more broadly, the literature on 'unconstitutional constitutional amendments', eg, Roznai, *Unconstitutional Constitutional Amendments* (n 48); R Albert, *Constitutional Amendments: Making, Breaking, and Changing Constitutions* (Oxford, Oxford University Press, 2019).

[58] *Movement for Quality Government v Knesset*, HCJ 5658/23 (1 January 2024) (Isr SC).

[59] ibid.

[60] Other examples could be mentioned, including the 'Nkandla' judgment of the Constitutional Court of South Africa, rendered in March 2016. See *Economic Freedom Fighters v Speaker of the National Assembly and Others* [2016] ZACC 11, as mentioned in, eg, Ginsburg and Huq (n 34) 189 and Huq (n 39) 24. Many more could also be mentioned, notably in the context of unconstitutional constitutional amendments. See, eg, *Interpretation No 499* of the Council of Grand Justices of Taiwan (24 March 2000) and the more complex *Mabiziri v Attorney General* (Uganda SC, 2018) 1, 11, 19–21, 101, upheld by *Mabirizi v Attorney General* (E Afr Ct J, 2019) 96, 136 in September 2020. Both examples are mentioned by Yaniv Roznai in Roznai, 'Who Will Save the Redheads?' (n 48) 341–343.

[61] The concept is discussed in more detail in ch 5.

[62] Ginsburg and Huq (n 34) 188.

[63] Kuo (n 12).

[64] Prendergast (n 50) 246 (and 261).

function as a useful stop sign or a speed bump against constitutional and legal reforms aiming to undermine or erode the democratic order'.[65]

The second camp, a more diverse group of legal scholars with different approaches and viewpoints, is generally much more sceptical vis-à-vis the role of courts against authoritarian populism and, more broadly, democratic erosion or backsliding. Mark Tushnet, for instance, is of the view that the protection of civil liberties against authoritarian excesses is not the preserve of judges, but, rather, a task, responsibility and commitment of the citizenry.[66] In arguing for the replacement of judicial supremacy with popular constitutionalism,[67] Tushnet firmly sits with Larry D Kramer and the latter's commitment to the idea that 'ordinary citizens [have] a central and pivotal role in implementing their Constitution'.[68] For Kramer, the final interpretative duty should rest with 'the people themselves' rather than with courts.[69] This has led to a different assessment of the relationship between populism and constitutionalism, broadly taken. In a book published in 2022, Mark Tushnet and Bojan Bugarič argue that in some instances, populism can in fact be consistent with a thin version of constitutionalism.[70] In a relatively similar vein, Richard Bellamy argues in a recent article that mechanisms of legal constitutionalism can be a driver of populism and can contribute to the production of different types of arbitrary rule. For him, '[c]ounter-majoritarian mechanisms, including entrenched constitutions and judicial review, form part of the problem rather than a solution'.[71] Rather than calling for a strengthening of legal constitutionalism, as many have, Bellamy argues that 'the solution lies in exploring how democratic politics might be deployed to enable the political constitution to renew itself'.[72] Moreover, in an analysis focused on the political implications of the different forms of judicial review in new and transitional democracies, Stephen Gardbaum raises the possibility that the active exercise of 'strong-form' powers of judicial review can trigger political backlash against courts, which can, in turn, reduce or even eliminate its independence.[73] In a similar vein, Roberto Gargarella warns against

[65] Roznai, 'Who Will Save the Redheads?' (n 48) 341. In this article, Roznai put a particular emphasis on judicial review powers, particularly in the context of constitutional amendments: 'Often, when courts declare constitutional amendments that would significantly harm the democratic constitutional order as unconstitutional, such judicial decisions may slow down – even if not completely stop – authoritarian initiatives until different political actors gain power.'

[66] Tushnet, 'Taking Back the Constitution' (n 14); Tushnet, 'Taking the Constitution Away' (n 14).

[67] ibid.

[68] LD Kramer, *The People Themselves: Popular Constitutionalism and Judicial Review* (Oxford, Oxford University Press, 2004) 8.

[69] ibid. This is also discussed in ch 2.

[70] M Tushnet and B Bugarič, *Power to the People: Constitutionalism in the Age of Populism* (Oxford, Oxford University Press, 2022).

[71] R Bellamy, 'Political Constitutionalism and Populism' (2023) 50 *Journal of Law and Society* 7, 23.

[72] ibid 25.

[73] Gardbaum (n 14) 320. Gardbaum thus presents a pragmatic argument for weak-form (rather than strong-form) review in the context of transitional democracies, with a view to minimising or reducing the pressures that judicial review places on the independence of the judiciary of new and transitional democracies.

an overly powerful judiciary, dangerously detached from the will of the people, particularly in newer democracies.[74] Tom Gerald Daly, for his part, questions the democracy-building function of courts in a post-authoritarian context and argues that the faith in courts as democracy-builders places excessive reliance on them and can, as such, often be counter-productive.[75]

Many others are also sceptical vis-à-vis the 'democracy-enhancing' function of courts against the threat of populist authoritarianism and (or) illiberalism.[76] Some in the European Union (EU) context, like Dariusz Adamski, doubt that domestic courts – even when aided by supranational institutions like the EU Commission and the tools at their disposal, such as the infringement procedure – can do much to sustain liberal constitutionalism against the forces (and successes) of illiberal governments.[77] For Adamski, domestic courts and the infringement procedure can, at best, 'only slow down the process of constitutional retrogression'.[78] Others, like Andrea Pin, even go as far as to suggest that courts themselves (particularly supranational courts) are 'partially responsible for the supranational malaise and the rise of populism' in Europe.[79]

However, both camps, I contend, generally paint an incomplete picture – particularly with regard to the relationship between populism, constitutionalism and the judiciary. Populism is often addressed in isolation, without a specific investigation into its implications for courts,[80] or as an element that forms part of a broader examination of democratic backsliding or erosion – that is to say, without a detailed analysis of the role that populism plays, more specifically, in the context of the latter two processes.[81] As Nicola Lacey has observed, there is a growing political theory and political science literature engaging with the rise of populism (notably on its causes and general implications), but this literature very rarely engages with the implications of populism for law, constitutionalism (or the rule of law) and, I would add, the courts.[82] This, of course, is changing, as Lacey

[74] R Gargarella, 'In Search of Democratic Justice – What Courts Should Not Do: Argentina, 1983–2002' in S Gloppen, R Gargarella and E Skaar (eds), *Democratization and the Judiciary: The Accountability Function of Courts in New Democracies* (London, Frank Cass, 2004).

[75] Daly, *The Alchemists* (n 14); and Daly, 'The Alchemists' (n 14).

[76] For a recent example regarding Prime Minister Benjamin Netanyahu's coalition government's attempts to overhaul the judiciary in Israel and curb its powers, see R Zinigrad, 'The False Hope of Israel's Protestors: Why the Supreme Court Is Not (and Never Was) the Last Bastion of Democracy' (*Verfassungsblog*, 8 September 2023) *Verfassungsblog*, www.verfassungsblog.de/the-false-hope-of-israels-protestors.

[77] Adamski (n 32) 659.

[78] ibid.

[79] A Pin, 'The Transnational Drivers of Populist Backlash in Europe: The Role of Courts' (2019) *German Law Journal* 225. That said, Pin also suggests in the same article, at p 243, that 'courts can contribute to the recovery of supranational constitutional projects by amending their legal doctrines on the relationship between human rights, democracy and progress'.

[80] See, eg, N Urbinati, *Me, The People: How Populism Transforms Democracy* (Cambridge, Harvard University Press, 2019); N Urbinati, 'Political Theory of Populism' (2019) 22 *Annual Review of Political Science* 111.

[81] See, eg, Ginsburg and Huq (n 34).

[82] N Lacey, 'Populism and the Rule of Law' (2019) 15 *Annual Review of Law and Social Science* 79, 80.

has herself noted,[83] but there are still few in-depth and contextual analyses of the implications of populism specifically for constitutionalism and, more particularly, for the courts.[84]

In addition, the literature on populism, courts and (or) constitutionalism tends to have little to say about 'effects' and 'effectiveness' – despite the fact that it uses these terms relatively frequently.[85] Indeed, the literature is somewhat silent on the effects (or consequences, or what Frederick Schauer has called the 'non-legal end-states') of laws, judicial decisions and legal doctrine.[86] In fact, the question of the relevant timescale (and space-scale) of analysis further complicates any search for 'effectiveness'.[87] To give an example, a court could manage to block a given piece of legislation or a policy today, but this could lead to backlash over a longer period of time, and vice versa. These questions intertwining frame and substance are thus, in my view, not sufficiently addressed in the existing literature. They will be addressed both theoretically and contextually, mainly in relation to the book's three main case studies.

IV. Notes on the Case Study Selection

The few existing studies on populism, courts and (or) constitutionalism often reveal a certain 'selection bias' (or 'selection effect'), akin to a confirmation bias, which Mark Tushnet and Bojan Bugarič have highlighted.[88] For instance, the scholarly work on populism and courts (and its implications for constitutionalism more broadly) usually portrays populism in a more negative or critical light when discussing cases like Hungary under Fidesz or Poland under the Law and Justice Party (*Prawo i Sprawiedliwość* or PiS). In simple terms, populism appears 'problematic', 'dangerous' or even 'anti-democratic' when mentioned in connection with recent examples of more authoritarian (and usually right-wing) forms of populism, mainly in Central and Eastern European countries such as

[83] ibid.

[84] For exceptions, ie, for academic discussions on the implications of populism for the judiciary, see, eg, D Giannoulopoulos and Y McDermott (eds), *Judicial Independence Under Threat* (Oxford, Oxford University Press, 2022); JW Müller, '"Enemies of the People": Populism's Threat to Independent Judiciaries' in ibid; 'Populist Rhetoric, False Mirroring, and the Courts' (2020) 18 *International Journal of Constitutional Law* 746; Arato (n 47); and Prendergast (n 50).

[85] See, eg, Kuo (n 12).

[86] F Schauer, 'Comparative Constitutional Compliance: Notes Towards a Research Agenda' in M Adams and J Bomhoff (eds), *Practice and Theory in Comparative Law* (Cambridge, Cambridge University Press, 2012).

[87] David Landau makes a similar point in D Landau, 'Personalism and the Trajectories of Populist Constitutions' (2020) 16 *Annual Review of Law and Social Science* 293, 302: 'One shortcoming of much of the recent literature on populism – and democratic decline more generally – is that comparative studies generally take the form of snapshots over relatively brief periods of time, usually centered around when regimes come to power.'

[88] See Tushnet and Bugarič (n 22) 4. This 'selection bias' was first identified by Paris Aslanidis, in P Aslanidis, 'Avoiding Bias in the Study of Populism' (2017) 2 *Chinese Political Science Review* 266.

Hungary, Slovakia and, until recently, Poland. The approach can be slightly more ambivalent when discussing cases of left-wing populism in Latin America, like Evo Morales' Bolivia or Rafael Correa's Ecuador, for instance, but only relatively so.[89] Also, albeit in rarer instances, populism might even be portrayed positively, especially when discussing its implications for courts in cases such as Franklin D Roosevelt's New Deal, and his (ultimately abandoned) court-packing plan,[90] or Syriza in Greece.[91] As such, one may question whether populism is in fact perceived through a political lens, which affects, influences and possibly distorts understandings of populism, notably in relation to its 'democratic' character and its implications for courts.

It is precisely for this reason, and to avoid the selection bias discussed above, that I have chosen to test the theoretical framework – based on spatiotemporality – elaborated in the first part of the monograph and explore, in the second part of my monograph, three more difficult or challenging case studies. These case studies reveal, in my view, a certain incompleteness in the existing literature on populism, law and courts. Indeed, the conceptual framework (including the language used in this literature) is often ill-adapted to analyse more complicated and ambiguous cases, such as the recent examples of Malaysia,[92] the Philippines[93] or Armenia,[94] to name a few. Imagine, for example, the ruler of a country who frequently uses anti-establishment rhetoric and outfits, tells supporters to blockade courts, and threatens constitutional court judges with dismissal if they do not resign – before ultimately removing them from office through a constitutional amendment. In the language of the existing literature on populism, constitutionalism and (or) democratic erosion, it would be hard to view and depict this leader as anything other

[89] See, eg, Loughlin (n 29) 440–442; M Tushnet, 'Varieties of Populism' (2019) 20 *German Law Journal* 383, 388, hinting that the constitutional changes in Ecuador (and recent Andean populism in general) might be an instance of (or the first step towards a form of) 'transformative "populism"', namely the transforming of subjects into citizens. By contrast, scholars like Catherine Conaghan, Carlos de la Torre, Tom Ginsburg and Aziz H Huq usually take a more critical stance on these events – particularly in Ecuador under Rafael Correa. See, generally, ch 5.

[90] See, eg, B Bugarič, 'Could Populism Be Good for Constitutional Democracy?' (2019) 15 *Annual Review of Law and Social Science* 41, 42; B Bugarič, 'The Two Faces of Populism: Between Authoritarian and Democratic Populism' (2019) 20 *German Law Journal* 390, 394–395. See also Ginsburg and Huq (n 34) 128–129. For an interesting historical take on Roosevelt's populism (and how his populist ideas were influenced by the late 19th century Populist Party), see T Frank, *People Without Power: The War on Populism and the Fight for Democracy* (London, Scribe, 2020), especially ch 3, and D Rodrik, 'What Does a True Populism Look Like? It Looks Like the New Deal' (*New York Times*, 21 February 2018) www.nytimes.com/2018/02/21/opinion/populism-new-deal.html.

[91] See, eg, Bugarič, 'Could Populism Be Good' (n 90) 46, 50–51. See also Tushnet and Bugarič (n 22) 140–147. For a slightly more critical stance on Syriza's relationship with the courts, see B Moffitt, *Populism* (Cambridge, Polity, 2020) 89–90.

[92] In Malaysia, courts – rather than populist political actors – have become active agents of a certain 'judicial Islamisation' of secular courts and the constitutional order more broadly. See Y Tew, 'Stealth Theocracy' (2018) 58 *Virginia Journal of International Law* 31.

[93] See, eg, D Gatmaytan, 'The Case of the Philippine Judiciary – Guardian of Democracy or Enabler of Populism?' in S Hardt, AW Heringa and HT Nguyen (eds), *Populism and Democracy* (The Hague, Eleven International Publishing, 2020).

[94] See ch 4.

than a populist with manifestly and pervasively anti-institutional (if not outright authoritarian) tendencies. Yet, and as discussed in the first chapter of the second part of this monograph (chapter four), the situation in this particular case – a case that mirrors this hypothetical scenario, namely Nikol Pashinyan's Armenia following the 2018 Velvet Revolution – is arguably far more complicated and nuanced than it might appear at first blush.[95]

Employing a combination of what Ran Hirschl describes as the 'prototypical cases' and the 'most difficult cases' principles of case study selection,[96] I propose to examine, first, the case of Armenia in the immediate aftermath of the 2018 Velvet Revolution, as an exemplar or prototype[97] of an understudied 'new' or 'third-wave' constitutional democracy – more specifically a post-1989 emerging (or consolidating) constitutional democracy. The emphasis of academic literature on constitutional democracy in post-communist states thus far has been on Central and Eastern European states, particularly Hungary and Poland.[98] Meanwhile, many post-Soviet states, particularly Armenia, Moldova, Kyrgyzstan and, albeit to a lesser extent, Georgia, have for the most part received scant attention in the academic literature on populism, constitutionalism, law and the courts.[99] Armenia has in fact been almost completely ignored in such literature over recent years.[100] Yet, the recent standoff between a newly elected populist leader and *ancien régime* judges in the direct aftermath of the 2018 Velvet Revolution raises many salient – and challenging – questions for scholars of constitutional democracy, constitutionalism, populism and the courts, both from theoretical and practical

[95] Other examples could be mentioned, from Franklin Delano Roosevelt's famous 'court-packing' plan to, more recently, former President Joe Biden's commission to study possible reforms to the US Supreme Court.

[96] See Ran Hirschl, 'The Question of Case Selection in Comparative Constitutional Law' (2005) 53 *American Journal of Comparative Law* 125.

[97] ibid 125.

[98] See, eg, M Krygier, 'The Challenge of Institutionalisation: Post-Communist "Transitions", Populism, and the Rule of Law' (2019) 15 *European Constitutional Law Review* 544; W Sadurski, *Poland's Constitutional Breakdown* (Oxford, Oxford University Press, 2019); B Bugarič, 'Central Europe's Descent into Autocracy: A Constitutional Analysis of Authoritarian Populism' (2019) 17 *International Journal of Constitutional Law* 597; B Bugarič and T Ginsburg, 'The Assault on Postcommunist Courts' (2016) 27 *Journal of Democracy* 69 (focusing mainly on Central and Eastern European post-communist states), etc.

[99] For a rare exception, see, eg, G Armas-Cardona, 'Context Matters: The Rule of Law and Armenia's Referendum to Remove Constitutional Court Justices' (*Verfassungsblog*, 29 February 2020) www.verfassungsblog.de/context-matters. On the post-Soviet world more generally, see, eg, W Partlett, *The Post-Soviet as Post-Colonial: A New Paradigm for Understanding Constitutional Dynamics in the Former Soviet Empire* (Cheltenham, Edward Elgar, 2022) and W Partlett, 'Post-Soviet Constitution Making' in D Landau and H Lerner (eds), *Comparative Constitution Making* (Cheltenham, Edward Elgar, 2019); and A Mazmanyan, 'Judicialization of Politics: The Post-Soviet Way' (2015) 13 *International Journal of Constitutional Law* 200.

[100] To give an example of the scarcity of legal analyses pertaining to Armenia and the 'Velvet Revolution' in particular, the 2019 Global Review of Constitutional Law, published in 2020 by I·CONnect and the Clough Center, which contains 73 country reports, does not make any references to Armenia, despite the importance of the legal-political changes that took place that year in that country. Armenia was also not included in the 2020 and the 2021 versions of the Review, but was finally included in the 2022 edition published in October 2023.

perspectives, questions which have not yet been discussed in depth in the comparative constitutional law literature.[101] This chapter aims to address, and in part fill, these important gaps. Beyond these difficult questions, the Armenian case study is relevant because of its complexity, as an example of populism that does not fit neatly into traditional left-right labels, especially as those are defined in Western political discourse.

The second case selected for analysis is the case of Ecuador under the presidency of Rafael Correa (2007–2017). Ecuador can be seen as an exemplar or prototype of a Latin American democracy with a long history of populism (and institutional/political instability). While there is some literature in political science focusing on Correa's populist discourse and actions, very few legal scholars outside Latin America have provided an in-depth and contextual analysis of Correa's populism from an institutional perspective, particularly in relation to its implications for the Ecuadorian judiciary.[102] Ecuador is also a difficult case, in part because of the democracy-enhancing features of some of Correa's actions and constitutional changes, as will be discussed in further detail later in this book. In addition, Ecuador provides a good example of fertile ground for Latin American left-wing populism, a form of populism that has often been overlooked in the literature, which instead tends to focus on instances of right-wing, authoritarian and (or) exclusionary populism in Europe and in the US.[103]

The third and final case study chosen is that of the UK in the aftermath of the Brexit vote. The latter can be seen as an exemplar or prototype of a well-established Western democracy in which significant political actors have had recourse to the ideal-typical populist discourse, from rhetoric[104] to action, including an increased use of and reliance on prerogative powers as well as plebiscitary instruments, amid a (disputed) backdrop of growing assertions of judicial authority in political affairs and, particularly, against executive powers. It is also a difficult case study, particularly given the political nature of the UK's Constitution and the absence of 'strong-form' mechanisms of judicial review, compared with many other established constitutional democracies.

[101] These questions include, for instance, the following: Can constitutional democracy and the rule of law be reconciled – as Armenian Prime Minister Nikol Pashinyan claims – with the mass removal of judges appointed by a previous, corrupt and semi-authoritarian regime? In other words, can a populist strengthen, or even vindicate, the rule of law? These questions are addressed – directly and indirectly – in Part II of this monograph.

[102] For a recent (and relatively short) exception, see Tushnet and Bugarič (n 22) 184–188.

[103] See, eg, WA Galston, *Anti-Pluralism: The Populist Threat to Liberal Democracy* (New Haven, Yale University Press, 2018); JW Müller, *What is Populism?* (London, Penguin, 2017). This is not to say, however, that *all* populisms in Latin America have been 'left-wing' populisms. Examples of Latin American 'right-wing' populisms (or, as some would call them, 'market reform populisms') since the 1940s include Alberto Fujimori's Peru (1990–2000) and Carlos Menem's Argentina (1989–1999). In that regard, see C de la Torre, *Populist Seduction in Latin America*, 2nd edn (Athens, Ohio University Press, 2010) xiii–xiv.

[104] There are, of course, strong similarities and links between 'rhetoric' and 'discourse'. My view on the distinction between both is the following: 'rhetoric' relates to style, or form, whereas 'discourse' is broader, referring to both form *and* substance, or both rhetoric *and* action(s).

Conducting a purely horizontal or holistic comparison is not, of course, the purpose of the three case studies. It goes without saying that the experiences discussed in the three case studies are rooted in very different sociopolitical and institutional contexts. The idea, rather, is to analyse these case studies with a view to evaluating and testing – in light of the framework established and described in the first part of this monograph – the broader literature, which affirms the power of constitutional courts to act as ramparts against authoritarian, self-aggrandising populists, including Kuo's hypothesis that courts can act as judicial decelerators against populist-driven impatience and 'instantaneous' democracy. To do so, instead of comparing these selections horizontally or holistically, as mentioned above, I investigate each case in terms of the relationship between the executive and the judiciary through the lens of space and time and, more specifically, in relation to the abovementioned claims regarding judicial deceleration and the role of the courts against populist and executive aggrandisement more broadly. The analysis conducted is therefore highly contextual and highlights populism's reach beyond established democracies, while bringing insights from two relatively understudied jurisdictions at the periphery or in the Global South, as well as one from the so-called 'established democratic order'.[105] In doing so, the monograph seeks to engage with – and reflect on – the various experiences of constitutionalism across the world and to avoid the pitfall of offering an analysis of populism through the (limited) lens of a globalised version of Northern constitutionalism.[106]

V. Scope and Limitations

This monograph concerns the character of contemporary populism and its implications for the judiciary in a constitutional democracy. As mentioned above, the analysis is conducted through a particular lens, namely that of the conjunction of space and time – or spatiotemporality. This book does not therefore aim to determine the origins or causes (sociolegal, sociological, economical, historical or otherwise) of populism.[107] As Issacharoff has noted, '[m]uch has been written on the economic preconditions for the current populist surge, and the role of failing economic fortunes in prompting a backlash in politics, particularly in

[105] The expression is from Samuel Issacharoff. See, eg, S Issacharoff, *Democracy Unmoored: Populism and the Corruption of Popular Sovereignty* (Oxford, Oxford University Press, 2023) 7.

[106] On this, see P Dann, 'Southern Turn, Northern Implications: Rethinking the Meaning of Colonial Legacies for Comparative Constitutional Studies' (2023) 1 *Comparative Constitutional Studies* 174, 176.

[107] For this, see, eg, P Norris and R Inglehart, *Cultural Backlash: Trump, Brexit, and Authoritarian Populism* (Cambridge, Cambridge University Press, 2019); Y Algan, E Beasley, D Cohen and M Foucault, *Les origines du populisme : Enquête sur un schisme politique et social* (Paris, Seuil, 2019); R Eatwell and Goodwin, *National Populism: The Revolt Against Liberal Democracy* (Elmwood, Pelican, 2018); B Eichengreen, *The Populist Temptation: Economic Grievance and Political Reaction in the Modern Era* (Oxford, Oxford University Press, 2018); D Rodrik, 'Populism and the Economics of Globalization' (2017) 1 *Journal of International Business Policy* 12.

the face of immigration'.[108] Instead, my focus in this monograph is on the legal – understood in a more open-textured way that abuts other disciplinary perspectives – rather than purely on the sociological, economical and (or) historical. In terms of institutions analysed, the emphasis is on courts (particularly apex courts, such as constitutional or supreme courts) and, to a lesser extent, executives and legislatures.

My aim in this monograph is not to make strong normative or definitive claims about the value of populism, nor to decisively answer the question of whether populism is a phenomenon with positive or negative implications. While many writers on populism have adopted a critical stance on the phenomenon and its implications, notably for constitutionalism,[109] others – most famously scholars like Ernesto Laclau and Chantal Mouffe – have characterised populism (more specifically its left-wing variant) as an 'emancipatory force' that is beneficial for democracy.[110] Populism has likewise been praised for its mobilisation effects.[111] In fact, some writers – including legal scholars – have even criticised the very use of the term 'populism' for its negative, pejorative and even disqualifying connotations.[112] Similarly, scholars such as Yannis Stavrakakis and Anton Jäger have criticised the 'limitations' of the 'mainstream' scholarship on populism, notably its 'moralistic stress'.[113]

[108] S Issacharoff, 'The Corruption of Popular Sovereignty' (2020) 18 *International Journal of Constitutional Law* 1109, 1111–1112.

[109] See, eg, JW Müller, 'Populism and Constitutionalism' in C Rovira Kaltwasser, P Ochoa Espejo, P Taggart and P Ostiguy (eds), *The Oxford Handbook of Populism* (Oxford, Oxford University Press, 2017); P Blokker, 'Populist Constitutionalism' in C de la Torre (ed), *Routledge Handbook of Global Populism* (Abingdon, Routledge, 2019) (although Blokker recognises, especially at p 115, that the relationship between populism and constitutionalism is not always a negative one and that populism can potentially allow forms of radical-democratic constitutional change). Other scholars, like Mark Tushnet and Bojan Bugarič, more clearly argue that while some forms of populism are inconsistent with constitutionalism, many others are not. See Tushnet and Bugarič (n 22).

[110] See, eg, C Mouffe, *For a Left Populism* (London, Verso, 2018); E Laclau, *On Populist Reason* (London, Verso, 2005). Others have also lauded the 'democratic' nature of certain types or forms of populism. See, eg, Tushnet and Bugarič (n 22); F Tarragoni, *L'Esprit démocratique du populisme* (Paris, La Découverte, 2019).

[111] R Jansen, 'Populist Mobilization: A New Theoretical Approach to Populism' (2011) 29 *Sociological Theory* 75, 82.

[112] See, eg, R Howse, 'Epilogue: In Defense of Disruptive Democracy – A Critique of Anti-Populism' (2019) 17(2) *International Journal of Constitutional Law* 641. Others have made similar arguments. For Jacques Rancière, for instance, critiques of populism hide a modern expression of the hatred of democracy: 'ce nom commode masque et révèle en même temps le grand souhait de l'oligarchie : gouverner sans peuple, c'est-à-dire sans division du peuple : gouverner sans politique'. See J Rancière, *La Haine de la démocratie* (Paris, La Fabrique, 2005) 88. See also C Colliot-Thélène, 'Quel est le peuple du populisme?" in C Colliot-Thélène and F Guénard (eds), *Peuples et populisme* (Paris, Presses universitaires de France, 2014). It is also worth noting that many, especially in the US, tend to perceive the epithet in a more positive way, with some authors criticising the negative, dismissive and sometimes instrumental use of the term by 'Anti-Populists'. See, eg, Frank (n 90); DA Johnson, 'In Defense of Democratic Populism' in GL Neuman (ed), *Human Rights in a Time of Populism: Challenges and Responses* (Cambridge, Cambridge University Press, 2020).

[113] Y Stavrakakis and A Jäger, 'Accomplishments and Limitations of the "New" Mainstream in Contemporary Populism Studies' (2018) 21 *European Journal of Social Theory* 547.

Recognising the risk of 'self-idealisation' by 'good democrats',[114] I therefore strive in this monograph to avoid making value judgments vis-à-vis populism. Rather, my aim is to take populism seriously, as a response proposal to contemporaneous problems that must be given proper attention, and to understand it as such.[115] As mentioned previously, I recognise that populism may take many forms;[116] and that it is therefore not desirable to make all-encompassing claims about its normative value. For the same reason, I do not believe it is particularly helpful to compartmentalise populism, or to create a hyperdetailed typology or 'taxonomy' of populism(s).[117] Instead, this monograph should be viewed as a contextual analysis of specific (and potentially 'difficult') instances of contemporary populism, particularly in the three chapters of Part II, which indicate three distinctive relationships between populism and constitutionalism, as well as three different institutional (judicial) responses to populism. Of course, certain conclusions can – and will – be drawn from these case studies; however, these conclusions are not necessarily intended to apply to *all* instances of populism. The same caveat applies to the first three (more theoretical) chapters: I recognise that the analysis in these chapters may not always apply equally to every variety of populism, right or left, bundled or unbundled.[118]

Moreover, while I occasionally refer to more historical instances of populism, mainly from the mid- to late twentieth century, my focus in this monograph is resolutely on contemporary populism. By 'contemporary', I refer mainly to actual or recent instances of populism, mostly from the twenty-first century – and more specifically in the two decades that preceded the publication of this monograph. This is not to say, of course, that earlier forms of populism – for example, in the context of the French Revolution, the Narodnik movement in Tsarist Russia or the People's Party (also known as the 'Populist Party') in late nineteenth-century America[119] – do not provide valuable insights into the current phenomenon.

[114] C Mouffe, 'The "End of Politics" and the Challenge of Right-Wing Populism' in F Panizza (ed), *Populism and the Mirror of Democracy* (London, Verso, 2005) 55. See also C de la Torre, 'Global Populism: Histories, Trajectories, Problems and Challenges' in de la Torre (ed) (n 109) 7.

[115] On the importance of applying the term 'populism' more responsibly, see Y Serhan, '*Populism* is Meaningless' (*The Atlantic*, 14 March 2020) www.theatlantic.com/international/archive/2020/03/what-is-populism/607600.

[116] Tushnet and Bugarič (n 22); Tushnet (n 89); Bugarič, 'Two Faces of Populism' (n 90); D Fontana, 'Unbundling Populism' (2018) 65 *UCLA Law Review* 1482; M Canovan, *Populism* (London, Junction Books, 1981).

[117] For such a taxonomy, see, eg, PB Guy and J Pierre, 'A Typology of Populism: Understanding the Different Forms of Populism and Their Implications' (2020) 27 *Democratization* 928. Cédric M Koch has also proposed a typology distinguishing 'communitarian' from 'cosmopolitan' types of populism. See CM Koch, 'Varieties of Populism and the Challenges to Global Constitutionalism: Dangers, Promises and Implications' (2021) 10 *Global Constitutionalism* 400. Other commentators have gone as far as to claim that there are up to 36 types, categories or 'families' of populism. See, eg, the April 2019 issue of *Éléments* (issue no 177).

[118] See Fontana (n 116). The distinction between 'bundled' and 'unbundled' populism is discussed below.

[119] According to Margaret Canovan, the origins of populism can be traced back to these two movements. See Canovan (n 116) 5–6.

In fact, many earlier populists, from Saint-Just, Jean-Paul Marat and Napoléon III in France to Andrew Jackson in the US, warned of the risks of ignoring the 'will of the people'.[120] Others, like Carl Schmitt in the 1920s, also provided important critiques of the liberal component of constitutional democracy and arguably laid out the theoretical foundations of contemporary populism, something that is discussed in more depth in Part I of this monograph.[121] Nevertheless, as I am interested (mainly in Part II of this monograph) in the contemporary judicial responses to populism (and the broader literature on judicial responses to democratic erosion and backsliding), I have chosen to limit the scope of this monograph to more recent or actual instances of populism. Similarly, the focus of the monograph is on populists in power, although I also occasionally refer to populists in opposition.[122]

Finally, while its contribution mainly lies within the academic discipline of law, more specifically constitutional theory[123] and comparative constitutional law,[124] this book can be viewed as a cross-disciplinary study of populism. Given that the concepts of time and space are not primarily (and inherently) legal[125] concepts, it only makes sense to draw on (and borrow from) other disciplines that have studied these concepts more extensively, including political science and sociology. In fact, the field of 'time studies' (and, although to a lesser extent, that of 'space studies') within the social sciences is extensive. Theory, especially political and social theory, can shed a new light on how space and time affect legal phenomena and concepts such as constitutions, constitutionalism and constitutional democracy, and vice versa. As such, this monograph offers a cross-disciplinary analysis of space and time, insofar as it takes inspiration – and borrows – from the work of political and social theorists such as Hartmut Rosa and William E Scheuerman,[126] only to name a few, to shed a different light on the abovementioned legal phenomena and

[120] In the American context, see, for instance, Johnson (n 112); M Kazin, *The Populist Persuasion: An American History* (Ithaca, Cornell University Press, 1998), especially ch 2; Frank (n 90) especially ch 3. On the 'illiberal democratic' character of France's First Republic and how, later (mainly after the 1848 Revolution and during the Second Empire), Louis-Napoléon Bonaparte (also known as Napoléon III) came to follow the 'standard authoritarian-populist playbook', notably by seeking 'direct endorsement by the people while bypassing and undermining representative institutions', see S Berman 'The Pipe Dream of Undemocratic Liberalism' (2017) 28 *Democracy* 29, 30–32. On the 'caesarist' and 'illiberal' character of democratic representation in France under Napoléon III (1848–1870), see P Rosanvallon, *Le Siècle du populisme : Histoire, théorie, critique* (Paris, Seuil, 2020), especially Part I, ch 1, 97–113.

[121] See chs 1 and 2.

[122] On the distinction between the two, see, eg, J Mansbridge and S Macedo, 'Populism and Democratic Theory' (2019) 15 *Annual Review of Law and Social Science* 59, 60.

[123] Which, I acknowledge, is as legal as it is political, given that it draws heavily on political theory – and can even be viewed as a subcategory of the latter.

[124] These two legal subfields offer a perspective that foregrounds the role of law, legal principle and legal concepts, which are themselves focused on the idea of law as an autonomous or semi-autonomous domain of rules and interpretive practices.

[125] 'Legal' here (and elsewhere in this book) does not refer to 'juridically compliant' and does not have a normative meaning but simply refers to the study of law as an academic discipline.

[126] These two authors are particularly relevant for this book, as their study of time has focused (at least in part) on political and legal institutions.

concepts, as well as politico-legal ones, such as populism. However, this monograph is not a work of social theory, nor of (political) philosophy.[127] The book is ultimately grounded in legal methodologies, including doctrinal, comparative and (to a lesser extent) empirical ones,[128] although it rejects narrowly legalistic interpretations and embraces cross-disciplinary readings. Put differently, the monograph does not aim to directly contribute to social theory or (political) philosophy but rather engages with their insights in a way that complements legal analysis.

VI. Conceptual Clarifications

Before discussing the abovementioned claims in more depth, it is important to introduce some conceptual clarifications, notably on what I mean when I refer to: (A) 'populism'; (B) 'constitutional democracy'; and (C) 'space,' 'time' and (or) 'chronotope'.

A. Populism

There are countless definitions of 'populism' in the academic literature. Arguably the most prominent (and the most widely cited[129]) definition has been formulated by Cas Mudde, who defines it as an ideology, more specifically one 'that considers society to be ultimately separated into two homogeneous and antagonistic groups, "the pure people" versus "the corrupt elite," and which argues that politics should be the expression of the *volonté générale* (general will) of the people'.[130] For Mudde, populism is not a full or thick ideology, but rather a 'thin-centred ideology', that is to say, one that exhibits 'a restricted core attached to a narrower range of political concepts'[131] and that can be combined with other (full or thin) ideologies.[132] Under that ideational approach, the core of populism is generally considered to be the concept of 'the people' and its antagonist or nemesis, the concept of 'the elite'.[133] Others, like Ben Stanley, claim that the common core of the ideology of populism is the idea of 'the people', but also the principle of sovereignty (and, one may add, more specifically, the idea of unrestricted or unconstrained popular sovereignty)

[127] Nor of analytical jurisprudence or normative legal theory. For an analysis of time grounded in legal philosophy, see, eg, F Ost, *Le Temps du droit* (Paris, Odile Jacob, 1999).

[128] See, eg, ch 4, particularly the paragraph based on an April 2024 interview with a constitutional court judge.

[129] P Aslanidis, 'Is Populism an Ideology? A Refutation and a New Perspective' (2016) 64 *Political Studies* 88, 88.

[130] C Mudde, 'The Populist Zeitgeist' (2004) 39 *Government and Opposition* 541, 543.

[131] M Freeden, 'Is Nationalism a Distinct Ideology?' (1998) 46 *Political Studies* 748, 750, as cited in Mudde (n 130) 544.

[132] Mudde (n 130) 544.

[133] ibid.

and, finally, the underlying dichotomy of 'us against them'.[134] However, and by contrast, some scholars, including Catherine Fieschi, view populism as a self-sufficient ideology.[135]

Beyond this understanding of populism as an ideology (whether thin-centred or self-sufficient), other scholars have defined populism in a myriad different ways, including as a mode of persuasion,[136] a political strategy,[137] a political style,[138] a political logic,[139] a political identity,[140] a particular type of constitutional pathology,[141] a moralistic imagination of politics,[142] a mode of political identification,[143] a representative process,[144] or a discourse,[145] to name a few. Paris Aslanidis, for instance, suggests abandoning the conception of populism as an ideology in favour of one that is a 'discursive frame'.[146] Aslanidis' discursive definition of populism is as follows: 'a discourse, invoking the supremacy of popular sovereignty to claim that corrupt elites are defrauding "the People" of their rightful political authority'.[147] It is, in other words, an 'anti-elite discourse in the name of the sovereign People'.[148] For Ernesto Laclau, a movement, politician or political party 'is not populist because in its politics or ideology it presents actual *contents* identifiable as populistic, but because it shows a particular *logic of articulation* of those contents – whatever those contents are'.[149]

[134] B Stanley, 'The Thin Ideology of Populism' (2008) 13 *Journal of Political Ideologies* 95.

[135] C Fieschi, *Populocracy: The Tyranny of Authenticity and the Rise of Populism* (New York, Columbia University Press, 2019).

[136] See Kazin (n 120) 3, 5.

[137] See K Weyland 'Clarifying a Contested Concept: Populism in the Study of Latin American Politics' (2001) 34 *Comparative Politics* 1, 14; HG Betz, 'Conditions Favoring the Success and Failure of Radical Right-Wing Populist Parties in Contemporary Democracies' in Y Mény and Y Surel (eds), *Democracies and the Populist Challenge* (London, Palgrave MacMillan, 2002) 197, 198.

[138] See, eg, Ginsburg and Huq (n 34) 72, 79. For a different understanding of populism as a political style, see B Moffitt and S Tormey, 'Rethinking Populism: Politics, Mediatisation and Political Style' (2014) 62 *Political Studies* 381, 381, 387, 389. See also B Crick, *Democracy: A Very Short Introduction* (Oxford, Oxford University Press, 2002) 77, 90.

[139] See E Laclau, 'Populism: What's in a Name?' in Panizza (ed) (n 114) 44. For a different, non-Laclauan account of populism as a 'political logic', see also JB Ludis, *The Populist Explosion: How the Great Recession Transformed American and European Politics* (New York, Columbia Global Reports, 2016) and JB Ludis, 'Us v Them: The Birth of Populism' (*The Guardian*, 13 October 2016) www.theguardian.com/politics/2016/oct/13/birth-of-populism-donald-trump. See also Ginsburg and Huq (n 34) 79.

[140] See Arato, 'Populism' (n 47) 326. This definition is derived, at least in part, from the work of Laclau.

[141] See NW Barber, 'Populist Leaders and Political Parties' (2019) 20 *German Law Journal* 129.

[142] See Müller (n 109) 592–593.

[143] More specifically, a 'mode of political identification that retroactively constructs and gives meaning to "the people" as a political actor'. See F Panizza, 'What is Contested and What Is Not in the Debate About Populism', paper presented at the LSE Graduate Conference on Populism (3 November 2017), referring to O Reyes, 'Skinhead Conservatism: A Failed Populist Project' in Panizza (ed) (n 114).

[144] Urbinati, *Me, The People* (n 80) 5.

[145] See, eg, Aslanidis (n 129).

[146] ibid.

[147] ibid 96.

[148] ibid.

[149] Laclau (n 139) 33.

This monograph adopts a 'content-free' understanding of populism. As highlighted by Ginsburg and Huq (in their analysis of Müller's account of populism), 'populism is less a matter of policy preferences and more a matter of the guiding assumptions about how democracy can and should work, and how leaders can and should relate to the people'.[150] In that (relatively narrow) sense, populism can perhaps be viewed as a 'thin' ideology, 'in the sense that it is consistent with many combinations of policies, only some of which are logically related to the representational claim on which populism is founded'.[151] This is not to say, however, that there is only one single version of populism. David Fontana, for example, urges students of populism to distinguish between two versions, namely what he calls 'unbundled' and 'bundled' populism. While the former focuses on the claim that a significant number of citizens have been unjustly and unnecessarily disempowered by a small and disconnected elite, the latter goes further by including authoritarian and xenophobic claims.[152] It goes without saying that not all populists are authoritarian and (or) nativist, as will become evident in the rest of monograph, particularly in Part II.[153]

In light of the above, and acknowledging that populism is a matter of degree[154] and may take many forms,[155] I adopt, for the purposes of this monograph, a 'minimalist'[156] definition of populism, comprising two key elements: (1) a discursive (and practical) framing of the political world divided into two opposing groups – between 'them' and 'us', between *gouvernants* and *gouvernés*, more specifically between the ruling elite and the 'real' or 'ordinary'[157] people; and (2) a focus on popular sovereignty and plebiscitary instruments – as the unitary articulation of public power – accompanied with a rejection of mediated politics and institutional intermediaries,[158] perceived as illegitimately and unjustly thwarting the direct expression of the 'will of the people'.[159]

[150] Ginsburg and Huq (n 34) 78.

[151] Urbinati, *Me, The People* (n 80) 82.

[152] Fontana (n 116) 1485–1486.

[153] Examples of non-authoritarian populisms abound. They include Brexit (see ch 6); Nikol Pashinyan's Armenia (see ch 4); Alexis Tsipras' Syriza party in Greece; Podemos in Spain; and Bernie Sanders in the US, to name a few. More historical examples include Franklin Delano Roosevelt's presidency (and court-packing plan) in the US. See, generally, Bugarič, 'Could Populism Be Good' (n 90).

[154] See, eg, Barber (n 141) 134. In fact, many (if not most) comparative-oriented scholars view populism as a matter of degree, on a continuous, 'more-or-less' scale rather than in a dichotomous, 'either-or' way. For a critique of that form of 'degreeism', however, see TS Pappas, 'Modern Populism: Research Advances, Conceptual and Methodological Pitfalls, and the Minimal Definition' (2016) *Oxford Research Encyclopedia of Politics*.

[155] See, eg, Tushnet and Bugarič (n 22); Tushnet (n 89); Bugarič, 'Two Faces of Populism' (n 90); Fontana (n 116); Canovan (n 116).

[156] See also Urbinati, 'Political Theory of Populism' (n 80).

[157] Other formulations include the 'forgotten' or 'silent' people, amongst others.

[158] The reference here is both to institutions of representative democracy and mediators such as traditional news media.

[159] See also R Girard, 'Populism, "the People" and Popular Sovereignty' in M Cahill, C Ó Cinnéide, Seán Ó Conaill and Conor O'Mahony (eds), *Constitutional Change and Popular Sovereignty: Populism, Politics and the Law in Ireland* (Abingdon, Routledge, 2021); R Girard, 'Accountability, Populism and

B. (Liberal Constitutional) Democracy

Beyond 'populism', this book also often refers to 'democracy' or 'constitutional democracy' (and, in some instances, to 'liberal democracy'). This monograph adopts Tom Ginsburg and Aziz Huq's three-pronged account of 'democracy' – what they call 'liberal constitutional democracy'.[160] Taking an institutional (rather than socio-cultural or economic) focus, this minimalist definition of democracy is comprised of three 'conceptually separate but functionally intertwined' components or traits. First, it requires the existence of a democratic electoral system, including periodic free and fair elections and, drawing on Joseph Schumpeter, a 'genuine possibility of alteration in actual political power' – namely, the potential transfer of power.[161] Second, it involves the presence and protection of 'first generation' rights, mainly the liberal rights to speech, assembly and association. These rights are arguably essential to the existence of meaningful political, multi-party competition.[162] Third, this definition of democracy is completed by the existence of a bureaucracy governed by the rule of law (in its 'thin', or content-free, procedural understanding) – what Ginsburg and Huq call the 'administrative rule of law'.[163]

This monograph adopts this definition for two main reasons. First, from a practical perspective, it is a relatively minimalist definition, which can translate into a wide range of applications, taking various shapes and forms. Second, while encompassing a variety of practical applications, institutional arrangements and policy preferences, it is also precise enough to exclude from its scope of application a range of competing models or 'alternatives' to democracy. These alternatives include, at one end of the spectrum, the pure (full-scale) authoritarian model, which is characterised by 'the complete absence of political competition'.[164] However, it is also specific enough to exclude more 'subtle' models, such as what political scientists Steven Levitsky and Lucan Way call 'competitive authoritarianism'[165] (referring to 'civilian regimes in which formal democratic institutions exist and are widely viewed as the primary means of gaining power, but in which incumbents' abuse of the state places them at a significant advantage vis-à-vis their opponents'[166]), as

Expertise: The United Kingdom Government's Response to Covid-19' (2021) *Public Law* 707; D Vitale and R Girard, 'Public Trust and the Populist Leader: A Theoretical Argument' (2022) 11 *Global Constitutionalism* 548; and R Girard, 'Populism, Executive Power and "Constitutional Impatience": Courts as Institutional Stabilisers in the United Kingdom' (2022) 8 *Constitutional Studies* 35.

[160] See Ginsburg and Huq (n 34) 10; Huq and Ginsburg (n 25) 87.

[161] Ginsburg and Huq (n 34) 10; Huq and Ginsburg (n 25) 88, referring to JA Schumpeter, *Capitalism, Socialism and Democracy* (Abingdon, Routledge, 2003 [1942]).

[162] Ginsburg and Huq (n 34) 11–12.

[163] ibid 12–13.

[164] ibid. This is also how Juan Linz understands it. See, generally, JJ Linz, *Totalitarian and Authoritarian Regimes* (Boulder, Lynne Rienner, 2000).

[165] See, generally, S Levitsky and L Way, *Competitive Authoritarianism: Hybrid Regimes After the Cold War* (Cambridge, Cambridge University Press, 2010).

[166] ibid 5. Levitsky and Way add that such competitive authoritarian regimes are 'competitive in that opposition parties use democratic institutions to contest seriously for power, but they are not democratic because the playing field is heavily skewed in favor of incumbents. Competition is thus real but unfair.' See ibid 5.

well as what Fareed Zakaria and, later on (albeit with a different meaning), Yascha Mounk, have called 'illiberal democracy' – generally understood as a reasonably 'democratic' regime, but without its liberal-constitutional components.[167]

C. Space, Time and Chronotope

Finally, and as mentioned above, the populist phenomenon has seldom been analysed through the prism of space and time.[168] The few that exist are usually non-legal analyses – and focus on a mainly symbolic or metaphorical understanding of space and (or) time. For example, from a spatial perspective,[169] some defenders of populism have claimed that the latter sometimes helps rebuild the 'spaces' of democracy.[170] Others, by contrast, have taken a more critical stance and have argued that populism attempts to appropriate and occupy democratic spaces and imaginaries.[171]

From a temporal perspective, populism is often depicted (perhaps erroneously) in the academic literature as a 'disruption'[172] or 'rupture',[173] both of which imply a certain (and potentially problematic) linear temporality for human history and a linear progress towards (Western) liberal democracy.[174] Perhaps more crucially,

[167] See, eg, Zakaria, 'Illiberal Democracy' (n 22); Mounk (n 22). Zakaria does not provide a clear definition of 'illiberal democracy'. He does, however, define illiberal democratic *regimes* as 'democratically elected, often ones that have been reelected or reaffirmed through referenda', but which are also 'routinely ignoring constitutional limits on their power and depriving their citizens of basic rights and freedoms'. See Zakaria 'Illiberal Democracy' (n 22) 22.

[168] For exceptions regarding time, see, eg, J Waldron, 'Rule-of-Law Rights and Populist Impatience' in GL Neuman (ed), *Human Rights in a Time of Populism* (Cambridge, Cambridge University Press, 2020); Kuo (n 12); H Bødker and C Anderson, 'Populist Time: Mediating Immediacy and Delay in Liberal Democracy' (2019) 13 *International Journal of Communication* 5948; LR Pierre Louis, *Communication et espace public : Une reconstruction à travers l'espace public haïtien* (Louvain-la-Neuve, Presses universitaires de Louvain, 2011); G Hermet, *Les Populismes dans le monde : Une histoire sociologique – XIXe-XXe siècle* (Paris, Fayard, 2001). For exceptions regarding populism (or public law) and considerations of space and place (at least in a metaphorical sense), see, eg, JW Müller, '"The People Must Be Extracted from Within the People": Reflections on Populism' (2014) 21 *Constellations* 483, 488; R Hirschl and A Shachar, 'Spatial Statism' (2019) 17 *International Journal of Constitutional Law* 387.

[169] Here I – like Bart van Klink – adopt a relatively broad understanding of (juridical) 'space', defined as 'the domain in which a legal norm is valid, geographically and legally speaking; the ordering and arrangement of legally relevant locations, among which court rooms, town halls and prisons; symbolic divisions of space, for instance between the public and the private domain'. See B van Klink, 'Law at the Right Time: A Plea for Slow Law in Hasty Times' in Corrias and Francot (eds) (n 9) 47.

[170] See, eg, L Grattan, 'Pierre Bourdieu and Populism: The Everyday Politics of Outrageous Resistance' (2012) 21 *The Good Society* 194.

[171] Müller (n 168) 488.

[172] See, eg, A Hira, *The Great Disruption: Understanding the Populist Forces Behind Trump, Brexit, and Le Pen* (Lausanne, Peter Lang, 2019); E Kaufmann, *White Shift: Populism, Immigration, and the Future of White Majorities* (London, Penguin, 2019).

[173] See, eg, P Langford, 'The Populist Disruption: Juridico-Political Reflections on Democracy, Law and Rights' (2018) 5 *Soft Power Revista euro-americana de teoría e historia de la política y del derecho* 79.

[174] This linear temporality can also be seen in concepts such as 'democratic backsliding'. Yet, it can be problematic. Beyond being often inadequate and/or inaccurate (with 'a strong Eurocentric or Western-centric bent'), this vision adopts, as Fabio Wolkenstein notes, 'an implausibly

salient elements relating to time – including the acceleration of political time and processes – are arguably central to the ideal-typical populist discourse. For French political scientist Guy Hermet, for instance, populism's unique relation to time constitutes one of its main distinctive characteristics. For Hermet, populism is first and foremost defined by its 'anti-political temporality', notably by its explicit or implicit claim of offering an 'instantaneous response to problems or aspirations that no governmental action has in reality the power to resolve or, at least, to immediately resolve'.[175]

Yet, despite the significance of these claims – notably on issues such as democratic participation, constitutional change and rights protection – the relationship between populism, space and time remains largely undertheorised and understudied, particularly in constitutional theory and in comparative constitutional law. Moreover, and perhaps more importantly, considerations related to space and time have often been studied separately, rather than in conjunction. As Mariana Valverde notes, legal scholars have often distinguished questions of space from those of time, notably in the literature on law and geography, which has the effect of 'reviving an old metaphysical fallacy, namely, treating space and time as abstract and separate entities'.[176] Yet, and as discussed in more detail in this monograph, considerations pertaining to time and space share crucial affinities in the context of the study of populism and should be analysed and understood together and relationally rather than separately – hence the use, in this monograph, of the term 'spatiotemporality'.[177]

Mikhail Bakhtin's literary notion of the 'chronotope' can guide us in that regard. This notion refers, in Bakhtin's words, to 'the intrinsic connectedness of spatial and temporal relationships that are artistically expressed in literature'.[178] Translated and adapted as a (socio)legal concept by Valverde, the chronotope can be of help, as the purpose of this notion is to analyse 'how the temporal and the spatial dimensions of life and governance affect each other'.[179] Indeed, a key contention in this monograph is that populism puts forward, and is shaped by, a distinct spatiotemporality or spacetime. This spacetime, in my view, is visible in at least three major ways, which will each be the object of a separate chapter. First, as

teleological vision of progress that casts history as moving unidirectionally toward a predetermined goal'. See F Wolkenstein, 'What is Democratic Backsliding?' (2022) 30 *Constellations* 261, 264. For another challenge of the linear temporality of democracy, see S Skinner, 'Fault Lines in the Rule of Law' (2024) 20 *International Journal of Law in Context* 133.

[175] Hermet (n 168) 50 (my translation).

[176] M Valverde, '"Time Thickens, Takes On Flesh": Spatiotemporal Dynamics in Law' in I Braverman, N Blomley, D Delaney and A Kedar (eds), *The Expanding Spaces of Law: A Timely Legal Geography* (Redwood, Stanford University Press, 2014) 72. See also Valverde (n 7) 9-ss.

[177] That said, I do not necessarily disagree with Harmut Rosa's postulation of a sociological priority of time (over an anthropological priority of space), namely his claim that 'the transformation of spatiotemporal structures is primarily driven by its temporal dynamic of change'. See Rosa, *Social Acceleration* (n 9) 29.

[178] M Bakhtin, *The Dialogic Imagination: Four Essays* (Austin, University of Texas Press, 1981) 84, as cited in Valverde (n 7) 9–10.

[179] Valverde (n 7) 9.

discussed in more depth in chapter one, the ideal-typical populist legal discourse aggregates the transient, temporal and inherently ephemeral electoral majorities with the revolutionary, mystical and eternal 'sovereign people', understood as the People-as-One, thereby imbuing the latter with the characteristics of timeless unity, permanency and immutability. Second, populism weakens the distinction between ordinary, day-to-day politics, on the one hand, and intemporal, timeless constitutional politics, on the other. By doing so, populists tend to emphasise the spaces of democratic self-rule and freedom from limitations of power, including internal and external institutional constraints, as discussed in chapter two. Third, a more normative claim – discussed at more length in chapter three – is that while populism aims (or claims) to narrow the spatiotemporal distance or gap between the leader and the people, between *gouvernants* and *gouvernés*, it eventually creates a regime of proximity, immediacy and occupation (what I call in that chapter 'constitutional impatience'[180]) which ultimately risks affecting or even distorting the constitutive features of constitutional democracy.

It is worth clarifying that I use the concept of 'space' in a broad sense in this monograph, to include any determination of community, polity and (or) people. In other words, I understand space both in the sense of concrete spaces *and* in the more abstract sense of the ambit of constitutional politics, discourse and reach, or type and scope of 'community of subjects' and (or) 'intended/participating audience'. As such, space, in my perspective, is both a matter of real, actual spaces *and* a matter of constructing, demarcating and delimiting a body of people with a real or imagined role in grounding, forming and participating in political processes. This is important, because determinations of what is 'in' or 'out' do not necessarily map onto easy or 'given' geographical notions. Therefore, references to space in this monograph will frequently be both concrete/actual and, simultaneously, metaphorical, given that many metaphors are somewhat grounded in reality. Put differently, law is often constitutive, or the result, of certain imaginaries; as such, metaphors can often shape actual or concrete spaces, and vice versa.

VII. Social Acceleration, Separation of Powers and the Spatiotemporal Contours of (Liberal Constitutional) Democracy

Lastly, before moving on to the analysis of the character and discourse of contemporary populism, as well as the content of the populist constitutional project (both discussed in Part I of this book), it is important to provide some context

[180] Kim Lane Scheppele also uses this expression, but in a different context (and with a different meaning), namely that of Russia's 'impatient constitutional history', or what she calls 'impatient constitutionalism'. See KL Scheppele, '"We Forgot About the Ditches": Russian Constitutional Impatience and the Challenge of Terrorism' (2005) 53 *Duke Law Review* 963, 967.

or background for my treatment of this subject. It is contended that relying on the space-time lens will shed light on the spatiotemporal claims of the populist critique of the liberal component of constitutional democracy – a fundamental part of this critique, I suggest – as well as on the content of the populist constitutional project.[181] The same approach will also be beneficial in understanding the institutional reaction or response, by judicial actors, to this very project – including the view that courts can act as democracy-enhancing institutional decelerators.[182]

As a critique of the liberal component of constitutional democracy, contemporary populism – like constitutional democracy itself – operates within a specific spatiotemporal context, that of acceleration, more specifically the compression of time and the shrinking of space. In the 1970s, French theorist Paul Virilio coined the term 'dromology' (from the Greek *dromos*, meaning 'race', 'racecourse', 'track' or 'run') to refer to the study of speed, describing how speed has become a structuring force, shaping many aspects of society, including politics, perceptions and space.[183] A few decades later, German sociologist and social theorist Hartmut Rosa elaborated a theory of 'social acceleration', a sociological framework for understanding how modernity affects and transforms time, more specifically how modern society is caught in a logic of acceleration.[184] Rosa identified three different, albeit interrelated, components of the social acceleration of contemporary life, namely: technological acceleration; social change or transformation; and the heightened tempo of everyday life.[185] Many of these elements are directly linked to the imperatives of temporal efficiency and rapidity of present-day capitalism.[186] However, this acceleration is not limited to the institutions of capitalism (such as production, distribution and consumption): in fact, almost all elements of contemporary society have experienced a 'substantial acceleration vis-à-vis earlier forms of social organization', from transportation to communication and information technology.[187]

This form of 'modernity as acceleration' has, I contend, important implications for constitutional democracy. Democratic institutions (which are often associated with 'inertia'[188]) are not mere passive bystanders in that context of acceleration; instead, they contribute to and are, indeed, confronted with the consequences of that very process.[189] Political institutions (including deliberative institutions such as parliaments and legislatures, whose role is to represent a wide array of interests)

[181] This populist constitutional project is discussed in more detail in Part I of this monograph, particularly in ch 3.
[182] This is discussed in more detail in Part II of this monograph.
[183] Virilio (n 9).
[184] Rosa, *Social Acceleration* (n 9); Rosa, 'Social Acceleration' (n 9).
[185] ibid.
[186] Scheuerman (n 9) 4.
[187] ibid.
[188] See, eg, Rosa, *Social Acceleration* (n 9) 92.
[189] L Francot, '"Suspended in Gaffa": Legal Slowness in the Acceleration of Society' in Francot and Corrias (eds) (n 9) 97.

seem overwhelmed, outdated and ill-equipped to adapt to these new imperatives of temporal efficiency and rapidity.[190] As political theorist William E Scheuerman explains, 'liberal democracy rests on a temporal separation of powers according to which distinct (legislative, executive, and judicial) functions of government presuppose different temporal horizons'.[191] Yet,

> [h]igh-speed society tends to favor high-speed political institutions, and traditional liberal democratic assumptions about temporality unwittingly aggrandize executive power and weaken broad-based popular legislatures. Albeit paradoxically, the traditional liberal democratic temporal separation of powers potentially generates antiliberal and antidemocratic results – in particular, the rise of executive discretion and decay of parliamentary legality – amid the intensified tempo of modern social and economic existence.[192]

Democratic politics and institutions thus appear overwhelmed by the very social acceleration they set forth (or at least contribute to).[193] Put differently, the social acceleration of time creates a situation in which 'the temporal patterns' of democratic politics may become 'irreconcilably out of step with the time structures of the global age'.[194]

I suggest, in this monograph, that it is precisely in the context of this social acceleration, and perhaps even in response to it, that populism emerges. As liberal institutions are seemingly ill-equipped to adapt to and face this trend, populism manifests itself as a powerful critique of the liberal component of constitutional democracy; populists perceive and depict the latter as fundamentally inefficient, distant, slow, elite-driven and opaque. Intertwining space and time, as it were, populism – in contrast to and in response to these identified shortcomings of liberal democracy – puts forward an alternative conception of representation, one that is based on proximity, authenticity and speed (or temporal efficiency). The populist alternative is thus depicted as spatially closer, temporally faster and more time-efficient than its liberal-democratic counterpart.

However, before elaborating on the populist alternative in more detail,[195] it is important to discuss, first, how social acceleration affects the spatiotemporal horizons of constitutional democracy and the separation of powers. In the next three sub-sections, I explain how two key liberal institutions of constitutional democracy – namely legislatures and courts – are singularly vulnerable to social acceleration given that they are designed according to distinct spatiotemporal frames or mindsets. Indeed, legislatures are depicted as spatially distant and

[190] Scheuerman (n 9) 4.

[191] ibid 26. See also AJ Wistrich, 'The Evolving Temporality of Lawmaking' (2012) 44 *Connecticut Law Review* 737, 750, 773.

[192] Scheuerman (n 9) 26.

[193] Rosa, 'Social Acceleration' (n 9) 21.

[194] H Rosa, 'The Speed of Global Flows and the Pace of Democratic Politics' (2005) 27 *New Political Science* 445, 454.

[195] I do this mainly in ch 3.

temporally slow-paced and prospective or future-oriented; whereas the executive is seen as spatially omnipresent, with a temporal orientation that is largely contemporaneous or present-oriented; and the judiciary is viewed as spatially distant, with judicial decisions that are perceived, temporally, as mainly retrospective or past-oriented.[196]

A. Distant, Slow-Paced, Deliberative and Future-Oriented Legislatures

First, primary law-making[197] is seen as future-oriented, 'futuristic'[198] or prospective in nature insofar as it requires parliamentarians, legislators and other elected officials to engage in a certain 'forward-looking process of trying effectively to plan or coordinate future state activities and, albeit to a more limited extent, future social trends'.[199] It is in this context, I would add, that deliberation, reflection and compromise take place – but most often with a view to 'predicting' future situations and (or) achieving a certain policy outcome viewed as desirable.[200]

To be sure, the idea for the legislature is not to anticipate *all* situations likely to arise in society. In the context of codification in the civil law tradition, for instance, the purpose of legislation is not to consolidate all the principles of civil law, nor to pre-empt every potential problem likely to arise in a given polity.[201] Such an objective, as Jean-Marie-Étienne Portalis wrote in 1801, would be purely utopian: 'The needs of society are so varied, the communication of men is so active, their interests are so multiplied, and their relationships so extensive, that it would be impossible for the legislator to meet all needs'.[202] This view mirrors that of John Locke, who conceded, in his *Second Treatise of Government*, that 'it is impossible to foresee, and so by Laws to provide for all Accidents and Necessities that may concern the Publick'.[203] Moreover, it can certainly be pointed out that pieces of

[196] Scheuerman (n 9) 29. See also Wistrich (n 191) 750, 773.

[197] On the relationship between time, change and law-making, see, generally, S Ranchordás and Y Roznai (eds), *Time, Law, and Change: An Interdisciplinary Study* (Oxford, Hart Publishing, 2020).

[198] J Přibáň, *Legal Symbolism: On Law, Time and European Identity* (Abingdon, Routledge, 2007) 55. See also Walker (n 20) 23–24.

[199] Scheuerman (n 9) 29.

[200] Of course, legislatures sometimes operate within different or additional spatiotemporal contours. One may think, for instance, of the legislative work done regarding the approval of annual budgets – which is, in a sense, present-focused. One may also think of parliamentary scrutiny of executive action, which is past-oriented. Moreover, delegated legislation can be seen as present- or future-oriented, as discussed below. I thank Winluck Wahiu for pointing this out. My focus here, however, is on what is arguably the main function of legislatures, namely law-making, particularly primary legislation.

[201] See R Girard, 'Réflexions sur la codification du droit des obligations au Québec' (2012) *Cahiers du PEQ* (student edition).

[202] JME Portalis, *Discours préliminaire du premier projet de Code civil* (Bordeaux, Confluences, 2004 [1801]) 5 (my translation).

[203] J Locke, *Second Treatise of Government* [1689] in J Locke, *Second Treatise of Government* and *A Letter Concerning Toleration* (Oxford, Oxford University Press, 2016) 82, para 160.

legislation are sometimes brought forward in response to an observed situation or social trend. Still, to be compliant with a thick – and, indeed, even a thin – conception of the rule of law, legislation cannot (or should not) be retroactive.[204] As such, the legislative process is inherently forward-looking: the idea is for legislators to respond to current and future situations, think ahead and, inevitably, to 'make predictions about the likely course of a potentially significant array of succeeding social trends'.[205] In other words, statutes are meant to be prospective, general, accessible and clear, so that they can provide determinative guidelines for future state actors such as judges and administrative bodies, at least in theory.[206]

In terms of speed, legislatures have long been viewed as prudent and slow-paced institutions. In fact, many modern political thinkers were already very well aware of the ingrained 'slowness' of legislatures.[207] For instance, in *Federalist No 70*, Alexander Hamilton remarked that '[i]n the legislature, promptitude of decision is oftener an evil than a benefit'.[208] In the same vein, Hamilton noted the deliberative functions of the legislature: 'The differences of opinion, and the jarrings of parties in that department of the government, though they may sometimes obstruct salutary plans, yet often promote deliberation and circumspection, and serve to check excesses in the majority'.[209] This slowness was thus depicted in a positive way, but not every modern political theorist saw things in the same light. To give an example, in his *Discourses on Livy*, Machiavelli pointed out that ordinary deliberative institutions like councils and assemblies are ill-equipped in urgent times:

> Because as the ordinary institutions of a commonwealth work but slowly, no council and no magistrate having authority to act in everything alone, but in most matters one standing in need of the other, and time being required to reconcile their differences, the remedies which they provide are most dangerous when they have to be applied in cases which do not brook delay.[210]

Of course, many legislatures or parliaments are constituted of separate chambers, which do not necessarily operate within the exact same spatiotemporal logic or orientation. One may argue, for instance, that the prudent, slow-paced nature of the legislature is more prominent in upper chambers (or senates) than in lower chambers (such as houses of commons or houses of representatives), which tend to be a bit more caught up in the 'heat of the moment' than their upper-chamber counterparts. Moreover, it is hard to deny, as Lord Bingham pointed out in 2006,

[204] See, eg, J Raz, 'The Rule of Law and its Virtue' in J Raz (ed), *The Authority of Law: Essays on Law and Morality* (Oxford, Clarendon, 1979).
[205] Scheuerman (n 9) 30.
[206] ibid 29.
[207] ibid ch 2.
[208] A Hamilton [Publius] (1788), 'Federalist No 70: The Executive Department Further Considered' (15 March 1788), as cited in Scheuerman (n 9) 39.
[209] ibid.
[210] N Machiavelli, *Discourses on Livy* (trans Ninian Hill Thomson [1883]) (1532 [c. 1517]) www.online-literature.com/machiavelli/titus-livius, ch XXXIV.

that we are now witnessing a certain 'legislative hyperactivity which appears to have become a permanent feature of our governance'.[211] Nevertheless, the fact remains that parliaments in general tend to be slower, more deliberative and more future-oriented than the executive, for instance. In fact, parliaments are often seen as reactive (rather than active) bodies, 'waiting for the executive to bring forward measures'.[212]

In the same vein, the outcome of deliberation in legislatures – that is to say, the legislative process – is also noted for being slow[213] and, in more extreme cases (such as instances of legislative deadlock or gridlock, for example), at a complete standstill. This is not to suggest, however, that legislation moves inherently more slowly than society, nor that it is completely ill-equipped to follow (and adapt to) social changes. In fact, legislation has often been used as a tool to implement important social changes: between the eighteenth century and even well into the twentieth century, it was used as a political instrument to 'dynamize or speed-up social developments; the prime tool of social engineering'.[214] Nevertheless, since the second half of the twentieth century, and particularly since the beginning of the twenty-first century, the legislature – among other democratic institutions – no longer appears to be the driver of social change par excellence and, thus, an engine of social acceleration. Rather, its role has 'shifted to a role of "fire-extinguisher" and to a mode of "muddling through", at best reacting to the pressures created elsewhere rather than shaping our shared world'.[215]

Many theories have been put forward to explain the (relative) temporal inefficiencies of the deliberative, elected parliament. Carl Schmitt, for instance, believed that the traditional precepts of separation of powers were out of sync with the needs of modern governance and of the 'total state'.[216] In 1936, Schmitt wrote that the industrialisation of society, the acceleration of legislation after 1914 and the ensuing broader delegations of legislative power to the executive had led to 'an insurmountable opposition between the concept of legislation in a parliamentary

[211] Lord Bingham here referred to the growing – and 'sheer' – volume of current legislation, both in terms of primary legislation and statutory instruments, which 'raises serious problems of accessibility, despite the Internet'. See Lord Bingham, 'The Rule of Law', Sixth David Williams Lecture, House of Lords (16 November 2006).

[212] In the case of the UK Parliament, see, eg, P Norton, 'Parliament: The Best of Times, the Worst of Times?' in J Jowell and C O'Cinneide (eds), *The Changing Constitution*, 9th edn (Oxford, Oxford University Press, 2019) 185–186.

[213] Even law as a discipline/institution is sometimes viewed as 'slow'. For instance, Bruno Latour highlights the essential 'slowness' of law: 'All those aspects of law that common sense finds so irritating – its tardiness, its taste for tradition, its occasionally reactionary attitudes – are essential to law's functioning'. See B Latour *The Making of Law: An Ethnography of the Conseil d'Etat* (trans M Brilman and A Pottage) (Cambridge, Polity, 2013) 242–243, as cited in van Klink (n 169) 36.

[214] H Rosa, 'Airports Built on Shifting Grounds?' (n 9) 83.

[215] ibid.

[216] P Lindseth, 'The Paradox of Parliamentary Supremacy: Delegation, Democracy, and Dictatorship in Germany and France, 1920s–1950s' (2004) 113 *Yale Law Journal* 1341, 1357.

regime and the evolution of public life over the course of the last decades'[217] – the latter requiring swift, decisive action by the executive rather than protracted deliberation by the legislature over abstract, general norms.[218] The inevitable and logical conclusion of this process, he wrote at the time, was to completely eliminate any (false or misleading) appearance of separation of powers and to opt, instead, for a system of 'governmental legislation'.[219]

This perception of legislatures as prudent, slow-paced and deliberative institutions, combined with industrialisation, population increase and the growth of the administrative state, arguably makes them particularly vulnerable to the social acceleration of time or, as Carl Schmitt put it later in 1950, to the speed-up or 'motorization'[220] of parliamentary legislation. Schmitt predicted that 'the motorization of lawmaking would engender a vast range of vague delegations of open-ended authority to the executive and administration, exceptional and emergency norms, as well as poorly crafted statutes possessing a limited half-life'.[221] Schmitt was right, at least to a certain extent, as the post-World War II era witnessed the rise of the administrative state and the exponential growth of delegated (secondary) legislation.[222] This is partly because, as Scheuerman has noted,

> [c]ontemporary law-making bodies are asked to handle significantly more legislation than their historical predecessors, but less time is available for general debate, and legislation is considered more quickly, even though legislatures now typically meet for longer periods of time than their nineteenth- and early-twentieth-century predecessors.[223]

From a spatial perspective, finally, this rise of the administrative state and the growth of delegated legislation has led to an impression – shared by many, including several contemporary populist leaders – that legislatures are both geographically (or physically) and symbolically distant and, perhaps, disconnected from the views of the public. This critique of liberal-democratic distance is discussed in more detail in chapter three.

[217] C Schmitt, 'Une étude de droit constitutionnel comparé : L'évolution récente du problème des délégations législatives' (trans P Roubier and H Mankiewicz) in *Introduction à l'étude du droit comparé : Recueil d'études en l'honneur d'Édouard Lambert* (Paris, Sirey: LGDJ, 1938 [1936]) 204, as mentioned in Lindseth (n 216) 1359. For his later views, see also C Schmitt, 'The Plight of European Jurisprudence' (trans GL Ulmen) (1990 [1943/44]) 83 *Telos* 35, 50.

[218] Lindseth (n 216) 1359.

[219] Schmitt, 'Une étude de droit constitutionnel comparé' (n 217) 205, as cited in Lindseth (n 216) 1359.

[220] See Schmitt (n 217) 50.

[221] As summarised in Scheuerman (n 9) 63. See also Schmitt, 'Une étude de droit constitutionnel comparé' (n 216).

[222] Lindseth (n 216) 1383.

[223] Scheuerman (n 9) 62. See also WE Scheuerman, 'Motorized Legislation? Statutes in an Age of Speed' (2002) 88 *ARSP: Archiv für Rechts- und Sozialphilosophie / Archives for Philosophy of Law and Social Philosophy* 379.

B. Omnipresent, Fast-Paced, Expeditious and Present-Oriented Executives

In contrast to the above, many have stressed the fast-paced, expeditious and 'present-oriented, or contemporaneous, temporal contours of modern executive power'.[224] The necessity of an omnipresent body capable of swift, expeditious and decisive action in situations of urgent danger has long been highlighted amongst modern political thinkers. Machiavelli, for instance, noting the slow pace of ordinary deliberative institutions, praised the Roman institution of the Dictator; and in the case of the Venetian Republic, the authority granted to a few citizens, in cases of 'urgent danger', the capacity to determine 'without further consultation' the further course of action required.[225] Machiavelli saw this power as fundamental to all republics: 'those republics which cannot in sudden emergencies resort either to a dictator or to some similar authority, will, when the danger is serious, always be undone'.[226] Put differently, emergency orders, decrees and regulations allow for 'high-speed political action and reaction', including an 'additional speed-up in legislation in times of crises, when speed is vital'.[227]

However, the fast-paced, contemporaneous temporal contours of executive power are not limited to situations of emergency; even in normal times, a present-oriented institution is required to execute the laws promulgated by Parliament and, sometimes, to use the executive prerogative or to enact decrees. John Locke, for instance, argued that it is precisely because legislation is 'too slow, for the Dispatch requisite to Execution' (and also because, as mentioned earlier, it is impossible to foresee all future needs of society) that it is necessary to endow the 'Executor of the Laws' with executive power – the Prerogative – that is to say, the 'Power to act according to Discretion, for the Publick Good, without the Prescription of the law, and sometimes even against it.'[228] As Scheuerman points out, '[t]he necessity of executive prerogative to act beyond and even against the law thus derives not merely from the need to acknowledge the limitations of inflexible and rigid legislative statutes but from an unduly slavish dependence on the dictates of the past'.[229] For him, '[t]he rigidity of the past is merely a manifestation of the domination of the present by the past'.[230]

Such executive power, being applied at short notice, sometimes contrary to the legislation, is in that sense viewed as inherently contemporaneous, responsive, active

[224] Scheuerman (n 9) 36.
[225] Machiavelli (n 210) ch XXXIV.
[226] ibid.
[227] Rosa, 'Airports Built on Shifting Grounds?' (n 9) 84.
[228] Locke (n 203) 81, para 160. Montesquieu also highlights the executive power's 'need of despatch' in Montesquieu (n 1) vol I, bk VI, ch II.
[229] Scheuerman (n 9) 38.
[230] ibid.

(if not even hyperactive), energetic and fast-paced. Alexander Hamilton, in *Federalist No 70*, noted the 'qualities in the Executive which are the most necessary ingredients in its composition – vigor and expedition'.[231] He characterised the executive as a fast-moving, energetic body, which he described as 'a leading character in the definition of good government'.[232] For Hamilton, the executive is, in fact,

> essential to the protection of the community against foreign attacks; it is not less essential to the steady administration of the laws; to the protection of property against those irregular and high-handed combinations which sometimes interrupt the ordinary course of justice; to the security of liberty against the enterprises and assaults of ambition, of faction, and of anarchy.[233]

However, the effects of executive power are not only experienced in the present; they are also, to a certain extent, felt in the future – with various commissions, committees and task forces entrusted with investigating and reporting a course of action. Yet, it is precisely in that regard that the effects of social acceleration are felt more prominently, with a certain reallocation of powers within different institutional and temporal contours. To be sure, there are different temporalities and different allocations between legislatures and executives, depending on the area (social, economic, etc) of policymaking.[234] Nevertheless, the fact remains, as Scheuerman has noted, that

> social acceleration potentially undermines core features of the temporal separation of powers, disfiguring liberal democracy as initially conceived. In particular, social acceleration presents a direct threat to the notion of prospective, or future-oriented, legislation, tending to undermine the paramount position of legislative rule making in the traditional liberal democratic temporal division of labor.[235]

The most obvious beneficiary of this indirect reallocation of powers within different institutions operating within different spatiotemporal contours appears to be the executive, 'whose contemporaneous and high-speed temporal contours appear to leave it particularly well-suited to decision making in a corresponding high-speed social environment'.[236] This is important because, as Scheuerman puts it, '[h]igh-speed society privileges high-speed institutions, and in the liberal democratic worldview it is typically the executive who is viewed as an especially energetic institutional agent'.[237] This is to be contrasted with more deliberative representative legislatures, which 'risk getting left at the wayside, as the ever faster pace of social and economic life conflicts with the conventional emphasis on the

[231] Hamilton (n 208).
[232] ibid.
[233] ibid.
[234] See, for instance, the spatial disjunctions (asymmetries) identified in relation to the EU by Fritz Scharpf in FW Scharpf, 'The Asymmetry of European Integration, or Why the EU Cannot Be a "Social Market Economy"' (2010) 8 *Socio-Economic Review* 211. I thank Jacco Bomhoff for pointing this out.
[235] Scheuerman (n 9) 45.
[236] ibid.
[237] ibid.

legislature's necessary reliance on careful, wide-ranging, and time-consuming deliberative exchange'.[238] The result, as discussed in more detail in chapter three, is a certain acceleration (and, perhaps, diminution in quality) of scrutiny, debate and deliberation.

It is also in the context of these recent shifts in the temporality of liberal democracy that we have witnessed the growth of delegated legislation – which, of course, favours the executive and raises a number of important issues pertaining to the principles of democracy, rule of law and separation of powers. Most notably, it raises questions concerning the democratic legitimacy of delegated legislation and the ability of the executive branch of government to legislate – via regulation, subject to little or no policy guidance from the primary democratic decision-making body and with very limited parliamentary scrutiny – on public policy matters of the highest importance. These important issues have been recently discussed in many jurisdictions across the world, including in the UK and Canada.[239]

As a result of these changes, and perhaps also due to the character of the populist critique of liberal democracy discussed in chapter three, the executive is often viewed and (or) depicted as spatially omnipresent and responsive, in contrast to legislatures which, as discussed previously, are seen as distant and detached. Indeed, the government (namely, the executive) can be seen almost everywhen and everywhere – in extraordinary times and situations of emergency, of course, but also increasingly in less-than-extraordinary situations, notably through an augmented use of executive or prerogative powers.[240] These ideas are discussed theoretically in chapter three and more practically in chapter six.

C. Detached, Slow-Paced and Past-Oriented Judiciaries?

Courts, for their part, were generally perceived – at least until recently – as retrospective or past-oriented, insofar as 'they would ideally be concerned exclusively with the ascertainment of past events and the relationship of those events to legal precedents or statutory rules that already have been declared valid' – thereby downplaying, of course, the creative (and future-oriented) character of judgment-making.[241] Ronald Dworkin referred to this past-oriented temporality when he wrote that judges are bound exclusively by the past, speaking in the

[238] ibid.

[239] In the UK, see, eg, the debates surrounding 'Henry VIII clauses', the Strathclyde Review 2015 and the House of Lords' Committee on the Constitution March 2016 report. In Canada, see, eg, AJ Johnson, 'The Case For a Canadian Nondelegation Doctrine' (2019) 52 *UBC Law Review* 817.

[240] See, eg, WE Scheuerman, 'President Trump's "Get it Done Faster" Emergency' (*Verfassungsblog*, 18 February 2019) www.verfassungsblog.de/president-trumps-get-it-done-faster-emergency.

[241] Scheuerman (n 9) 34.

name of the dead.[242] Of course, Dworkin had the US Supreme Court in mind, with its focus on (or perhaps obsession with) originalism, when writing this. Neil Walker, for his part, wrote that '[c]ommon law seeks typically to sponsor its situation as the accumulation of the past knowledge, wisdom and practice in common'.[243] He added: 'Under the common law, then, the present is justified by the past rather than by the future, and indeed the future does not come into the picture except as the indistinct and unprojected time of the inevitable continuity of the past-in-the-present'.[244] This situation is compounded, it could be argued, by the fact that there is an inevitable discrepancy between the orientation of the judges – appointed at a given moment in time – and subsequent parliamentary majorities.[245]

In recent decades, however, courts have increasingly been perceived as creative bodies, oriented not only towards the past, but also the present and, in certain instances, even the future. The growth of judicial and especially constitutional review has arguably exacerbated this trend, which has led some scholars and commentators to raise some concerns pertaining to the discretionary power of judges.[246] In any event, many post-World War II courts – especially those endowed with powers of constitutional review – are arguably much more forward-looking and creative than this vision (or impression) of courts as 'past-oriented' would lead us to believe. For example, Canada's living tree/ living instrument methods of interpretation give rise to a very different temporal framework, one that is not exclusively focused on the past, but also on the present and the future – albeit in a relatively cautious way. Canadian Supreme Court Justice Nicholas Kasirer discussed the need for a balance between 'caution' (or perhaps 'prudence') and future-looking 'imagination' and 'courage' when he said during his appointment process that the 'call for caution' in the exercise of judicial power 'is complemented by an unspoken injunction for judges to take up their public duty by showing imagination, and indeed some courage, in the pursuit of justice'.[247] Noting that judges usually benefit from a significant level of independence and a presumption of impartiality, Justice Kasirer stressed the importance of

[242] R Dworkin, *Law's Empire* (Cambridge, Harvard University Press, 1986) 225, 242, as mentioned in L Barshack, 'Interpretation and the Legal Fabrication of Time' in Ranchordás and Roznai (eds) (n 197) 13.
[243] Walker (n 20) 24.
[244] ibid.
[245] Frédéric Rouvillois makes a similar point in F Rouvillois, *Le gouvernement des juges : Histoire d'un mythe politique* (Paris, Desclée de Brouwer, 2023) 251–252.
[246] For instance, Scheuerman is sceptical or suspicious of the role of the judiciary in the context of social acceleration – see, eg, Scheuerman (n 9) 48, 58: 'What would prevent courts from becoming a new source of illegitimate form of discretionary power? Like parliament, the judiciary might imitate the executive and thereby streamline its tempo in accordance with social acceleration but only at the cost of abandoning its special normative and institutional attributes.'
[247] N Kasirer, 'The Honourable Nicholas Kasirer's Questionnaire' (Office of the Commissioner for Federal Judicial Affairs Canada, 2019) www.fja-cmf.gc.ca/scc-csc/2019/nominee-candidat-eng.html.

> [s]triking the right balance between these competing calls to caution and to courage is a central challenge in the exercise of judicial responsibility in a constitutional democracy. In my experience, they are not incompatible – there is an immense satisfaction in moving law resolutely forward, but only so far forward as is necessary to solve the problem at hand, leaving the rest for another day.[248]

This highlights the future- and forward-looking nature of certain courts. In Europe, apex courts – especially courts vested with powers of constitutional review – are also impacted by the human rights dimension, which underpins European constitutionalism and constitutional democracy more broadly and which makes courts more present- and future-looking than what is often assumed.[249]

From the perspective of space, courts are sometimes perceived as 'distant' and (or) detached, at least compared with (democratically elected) bodies such as parliaments. Sitting judges rarely interact with members of the public or with the media, at least compared with elected political actors. Moreover, and as Andrea Pin has highlighted, the judicial sense of distance is 'further aggravated by the language factor'.[250] For Pin, while both legislation and case law employ highly technical words and legal concepts, 'parliamentary deliberations can host narratives that are more easily accessible to the people, and with which individuals and groups can entertain a dialogue'.[251] By contrast, courts and judges 'sustain themselves with their skill in reasoned judgments, and cannot detach themselves from technicalities without running the risk of imprecision or triviality'.[252] This, in turn, can create a 'disconnection' between the judiciary and the public.[253] In terms of speed (and temporal efficiency), courts, like legislatures, are sometimes perceived as relatively 'slow' and 'inefficient' institutions that are required to follow a set of time-consuming rules and procedures.[254] One may think, for example, of civil and criminal procedures, court rules of practice and appeal processes, to name a few. Yet, simultaneously, courts have to deal with an increased volume of legislation and court cases,[255] which could explain – at least in part – this perception of courts as relatively slow and time-inefficient liberal institutions.

[248] ibid.

[249] In fact, one could argue that it is precisely this present- and future-looking approach that some populists find problematic.

[250] Pin (n 79) 237.

[251] ibid.

[252] ibid.

[253] ibid 243. Such sense of 'disconnection' or 'distance' has led some apex courts to organise sittings outside their main building and (or) capital cities. The example of the Canadian Supreme Court, which has recently sat outside Ottawa, in cities like Winnipeg and Québec City.

[254] See, eg, Francot (n 189).

[255] This has also led to an increase in international and commercial arbitration, whose cheaper and less time-consuming procedures appear advantageous to private actors and other corporations. See, eg, Y Dezalay and BG Garth, *Dealing in Virtue: International Commercial Arbitration and the Construction of a Transnational Legal Order* (Chicago, University of Chicago Press, 1996), particularly ch 3.

Combining space and time, the seemingly slow pace of judicial procedures and processes may make courts – whose judges are often demarcated as belonging to 'the elite' and therefore not 'of the people', particularly because they are generally not elected by popular vote – appear as both distant, detached and/or unresponsive *and*, simultaneously, out of sync with the acceleration of political time and processes. This sense of distance, detachment and unresponsiveness, combined with a (founded or unfounded) view that courts are inherently slow-paced and past-oriented, may make them potentially more vulnerable to populist impatience, as the depiction of British judges (in the Brexit context) as 'enemies of the people' suggests.[256] These ideas are discussed in more detail in chapter three and in Part II (particularly in chapter six) of this monograph.

In short, societies have witnessed, in recent years, a heightened social acceleration, which has led to a gradual transfer or delegation – for speed- and efficiency-related reasons – of discretionary power from the legislature to the executive. The omnipresent, fast-paced, expeditious and present-oriented character of the executive makes it, at face value, the most suited to respond to new political and economic situations, social experiences and trends – from the development of new technologies to military operations, economic crises and even pandemics and other health emergencies. Thus, I contend that social acceleration changes the relationship vis-à-vis space and time, including the pace of democratic politics[257] and the spatiotemporal contours of liberal-democratic institutions.

As we have seen, and as Ming-Sung Kuo puts it, '[t]he constitutional design of separation of powers works on the assumption that democratic decisions are made over a period of time, not at a transient moment'.[258] Yet, and as it is argued in more detail in this monograph (theoretically, particularly in chapter three, but also practically, especially in chapter five), populists sometimes manage to navigate through these contours, notably to accelerate certain political processes. In doing so, they: (1) contribute to (or participate in) the redrawing of the temporal horizons of liberal constitutional democracy; and (2) put forward an alternative conception of democratic representation – one that is based on politics of immediacy[259] as well as what I call 'constitutional impatience'. These ideas are discussed further in the next three chapters.

[256] See J Slack, 'Enemies of the people: Fury over "out of touch" judges who have "declared war on democracy" by defying 17.4m Brexit voters and who could trigger constitutional crisis' (*Daily Mail*, November 2016) www.dailymail.co.uk/news/article-3903436/Enemies-people-Fury-touch-judges-defied-17-4m-Brexit-voters-trigger-constitutional-crisis.html and ch 6.

[257] H Rosa (n 194).

[258] Kuo (n 12) 564.

[259] See, eg, L Corrias, 'Populism in a Constitutional Key: Constituent Power, Popular Sovereignty and Constitutional Identity' (2016) 12 *European Constitutional Law Review* 6, 12.

PART I

Understanding Populism: Towards a Constitutional Theory of Populism

1

Identifying Populism: Law, Popular Sovereignty and 'the People'

La volonté nationale est un des mots dont les intrigants de tous les temps et les despotes de tous les âges ont le plus abusé.[1]

I. Introduction

As discussed in the introductory chapter, the first part of this monograph analyses, theorises and conceptualises contemporary populism from a legal-constitutional perspective and using a spatiotemporal lens. The development of such a theoretical framework for the legal study of populism will contribute to a re-conceptualisation of contemporary populism as a serious and at least somewhat coherent constitutional theory.[2]

In this first chapter, I will identify the key elements of the ideal-typical populist legal discourse, particularly as they relate to popular sovereignty and the concept of 'the people'. Through an analysis of various contemporary populist discourses, this chapter will pave the way for a more institutional analysis of the populist approach to constitutions, as well as of the content of the populist constitutional project, which are discussed in more detail in chapters two and three. The main argument of this chapter is that the ideal-typical populist discourse tends to aggregate the transient, temporal and inherently ephemeral electoral majorities with the revolutionary, mystical and eternal 'sovereign people', understood as the People-as-One, thereby imbuing the latter with the characteristics of timeless unity, permanency and immutability. This aggregation – and the weakening of the distinction between ordinary, day-to-day politics, on the one hand, and intemporal, timeless

[1] A de Tocqueville, *De la Démocratie en Amérique*, vol 1 (Paris, Michel Lévy, 1864 [1835]) 88.

[2] Of course, some scholars would disagree and would argue, like Giuseppe Martinico, that 'there is no populist constitutional theory at all'. See, eg, G Martinico, *Filtering Populist Claims to Fight Populism: The Italian Case in a Comparative Perspective* (Cambridge, Cambridge University Press, 2022) 27. Similarly, Cesare Pinelli argues that 'contemporary populism does not follow a single constitutional theory, but a pragmatic approach varying from country to country'. See C Pinelli, 'The Rise of Populism and the Malaise of Democracy' in S Garben, I Govaere and P Nemitz (eds), *Critical Reflections on Constitutional Democracy in the European Union* (Oxford, Hart Publishing, 2019) 27, 29, as cited in Martinico, *Filtering Populist Claims* 27.

constitutional politics, on the other – has important constitutional ramifications, which will become clear in the three chapters that form Part I of this monograph.

This chapter is structured in the following way: section II discusses the ambiguous concept of 'the people' and how populists employ this notion in their legal discourse. Section III examines the populist conception of sovereignty, contrasting it with the modern or liberal-constitutionalist conception, and discusses whether 'the people' can be institutionalised as a sovereign in a legal sense.

II. Who are 'the People'?

Most populist movements claim that 'the ultimate source of authority is the sovereign people; that all legitimate political power is based on occasion of withdrawing legitimacy from one regime and bestowing it upon another'.[3] This idea is not new. In fact, it is a persistent theme in modern constitutional thought that political power is ultimately vested in 'the people'.[4] The idea that sovereignty rests with the people – rather than with legislatures and governments, for instance – was even the object of a US Supreme Court decision dating as far back as 1793.[5] But who are 'the people'?

A. The Ambiguous Nature of 'the People'

There is a certain indeterminacy in the concept of 'the people' as the ultimate source of authority.[6] Under the populist logic, the concept of 'the people', and to whom it refers, is self-evident: the people are to be distinguished from significant 'others', including the elite, the ruling class and other power wielders, foreigners as well as the media.[7] For populists, the people are the 'common', 'ordinary', 'forgotten', 'invisible' or 'anonymous' people of a polity, or sometimes the 'silent majority'.[8] They are conceived as the 'pure people' (in contrast to the 'corrupt elite'), whose unified will and common self-interest have been largely ignored by the political, social, institutional and economical elite. Therefore, the populist definition of the

[3] M Canovan, *The People* (Cambridge, Polity, 2005) 84.

[4] M Loughlin, 'The Concept of Constituent Power' (2014) 13 *European Journal of Political Theory* 218, 218. For example, Locke holds that no government is legitimate if it does not have the consent of the people. See J Locke, *Second Treatise of Government* in *Second Treatise of Government and A Letter Concerning Toleration* (Oxford University Press, 2016 [1689]).

[5] *Chisholm v Georgia* 2 US (2 Dall) 419 (1793). In this case, Justice Wilson opined that 'the Supreme Power resides in the body in the body of the people' [457].

[6] See, eg, L Jaume, 'Le nom du peuple dans la révolution française et sa représentation politique' (2014) 57 *Cahiers du CEVIPOF* 43, 43.

[7] Other variations include oligarchies, immigrants, non-natives, foreign forces, etc.

[8] See, eg, US President Donald Trump's tweet on 14 June 2020: 'THE SILENT MAJORITY IS STRONGER THAN EVER!!!' (*Twitter/X*, 14 June 2020) x.com/realDonaldTrump/status/1272286399752855552.

people is, in one sense, exclusionary: populists appeal to the excluded 'people-as-part' (that is, the 'common' or 'ordinary' people referred to above).[9] Yet, while they mobilise the excluded people-as-part, populists implicitly summon the authority of the larger 'people-as-whole'.[10] In other words, populists assert that they represent the unitary and undivided will of the people, the (common) general interest of 'the people', re-conceptualised as unity.[11]

This re-conceptualisation of the people as people-as-whole – or People-as-One, as I would call it – has, from a populist viewpoint, some important advantages. From this perspective, the re-conceptualisation of the people develops important mobilisation effects, notably through the way it valorises ordinary people.[12] From a spatial point of view, populism also contributes to the reconstruction of democratic spaces. For example, Laura Grattan, drawing on Pierre Bourdieu,[13] suggests that populism (notably what she calls 'everyday populism') can help build parallel 'spaces of democratic practices and imagination'.[14] From the standpoint of time, this re-conceptualisation of populism as unity also has immediate effects: it manifests itself in the instantaneous creation of a majority and minorities, seemingly easy to determine (and to distinguish from each other).[15]

However, the populist claim to represent the unitary will of the people is prone to criticism, notably by liberal constitutionalists. A first important nuance to the populist claim is linked to the intrinsically ambiguous nature of the notion of 'people' itself.[16] In populist discourse, the concept of 'the people' conflates – I would contend – into a single entity three different concepts, namely: (1) the 'revolutionary' people, or people as *pouvoir constituant* (constituent power); (2) the 'electoral' people, or the electorate in general; and (3) the 'representative' people, or temporal majorities. From a legal standpoint, these three concepts (or 'peoples', if you will) are distinct, both conceptually and with regard to their composition.

First, the 'revolutionary' people, or people as *pouvoir constituant*, refers to the people as the ultimate holder of sovereignty, or political power.[17] It is an abstract,

[9] Canovan (n 3) 90.

[10] ibid.

[11] That said, the expression 'will of the people' is not exclusively used in populist discourses. This is discussed in more detail below.

[12] For a conceptualisation of populism as a mode of political practice, more specifically a 'sustained, large-scale political project that mobilizes ordinarily marginalized social sectors into publicly visible and contentious political action, while articulating an anti-elite, nationalist rhetoric that valorizes ordinary people', see, generally, RS Jansen, 'Populist Mobilization: A New Theoretical Approach to Populism' (2011) 29 *Sociological Theory* 75.

[13] P Bourdieu, *Outline of a Theory of Practice* (trans Richard Nice) (Cambridge, Cambridge University Press, 1977) 170–171.

[14] L Grattan, 'Pierre Bourdieu and Populism: The Everyday Politics of Outrageous Resistance' (2012) 21 *The Good Society* 194.

[15] P Rosanvallon, *Le Siècle du populisme: Histoire, théorie, critique (Paris, Seuil, 2020)* 148.

[16] See, eg, Y Mény and Y Surel, 'The Constitutive Ambiguity of Populism' in Y Mény and Y Surel (eds), *Democracies and the Populist Challenge* (London, Palgrave MacMillan, 2002) 6.

[17] '[L]a constitution n'est pas l'ouvrage du pouvoir constitué, mais du pouvoir constituant. Aucune sorte de pouvoir délégué ne peut rien changer aux conditions de sa délégation'. See EJ Sieyès, *Qu'est-ce que le Tiers État?* (Paris, Éditions du Boucher, 2002 [1789]) 53.

collective, dignified and mystical entity that is hardly visible, except in specific space-times – that is to say, mainly during revolutionary or foundational moments.[18] It also often appears in hindsight.[19] Second, the 'electoral' people, or the electorate, is an entity that is, by contrast, a bit more tangible. It is the sum of all electors (usually citizens aged 18 and above) in a polity. It includes people of different backgrounds and views. It is a 'collection of ordinary, ever-changing people with their separate lives, interests and views'.[20] Third, the 'representative' people, or temporal majorities, refers to electoral majorities at a given time and place, as expressed through the outcome of referendums or the election of representatives. They are, by definition, temporal (and temporary): they act, and exist, only during elections or referendums, and through elected representatives for the duration of their term.[21]

Under the populist discourse (and worldview), the differences between these three peoples tend to disappear; they are mingled into one, single notion of people, understood as the People-as-One. This is particularly the case after an election or a referendum. To give an example, several British politicians have used the outcome of the 2016 EU membership referendum (the 'Brexit referendum') in the UK, where 51.89 per cent of voters cast their vote in favour of leaving the EU, to claim that 'the people have spoken' or that the outcome of the referendum was 'the will of the people'.[22] Similarly, in a White Paper presented to Parliament in February 2017, then-Prime Minister Theresa May even claimed to have '[t]he strength and support of 65 million people' willing to make Brexit happen, thereby conflating the size of the 'Leave' voters (approximately 17 million out of 46.5 million registered voters) with the entire UK population (approximately 65 million people at the time).[23] Yet,

[18] See, eg, Canovan (n 3) 121.

[19] See, eg, H Lindahl, 'Constituent Power and Reflexive Identity: Towards an Ontology of Collective Selfhood' in M Loughlin and N Walker (eds), *The Paradox of Constitutionalism: Constituent Power and Constitutional Form* (Oxford, Oxford University Press, 2008) 19: '[I]f the activity of constituent power discloses an irreducible passivity in political unity, a no less irreducible passivity is embedded in constituent power's activity. This insofar as this activity only constitutes a polity if taken up again and carried forward by further acts. Thus, an act of constitution-making can only be viewed retroactively – and provisionally – as an act *by* the collective'.

[20] Canovan (n 3) 6. See also M Canovan, 'Populism for Political Theorists?' (2004) 9 *Journal of Political Ideologies* 241, 250.

[21] On the temporal dimension of popular sovereignty – and the distribution of democracy through time, see also DJ Thompson, 'Democracy in Time: Popular Sovereignty and Temporal Representation' (2005) 12 *Constellations* 245.

[22] See, eg, S Beer, '"The people have spoken": Theresa May issues warning to MPs as she takes axe to EU laws' (*Express*, 2 October 2016) www.express.co.uk/news/uk/716723/Theresa-May-Article-50-Brexit-Great-Repeal-Act.

[23] See May's foreword in HM Government, 'The United Kingdom's exit from and new partnership with the European Union' (*HM Government*, February 2017) assets.publishing.service.gov.uk/government/uploads/system/uploads/attachment_data/file/589191/The_United_Kingdoms_exit_from_and_partnership_with_the_EU_Web.pdf, 3. May however qualified this statement by adding that 'one of the reasons that Britain's democracy has been such a success for so many years is that the strength of our identity as one nation, the respect we show to one another as fellow citizens, and the importance we attach to our institutions means that when a vote has been held we all respect the result […]. The House of Commons has voted overwhelmingly for us to get on with it. And the overwhelming majority of people – however they voted – want us to get on with it too. So that is what we will do'.

the outcome of elections and referendums is usually the result of the expression of temporal majorities (namely, of a plurality or majority of voters at one particular time), not the expression of the (intemporal) people as *pouvoir constituant*.[24]

This is not to say, of course, that liberal constitutionalists work with one single coherent and 'un-manipulated' concept of 'the people', nor that the liberal-constitutionalist discourse is always entirely honest about the tensions inherent in its own project. In fact, several liberal-constitutionalist-oriented politicians have themselves borrowed important parts of the ideal-typical discourse relating to the concept of 'the people', for instance by referring to the outcome of an election as the 'will of the people'. To give a concrete example, former US President Joe Biden referred to the 'will of the people' in his 2021 presidential inauguration speech.[25] Similarly, in a January 2022 speech marking the first anniversary of the 2021 Capitol insurrection by Donald Trump supporters, then-President Biden referred to 'the people' on no less than 12 separate occasions, including six references to the 'will of the people'.[26] He described the insurrection and riots as an 'assault' on the 'will of the people', the latter being a direct reference to the outcome of the November 2020 presidential election, which he won. For Biden, those who stormed the Capitol on 6 January 2021 'weren't looking to uphold the will of the people; they were looking to deny the will of the people'.[27] This rhetoric (and, arguably, May's rhetoric on the outcome of the Brexit referendum as well) gives weight to the argument that populism is a matter of degree[28] and, one may add, to the argument that the separation between populist and liberal-constitutionalist discourses is not always watertight.

Nevertheless, it could plausibly be argued, at least from a liberal-constitutionalist perspective, that the ideal-typical populist discourse instrumentalises (and even manipulates, distorts and/or misrepresents) the concept of 'the people'. Indeed, by summoning the authority of the People-as-One on the basis of a temporal majority at a specific point in time, populist leaders tend to exploit the ambiguous nature of 'the people' to increase the legitimacy of a given political act or electoral outcome. In other words, populists tend to rely on empirical (and partial) manifestations of the people, such as temporal (electoral) majorities, to summon the authority of 'the people' in its mythical and perhaps even mystical sense, that is to say, the people as a *corpus mysticum*, a sort of fictitious or juristic collective person with a single body (and a single will).[29]

[24] That said, certain referendums – such as referendums for the setting of a new constituent assembly or for national independence – could, in some circumstances, be viewed as the expression of the *pouvoir constituant*. This possibility is further discussed below.

[25] JR Biden, 'Full transcript of Joe Biden's inaugural speech' (*BBC*, 20 January 2021) www.bbc.co.uk/news/world-us-canada-55656824.

[26] JR Biden, 'Statuary Hall Speech' (*USA Today*, 6 January 2021) eu.usatoday.com/story/news/politics/2022/01/06/biden-jan-6-capitol-riot-speech-transcript/9115459002.

[27] ibid.

[28] See, eg, NW Barber, 'Populist Leaders and Political Parties' (2019) 20 *German Law Journal* 129, 134.

[29] EH Kantorowicz, *The King's Two Bodies: A Study of in Medieval Political Theology* (Princeton, Princeton University Press, 1997 [1957]) 209, as mentioned in J-W Müller, 'Populism and

B. 'The People' as Unity: Populism as Monism

A second, related populist claim to popular sovereignty pertains to populism's monist (or, as some liberal constitutionalists would say, anti-pluralist[30]) conception of 'the people'. Under the populist logic, 'the people' can only exist as a political unity – they hold a common interest and one single, unified will and, as such, can only act as one. This idea of the people as unity can be traced back to certain thinkers, including Abbé Sieyès[31] and Jules Michelet,[32] but perhaps most notably Carl Schmitt.[33] Schmitt's conception of popular sovereignty bases the general will on the unity of the people, which, in turn, is based on a homogeneous conception of the people; those who do not belong to this homogeneous people are thus excluded (or, in Schmitt's terms, 'eliminated') from it.[34] Of course, populists could respond to this by questioning the extent to which this view is different from the traditional Western view of constitutionalism, where the laws of the state conform to the geographic territory of that state and rest on a socio-cultural substrate that gives rise to the nation state in several polities.[35] Nevertheless, at least from a liberal-constitutionalist point of view, the populist emphasis on the unification of the people, more specifically the 'real', 'true' or 'forgotten' people, is inherently exclusionary: from a spatial perspective, it requires the 'extraction'[36] of the 'morally pure people' from the citizens who inhabit a given polity. In other

Constitutionalism' in C Rovira Kaltwasser, P Ochoa Espejo, P Taggart and P Ostiguy (eds), *The Oxford Handbook of Populism* (Oxford, Oxford University Press, 2017) 595. See also Claude Lefort's account of Kantorowicz's image of the king's body as two bodies (both mortal and immortal, individual and collective) in C Lefort, *The Political Forms of Modern Society: Bureaucracy, Democracy, Totalitarianism* (Cambridge, Polity, 1986) 302.

[30] See, eg, WA Galston, *Anti-Pluralism: The Populist Threat to Liberal Democracy* (New Haven, Yale University Press, 2018); C Mudde, 'The Populist Zeitgeist' (2004) 39 *Government and Opposition* 541, 543. For reasons discussed at the end of this subsection, however, I believe the term 'monist' is more accurate than 'anti-pluralist'. This is because there certainly are instances of contemporary populism that do not deserve the 'anti-pluralist' epithet, such as the example of Podemos in Spain. On this, see, eg, J Mansbridge and S Macedo, 'Populism and Democratic Theory' (2019) 15 *Annual Review of Law and Social Science* 59, 63.

[31] 'L'assimilation des hommes est la première condition de la grande réunion nationale, en un peuple *un*'. EJ Sieyès, 'Sur le projet de décret pour l'établissement de l'instruction nationale' (1793) 5 *Journal d'instruction sociale* (6 July), as cited in P Rosanvallon, *Le Peuple introuvable: Histoire de la représentation démocratique en France* (Paris, Gallimard, 1998) 39. In English, see P Rosanvallon, *Democracy Past and Future* (New York, Columbia University Press, 2006) 90.

[32] See J Michelet, *Le Peuple* (Paris, Flammarion, 1974 [1846]).

[33] C Mudde and C Rovira Kaltwasser, *Populism: A Very Short Introduction* (Oxford, Oxford University Press, 2017) 18. For a detailed analysis of how contemporary populism rests on a 'distinctly Schmittian logic', see, eg, WE Scheuerman, 'Donald Trump meets Carl Schmitt' (2019) 45 *Philosophy and Social Criticism* 1170.

[34] See, eg, C Schmitt, 'The Liberal Rule of Law' in AJ Jacobson and B Schlink (eds), *Weimar: A Jurisprudence of Crisis* (Berkeley, University of California Press, 2000 [1928]) 299–300. In an earlier work, Schmitt went as far as to write that '[e]very actual democracy rests on the principle that not only are equals equal but unequals will not be treated equally. Democracy requires, therefore, first homogeneity and second – if the need arises elimination or eradication of heterogeneity'. See C Schmitt, *The Crisis of Parliamentary Democracy* (Cambridge, MIT Press, 2000 [1923]) 9.

[35] I thank Jo Murkens for pointing this out.

[36] See C Lefort, *Democracy and Political Theory* (Cambridge, Polity, 1988) 79.

words, 'the people', under the populist logic, must be purified and removed of their heterogeneous components. As a result, those who are not part of this homogeneous entity (comprised of 'real' or morally 'pure' people), or those who do not support them, do not belong to the political community and are thus excluded from it; political opponents and contenders, for their part, are viewed as illegitimate, corrupt and/or incompetent.

Illustrations of the exclusionary nature of the populist conception of 'the people' abound. They include, for instance, Nigel Farage's claim that the result of the referendum on the withdrawal of the UK from the EU was a 'victory for the *real* people'[37] or President Recep Tayyip Erdoğan's statement that Turkish citizens protesting in Gezi Park in 2013 did not belong to the people.[38] In perhaps even bolder terms, Donald Trump clearly stated during his 2016 presidential campaign that 'the only important thing is the unification of the people – because the *other* people don't mean anything'.[39] More liberal-constitutionalist-leaning politicians, such as Prime Minister Keir Starmer in the UK, have also engaged in populist discourses, as evidenced by Starmer's statement in May 2025 that without curbs on immigration, Britain risks becoming an 'island of strangers'.[40] Populist exclusion (or, in some cases, expulsion – metaphorical or actual[41]) can also sometimes be drawn along ethnic or religious lines. For instance, Prime Minister Narendra Modi of India has defined Indian Muslims as 'external invaders who gained too much power over a pure Hindu culture'.[42] The populist 'people', therefore, is defined as *communitas*, but along ethnic, religious, linguistic and (or), sometimes, notably in the case of

[37] J-W Müller, *What is Populism?* (London, Penguin, 2017) 21–22 (emphasis added). It should be added that this type of rhetoric can also sometimes be found in certain liberal-constitutionalist discourses. One may think, for example, of the movement advocating for a second Brexit referendum under the banner of a 'People's Vote', thereby prompting the question as to who exactly voted in the first referendum.

[38] Müller, '"The People Must Be Extracted from Within the People": Reflections on Populism' (2014) 21 *Constellations* 483, 487.

[39] Müller (n 37) 22 (emphasis added). Müller adds, in a later piece, that '[p]opulists talk incessantly about unifying the people, but their political strategy involves dividing societies and waging culture wars: whoever doesn't want to be unified on their terms is cast out'. See JW Müller, 'Populism and the People' (2019) (*London Review of Books*, 23 May 2019) www.lrb.co.uk/the-paper/v41/n10/jan-werner-mueller/populism-and-the-people.

[40] See, eg, R Syal, 'UK risks becoming "island of strangers" without more immigration curbs, Starmer says' (*The Guardian*, 12 May 2025) www.theguardian.com/world/2025/may/12/uk-risks-becoming-island-of-strangers-without-more-immigration-curbs-starmer-says.

[41] One can think, for example, of Trump's mass deportations of 'undocumented' migrants in his second presidential term in 2025, including deportations to El Salvador on the basis of an 18th-century wartime law, the Alien Enemies Act 1798, ch 66, 1 Stat 577. While these were blocked by Judge James Boasberg of the US District Court for the District of Columbia (DC) through temporary restraining orders (TROs) (which were later upheld by the US circuit court of appeals for DC), these TROs were, however, vacated by a 5–4 majority at the US Supreme Court in April 2025, which paved the way for the deportations. See *Trump v JGG* 604 US 670 (2025).

[42] DA Johnson, 'In Defense of Democratic Populism' in GL Neuman (ed), *Human Rights in a Time of Populism: Challenges and Responses* (Cambridge, Cambridge University Press, 2020) 206. That said, Johnson would argue that this rhetoric or discourse is not a feature of populism *as such* but, rather, a feature of 'nativist authoritarianism'.

left-wing populism, socioeconomic lines, acting towards the realisation of the 'common good'.[43]

This is not to say, of course, that this exclusionary conception of the people is necessarily and inevitably based on ethnic, linguistic and (or) religious homogeneity. In fact, several left-wing populist leaders, notably in Latin America, have been noted for receiving the support of diverse ethnic minority groups, including indigenous peoples.[44] In the same vein, it would be a mistake to fail to recognise that traditional, liberal-democratic representation also frequently comes with its own forms of exclusion(s), including economic exclusion. In fact, it is precisely in such a context of economic exclusion that left-wing populists like Hugo Chávez (in Venezuela), Evo Morales (in Bolivia) and Rafael Correa (in Ecuador) successfully mobilised – at least initially – mass constituencies,[45] including indigenous peoples, against the 'oligarchy' and the 'neoliberal exclusionary system'.[46] It should be noted that these forms of 'exclusionary mobilisation' have sometimes led to social advances and, perhaps ironically, some forms of 'social *inclusion*'. In the words of Yannis Stavrakakis and Anton Jäger, 'most advances on this front – from voting rights to social, racial and sexual inclusion – have been the result of political struggles in which excluded popular sectors have managed to transform their diversity into a unity (at least partial)'.[47] This shows there is a certain emancipatory potential in grassroots populism, which can emanate, it appears, from the 'fostering [of] unlikely alliances between marginalized groups'.[48]

Nevertheless, even these cases of successful mobilisation and inclusion involve, I contend, a certain form of exclusion or expulsion. Indeed, the 'inclusion' (the 'us') necessary for political unity inevitably requires a concomitant 'exclusion' (a 'they' or an 'Other') or, as Hans Lindahl points out, 'the exclusion of other possible legal instantiations of political unity'.[49] This is also apparent in the way political power is monopolised – at least to a certain extent – by one influential and charismatic leader, claiming to speak on behalf of the (entire) people or nation (and/or to mirror the

[43] In a somewhat similar way, Ulrich Preuß describes this as 'the notion of the people as an ethnos', in contrast to the notion of the people as 'demos' which 'consists of the entirety of the citizens who form a community by the bonds of common laws'. See UK Preuß, 'Judicial Power in Processes of Transformation' in C Landfried (ed), *Judicial Power: How Constitutional Courts Affect Political Transformations* (Cambridge, Cambridge University Press, 2019) 357.

[44] See, eg, C Mudde and C Rovira Kaltwasser, 'Exclusionary vs. Inclusionary Populism: Comparing Contemporary Europe and Latin America' (2013) 48 *Government and Opposition* 147.

[45] On anti-establishment appeals, mobilisation and competitive authoritarianism, see S Levitsky and J Loxton, 'Populism and Competitive Authoritarianism in the Andes' (2013) 20 *Democratization* 107, 108.

[46] See, eg, M Becker, 'Correa, Indigenous Movements, and the Writing of a New Constitution in Ecuador' (2011) 38 *Latin American Perspectives* 47, 60.

[47] Y Stavrakakis and A Jäger, 'Accomplishments and Limitations of the "New" Mainstream in Contemporary Populism Studies' (2018) 21 *European Journal of Social Theory* 556.

[48] T Riofrancos, 'Democracy Without the People' (*N+1*, 6 February 2017) www.nplusonemag.com/online-only/online-only/democracy-without-the-people. See also L Grattan, *Populism's Power: Radical Grassroots Democracy in America* (Oxford, Oxford University Press, 2016).

[49] See Lindahl (n 19) 20.

latter's sentiments[50]), often to the detriment of other competing claims to authority and representation.[51] From a spatiotemporal perspective, therefore, and to draw a parallel with literary studies, the ideal-typical populist discourse is sometimes akin to the 'epic' literary genre, with its grand-scale narrative invoking a unified and heroic people, often consisting of a 'one-voice story told by a single, all-knowing narrator'.[52] The populist discourse thus emulates the epic, with its world that – to re-employ Mikhail Bakhtin's account – 'knows only a single and unified world view, obligatory and indubitably true for heroes as well as for authors and audiences'.[53]

By contrast, under a liberal-constitutionalist perspective, the concept of 'the people' is said to be pluralist in nature – at least in theory and in its idealised form – with multiple (if not infinite) claims to representation. From a spatiotemporal perspective, the boundaries of 'the people' are constantly subject to contestation and capable of changing over time. In other words, instead of existing as one, 'the people' can only exist through a wide range of partial manifestations, each with their own irreducible individuality, and which reflect the identity of a community and the diversity of its citizens.[54] This pluralism (again, at least in its theoretical and idealised form) clashes with the populist conception (also in its theoretical and idealised form) of the 'people' as unity. It is in this context that Pierre Rosanvallon has argued that populists oversimplify the concept of 'the people' when they explicitly or implicitly claim that 'the people' are the authentic and unified (and, sometimes, purified) part of a society that emerges and comes together in opposition to elitist, cosmopolitan groups or oligarchies. In fact, for Rosanvallon, a people or a society cannot be defined negatively; contrary to Schmitt's belief,[55] it is not simply by removing or extracting (or, as one might say, 'expulsing') oligarchies or certain groups of society – notably the elite, foreigners, etc – that 'the people' will suddenly emerge as a unified mass with one common, undivided will.[56] For him, the conception of 'the people' (or of the general interest) should encompass society as a whole and not simply the majority of the electorate. Rosanvallon therefore argues that the populist conception of democracy rests, in that regard, on a form of fiction, namely that the electoral majority represents society as a whole.[57]

Therefore, and to continue the parallel with literary studies begun above, the liberal-constitutionalist conception of democracy – like the novel and in contrast to the epic, briefly discussed previously – is based on the idea that there

[50] A Harel and N Kolt, 'Populist Rhetoric, False Mirroring, and the Courts' (2020) 18 *International Journal of Constitutional Law* 746.

[51] See chs 2 and 3.

[52] M Valverde, *Chronotopes of Law: Jurisdiction, Scale and Governance* (Abingdon, Routledge, 2015) 7.

[53] M Bakhtin, *The Dialogic Imagination: Four Essays* (Austin, University of Texas Press, 1981) 35, as cited in ibid 7.

[54] K Abts and S Rummens, 'Populism versus Democracy' (2007) 55 *Political Studies* 405, 413.

[55] See, eg, Schmitt, 'Liberal Rule of Law' (n 34) 299–300.

[56] P Rosanvallon, 'Penser le populisme' in C Colliot-Thélène and F Guénard (eds), *Peuples et populisme* (Paris, Presses universitaires de France, 2014) 34–36.

[57] ibid.

is no single, unique point of view, nor a single, unitary people. On that view, democratic representation, just like the novel genre, is based on a multiplicity of narratives, modes of speech, viewpoints and worldviews. To re-employ Mariana Valverde's framework, liberal constitutional democracy (again, in its idealised form) thus performs what Bakhtin calls 'heteroglossia', as it gives its audience – namely, the citizenry – 'a whole cast of characters with distinct, individual voices, thus offering that audience a wide variety of perspectives and mini-languages'.[58]

In short, populists often have a monist – and, to a certain degree, exclusionary – conception of 'the people', that is to say, a conception under which 'the people' are a pre-constitutional entity with one will; a single entity, acting and speaking through a unified voice.[59] This monist conception also has important mobilisation effects, notably in the way it valorises ordinary people through identity- and authenticity-based identification.[60] Yet, liberal constitutionalists would retort that this conception is limited, or at least partial, insofar as the 'people' populist leaders refer to are, too often, only a 'mythical and constructed sub-set of the whole population'.[61] This constructed sub-set, they would argue, does not reflect the pluralist nature of a community or the diversity of the people who inhabit that said community. Moreover, and in the same vein, many liberal constitutionalists would argue that the voice of the people (or the expression of their political power) is better expressed not through acclamation or the will of an authoritative leader, contrary to what some populists often argue or imply, but rather through deliberation, compromise and institutional arrangements. In the words of the leading deliberative constitutional democrat, Jürgen Habermas, '[t]he people from whom all governmental authority is supposed to derive does not comprise a subject with will and consciousness. It only appears in the plural, and *as* a people it is capable of neither decision nor action as a whole'.[62]

C. The 'Other' as Constitutive of the Identity of 'the People'

As alluded to above, it is worth emphasising that the populist conception of 'the people' as unity does not necessarily mean (or imply) *Artgleichheit*, that is to say, racial homogeneity or identity.[63] While it is true that many right-wing populist

[58] Valverde (n 52) 7.

[59] L Corrias, 'Populism in a Constitutional Key: Constituent Power, Popular Sovereignty and Constitutional Identity' (2016) 12 *European Constitutional Law Review* 19.

[60] See, eg Jansen (n 12) and ch 3 of this monograph.

[61] Mudde (n 30) 546.

[62] J Habermas, 'Popular Sovereignty as Procedure' in J Habermas, *Between Facts and Norms: Contributions to a Discourse Theory of Law and Democracy* (trans W Rehg) (Cambridge, Polity, 1996) 469. That said, the sovereign people may, in certain limited circumstances, (re-)appear. This is discussed further below.

[63] On this, see Müller (n 38) 486.

parties in Europe have indeed adopted an exclusionary, nativist and/or sometimes racialised conception (which often excludes non-native and immigrant populations), many populist parties and leaders, especially in Latin America, have been more inclusionary (and, in some cases, more multicultural) in their definition of 'the people' – and in the legal institutions they have set up.[64] For instance, Article 1 of the Bolivian Constitution, promulgated in 2009 by then-President Evo Morales, provides that Bolivia is a 'pluri-national', 'inter-cultural' and 'decentralised' state, 'founded on plurality and on political, economic, juridical, cultural and linguistic pluralism'.[65] Similarly, the preamble to the Constitution of Venezuela, promoted by then-President Hugo Chávez, recognises the 'multiethnic and multicultural' nature of the Venezuelan society.[66] As Cristóbal Rovira Kaltwasser has pointed out, '[European] populist leaders are prone to define "the people" in ethnic terms, while in Latin America populist forces tend to conceive 'the people' as the socioeconomic underdog'.[67] Given this distinction, it would probably be an oversimplification to claim that the populist conception of 'the people' is, in and of itself, (always) anti-pluralist.

What both European and Latin American (or right-wing and left-wing)[68] populist conceptions of 'the people' have in common, however, is that they arguably both require the creation of an Other. As Claude Lefort has argued in the context of his discussion on democracy and totalitarianism, 'the People-as-One can both be represented and affirmed only by a great Other'.[69] This Other, or enemy, is 'constitutive of the identity of the people'.[70] Of course, the composition of the populist Other may vary. It can include, for example, ethnic or religious minorities, such as Roma and Muslim refugees, according to Viktor Orbán's Hungary. It can also include criminals, drug dealers and even drug users, who were depicted by former President Rodrigo Duterte of the Philippines – recently arrested for crimes against humanity[71] – as 'outsiders' who need to be 'expunged from society'.[72] In

[64] See, generally, Mudde and Kaltwasser (n 44).

[65] Constitution of the Plurinational State of Bolivia (adopted 7 February 2009), art 1.

[66] Constitution of the Bolivarian Republic of Venezuela (adopted 15 December 1999) (as amended to 2009), Preamble.

[67] C Rovira Kaltwasser, 'Explaining the Emergence of Populism' in C de la Torre (ed), *The Promise and Perils of Populism: Global Perspectives* (Lexington, University Press of Kentucky, 2014) 209.

[68] As mentioned in the introductory chapter, this is not to say that *all* populisms in Latin America have been 'left-wing' populisms. Examples of Latin American 'right-wing' populisms (or, as some would call them, 'market reform populisms') since the 1940s include Alberto Fujimori's Peru (1990–2000) and Carlos Menem's Argentina (1989–1999). Conversely, while many European populisms in Europe have been 'right-wing' populisms, recently examples of European 'left-wing' populist parties include Syriza in Greece, Podemos in Spain and Jean-Luc Mélenchon's La France insoumise.

[69] Lefort (n 29) 287.

[70] ibid.

[71] J Guinto, 'Philippines' Duterte in The Hague after ICC arrest over drug war' (*BBC*, 12 March 2025) www.bbc.co.uk/news/articles/c9819r2en4do.

[72] DA Johnson, 'In Defense of Democratic Populism' in GL Neuman (ed), *Human Rights in a Time of Populism: Challenges and Responses* (Cambridge, Cambridge University Press, 2020) 206. However, and as mentioned above, Johnson argues that this exclusionary discourse is more a feature of 'nativist authoritarianism' than a feature of populism per se. Other populists employing similar rhetoric

such cases, the populist 'enemy' is portrayed, in a way reminiscent of Schmitt's views, as a threat to a nation's existence, to a way of life.[73] It may also include universities, as seen in Türkiye (with the purge of critical academics, especially in the aftermath of the failed 2016 coup attempt),[74] Hungary (the case of the Central European University, which had to move from Budapest to Vienna in Austria, provides an example[75]) or, more recently, in the US (with the Trump administration's decision to cut funding and threaten what it views as liberal bastions, such as Columbia University, and their diversity, equity and inclusion programmes).[76] In many instances, these various and eclectic groups are merged into one, as US Vice-President JD Vance's speech at the February 2025 Munich Conference reveals, with his concerns about what he depicted as the 'threat from within',[77] a discourse reminiscent of Senator Joseph McCarthy's 'enemies from within' speech delivered in 1950.

As will become clear in Part II of this book, judges – especially those who rule against the regime or are against it – are also a particular target for populists, who will not hesitate to depict them as 'enemies'. Examples abound, but one may think, for instance, of Maria Lourdes Sereno, then serving as chief justice of the Supreme Court of the Philippines, who took a stance against the country's 'drug war', calling for due process for people included in Duterte's extensive list of people suspected of being involved in the illegal drug trade. In response, in a 2018 televised speech, then-President Duterte addressed her and said: 'So I'm putting you on notice that I am now your enemy. And you have to be out of the supreme court.'[78] Shortly thereafter, she was indeed removed from office, with the help of quiescent judges,[79] over a *quo warranto* petition that many saw as politically motivated.[80]

and actions (albeit to a lesser extent) include Thaksin Shinawatra, Thailand's former Prime Minister (2001–2006), Joko Widodo (Jokowi), Indonesia's former president (2014–2024) and, more recently, US President Trump's recent emphasis on the 'war on fentanyl'.

[73] M de Wilde, 'Uncertain Futures and the Problem of Constraining Emergency Powers: Temporal Dimensions of Carl Schmitt's Theory of the State of Exception' in Corrias and Francot (eds), *Temporal Boundaries of Law and Politics: Time Out of Joint* (Abingdon, Routledge, 2018). See, generally, C Schmitt, *The Concept of the Political: Expanded Edition* (trans by George Schwab) (University of Chicago Press, 2007 [1932]).

[74] See, eg, M Kaya, 'Turkey's Purge of Critical Academia' (*MERIP*, December 2018) www.merip.org/2018/12/turkeys-purge-of-critical-academia.

[75] See, eg, G Gőbl, 'Orbán vs. the World: The Background Context of the Lex CEU' (*Heinrich Böll Stiftung*, 3 May 2017) www.boell.de/en/2017/05/03/orban-vs-world-background-context-lex-ceu.

[76] See, eg, C McGreal, 'A graduate's arrest and Trump's 'pincer attack' on higher education' (*The Guardian*, 15 March 2025) www.theguardian.com/us-news/2025/mar/15/universities-columbia-trump.

[77] See, eg, P Wintour, 'JD Vance stuns Munich conference with blistering attack on Europe's leaders' (*The Guardian*, 14 February 2025) www.theguardian.com/us-news/2025/feb/14/jd-vance-stuns-munich-conference-with-blistering-attack-on-europes-leaders.

[78] AP, 'Fear for democracy after top Philippine judge and government critic removed' (*The Guardian*, 12 May 2018) www.theguardian.com/world/2018/may/12/fear-for-democracy-after-top-philippine-judge-and-government-critic-removed.

[79] *Republic of the Philippines v Sereno* (2018) G R No 237428 (Phil SC).

[80] AP (n 78).

In other cases, as we have seen earlier in some examples of left-wing populism, the populist Other can be defined on socioeconomic grounds – namely, as the socioeconomic underdog. That said, while the composition of the populist Other, or enemy, may vary depending on the region and socioeconomic circumstances, it almost inevitably includes the 'elite', more particularly the economic and political elite, as well as other wielders of power, who – as 'enemies' – are opposed to the 'real' or 'pure' people. As Albert Weale summarises, there is a superficial plurality behind both the notions of 'people' and 'elite', but in both cases, the reference is singular.[81] Furthermore, and as Slavoj Žižek points out, populist discourses construct and externalise (or even reify) the enemy into a 'positive ontological reality', even if this entity is spectral or mythical.[82]

With their ability to determine who is part of the people (and, by extension, who is *not* – that is to say, the Other or the enemy), populist leaders are therefore instrumental in determining the boundaries of 'the people' as a construct.[83] Indeed, and in the words of Ernesto Laclau, 'the "people", as operating in populist discourses, is never a primary datum but a construct – populist discourse does not simply *express* some kind of original popular identity; it actually *constitutes* the latter'.[84] This constitutive function is done through a mode of identification. For Francisco Panizza, the latter 'requires the performative drawing of an internal frontier of exclusion within society': the people, arguably, are a 'partial component of society (the plebs) that nevertheless aspires to be conceived as the only legitimate totality (the demos)'.[85] For Panizza, this process is accomplished through a populist leader who appeals to the members of a community who feel politically excluded from the political system and elevates them to the status of the (only) legitimate holders of sovereignty.[86] This leader will often claim to have a 'direct rapport with the people that allows him to advance their interests without becoming prisoner to the powerful'.[87] This focus on identity-based identification over liberal-democratic representation is discussed in more detail in the next two chapters. It should be added that this constitutive function, performed through a mode of identification, is not always done explicitly; in

[81] See, eg, A Weale, *The Will of the People: A Modern Myth* (Cambridge, Polity, 2018) 34–35.

[82] S Žižek, 'Against the Populist Temptation' (2006) 32 *Critical Inquiry* 551, 555.

[83] In fact, many populist leaders expressly acknowledge this. One may think, for instance, of Orbán's well-known 'illiberal democracy' speech in Băile Tuşnad (Tusnádfürdő) in July 2014, in which he said: 'The Hungarian nation is not simply a group of individuals but a community that must be organized, reinforced and in fact *constructed*' (emphasis added). See 'Full text of Viktor Orbán's speech at Băile Tuşnad (Tusnádfürdő) of 26 July 2014' (trans Csaba Tóth) (*The Budapest Beacon*, 29 July 2014), as cited in P Blokker, 'Populism as a Constitutional Project' (2019) 17 *International Journal of Constitutional Law* 535, 543.

[84] Laclau, 'Populism: What's in a Name?' in F Panizza (ed), *Populism and the Mirror of Democracy* (London, Verso, 2005) 48. See also Laclau, *On Populist Reason* (London, Verso, 2005) 68-ss.

[85] F Panizza, 'What is Contested and What Is Not in the Debate About Populism', paper presented at the LSE Graduate Conference on Populism (3 November 2017) (unpublished manuscript; on file with author) 6.

[86] ibid.

[87] ibid 22.

fact, the ideal-typical populist discourse often precisely denies the constructed character of 'the people'.

The above paragraphs can be summarised in two points. First, the boundaries of 'the people' tend to be shaped by the populist discourse, which almost always involves the creation of an Other, or, sometimes, an enemy. This is not to deny, of course, that liberal-constitutionalist discourses also come with their own forms of othering. In fact, one might even argue that populism is liberal constitutionalism's Other: it is indeed hard to deny that the 'populist' epithet or label can also be, in certain circumstances, 'a form of "othering" that eschews serious engagement with those who see more promise than peril in today's disruptive politics'.[88] Nevertheless, the populist conception of 'the people' as unity, and its accompanying form of othering, is prone to criticism from a liberal-constitutionalist perspective on the grounds that it is singular, rigid and that it often disregards the pluralistic nature of society. Second, the ideal-typical populist discourse does not refer to a pre-existing people; this discourse, in fact, constitutes the people, notably through a mode of identification. In other words, populists discursively constitute – without necessarily acknowledging it – the very 'people' they claim to (sometimes exclusively) represent. From a spatial perspective, therefore, populists tend to shape the boundaries of the 'people' they invoke. This, of course, is not limited to populist discourses as such. Constitutional and (or) revolutionary moments, or even some liberal-democratic institutions, also have a constitutive effect. One may think, for instance, of the American people, who were arguably constituted by the enactment of the US Constitution itself.[89] As Jacques Derrida said about the 'We the people' preamble, the people 'do *not* exist as an entity, the entity does not exist *before* this declaration, not *as such*.'[90] Therefore, Derrida added, '[i]f it gives birth to itself, as free and independent subject, as possible signer, this can hold only in the act of the signature. The signature invents the signer'.[91]

In other words, 'the people', as *pouvoir constituant*, can and will indeed sometimes overthrow an existing order, enact a (new) constitution and establish democratic and representative institutions. Moreover, these democratic and representative institutions will sometimes have a constitutive effect – leading to the creation of a new 'people', as in the case of the American people. However, in both cases, the establishment of the boundaries of 'the people' (that is to say, who is included and who is not) requires a constituted legal and political order, with

[88] See R Howse, 'Epilogue: In Defense of Disruptive Democracy – A Critique of Anti-Populism' (2019) 17 *International Journal of Constitutional Law* 642, 650. In the same vein, '[b]y removing those with unconventional or dissonant voices from the legitimate realm of political discussion, in order to preserve some kind of vague centrist liberal consensus, one might say the [liberal] elites excused these unconventional or dissonant voices from political responsibility', pushing them farther from the mainstream.

[89] See ES Morgan, *Inventing the People: The Rise of Popular Sovereignty in England and America* (New York, Norton, 1989) 267.

[90] J Derrida, 'Declarations of Independence' in J Derrida and E Rosenberg (eds), *Negotiations: Interventions and Interviews, 1971–2001* (Redwood, Stanford University Press, 2001) 49.

[91] ibid.

its own set of procedures and institutional arrangements – and in any event, these boundaries can never be fully established nor clarified. Indeed, it could be said that democracy 'is in many ways an ongoing political contest to define the people and their powers'; as such, the boundaries of 'the people', just like a national territory, can also 'be tightened and secured, or they can be disrupted and expanded by the excluded'.[92] However, from a liberal-constitutionalist perspective, the will of the people as a whole is ephemeral and elusive, and as such, it can hardly be interpreted. In the words of Paulina Ochoa Espejo, 'if the people can (and probably will) change, then any appeal to its will is also fallible, temporary and incomplete'.[93]

III. The Sovereign People (or the Nation) as the Ultimate Source of Authority

In this third section of chapter one, I explain how the ideal-typical populist discourse views 'the people' (or the nation) as the ultimate (and only) holder of sovereignty. Through an exploration of the similarities and distinctions between the modernist and populist conceptions of sovereignty, I raise the hypothesis that populism seeks to refashion – and streamline – the (existing) relationships of sovereignty. I finish this section by asking whether 'the people' can be institutionalised as a sovereign in a legal sense.

A. The Populist Conception of Sovereignty

Another distinctive element of the populist discourse is its peculiar understanding of the concept of sovereignty. Under the modernist conception, sovereignty is 'entirely inseparable from the state'.[94] It is an expression of public power, manifested through a 'formal constitutional framework which allocates legislative, executive, and judicial powers of the state to designated institutions'.[95] As such, the legal system and the constitution may be viewed as an elaboration of legal sovereignty through institutional arrangements.[96]

At first sight, the populist conception of sovereignty seems to share some important similarities with the modernist conception. For instance, both conceptions put forward the idea that the authority of the final word for the expression of

[92] Riofrancos (n 48).

[93] P Ochoa Espejo, 'Power to Whom? The People between Procedure and Populism' in de la Torre (ed) (n 67) 61.

[94] C Loyseau, *Traicté des Seigneuries* (Paris, Abel l'Angelier, 1614) ii.4: 'la Souveraineté est du tout inseparable de l'Estat', as cited in M Loughlin, *The Idea of Public Law* (Oxford University Press, 2003) 73.

[95] Loughlin (n 94) 84.

[96] ibid.

political power resides in the political will of 'the nation'[97] or in the consent of 'the people', an idea that goes back to the eighteenth century and French revolutionary discourse.[98] In *The Rights of Man*, for example, Thomas Paine expressed the view that '[t]he Nation is essentially the source of all sovereignty; nor can any individual, or any body of men, be entitled to any authority which is not expressly derived from it'.[99] Similarly, the French Constitution of 1791, drawing on Jean-Jacques Rousseau,[100] promulgated that '[s]overeignty is one, indivisible, inalienable, and imprescriptible; it belongs to the Nation; no group can attribute sovereignty to itself nor can an individual arrogate it to himself'.[101]

What distinguishes the populist conception of sovereignty from the modernist (or liberal-constitutionalist) conception is that under the populist vision, sovereignty is situated 'squarely [and only] in the "nation" or the People, which remains ultimately unbound by the law'.[102] In other words, under the populist conception of sovereignty, 'the people' not only act as *pouvoir constituant*; they also act as an entity above the law, or *populus legibus solutus est*, which cannot ultimately be bound by legal, constitutional or institutional constraints. According to the populist logic, liberal democracy illegitimately fragmentises sovereignty through institutions and procedures. Of course, this is something that most liberal democrats would acknowledge themselves: this 'fragmentation' of sovereignty is often seen as liberal constitutionalism's central point and main virtue.[103] Yet, for populists, this fragmentation of sovereignty (and/or dispersion of power) is both illegitimate and a weakness: it prevents 'the people', as holders of sovereignty, from truly exercising the powers that belong to them. Because sovereignty resides ultimately in the people or nation, populism rejects the 'divided' sovereignty of liberalism, more particularly its jurisdictional divisions of powers and constitutional limitations on political power. For populists – and by contrast to liberal constitutionalists, who often have an uneasy relationship with constituent power – sovereignty does not emerge 'from within empirical, modern, actually existing society as such'.[104] Rather, it 'has extra-societal, transcendental origins in the People or "the eternal nation", and is in turn represented or embodied by the populist leader'.[105] Populists therefore seek to re-centralise political power in the hands of the people (or, as some critics would say, in the hands of a populist leader who impersonates the people), away

[97] For the purpose of the present discussion, 'the people' and 'the nation' can be used interchangeably. In both cases, as Rosanvallon explains, the reference is to a political and historical force rather than a sociological reality. See Rosanvallon (n 31) 41.

[98] See, eg, R Jackson, *Sovereignty: The Evolution of an Idea* (Cambridge, Polity, 2013).

[99] T Paine, *The Rights of Man* (London, JS Jordan, 1791).

[100] See JJ Rousseau, *On the Social Contract, or Principles of Political Right* in JJ Rousseau (ed), *The Basic Political Writings* (Indianapolis, Hackett, 1986 [1762]) 153–155.

[101] French Constitution of 1791, as cited in Jackson (n 98) 93.

[102] Blokker (n 83) 550.

[103] I thank Conor Gearty and Thomas Poole for raising this point.

[104] Blokker (n 83) 550.

[105] ibid.

from liberal institutions, including the judiciary, which are seen as illegitimate obstacles to the expression of the popular will.[106]

B. Populism, Rousseau, Schmitt and the 'General Will'

The conception of popular sovereignty relied upon by populist leaders echoes the conception put forth by Jean-Jacques Rousseau in *The Social Contract*. Populists tend to rely upon a conception of popular sovereignty that puts the emphasis on the *volonté générale* (general will), the idea that the people can act in unison and rule in the manner of a sovereign,[107] acting 'utterly on the basis of common interest'.[108] The general will, which focuses on the 'general interests' and 'tends toward equality',[109] must be distinguished from the *volonté de tous* (will of all), 'which considers private interest and is merely the sum of private wills'.[110] Contrary to private (or particular) wills, which may err, the general will is objective and infallible: 'the general will is always right and always tends toward the public utility'.[111] Moreover, under the Rousseauian conception, the general will cannot be expressed by Parliament; it is fundamental law, and, as such, it cannot be represented, determined or expressed by an institution. In short, for Rousseau, sovereignty is understood as 'the exercise of the general will',[112] as well as being inalienable[113] and indivisible.[114]

The idea that the general will is the source of sovereignty (unconstrained by institutions) is appealing to populists, particularly as they appear to reject liberal (or external) constraints on the popular will. For Schmitt,

> Rousseau's general will has godlike dignity uniting power and justice; it is an unlimited and unlimitable legislator, the source of the laws of the state as God is of the laws of nature; it is undivided, and indivisible, indestructible, morally pure, incapable of error or even of willing a wrong.[115]

Rousseau's legislator is thus, from a spatiotemporal perspective, a figure that straddles the boundary between immanence and transcendence.[116]

[106] ibid. See also I Krastev, 'Eastern Europe's Illiberal Revolution: The Long Road to Democratic Decline' (*Foreign Affairs*, 16 April 2018) www.foreignaffairs.com/articles/hungary/2018-04-16/eastern-europes-illiberal-revolution?cid=int-now&pgtype=hpg&region=br2. These ideas are discussed later in this monograph, including in ch 2 and in Part II.

[107] Jackson (n 98) 94.

[108] Rousseau (n 100) 153.

[109] ibid 154.

[110] ibid 155.

[111] ibid.

[112] ibid 153.

[113] ibid.

[114] ibid 154.

[115] C Schmitt, *Die Diktatur* (Berlin, Duncker & Humblot, 1994 [1921]) 118–119, as cited in A Arato, 'Political Theology and Populism' in de la Torre (ed) (n 67) 33.

[116] See Social Contract, bk II, 7; OCP III, 383 ('Ainsi l'on trouve à la fois dans l'ouvrage de la Législation deux choses qui semblent incompatibles: une entreprise au-dessus de la force humaine, & pour

Populists, in their view, rely on this very Rousseauian conception of sovereignty when they invoke the authority of 'the people' to claim that the outcome of an electoral vote is the 'general will' of the people, and tend to emphasise its nature as 'inalienable',[117] 'indivisible'[118] and 'incapable of erring'.[119] To give a concrete example, this Rousseauian-Schmittian idea that the people as a whole simply cannot err was clearly echoed in Hugo Chávez's inaugural speech in 2007, in which he said:

> All individuals are subject to error and seduction, but not the people, which possesses to an eminent degree of consciousness of its own good and the measure of its independence. Because of this its judgment is pure, its will is strong, and none can corrupt or even threaten it.[120]

From a populist perspective, this idea is certainly very attractive: it sends a positive message of self-trust[121] to the electorate, namely the idea that the public is competent enough to take an active part in government, thereby appealing to 'Rousseau's republican utopia of self-government, i.e., the very idea that citizens are able to both make the laws and execute them'.[122] This desire to directly decide on a broad spectrum of sociopolitical, legal and economic issues – some of which are technical in nature – and the corresponding decline, if not outright rejection of, deference and expertise, are particularly evident in matters pertaining to criminal law, a phenomenon often referred to as 'penal populism'.[123] Implicit in this message of self-trust, also, is the claim that representative government is an illegitimate, elite-based 'aristocratic form of power, in which citizens are treated as passive entities, mobilized periodically by elections, in which they do nothing more than elect their representatives'.[124]

Yet, it could be retorted – at least from a liberal-constitutionalist perspective – that this conception of the general will is incomplete or even misconceived. The general will is not the numerical majority, nor simply the outcome of an election or a referendum. In the words of Rousseau himself, '[w]hat makes the general will is not so much the number of votes as the common interest that unites them'.[125] In the same vein, Jan-Werner Müller points out that the formation of

l'exécuter, une autorité qui n'est rien'), as mentioned in J Bomhoff, 'Immanence and Irreconcilability: On the Character of Public Law as Political Jurisprudence' in M Wilkinson and M Dowdle (eds), *Questioning the Foundations of Public Law* (Oxford, Hart Publishing, 2018) 78.

[117] Rousseau (n 100) 153.

[118] ibid 154.

[119] ibid 155.

[120] Hugo Chávez, 2007 inaugural address, as cited in C Mudde and C Rovira Kaltwasser, 'Populism and (Liberal) Democracy: A Framework for Analysis' in C Mudde and C Rovira Kaltwasser (eds), *Populism in Europe and the Americas: Threat or Corrective for Democracy?* (Cambridge, Cambridge University Press, 2012), 17.

[121] On populism and (public) self-trust, see D Vitale and R Girard, 'Public Trust and the Populist Leader: A Theoretical Argument' (2022) 11 *Global Constitutionalism*.

[122] Mudde and Kaltwasser (n 120) 17.

[123] See ch 2, section IV, subsection C.

[124] Mudde and Kaltwasser (n 120) 17.

[125] Rousseau (n 100) 158. See also R Dagger, 'Understanding the General Will' (1981) 34 *The Western Political Quarterly* 359.

the Rousseauian general will requires actual participation by citizens[126] – and, arguably, by *all* citizens. In other words, even when adopting a Rousseauian perspective, populists appear to conflate the general will, understood as the 'capacity of the people to join together into a community and legislate to enforce their common interest', with the 'will of all', understood as 'the simple sum of particular interests at a specific moment in time'.[127] The general will, in reality, does not emerge in the outcome of an election (or a referendum); it builds itself over time (*la volonté générale se construit dans le temps*)[128] – and, I would add, through the output of the entire citizenry.

C. Can 'the People' be Institutionalised as a Sovereign in a Legal Sense?

The above analysis begs the question as to whether 'the people', even as the ultimate holders of political power, can really be institutionalised as a sovereign in a legal sense. One may indeed wonder if 'the people' are not too occasional and, perhaps more importantly, rarely comprehensive enough to be institutionalised as the 'legal' sovereign.[129] In fact, the idea of a 'sovereign people' arguably refers to two sets of related, yet distinct, bodies: on the one hand, a body of transitory individuals, those who inhabit a polity at a given time; on the other, a larger-encompassing 'collective entity that continues over the generations'.[130] This second body is characteristically more abstract and mysterious; it refers to a collective abstraction 'that has continuous existence and history, transcending and outliving its individual members'.[131] Despite this distinction, and as discussed earlier, populist discourses often tend to 'exploit the ambiguity according to which "the people" is first understood by contrast with the power-holders (and therefore as something less than the population at large) and then expanded to wield the authority of the sovereign people as a whole'.[132]

This is not to say, however, that there is no such thing as a sovereign people. The sovereign people, understood as the 'revolutionary' people,[133] have arguably manifested themselves as an 'occasional community of action'.[134] They have, on a few (albeit rare) occasions, appeared 'on the public stage of a large-scale movement' in which the individual members of a polity were mobilised for common action, 'consciously united as the people and act[ing] as a collective body'.[135] Pierre-Joseph

[126] Müller (n 37) 29.
[127] Mudde and Kaltwasser (n 120) 16.
[128] Rosanvallon, 'Penser le populisme' 38.
[129] This view was expressed in Canovan (n 3).
[130] ibid 7. On the distinction between present and future sovereigns, see Thompson (n 21).
[131] Canovan (n 3) 6.
[132] ibid 5.
[133] See section II of this chapter, above.
[134] Canovan (n 3) 121.
[135] ibid. See also Canovan, 'Populism for Political Theorists' (n 20) 251.

Proudhon once noted that while they have a mystical existence and only manifest themselves at intervals, 'the People are not for that a ghost, and when they get up, no one can ignore them'.[136] Proudhon, of course, was writing in the context of the 1848 revolution and was explicitly referring to the events of 14 July 1789, 10 August 1792 and July-August 1830 in France. Others may add events such as the Revolutions of 1989 in Central and Eastern Europe, the Arab Spring, as well as certain independence movements, for example. Other more recent large-scale mobilisations could perhaps be added to that list, including, for instance, the 2019–2020 protests in Lebanon, in which protesters from various religious and social affiliations united against the ruling elite of the country and often portrayed themselves as 'the people as one'.[137] That said, even in the case of large-scale mobilisations or revolutions, it is often hard to determine precisely whether a given movement was broad enough to be considered as a demonstration of the sovereign people in action, that is to say 'a united people able to take collective action'.[138] Some would even argue that the sovereign people simply cannot be embodied as a subject or body with a 'will'.[139]

Yet, even if we accept the premise that there exists such a thing as a sovereign people in action, it remains extremely difficult to determine whether a particular action, performed by a particular people at a particular time, amounts to collective action by a united people. For instance, the American Revolution 'relied on the assumption (made explicit in *The Federalist*) that there *was* a united people able to take collective action'.[140] However, in reality, the collective action was undertaken only by a particular fringe of the population – notably, the white, male 'common people'. While the outcome of the American Revolution – particularly the enactment of the American Constitution – seemed to 'excuse the boldness' of the assumption that the Revolution was the result of the sovereign people in action,[141] it remains unclear whether this assumption was justified. In any event, once the constitutional order had been instituted in the US, it quickly became clear that the sovereign people in action – who had started the Revolution – had been sent back to their original position as 'sovereign in reserve'. Indeed, through the establishment of a republic[142] and of representative democracy, the people were redefined

[136] (My translation). See PJ Proudhon, *Solution du problème social* in PJ Proudhon, *Œuvres complètes* (Paris, Marcel Rivière, 1929 [1884]) 62, as cited in Rosanvallon (n 31) 61: 'Le Peuple n'a qu'une existence mystique; il ne se manifeste qu'à de rares intervalles, à des épiques prédestinées! Mais le Peuple n'est pas pour cela un fantôme, et quand il se lève, nul ne peut le méconnaître. Le Peuple s'est montré le 14 juillet, le 10 août, en 1830'.

[137] '"The people are one": Lebanese unite against political elite' (*Aljazeera*, 21 October 2019) www.aljazeera.com/news/2019/10/lebanon-protesters-streets-gov-leave-191020171622869.

[138] Canovan (n 3) 27.

[139] See, eg, Habermas (n 62).

[140] Canovan (n 3) 27, referring to A Hamilton, J Jay and J Madison. *The Federalist: A Commentary on the Constitution of the United States* (London, T Fisher Unwin, 1886 [1788]) 135, 552.

[141] Canovan (n 3) 27.

[142] See J Madison, 'Federalist No 14: Objections to the Proposed Constitution from Extent of Territory Answered' (30 November 1787), which discusses the exercise of power in a republic – notably through representatives and 'agents' of the people.

as 'voters': they were to have a role in government through the election of representatives and agents, but would also be kept at a distance.[143] From this moment onwards, while the new government would be a 'popular government' – rather than the King's government, for instance – the active role of the sovereign people would nonetheless be limited to electing representatives during elections, alongside the passive role of the 'revolutionary' people (or, in the words of this chapter, the people as *pouvoir constituant*), ready to intervene in case the gap between the government and the sovereign people would become too egregious.[144]

From a liberal-constitutionalist perspective, the problem with the populist conception of popular sovereignty is that it attributes 'ultimate political authority to "a people" that manages somehow to be both a set of concrete individuals, taking action in a particular place at a particular time, *and* an abstract collective entity with a life beyond such limitations'.[145] Using the framework described at the beginning of this chapter, the populist concept of 'people' thus fails to acknowledge the differences between temporal majorities (as a subjection of the electorate) and their representatives as *pouvoir constitué* (constituted power), on the one hand, and the people as *pouvoir constituant* (constituent power), on the other. It is indeed debatable whether a people, understood as a set of concrete individuals in a particular place and time, can really speak and act on behalf of the larger, all-encompassing and eternal People-as-One. In fact, some, like Jeremy Waldron, have even questioned whether there is actually such a thing as 'the people'.[146] In any event, the vague and ambiguous nature of 'the people' is surely a mark of its political usefulness for populists; 'captured at different times by many different political causes, it has been stretched to fit their different shapes'.[147]

It could therefore be argued that the populist conception places the 'sovereign people' as the ultimate (and only) holders of sovereignty. By doing this, one may add, populists refashion – and streamline – the (existing) relationships of sovereignty, notably by rejecting liberalism's 'divided' (and fragmented) sovereignty. For populists, therefore, sovereignty resides in a specific locus, that of 'the people'. Yet, what populists – and, arguably, several liberal constitutionalists as well – arguably fail to acknowledge is the relational nature of sovereignty. As Martin Loughlin points out, 'it would be a mistake to assume that sovereignty resides in a specific locus, whether that be the king, the people or an institution such as parliament'.[148] Instead, 'political power is generated from the particular relationship that evolves between the sovereign and subject, government and citizens';[149] it 'becomes

[143] Canovan (n 3) 28.

[144] ibid 29, 81.

[145] ibid 91–92.

[146] See, eg, J Waldron, 'Bicameralism and the Separation of Powers' in J Waldron (ed), *Political Political Theory: Essays on Institutions* (Cambridge, Harvard University Press, 2016) 77.

[147] Canovan (n 3) 3.

[148] Loughlin (n 94) 83. For a more recent analysis, see M Loughlin and S Tierney, 'The Shibboleth of Sovereignty' (2018) 81 *MLR* 989.

[149] Loughlin (n 94) 81.

public power only when assuming an institutional form'.[150] Following the same reasoning, constitutional constraints – including counter-majoritarian checks on majoritarian politics – should not be seen simply as limitations on the exercise of public power; rather, they simultaneously act as a method of generating political power.[151] In other words, the establishment of a formal constitutional framework is an exercise of the constituent power of 'the people' or 'the nation' to constitute a system of government.[152] Understood that way, allocations of power to the legislative, executive and judicial powers of the state, established through such a formal constitutional framework, should not be seen as a 'division' of sovereignty, but rather as its expression or elaboration.[153]

In short, populists attempt to refashion and streamline the existing relationships of sovereignty: they rely on and invoke the sovereign people in a legal sense, more specifically as *populus legibus solutus est*, or as an entity above the law, which cannot ultimately be bound by legal, constitutional or institutional constraints. However, many would question or criticise this reliance on and invocation of the (sovereign) people, notably on the basis that the latter are arguably too ambiguous to be institutionalised as a sovereign in a legal sense.[154] To borrow the words of Margaret Canovan, there is indeed an important 'gulf between *occasional* appearances of what may be plausibly regarded as the sovereign people, and the regular institutionalization that the notion of active sovereignty seems to demand'.[155] In reality, once a constitutional order has been put in place, the more active role of 'the people' is transferred to representation and institutions, such as the legislature, the executive and the judiciary, as established and elaborated through the constitutional and institutional framework of the state. In light of this, it can be plausibly argued that sovereignty does not solely reside in 'the people', as many populist leaders would claim, nor in institutions like parliaments; but rather in the political relationship between the people and the state.[156]

IV. Conclusion

The aim of this chapter was to identify and explain the defining features of the 'ideal-typical' populist legal discourse, particularly as they relate to popular sovereignty and the concept of 'the people'. It was argued that populism has two

[150] ibid 78.
[151] ibid 86. See also H Arendt, *The Human Condition* (Chicago, University of Chicago Press, 1958) 201. See also, generally, S Holmes, *Passions and Constraint: On the Theory of Liberal Democracy* (Chicago, University of Chicago Press, 1995).
[152] Loughlin (n 94) 84.
[153] ibid.
[154] Canovan (n 3) 121.
[155] ibid 108.
[156] Loughlin (n 94) 83.

main characteristics that relate to these two key concepts. First, the ideal-typical populist legal discourse heavily draws on the concept of 'the people', an ambiguous concept prone to instrumentalisation. Second, populism puts forward a conception of 'the people' as *populus legibus solutus est*, or as an entity above the law, which, as such, cannot ultimately be bound by legal, constitutional or institutional constraints.

From a spatiotemporal perspective, therefore, the ideal-typical contemporary populist legal discourse has two main effects in relation to popular sovereignty and 'the people'. First, populists discursively constitute the very 'people' they claim to (sometimes exclusively) represent. Put differently, populists tend to shape the boundaries of the 'people' they invoke. Second, the ideal-typical populist discourse appears to aggregate the transient, temporal and inherently ephemeral electoral majorities with the revolutionary, mystical and eternal 'sovereign people', understood as the People-as-One, thereby imbuing the latter with the characteristics of timeless unity, permanency and immutability. This *pars pro toto* aggregation, as we will see in the next chapter, has important implications for constitutionalism and the institutions of constitutional democracy, notably in the way populism weakens the distinction between ordinary, day-to-day politics, on the one hand, and intemporal, timeless constitutional politics, on the other. By doing so, it will be argued, populists tend to emphasise the spaces of democratic self-rule and freedom from limitations of power, including internal and external institutional constraints.

2

Implementing Populism: Constitutions, Constitutionalism and 'Constitutional Timelessness'

I. Introduction

Many liberal constitutions are ordained and established in the name of 'the people'. One may think, for instance, of the preambles to the constitutions of the US, Germany and Ireland. In the same vein, many liberal constitutions contain important promises regarding the exercise of popular sovereignty, for instance through claims that political power derives from – and ultimately resides in the hands of – 'the people'. The Constitution of Ireland, enacted in 1937 by way of a plebiscite, provides an example. Its article 6(1) provides that '[a]ll powers of government, legislative, executive and judicial, derive, under God, from the people, whose right it is to designate the rulers of the State and, in final appeal, to decide all questions of national policy, according to the requirements of the common good'.[1] In fact, a 1978 study revealed that more than half of all national constitutions around the world at that time referred explicitly to the sovereignty of the people.[2]

However, an important part of the ideal-typical populist discourse is that the promises regarding the exercise of sovereignty by the people contained in many of those liberal constitutions have not materialised in practice. In fact, one of the main populist critiques of liberal democracy is that real political power stems from – but does not truly reside in – 'the people': rather, it is in the hands of a small number of 'elites' and 'unaccountable institutions', which do not act for 'the people', but rather rule above them.[3] In other words, the voice of the people disappears – or at least, is muted – through procedures, representation and institutions such as Parliament and the judiciary. This populist critique raises important legal

[1] Ireland, Bunreacht na hÉireann (Constitution of Ireland) 1937, art 6(1). See also Constitution of the Irish Free State (Saorstát Éireann) Act 1922 (No 1 of 1922), art 2.

[2] H van Maarseveen and G van der Tang, *Written Constitutions: A Computerized Comparative Study* (Dobbs Ferry, Oceana, 1978) 93, as cited in Roznai, *Unconstitutional Constitutional Amendments: The Limits of Amendment Powers* (Oxford, Oxford University Press, 2017) 105.

[3] This is made explicit in the objective of the PiS-led judicial reform in Poland, which was to 'make judges equal to people, not above them'. See M Scislowska and V Gera, 'Polish Govt Gets More Power Over the Courts, Defying EU' (*US News*, 8 December 2017) www.usnews.com/news/world/articles/2017-12-08/polands-outgoing-pm-vows-to-keep-serving-populist-govt.

questions, including those regarding what is perhaps the oldest and most critical feature of a constitutional order, namely 'the place of the people and their relationship with the institutions of government' or, as David Hume put it, '[t]he relationship between the few who rule and the many who are ruled'.[4]

The avowed aim of populism, in this context, is to 'give government back to the people'.[5] The objective, in other words, is to 'close' the (spatial) gap, as it were, between *gouvernants* and *gouvernés*, notably by putting a strong emphasis on the immediate exercise of popular sovereignty. This is often done through majoritarianism and plebiscitarian instruments, such as referendums, but also through the actions of a strong leader and a form of (re-)engagement with the constitution, which is often re-politicised. To justify their project, populists often invoke the eternal and transcendent People-as-One, discussed in more detail in the previous chapter, which is seen as above and beyond transient constitutions – the latter being viewed as inherently momentary and sometimes ephemeral. In so doing, populist discourses tend to rely on a 'decisionist' conception of the constituent power, under which the 'legal order rests on a decision and not on a norm'.[6] As such, pre-determined legal, constitutional and institutional constraints are deemed to be illegitimate and obstacles to the expression of the will of the people.

Against this backdrop, the aim of this second chapter is to explain how populist actors engage with constitutions and constitutionalism, as well as plebiscitarianism and instruments of direct democracy. Building on the previous chapter, I argue that populism tends to weaken the distinction between ordinary, day-to-day politics, on the one hand, and intemporal, timeless constitutional politics, on the other.[7] I call this approach to constitutions (and constitutionalism more broadly) the populist 'constitutional timelessness'. By doing so, I argue, populists tend to emphasise the spaces of democratic self-rule and freedom from limitations of power, including internal and external institutional constraints.

This chapter is divided into four sections. The second section builds on the previous chapter and explains how (and why) populism puts a strong emphasis on the immediate exercise of popular sovereignty, notably through plebiscitarian instruments such as referendums. The third section expands on what I have called above the populist 'constitutional timelessness', discussing how populism tends to reject liberal constraints on popular sovereignty, presupposing the primacy of politics over law and that of *pouvoir constituant* over *pouvoir constitué*. In the fourth and final section of the chapter, I discuss the practical implications of the above for constitutions, constitutionalism and liberal institutions, particularly courts.

[4] DJ Galligan, 'Introduction' in DJ Galligan (ed), *Constitution in Crisis: The New Putney Debates* (London, I.B. Tauris, 2017) 6. See, eg, D Hume, 'Essay IV: Of the First Principles of Government' in D Hume, *Essays, Moral, Political, and Literary* (1777 [1741]).

[5] See, eg, JB Ludis, *The Populist Explosion: How the Great Recession Transformed American and European Politics* (New York, Columbia Global Reports, 2016).

[6] C Schmitt, *Political Theology: Four Chapters on the Concept of Sovereignty* (trans George Schwab) (Chicago, University of Chicago Press, 2006) 10.

[7] See also, eg, P Blokker, 'Populism as a Constitutional Project' (2019) 17 *International Journal of Constitutional Law* 545.

II. Populism, Plebiscitarianism (Referendums) and the Expression of the Popular Will

Consistent with Carl Schmitt's conception of the people 'as an existential reality as opposed to mere liberal representation of voters in parliament',[8] populist discourses and imaginaries are often sceptical of representative democracy. Directly or indirectly, populism tends to criticise the liberal methods in which popular sovereignty is exercised in a representative democracy. For many populists, especially populists in opposition, representative democracy tends to shield the people from political decision-making or, even worse, make the people disappear altogether.[9] The goal allegedly pursued by populists is therefore to 'give government back to the people', away from the elites, 'money power' or 'plutocracy'[10] and, of course, unelected and (or) unaccountable liberal institutions.

The populist project to put power back into the hands of the people arguably goes back – at least in America – to the 1830s, when Jacksonian Democrats became mobilised to 'take back' power that had been 'stolen' from the people, defined as 'the planter, the farmer the mechanic, and the laborer'.[11] A similar idea was put forward in 1892, with the creation of the People's Party – arguably the first populist party in America[12] – which claimed, in its Omaha Platform, to 'seek to restore the government of the Republic to the hands of "the plain people", with whose class it originated'.[13] Several contemporary populist movements and actors have also put this idea – of giving government back to the people – at the forefront of their platforms. Donald Trump, for instance, embodied this idea by claiming, during his 2016 presidential campaign, that his movement was 'about replacing a failed and corrupt political establishment with a new government controlled by

[8] G Halmai, 'Is There Such Thing As "Populist Constitutionalism"? The Case of Hungary' (2018) 11 *Fudan Journal of Humanities and Social Sciences* 328.

[9] This view echoes Schmitt's views on representative democracy: 'Democracy today is a democracy without a *demos*, without a people. The democratic principle demands that people in its entirety decides and governs responsibly. But the methods in which today's democracy attempts to put the people's sovereignty into practice are not democratic, but liberal, methods. [...] The amazing thing is that nowhere in our democratic constitution does the assembled people appear; there are always only assembled representatives, the individual taken out of the mass. Where, in the text of the constitution and in the reality of the state based on the liberal rule of law does the people appear at all? Where is there room for an acclamation that can occur only if a public is created by the people assembled and present? There is no public without the people, and there is no people without a public. Where today, in the method of the secret ballot, is there a public, and where is the people?' See C Schmitt, 'The Liberal Rule of Law' in AJ Jacobson and B Schlink (eds), *Weimar: A Jurisprudence of Crisis* (Berkeley, University of California Press, 2000 [1928]) 298.

[10] Ludis, 'Us v Them: The Birth of Populism' (*The Guardian*, 13 October 2016) www.theguardian.com/politics/2016/oct/13/birth-of-populism-donald-trump.

[11] JL Blau (ed), *Social Theories of Jacksonian Democracy: Representative Writings of the Period 1825–1850* (New York, Hafner, 1947) 13–17, as cited in Canovan, *The People* (Cambridge, Polity, 2005) 29 (see also 81).

[12] Ludis (n 10).

[13] *The World Almanach 1893*, 83–85, reprinted in G Brown Tindall (ed), *A Populist Reader, Selections from the Works of American Populist Leaders* (New York, Harper & Row, 1966) 90–96, as cited in ibid.

you, the American people'.[14] In his inauguration speech, in 2017, he continued along the same lines and, adding a spatial element to his discourse, said: '[t]oday we are not merely transferring power from one administration to another, or from one party to another, but we are transferring power from Washington, DC, and giving it back to you, the people'.[15] Even after securing a second presidential term, Trump maintained a similar rhetoric. For example, in his 6 November 2024 election victory speech, he said: 'This will forever be remembered as the day the American people regained control of their country.'[16]

Populist discourses often attempt to divert attention from the relatively ambiguous nature of popular sovereignty and the concept of 'the people' – discussed in the previous chapter – by putting a strong emphasis on the immediate exercise of popular sovereignty, notably through majoritarianism and means of direct democracy, most particularly plebiscitary instruments such as referendums.[17] The latter can, it is said, 'correct some of the elite filtering and unrepresentativeness of status quo representative democracy'.[18] The referendum, in particular, is seen as the plebiscitary instrument par excellence to achieve this goal; for populists, there is no doubt that the people actually exercise their sovereignty when they are asked to cast their ballot in a referendum. In fact, some right-wing populists like Jean-Marie Le Pen have even claimed that the referendum is *l'expression parfaite de la démocratie* ('the perfect expression of democracy').[19] It follows, under the same logic, that the authoritative outcome of a referendum is a verdict of the people, expressing their sovereignty.[20] On the other side of the political spectrum, left-wing populists have also voiced their support for referendums as democratic instruments. One may think, for example, of Jean-Luc Mélenchon, leader of *La France insoumise* – which adopted '*Redonner du pouvoir au peuple*' ['Giving power back to the people'] as one of its slogans in the 2022 presidential election. Mélenchon has voiced on several occasions in the past decade his support for recall referendums to remove elected officials as a response to 'the democratic crisis and the discrediting of the political system'.[21]

[14] Trump, then presidential candidate, used those words at a rally in Florida in 2016. See DJ Trump, 'Remarks at the South Florida Fair Expo Center in West Palm Beach, Florida' (*The American Presidency Project*, 13 October 2016) www.presidency.ucsb.edu/documents/remarks-the-south-florida-fair-expo-center-west-palm-beach-florida.

[15] DJ Trump, 'Full text: 2017 Donald Trump inauguration speech transcript' (*Politico*, 20 January 2017) www.politico.com/story/2017/01/full-text-donald-trump-inauguration-speech-transcript-233907.

[16] F Nicholls, 'Donald Trump's Victory Speech in Full: Transcript' (*Newsweek*, 6 November 2024) www.newsweek.com/donald-trump-victory-speech-full-transcript-1981234.

[17] Art B(3) of the Fundamental Law of Hungary provides that the source of public power is the people. Yet, interestingly, art B(4) provides that this 'power shall be exercised by the people through elected representatives or, in exceptional cases, directly'.

[18] R Howse, 'Epilogue: In Defense of Disruptive Democracy – A Critique of Anti-Populism' (2019) 17 *International Journal of Constitutional Law* 648.

[19] See JM Le Pen, 'Pour une vraie révolution française' (26 September 1985) *National Hebdo*, as cited in P Rosanvallon, *Le Siècle du populisme: Histoire, théorie, critique* (Paris, Seuil, 2020) 39.

[20] For instance, and as discussed in the previous chapter, the result of the 2016 Brexit referendum is often portrayed as a manifestation of the 'will of the people'.

[21] See, eg, A Corlay, 'Comment s'appliquerait le référendum révocatoire de Jean-Luc Mélenchon?' (*LeMonde*, 21 April 2017) www.lemonde.fr/election-presidentielle-2017/article/2017/04/21/comment-s-appliquerait-le-referendum-revocatoire-de-jean-luc-melenchon_5115264_4854003.html. See also, eg,

This is not to say, of course, that the referendum (or plebiscite) is necessarily, in and of itself, a populist instrument. One may think, for example, of the abovementioned Constitution of Ireland, which has been amended multiple times by referendum – and, recently, in combination with other deliberative modes of democracy in the run-up to the referendums, such as in the case of the 34th and 36th amendments to the Constitution, which respectively legalised same-sex marriage (2015) and repealed the constitutional ban on abortion (2018).[22] These referendums were preceded by extensive public pressure, advocacy campaigns and recommendations from a constitutional convention (2012–2014) or a citizens' assembly (2016–2017).

The origins of the (modern) referendum go back as far as the mid-to-late nineteenth century and can be linked to socialist thought.[23] More conservative or centrist thinkers, such as Albert V Dicey and Raymond Carré de Malberg, also lauded it. For instance, Dicey defended the referendum in 1890, notably on the party-sceptic view that it 'does not hurry on a single law, nor facilitate any legislation which Parliamentary wisdom or caution disapproves'.[24] For him, the referendum 'merely adds an additional safeguard against the hastiness or violence of party. It is not a spur to democratic innovation; it is a check placed on popular impatience'.[25] Carré de Malberg, for his part, wrote that one of the advantages of the institution of the referendum is that it reduces Parliament from a position of sovereignty to one of mere authority, subject to the people's sovereignty and the constitution – no longer dominating it, but instead being dominated by it.[26]

In the same vein, it should be noted that populist discourses, while favouring the use of plebiscitary means such as referendums, do not necessarily advocate the widespread use of popular initiative measures, such as the ones in place in Switzerland. In fact, the populist conception of the referendum is probably more closely aligned with Schmitt's understanding of the *Volksentscheide* ('referendum' or 'popular decision'), which is to be distinguished from the *Volksbegehren* ('popular legislative initiative').[27] Schmitt rejects the latter on the basis that, much like parliamentary government, it transfers decisional initiatives from the executive to other agents and, as such, risks

his post on X on 31 March 2025, x.com/JLMelenchon/status/1906673335796146412: '[L]a décision de destituer un élu devrait revenir au peuple. C'est à cela que servirait le référendum révocatoire dans une 6e République démocratique'.

[22] I thank Julian Scholtes for pointing this out.

[23] L Rubinelli, 'Democracy, Parliamentarism and the Referendum, 1890–1940' in C Meckstroth and S Moyn (eds), *The Cambridge History of Democracy* (Cambridge, Cambridge University Press, forthcoming).

[24] AV Dicey, 'Ought the Referendum to Be Introduced into England?' (1890) 57 *Contemporary Review* 48, 496.

[25] ibid. Interestingly, this view implies, from a temporal perspective, that referendums 'slow down' (rather than accelerate) politics. As will become clear in this monograph, particularly in Part II (especially in chs 5 and 6), I disagree with this view.

[26] C de Malberg, *Considérations théoriques sur la question de la combinaison du référendum avec le parlementarisme* (Paris, Marcel Giard, 1931).

[27] C Schmitt, *Volksentscheid und Volksbegehren: Ein Beitrag zur Auslegung der Weimarer Verfassung und zur Lehre von der unmittelbaren* (Berlin, Walter de Gruyter, 1927), as mentioned in L Vinx, 'Carl Schmitt on the Limits of Direct Democracy' (2021) 42 *History of Political Thought* 157.

undermining the unity and general coherence of state policy.[28] Simply put, while some populist actors will allow some form of direct democracy (particularly in the form of spectacular demonstrations of democratic participation, such as high-profile referendums) to confirm or reject certain proposals, they nonetheless often have a somewhat restricted view of the permissible scope of popular initiatives in the broader frame of constitutional governance. By contrast, several jurisdictions generally led by liberal-constitutionalist political actors – like Switzerland and California, for example – make extensive use of such popular initiatives.[29]

In short, populist discourses and imaginaries are often sceptical about representative democracy. Populists often favour the use of plebiscitary instruments such as referendums, which are often depicted as the 'true' and 'spontaneous' expression of the 'will of the people'. While I do not believe that instruments of direct democracy such as referendums are *necessarily* at odds with liberal constitutionalism, I would argue that one must be cautious of the way these instruments are sometimes used by populist actors to undermine representative institutions and democracy more broadly. On the one hand, both populists and liberal constitutionalists would agree that democracy is premised on a promise of popular sovereignty, the idea of 'power to the people' – a promise that has not always been fulfilled. On the other, the resort to referendums by populists could be criticised on the basis that despite grandiose talks of 'giving the power back to the people' by way of direct democracy and referendums, the actual use of plebiscitary instruments by populist actors has, in fact, often been limited to consultations intended to arrive at a pre-ordained result. One may think, for example, of Hungary, where despite Orbán's promise to resort to instruments of direct democracy,[30] the use of plebiscitary instruments has been limited to two referendums in 15 years – one in 2016 on EU migrant quotas and another in 2022 on the so-called 'child protection' against LGTBQ+ content in education, both of which did not meet the turnout threshold for validity – as well as a few non-binding 'national consultations' (*nemzeti konzultációk*), often criticised as propaganda tools whose main purpose is 'to demonstrate popular support for the (ideological) position held by the government'.[31]

[28] Vinx (n 27) 181.

[29] This is not to say, however, that these popular initiatives have not been used (or instrumentalised, as one could say) for populist and (or) exclusionary purposes. One may think, for example, of the November 2009 minaret referendum in Switzerland. Moreover, and as Mény and Surel have noted, '[n]either the United States nor Switzerland, which both make extensive use of the tools of direct democracy, have escaped the pitfalls of popular claims and protests'. See Y Mény and Y Surel, 'The Constitutive Ambiguity of Populism' in Y Mény and Y Surel (eds), *Democracies and the Populist Challenge* (London, Palgrave MacMillan, 2002) 15.

[30] See, eg, Orbán's speech in S Kim, 'Hungary before the Elections: Understanding the Hegemony Project of Fidesz (*WZB Democracy Blog*, 6 April 2018) democracy.blog.wzb.eu/2018/04/06/hungary-before-the-elections-understanding-the-hegemony-project-of-fidesz, originally found in J Debreczeni, *Arcmás* (Budapest, Noran-Libro Kiadó, 2009) 336.

[31] S Svensson, A Molnar and A Batory, '(e-)Participation and Propaganda: The Mix of Old and New Techology in Hungarian National Consultations' in T Randma-Liiv and V Lember (eds), *Engaging Citizens in Policy Making: e-Participation Practices in Europe* (Cheltenham, Edward Elgar, 2022) 66. I thank Julian Scholtes for raising the broader point.

This is not to say, of course, that populists are wrong in pointing out that popular sovereignty and the place of direct democracy are often elided under liberal constitutionalism, partly because of the latter's emphasis on institutions. Nevertheless, it could be argued that democracy's promise of popular power can only be fulfilled 'through institutions that make that power effective and lasting'.[32] After all, democracy can be, as Margaret Canovan puts it, 'a very powerful form of government insofar as it does have the legitimacy of being recognised as *our* government. But to work as a government, it has to take institutional forms that are very far removed from spontaneous popular expression'.[33] These ideas are discussed further in the next section, as well as in the next chapter.

III. The Populist 'Constitutional Timelessness': A Rejection of Liberal Constraints on Popular Sovereignty

One important consequence of this particular form of anti-institutionalism – at least in the exercise of popular sovereignty, as evidenced by the abovementioned emphasis on plebiscitary instruments – is the way in which populists (re-)engage with constitutions. This form of engagement with the constitution is viewed as a 'necessary response to the rapid changes of "post-modern" society (in which politics needs to respond rapidly to societal change)' and (or) as an 'urgent answer to imminent threats to the political community'.[34] As discussed in this third section, this means that, in practice, populists often engage in a certain (re-)politicisation of constitutions, which are understood and depicted as 'vehicles *of* the popular will, rather than as significant constraints *on* that will'.[35] To do so, populists often invoke the eternal People-as-One, discussed in more detail in the previous chapter, which is seen as above and beyond transient constitutions – the latter being viewed as inherently momentary and (or) ephemeral.[36]

In fact, I would argue that populism adopts, from a temporal perspective, what could be described as a 'timelessness' understanding of the constitution, with a transcendental conception of the People-as-One at the forefront.[37] In his study of the temporal dimensions of constitutions, Thomas Poole (drawing on Bernard Williams) distinguishes between time and timelessness. The first view,

[32] M Canovan, 'Trust the People! Populism and the Two Faces of Democracy' (1999) 47 *Political Studies* 1, 13.

[33] ibid (emphasis in the original; bold characters have been replaced with italics).

[34] P Blokker, 'Populist Constitutionalism' in C de la Torre (ed), *Routledge Handbook of Global Populism* (Abingdon, Routledge, 2019) 124. See also R Prandini, 'The Future of Societal Constitutionalism in the Age of Acceleration' (2013) 20 *Indiana Journal of Global Legal Studies* 731.

[35] ibid 124.

[36] See ch 1.

[37] See ibid and Blokker (n 7) 551.

called 'time', is 'the notion that a constitution exists and can only exist in a concrete spatial-temporal setting'.[38] This view depicts constitutions as products of a given time, a sort of 'historical accident' and inherently unstable.[39] The second one, 'timelessness', is by contrast disengaged from material roots.[40] It refers to the conception of a constitution as 'transcendent, operating in a sense somehow out of time'.[41] Of course, populist constitutions could be viewed, at first blush, as 'time', given the populist focus on present time (discussed in more detail in the next chapter), as well as the populist reliance on plebiscitary instruments and their quasi-'instantaneous' effect, for instance. In the same vein, populism does not necessarily value constitutional endurance or stability (particularly when the constitution has been enacted by a different regime),[42] nor static constitutionalism.[43] On the other hand, however, the main powerholder in the populist legal discourse – that is, 'the people' – is presented in clear 'timeless' terms, as an immutable and transcendent people, the People-as-One. As we have seen in the previous chapter, populists tend to aggregate the mystical (if not mythical) and perpetual people with the people as represented in temporal (and by definition temporary) electoral majorities, elevating the decisions of the latter to the status of 'eternal word'.[44] Under the populist discourse, 'the people', as an ever-present, immutable and transcendent entity, sit above and beyond transient constitutions. It could thus be argued that populists follow Schmitt's distinction between 'the Constitution' (*die Verfassung*), understood as the fundamental political decision of the people regarding the form and identity of the political unity – the expression, in other words, of the concrete political existence of the people, on the one hand, and 'constitutional laws' (*Verfassungsgesetze*), referring to the set of positive legal norms contained in a constitutional document, which is viewed as changeable and secondary to the fundamental decision, on the other.[45] The result of this populist emphasis on the immutable Constitution (as a political decision) over the ever-changing 'constitutional laws', I would argue, is a form of 'constitutional timelessness' grounded in a 'timeless' conception of popular sovereignty (and, as we will see, a 'fixed' or 'intemporal' constitutional identity).

This form of 'constitutional timelessness' rooted in popular sovereignty has important effects, I contend, notably on the way populism weakens the distinction between ordinary, day-to-day politics, on the one hand, and intemporal, timeless constitutional politics, on the other. Indeed, many populists view existing liberal

[38] T Poole, 'Time and Timelessness in Constitutional Thought' (2020) 27 *Res Publica* 255.
[39] ibid 257.
[40] ibid.
[41] ibid. 256.
[42] See, eg, ch 5 (and the long history of constitutional changes in Ecuador).
[43] Blokker (n 34) 124.
[44] M Cahill, 'The Reign of Popular Sovereignty in Ireland: An Antidote to Populism?' in Cahill et al, *Constitutional Change and Popular Sovereignty* 16, referring to Girard, 'Populism, "the People" and Popular Sovereignty'.
[45] See Schmitt, *Constitutional Theory* 76. I thank Julian Scholtes for reminding me of this.

constitutions as 'rootless and arid' political decisions – as mere regulative 'constitutional laws' and, therefore, as sitting below (rather than above) the transcendent People-as-One. As such, they can be changed or amended at will, in contrast to the liberal-constitutionalist emphasis on (or advocacy for) constitutional endurance. This populist view is grounded, I would argue, on two main interrelated ideas, discussed in the next two subsections, namely (A) the primacy of politics over law; and (B) the populist conception of constituent power.

A. The Primacy of Politics Over Law

Populism presupposes the primacy of politics over law insofar as it rejects predetermined legal, institutional and constitutional constraints on the will of the people.[46] An example of this vision of politics as superior to law is the way Jarosław Kaczyński, the leader of the then-ruling PiS party in Poland, described constraints on majoritarian politics as 'legal impossibilism' (*prawny imposybilizm*).[47] Using words that unambiguously affirm the primacy of politics over law, the honorary speaker (Sejm Marshal) of the Lower House of the Polish Parliament (Sejm) also said in November 2015 that 'it is the will of the people, not the law that matters, and the will of the people always tramples the law'.[48] In the same vein, under the populist logic, the main function of the law is not to constrain (nor provide protection against) the arbitrary nature of political will; on the contrary, the law serves precisely to *express* political power in a given polity.

This primacy of politics over law – and its accompanying rejection of the liberal order (or constraints) – mirrors, at least to a certain extent and at a conceptual level, Schmitt's critique of the liberal rule of law. For Schmitt, the latter 'purposely balances contrary principles in the interest not of political unity but of individual freedom'.[49] In that sense, the populist rejection of the liberal constraints on popular sovereignty echoes Schmitt's critique that the liberal rule of law undermines the substance of the political and the unity of the people.[50] The avowed goal of populism is thus to promote an alternative constitutional order, one which 'puts the sovereignty of the people and its self-governing power upfront'.[51]

This emphasis on politics – and the rejection of liberal constraints on popular sovereignty – can arguably have positive effects, at least in some cases, 'positive' here meaning beneficial to the quality of democracy. To give an example, populism

[46] See, eg, Mény and Surel (n 29) 10.
[47] 'Poland's ruling Law and Justice party is doing lasting damage' (*The Economist*, 21 April 2018): www.economist.com/europe/2018/04/21/polands-ruling-law-and-justice-party-is-doing-lasting-damage.
[48] T Gyorfi, *Against the New Constitutionalism*, (Cheltenham, Edward Elgar, 2016) 62–63.
[49] Schmitt (n 9) 296.
[50] See, eg, ibid 298.
[51] P Blokker (n 34) (4) The Populist Threat to Democratic Constitutionalism' (*Constitutionalism and Politics [EUI Blog]*, 14 November 2017) blogs.eui.eu/constitutionalism-politics-working-group/populist-constitutionalism-4-populist-threat-democratic-constitutionalism.

can potentially increase mobilisation and political participation by giving a voice to those who feel excluded by the existing political-representative system, which includes the elite and (or) the establishment.[52] Similarly, the primacy of politics over law can arguably 'increase democratic accountability', notably by taking some issues and policies away from seemingly 'unresponsive'[53] or 'technocratic' institutions and courts, and re-politicising them.[54]

Nevertheless, this rejection of liberal constraints could be criticised, at least from a liberal-constitutionalist perspective, on the basis that it involves a call for – and (or) can possibly lead to – concentration of power, notably through exclusion and antagonistic polarisations. For liberal constitutionalists, and in contrast to the populist worldview, democracy requires power to be dispersed – hence the need for 'checks and balances', including constraints on the power of the executive, and the very idea of legal autonomy in 'the rule of law' – namely, the belief that it is the law that rules, not an individual or political institution or party.[55] These elements are discussed below and in the next chapter.

B. The Populist Conception of Constituent Power

Often implicit in the populist claim of the primacy of law over politics is a reliance on (or invocation of) the notion of *pouvoir constituant*, or constituent power, briefly discussed in the previous chapter. This notion refers to the authority to make and unmake institutional arrangements through which the people are governed and thus, to institute a legal order in a given polity.[56] This authority is vested in 'the people' as a body that exists prior to – and is independent from – a constitutional order.[57] The concept of constituent power rests on two fundamental assumptions, namely the 'recognition that the ultimate source of political authority derives from an entity known as "the people"' and the 'acceptance of the idea of the constitution

[52] See, eg, C Mudde and C Rovira Kaltwasser, 'Populism and (Liberal) Democracy: A Framework for Analysis' in C Mudde and C Rovira Kaltwasser (eds), *Populism in Europe and the Americas: Threat or Corrective for Democracy?* (Cambridge, Cambridge University Press, 2012) 21.

[53] See, eg, M Zürn, 'How Non-Majoritarian Institutions Make Silent Majorities Vocal: A Popular Explanation of Authoritarian Populism' (2022) 20 *Perspectives on Politics* 788.

[54] See, eg, Mudde and Kaltwasser (n 52) 21. One can also think of political constitutionalists, like Richard Bellamy, who argue that constitutionalism should primarily be understood as political rather than legal, as it is the political order that really matters. This is discussed further below.

[55] I thank Stephen Skinner for raising the latter point.

[56] M Loughlin, 'The Concept of Constituent Power' (2014) 13 *European Journal of Political Theory* 218, 219.

[57] See, eg, EJ Sieyès, *Qu'est-ce que le Tiers État?* (Paris, Éditions du Boucher, 2002 [1789]) / (Presses universitaires de France, 1982 [1789]) 53: 'La nation existe avant tout, elle est l'origine de tout. Sa volonté est toujours légale, elle est la loi elle-même. [...] la constitution n'est pas l'ouvrage du pouvoir constitué, mais du pouvoir constituant. Aucune sorte de pouvoir délégué ne peut rien changer aux conditions de sa délégation'. See also, eg, JEK Murkens, *From Empire to Union: Conceptions of German Constitutional Law since 1871* (Oxford, Oxford University Press, 2013) 48, referring to C Schmitt, *Verfassunglehre* (Berlin, Duncker & Humblot) 61.

as something that is created'.[58] Populists often rely upon this notion of constituent power, albeit not always expressly. For Luigi Corrias,

> populists implicitly claim that there is an absolute primacy of constituent power vis-à-vis the constitution and the rules and powers derived from it. The people as constituent power is ultimately not bound by [existing] constitutional constraints because it is the source from which the constitution receives its legitimacy.[59]

The populist conception of constituent power thus appears to be based on a decisionist approach. Under this approach, the constitutional order of a polity is 'a political decision', made by 'the people' as unity, 'concerning the type and form of its own being'.[60] In other words, and as Schmitt puts it, the essence of the constitution 'cannot be found in a law or a norm, but in the political decision of the [constituent] power'.[61] Under this view, the free will of the people 'remains alongside and above the constitution'.[62] In other words, a constitution is a political decision of a people who are ever-present and whose political existence precedes the constitution:[63] as such, the people as a unit 'can express its will and at the decisive moment can secure its wholeness and integrity in spite of pluralistic divisions'.[64] Thus, if previously political issues could be legalised or constitutionalised, it follows that the constitution itself can be deconstructed, and that previously political issues can be de-legalised or de-constitutionalised and therefore reappear in the political realm.[65]

However, and perhaps crucially, once de-legalised or de-constitutionalised, these issues do not permanently stay in the political realm; rather, they are often subsequently re-legalised or re-constitutionalised, notably through the enactment of new constitutions drafted by constituent assemblies. One may think, for example, of the constituent assemblies in Peru, Venezuela and Ecuador.[66] This approach appears relatively common amongst left-wing forms of populism. For example, in France, Jean-Luc Mélenchon emphasised the role and importance of constituent assemblies in his book *L'Ère du peuple*. For him, the constituent process is the 'founding act of the conquest of sovereignty by the people'; as such, the constituent process is the 'political vehicle' of the people.[67] In that sense, he wrote, 'fighting for the convocation of a Constituent Assembly is first

[58] Loughlin (n 56) 219.

[59] L Corrias, 'Populism in a Constitutional Key: Constituent Power, Popular Sovereignty and Constitutional Identity' (2016) 12 *European Constitutional Law Review* 9.

[60] C Schmitt, *Constitutional Theory* (Durham, Duke University Press, 2008 [1928]) 125, as cited in J Scholtes, 'The Complacency of Legality: Constitutionalist Vulnerabilities to Populist Constituent Power' (2019) 20 *German Law Journal* 351, 358.

[61] Schmitt (n 57) 20–21, as referred to in Murkens (n 57) 46.

[62] Schmitt (n 60) 125–126, as cited in Scholtes (n 60).

[63] Schmitt (n 57) 61, as referred to in Murkens (n 57) 48.

[64] ibid.

[65] Scholtes (n 60).

[66] See, for instance, ch 5 in relation to Ecuador. See also D Landau, 'Populist Constitutions' (2018) 85 *University of Chicago Law Review* 521, 528 (regarding the replacement of Venezuela's constitution in 1999).

[67] JL Mélenchon, *L'Ère du peuple* (Paris, Pluriel, 2017) 97.

and foremost fighting for the very existence of the people as an historical actor. The people are constituent, or they are nothing.'[68] It could therefore be argued that the populist approach to constituent power is, in essence, a claim of the primacy of politics over law. However, as Julian Scholtes explains, '[p]opulists, in their own view, are not "politicising the constitution" – they are simply exercising the constituent power that was naturally vested in the people in the first place'.[69] This points to a sort of limitless and permanent, Jacobin-like constituent power vested in the people as an entity.[70]

Yet, it could be argued that this populist approach has important limits.[71] First, it is unclear whether the political existence of the people precedes the constitution; one could also highlight the paradox of constituent power, namely the question as to how 'can "the people" act as the constituent power to establish the form of the political union if they can be identified as such only by virtue of the pact?'[72] Second, the populist 'constitutional timelessness' idea, focusing on an idea of the eternal people as a means of overcoming transient constitutions, is nevertheless nearly always 'immediate' in the sense of being presentist in its orientation and focus, ignoring the idea that 'the people in the past' had specific ideas or constraints in mind, and not really being mindful of any 'people in the future'.[73] These considerations are not merely theoretical; they also have concrete implications, notably with regard to constitutional and institutional arrangements. This is discussed in more detail in the next and final section of this chapter.

IV. Practical Implications: Constitutions, Constitutionalism and the Courts

A. Constitutions under Populism

By weakening the distinction between ordinary and constitutional politics, populists tend to emphasise democratic self-rule and freedom from external constraints, often at the expense of order and limitations of power.[74] This focus on *pouvoir constituant* (constituent power) over *pouvoir constitué* (constituted power) has led

[68] ibid (my translation).

[69] Scholtes (n 60) 359.

[70] G Martinico, *Filtering Populist Claims to Fight Populism: The Italian Case in a Comparative Perspective* (Cambridge, Cambridge University Press, 2022) 28.

[71] For a critique of left-wing populism's decisionism, see P Urfalino, 'Un nouveau décisionnisme politique : La philosophie du populisme de gauche' (2019) 82 *Archives de philosophie : recherches et documentation* 291.

[72] Loughlin (n 56) 228. Loughlin argues that this paradox can be solved by adopting a relational approach to the constituent power.

[73] This can, in some ways, be contrasted with the Italian Fascist ideology of an organic model of society – which spans all generations, back to Imperial Rome and into an eternal future. I thank Stephen Skinner for raising this.

[74] Blokker (n 7) 544–545.

some scholars to argue that populism favours a model of 'weak constitutionalism',[75] in that it seeks – at least to a certain extent – to balance the need for constitutional stability with the exigency of popular engagement in constitutional processes. This, as we have seen, often leads to a re-politicisation of the constitution. This is not to say, however, that populism is necessarily against *constitutions* as such.[76] When in power, populists will sometimes invoke that very same constituent power to enact a new (or heavily amended) constitution, as in the cases of Hungary's Viktor Orbán, Türkiye's Recep Tayyip Erdoğan, Tunisia's Kais Saied, Venezuela's Hugo Chávez or Ecuador's Rafael Correa, to name a few examples.

Compounded by the populist constitutional impatience, discussed in detail in the next chapter, these populists have engaged in 'hasty' constitution-making, sometimes using a fast-track legislative procedure, as in the case of Hungary's 2011 Fundamental Law,[77] which was adopted by the ruling Fidesz party and replaced the 1949 Constitution, and with little or no input from the opposition, as in the cases of both Hungary's Fundamental Law and Venezuela's 1999 Constitution.[78] These populists will then not hesitate to amend the new constitution, as illustrated by the case of the Fundamental Law, which was amended no less than five times in the year and a half that followed its adoption.[79]

This new (or heavily amended) constitution can serve multiple functions for populists. First, it can contribute to the deconstruction of the existing political system and regime;[80] and, correlatively, to the creation of a new constitutional order that is more in line with the populists' constitutional identity.[81] There is a strong temporal dimension to this function – and its corresponding constitutional identity. As Corrias puts it, '[p]opulism usually depicts constitutional identity as something fixed once and for all, pre-determined before the enactment of a legal order and stored away, untouchable by the ravages of time'.[82] This is another component of the populist 'constitutional timelessness' mentioned above. Second, the new or heavily amended constitution can serve as an 'ideological critique that promises to overcome flaws in the prior constitutional order'[83] – and more notably, in the case of left-wing populism, a response to 'historic patterns of socioeconomic inequality, elitism, and exclusion'.[84]

[75] See, eg, A Arato and JL Cohen, *Populism and Civil Society: The Challenge to Constitutional Democracy* (Oxford, Oxford University Press, 2022) 195, referring to J Colón-Ríos, *Weak Constitutionalism: Democratic Legitimacy and the Question of Constituent Power* (Abingdon, Routledge, 2012).

[76] See, eg, N Walker, 'Populism and Constitutional Tension' (2019) 17 *International Journal of Constitutional Law* 519.

[77] Fundamental Law of Hungary (adopted 18 April 2011, entered into force 1 January 2012).

[78] See, eg, W Sadurski, *A Pandemic of Populists* (Cambridge, Cambridge University Press, 2022) 69, 84–86.

[79] ibid 86.

[80] Landau (n 66) 522, 526–529.

[81] See, eg, Corrias (n 59) 13, 22. On the different types of abuse of constitutional identity by populists and authoritarians, see J Scholtes, 'Abusing Constitutional Identity' (2021) 22 *German Law Journal* 534.

[82] Corrias (n 59) 22.

[83] Landau (n 66) 529–532.

[84] ibid 529.

The invocation of the constituent power by populists to enact new constitutions, however, is prone to criticism, notably by liberal constitutionalists, on the basis that it can be used to 'perpetuate what [populists] regard as the proper image of the morally pure people' and to 'constitutionalize policies which they find to conform to that image of the people'.[85] One could probably refer, as an example, to the abovementioned Hungarian Fundamental Law, which puts forward an ideologically charged vision of national identity, history and moral order, for instance through its preamble ('National Avowal') that emphasises the country's Christian heritage and the unity of Hungarians, including those who live beyond its borders, as well as through one of its provisions which defines marriage as 'the union of one man and one woman' and a traditional gender-based conception of family.[86] Of course, populists could respond to this liberal-constitutionalist critique by saying they are simply using the liberal-constitutionalist's own framework of constitutional authority, albeit for a – substantively and (or) ideologically – different project, one which liberal-constitutionalists simply disagree with.[87] In other circumstances, populists will prefer to maintain the existing constitution, while favouring a specific interpretation, one that will help them retain power.[88] In both cases, as David Landau argues, '[p]opulist constitutions do not abandon the trappings of key liberal institutions, such as constitutional courts, and go to great lengths to justify their choices as acceptable within liberal democracies'.[89]

From a liberal-constitutionalist perspective, this latter aspect of some populist constitutions could also be criticised on the basis that they are sometimes devoid of *garantiste* features. By this, I mean, following Giovanni Sartori, that these constitutions may well accurately describe the formal organisation of the state and its correlative institutional arrangements, but they are often devoid of the *telos* of constitutionalism – namely, the idea of a government limited by the constitution (as opposed to arbitrary power). To borrow the words of Sartori, a 'constitution cannot effectively limit the will of power holders if they can outflank constitutional impediments by making direct appeals to the will of the people'.[90]

In short, what populists tend to reject in liberal constitutions, in particular, are the pre-determined legal, constitutional and institutional restraints on majority rule, which are seen as illegitimate constraints on popular sovereignty – more specifically on the exercise and expression, as we have seen, of the 'will of

[85] J-W Müller, 'Populism and Constitutionalism' in C Rovira Kaltwasser, P Ochoa Espejo, P Taggart and P Ostiguy (eds), *The Oxford Handbook of Populism* (Oxford, Oxford University Press, 2017) 598, referring to GJ Jacobsohn, *Constitutional Identity* (Cambridge, Harvard University Press, 2010).

[86] Fundamental Law of Hungary, art L).

[87] I thank Julian Scholtes for pointing this out.

[88] See, eg, C Rovira Kaltwasser, 'Populism vs Constitutionalism? Comparative Perspectives on Contemporary Western Europe, Latin America, and the United States' (2013) Policy Brief, The Foundation for Law, Justice and Society 6.

[89] Landau (n 66) 537.

[90] G Sartori, 'Constitutionalism: A Preliminary Discussion' (1962) 56 *American Political Science Review* 853, 862.

the people'. Instead, they put forward a 'timeless' conception of the constitution, which, in their view, puts the transcendent and immutable 'people' at the forefront, above liberal (and 'illegitimate') constraints.

B. Courts under Populism: Populist, Popular and (or) Political Constitutionalism?

Beyond constitutions and other legal restraints, many populists view independent institutions – particularly the judiciary – as illegitimate hurdles on (what they perceive as) the will of the majority. In fact, and as will become clear in the rest of this monograph, especially in Part II, populists often have an uneasy relationship with the courts, particularly when judges side against them. One may think, for example, of the recent allegation by the US White House Press Secretary Karoline Leavitt, in March 2025, that judges who have recently issued rulings against Trump's administration are '[n]ot only usurping the will of the president and the chief executive of our country, but they are undermining the will of the American public'.[91] Calling for the removal of judges against what he viewed as a 'judicial coup', the then-senior advisor to Trump and de facto head of the Department of Government Efficiency (DOGE), Elon Musk, also wrote on X: 'We need 60 senators to impeach the judges and restore rule of the people'.[92]

Yet, this conception of the 'will of the people' as sitting above independent institutions such as the judiciary is by no means unique to populism. One may think, for example, of countries such as the UK, where the principle of parliamentary sovereignty can ultimately put political decision-making above a ruling by the highest courts.[93] More broadly, this conception is reminiscent, at least to a certain extent, of the idea of popular constitutionalism, namely the view that 'ordinary citizens [have] a central and pivotal role in implementing their Constitution'.[94] Under this vision, the final interpretative duty should rest with 'the people themselves' – and courts are 'no less than elected representatives [who should be] subordinate to their judgments'.[95]

In fact, both populism and popular constitutionalism arguably share some important characteristics. First, they both claim that the locus of constitutional authority is the notion of 'the people', understood as a concrete socio-political

[91] AFP, 'White House Says US Judges "Usurping" Trump's Authority' (*France24*, 19 March 2025) www.france24.com/en/live-news/20250319-white-house-says-us-judges-usurping-trump-s-authority.

[92] ibid.

[93] I thank Stephen Skinner for pointing this out.

[94] LD Kramer, *The People Themselves: Popular Constitutionalism and Judicial Review* (Oxford, Oxford University Press, 2004) 8. That said, it could also be argued that 'popular constitutionalism' is a broader idea, one developed and popularised by English and American radicals in the early 19th century. See, eg, T Frank, *People Without Power: The War on Populism and the Fight for Democracy* (London, Scribe, 2020).

[95] Kramer (n 94) 8.

force and assumed to be a continuous empirical entity.[96] Second, both populism and popular constitutionalism question judicial supremacy, although the relationship between populism and the courts is, as we will see in greater detail in Part II of this monograph, more complex than it appears at first sight. Third, and in relation to the previous point, they both focus on the role of the people, more specifically the 'ordinary people'. Indeed, popular constitutionalists argue that judicial supremacy 'has fundamentally altered the meaning of republican citizenship by, as a conceptual matter, taking *ordinary people* out of the process of shaping constitutional law'.[97] Fourth, and in the same vein, both populism and popular constitutionalism pit democracy and judicial supremacy in two separate camps, as antitheses – with judicial supremacy (and, arguably, other liberal institutions and procedures) viewed as fundamentally and profoundly 'anti-democratic'.[98] Many liberal constitutionalists, by contrast, would acknowledge the representational role of courts (in the sense that they represent the public interest and common good by virtue of their independence, impartiality, professionalism and public trust in the institution) and would generally not view judicial review as undemocratic.[99] They would also highlight the role of the judiciary in demanding more information[100] (which, in turn, can make government more transparent vis-à-vis its citizens) or, alternatively, in facilitating the rotation of power (thereby meeting the people's demands for political change) by rejecting legal and constitutional changes that could potentially lead to executive entrenchment.[101] This role can be exercised, of course, by means of judicial review.[102] Fifth, both populism and popular constitutionalism are sceptical of preconditions for legitimate rule and deliberative democracy, which Kramer characterises bluntly as a 'philosophical school' which 'turns out to be mostly about deliberation and hardly at all about democracy'.[103] Finally, both criticise what Richard Parker has called the dominant 'Anti-Populist' sensibility amongst lawyers, judges, scholars and others – namely the view that

[96] Walker (n 76) 527.

[97] Kramer (n 94) 233.

[98] See, eg, ibid 242. Examples of populists calling judicial interventions as 'anti-democratic' abound. A recent example is White House deputy chief of staff Stephen Miller criticising the suspension, by a court, of the Pentagon's ban on transgenders serving in the military as 'pure lawlessness' and 'the gravest assault on democracy'. See AFP, 'White House Says US Judges "Usurping" Trump's Authority'.

[99] See, eg, JEK Murkens, 'Judicious Review: The Constitutional Practice of the UK Supreme Court' (2018) 77 *Cambridge Law Journal* 349. For Murkens, the democratic legitimacy of courts (and of constitutional review) 'depends on constitutional principle as a normative reference point, on the courts as representational organs, and on the law as "a continuous, historical process in which the law is developing through constant efforts of reform"'. See ibid 354, citing PW Kahn, *The Cultural Study of Law: Reconstructing Legal Scholarship* (Chicago, University of Chicago Press, 1999) 15. See also, generally, P Rosanvallon, *Counter-Democracy: Politics in an Age of Distrust* (trans Arthur Goldhammer) (Cambridge, Cambridge University Press, 2018); A Arato, 'Populism, Constitutional Courts, and Civil Society' in C Landfried (ed), *Judicial Power: How Constitutional Courts Affect Political Transformations* (Cambridge, Cambridge University Press, 2019) 338, 339.

[100] See, eg (and at a broader level), A Barak, 'A Judge on Judging: The Role of a Supreme Court in a Democracy' (2002) 116 *Harvard Law Review* 19.

[101] I thank Kim Lane Scheppele for raising these points.

[102] See, eg, ch 6.

[103] Kramer (n 94) 244.

'ordinary political energy [...] is problematic because of attributes that set it apart from, and identify it as qualitatively inferior to, more "refined" sources of political participation'.[104] In that regard, Kramer builds on Parker and argues that '[t]he modern Anti-Populist sensibility presumes that ordinary people are emotional, ignorant, fuzzy-headed, and simple-minded, in contrast to a thoughtful, informed, and clear-headed elite'.[105] In short, by pitting the 'ordinary people' against the 'elite', popular constitutionalism thus emulates the populist dichotomy between the (pure) people and the (corrupt) elite (including judges) who illegitimately thwart, through their use of procedures and institutions, the expression of the 'will of the people'.

That said, there are important distinctions between populism and popular constitutionalism. First, popular constitutionalism recognises more clearly than populism the need for representation and, from a spatiotemporal perspective, '[does] not object to institutional arrangements designed to slow politics down', including the separation of powers.[106] Second, as we have seen, many liberal constitutionalists have pointed out that populism is concerned with unity of voice, thereby leaving little room for disagreement.[107] Popular constitutionalism, by contrast, arguably leaves greater room for dissenting voices – so long as they are expressed through political (rather than judicial) channels. Lastly, populism is not *necessarily* against judicial supremacy and courts in general, particularly when the latter support the will of the leader or party.[108] In other words, the populist opposition to courts is often more outcome-based than principled: many populists will not necessarily object to a court having the last word on a legal-political issue (namely, the idea of the court as the ultimate authority), provided that said court is viewed as a friendly (rather than a hostile) institution and, ideally, rules in their favour.[109]

In short, populism and popular constitutionalism share some important similarities insofar as the locus of constitutional authority, in both cases, is the notion of 'the people', understood as a concrete socio-political force. The main difference, however, is that populism tends to be a bit less sceptical about judicial supremacy than popular constitutionalism, particularly when courts are viewed as friendly to the regime and (or) support the 'right' decision, that is to say, the 'will of the people' (either expressed through plebiscitary instruments or through a charismatic and influential leader, sometimes by acclamation). In fact, some apex courts captured by populists will not hesitate to use their constitutional review powers for

[104] RD Parker, '"Here, the People Rule": A Constitutional Populist Manifesto' (1993) 27 *Valparaiso University Law Review* 531, as cited in ibid 241–242.

[105] Kramer (n 94) 242.

[106] ibid 245.

[107] See ch 1.

[108] It is for that reason that populists often engage in court-packing, something popular constitutionalists would probably be opposed to.

[109] The recent situation of the packed Constitutional Tribunal in Poland under PiS rule (2015-2023) provides an example. See, eg, W Sadurski, *Poland's Constitutional Breakdown* (Oxford, Oxford University Press, 2019). See also ch 5.

the benefit of the populist regime and engage in what David Landau and Rosalind Dixon call 'abusive judicial review', namely the use of judicial review powers to actively undermine (rather than protect) liberal democratic constitutionalism.[110] This possibility is discussed in more depth in chapter five.

In a relatively similar way, it could be said that populism has some affinities with political constitutionalism, insofar as it shares a strong belief in the role of 'the people' (as an entity and political actor) in the political life of the polity, a certain scepticism towards the involvement of unelected judges and unaccountable courts, and, to a certain extent, towards judicial review more broadly.[111] There are, nonetheless, important differences between political constitutionalism and populism, as Ana Micaela Alterio has pointed out, namely: '(i) the notion of the people they support; (ii) how they propose to mediate the popular will; and (iii) how the framers of the constitution conceive the idea of popular participation'.[112] Giuseppe Martinico has built on the above to argue that populism, contrary to political constitutionalism, is 'deeply rooted in a kind of pre-political understanding of the "People", seen as the direct and automatic source of political truth, and this inevitably results in questioning representative institutions as well'.[113]

Of course, the populist conception of constitutionalism – with its emphasis on the notion of 'the people', understood as a concrete socio-political force and the main locus of constitutional authority – is interesting and, for many, very appealing. Nevertheless, it could be retorted that this conception has its limits, at least from a liberal-constitutionalist perspective, insofar as it leaves little room for checks and balances on the arbitrary exercise of power. As we have seen in the previous chapter, through its emphasis on majoritarianism and unity, this conception of popular participation gives little to no voice to the excluded members of a polity, most notably minorities and others who do not belong to temporal majorities. In the same vein, it could be argued that the populist critique of liberal constitutionalism is focused on 'negative constitutionalism', that is to say, the 'doctrine that constitutions are primarily preventive or inhibitory devices, meant to check or repress tyranny and other abuses of power'.[114] By contrast, many liberal constitutionalists

[110] D Landau and R Dixon, 'Abusive Judicial Review: Courts Against Democracy' (2020) 53 *University of California, Davis Law Review* 1313.

[111] See, generally, R Bellamy, *Political Constitutionalism: A Republican Defence of the Constitutionality of Democracy* (Cambridge, Cambridge University Press, 2007). Bellamy, however, would argue that while the appeals to [majoritarian] democracy found in populism create 'a certain superficial similarity with political constitutionalism', which could potentially be justified in the case of left-wing populism, but not in the case of right-wing populism which 'proves opposed to the very features of democracy that provide it with the constitutional features political constitutionalists admire and advocate'. See R Bellamy, 'Political Constitutionalism and Populism' (2023) 50 *Journal of Law and Society* S19.

[112] AM Alterio, 'Reactive vs Structural Approach: A Public Law Response to Populism' (2019) 8 *Global Constitutionalism* 270, 283.

[113] Martinico (n 70) 21.

[114] S Holmes, *Passions and Constraint: On the Theory of Liberal Democracy* (Chicago, University of Chicago Press, 1995) 7.

view constitutions not merely as disabling devices meant to fetter the will of the sovereign, but as enabling ones as well.[115] Under this conception, first articulated by Jean Bodin and known as 'positive constitutionalism', constitutions are facilitative documents that can reinforce sovereignty.[116] Rather than constraining or subverting the will of the people, constitutions can, in fact

> ensure that the will of the sovereign people is formed through open public debate where criticism of the past mistakes is more or less inhibited and where individuals inside or outside the government can propose and advocate new ways to attack common problems.[117]

From a liberal constitutionalist perspective, therefore, the popular will, or at least the will of (temporal) electoral majorities, cannot be coherently expressed without some sort of institutional framework and procedural mechanisms.[118] Without these legal and constitutional prearrangements, the popular will would be difficult to identify and channel. In fact, without this institutional framework and these prearranged procedures, 'the people' (and their will) would arguably become Schmitt's unstructured (and mystical) *Urgrund*, with the practical consequence that the popular will would be unidentifiable other than by acclamation and/or through the leadership of a strong, authoritarian (if not totalitarian) leader.[119] In that sense, constitutional and legal prearrangements, notably those that secure the equal protection of the laws to all citizens, including minorities, should not, at least from a liberal-constitutionalist perspective, be perceived as hindrances to the power of the people, as many populists do, but rather as some of its most fundamental conditions.

C. Populism Outside and within the Courts: Penal and Judicial Populism

As we have seen, courts – as liberal, independent and unelected bodies – are often (rightly or wrongly) portrayed as obstacles to the implementation of populist measures, described as the 'will of the people'. Judicial autonomy in matters relating to criminal justice, in particular, has sparked populist outrage and has sometimes led to populist-led legislative measures requiring a much more punitive approach to law breaking, while reducing margins of flexibility for judges, particularly in relation to sentencing. Criminologists and criminal law scholars have referred to this phenomenon as 'populist punitiveness' and, more recently, as 'penal populism', the latter generally understood as the pursuit of a set of penal policies for electoral advantage rather than for their penal effectiveness in reducing crime or promoting

[115] ibid 8.
[116] ibid 133.
[117] ibid 8.
[118] ibid 168.
[119] ibid 167.

justice.[120] Expanding on this definition, John Pratt has argued that 'disillusionment with existing political processes and declines in deference to elite opinion-formers' have led, in recent decades, in the Anglophone world but also elsewhere,[121] 'to a dramatic redrawing of the processes of government and democracy, with the effect that "people are less and less prepared to leave questions, including difficult penal questions to their masters"'.[122] This decline of deference is in line with Rousseau's republican utopia of self-government discussed in the previous chapter, particularly the idea that the public is competent enough to make important decisions *themselves* in nearly all political (and legal) spheres, including those that (usually) require a level of expertise, such as criminal justice.

Far from being the exclusive resort of populist actors, penal populism is now, arguably, very much part of mainstream politics[123] and can be reflected in legislative measures, particularly in relation to sentencing. Sometimes (but not exclusively) following the outcome of the populist instrument par excellence, the referendum,[124] a number of statutes have reduced the courts' autonomy in relation to sentencing. For example, in New Zealand, the Sentencing Act 2002 – which introduced provisions for mandatory minimum sentences – was enacted in the aftermath of a 1999 referendum in which 91.7 per cent of voters approved a proposal to the country's criminal justice system by 'placing greater emphasis on the needs of victims, providing restitution, and compensation for them and imposing minimum sentences and hard labour for all serious violent offences'.[125] As Pratt explains, the referendum was 'contradictory', 'incoherent' and 'non-binding' and, as such, could have been ignored.[126] Yet, the Ministry of Justice felt obliged to act in response to the outcome of the referendum, which, according to the Ministry, 'revealed public concern over the sentencing of serious violent offenders'.[127]

Under penal populism, individual judges who get in the way of the 'will of the people' or popular sentiments are often singled out. One may think of the above-mentioned example of Chief Justice Maria Lourdes Sereno, in the Philippines, who

[120] See, eg, JV Roberts, LJ Stalans, D Indermaur and M Hough, 'Introduction' in JV Roberts et al (eds), *Penal Populism and Public Opinion: Lessons from Five Countries* (Oxford, Oxford University Press, 2003) 5; N Lacey, *The Prisoners' Dilemma: Political Economy and Punishment in Contemporary Democracies* (Cambridge, Cambridge University Press, 2011) ch 1; AE Bottoms, 'The Philosophy and Politics of Punishment and Sentencing' in C Clarkson and R Morgan (eds), *The Politics of Sentencing Reform* (Oxford, Clarendon Press, 1995) 17–49; N Lacey, 'Populism and the Rule of Law' (2019) 15 *Annual Review of Law and Social Science*.

[121] See, eg, RH Heydarian, 'Penal Populism in Emerging Markets: Human Rights and Democracy in the Age of Strongmen' in GL Neuman (ed), *Human Rights in a Time of Populism: Challenges and Responses* (Cambridge, Cambridge University Press, 2020).

[122] J Pratt, *Penal Populism* (Abingdon, Routledge, 2007) 4, citing M Ryan, 'Red Tops, Populists and the Irresistible Rise of the Public Voice' (2004) 1 *Journal for Crime, Conflict and the Media* 1.

[123] See, eg, Pratt (n 122) 22. I also thank Julian Scholtes for pointing this out.

[124] See ch 1 and the previous sections of this ch.

[125] Pratt (n 122) 25–26. This is the wording of the referendum question.

[126] ibid 26.

[127] ibid, referring to Ministry of Justice of New Zealand, *Reforming the Criminal Justice System* (Wellington, Ministry of Justice, 2002).

was removed from office under Rodrigo Duterte's presidency after calling for more due process in the country's 'war on drugs'.[128] More recently, US President Donald Trump has publicly called for the impeachment of District Judge James Boasberg after the latter temporarily suspended the deportation flights of Venezuelan migrants to El Salvador.[129] Despite a rare rebuke from Supreme Court Chief Justice John Roberts – who said that 'impeachment is not an appropriate response to disagreement concerning a judicial decision' – Trump doubled down and wrote on his Truth Social network: 'If a President doesn't have the right to throw murderers, and other criminals, out of our Country because a Radical Left Lunatic Judge wants to assume the role of President, then our Country is in very big trouble, and destined to fail!'[130]

From an institutional perspective, the result of penal populism is a reduced autonomy for criminal justice – and for the judiciary as an institution. That said, the strategy under penal populism is not always (just) to remove judges and (or) limit or weaken institutions as such. In some cases, and paradoxically, significant resources have been allocated to, in fact, *strengthen* institutions, particularly prosecutorial offices. In Brazil, for instance, institutions such as the Public Prosecutor's Office and the Advocacy General of the Union secured independence and resources under various governments, eventually becoming powerful and activist actors that could not be contained by politicians, especially those on the left.[131] This became particularly clear in the context of the famous anti-corruption investigation known as *Lava Jato* (Operation Car Wash), when lead prosecutors and judges took a very aggressive stance towards politicians. While many have lauded the investigation and described it as successful, particularly considering its scope and 'the long-lasting tradition of impunity for corruption in Brazil',[132] others have criticised it for engaging in what they have described as 'prosecutorial [and] investigative overreach'[133] and 'degradation of legal norms',[134] with some decisions (such as the preventive imprisonment of former President Michel Temer) viewed as an 'act of will, rather than an act of law'.[135] In the course of the investigation,

[128] AP, 'Fear for democracy after top Philippine judge and government critic removed' (*The Guardian*, 12 May 2018) www.theguardian.com/world/2018/may/12/fear-for-democracy-after-top-philippine-judge-and-government-critic-removed.

[129] AFP, 'White House Says US Judges "Usurping" Trump's Authority'.

[130] ibid.

[131] I thank Fabio de Sá e Silva for this point and Laeticia Kreuz for an explanation of the broader context.

[132] MM Prado and MR De Assis Machado, 'Using Criminal Law to Fight Corruption: The Potential, Risks, and Limitations of Operation Car Wash (*Lava Jato*)' (2022) 69 *The American Journal of Comparative Law* 834, 836–837.

[133] G Mészáros, 'Caught in an Authoritarian Trap of Its Own Making? Brazil's "Lava Jato" Anti-Corruption Investigation and the Politics of Prosecutorial Overreach' (2020) 47 *Journal of Law and Society* S54.

[134] ibid, referring to lawyer Marcelo Nobre's views in R Gentile, 'Lava Jato tem passado como um trator sobre a Constituição, diz advogado' (*Folha de São Paulo*, 4 April 2019) www1.folha.uol.com.br/poder/2019/04/lava-jato-tem-passado-como-um-trator-sobre-a-constituicao-diz-advogado.shtml.

[135] ibid.

high-profile prosecutors have engaged in actions that could perhaps be described as 'prosecutorial populism': with a view to garner public support and appear 'close to the public', they had recourse to the 'creative use of legal tools and media mobilization', such as 'coercive questioning' (with media coverage) and the publicisation of evidence and privileged information, ostensibly to foster 'transparency'.[136]

Over the course of the investigation, many judges acted in a similar way, including Sérgio Moro, the judge heading *Lava Jato*: he was noted for his frequent use of 'accessible language, rather than the complicated technical terms and obtuse constructions that make most judicial decisions in Brazil inaccessible to the lay person',[137] but also for 'bending' legal rules – including due process – in order to achieve desired results.[138] Moro's decision, in 2019, to join then-President Jair Bolsonaro's cabinet as Minister of Justice further drew suspicions that some of his previous actions as a judge were politically motivated.[139]

In the end, *Lava Jato*'s unique form of 'punitivism' (understood as 'a punishment-centred conception of justice')[140] had repercussions beyond the fight against corruption: the 'political grammar'[141] prosecutors developed – including the view, put forward by actors such as lead prosecutor Deltan Dallagnol, that the legal system (and due process in particular) 'takes the side of defendants at the expense of victims and society'[142] – bolstered penal populism, anti-politics and ultimately strengthened Bolsonaro's far-right discourse.[143]

In other contexts, courts have, on their own, engaged in forms of populism – or what some scholars have described as 'judicial populism', referring to the incorporation, by judges, of 'public sentiment and popular opinion into their decision-making'.[144] Examples of judicial populism abound. The concept is spectacularly captured by an Israeli judge, Justice Mishael Cheshin, who wrote in a High Court ruling:

> *Vox populi, vox dei*. The voice of the people is the voice of God. [...] I am referring to the voice of the people, in the simple sense of the phrase. [...] It is incumbent upon us,

[136] MM Prado and MR Machado, 'Turning Corruption Trials into Political Tools in the Name of Transparency: The Lava Jato Case' in S Botero, DM Brinks and EA Gonzalez-Ocantos (eds), *The Limits of Judicialization: From Progress to Backlash in Latin America* (Cambridge, Cambridge University Press, 2022).

[137] ibid 267.

[138] ibid 266.

[139] ibid 267–268. In 2021, the Supreme Federal Court ruled that Judge Moro was biased in his handling of Lula's corruption conviction; as a result, the conviction was annulled.

[140] JGB dos Santos and E Solano Gallego, 'Fighting Corruption, Dismantling Democracy: Antagonism, Communication and the Political Use of Lava Jato in Brazil' in Botero, Brinks and Gonzalez-Ocantos (eds) (n 136) 290.

[141] F de Sá e Silva, 'From Car Wash to Bolsonaro: Law and Lawyers in Brazil's Illiberal Turn (2014-2018)' (2020) 47 *Journal of Law and Society* S90.

[142] ibid S103.

[143] dos Santos and Solano Gallego (n 140) 290. Another example could also be mentioned in this regard, namely the famous 'Mani Pulite' ('Clean Hands') investigation in the 1990s, which contributed to the emergence of right-wing actors such as Silvio Berlusconi, amongst others.

[144] A Arel and N Kolt, 'Populist Rhetoric, False Mirroring, and the Courts' (2020) 18 *International Journal of Constitutional Law* 749.

> the judges, to go out into the street, to literature, to poetry, to the press, to the radio and television, to everyday conversation.[145]

In doing so, Justice Cheshin – and other judges in Israel and elsewhere – chose to mirror public sentiment in their judicial decisions.[146] From a spatial perspective, it thus appears that courts can sometimes – just like many populist political actors themselves – act in a way that 'departs from technocratic procedural and communicational norms in favor of public proximity and orientation',[147] an element of (real or performative) proximity which is discussed in more detail in the next chapter.

Of course, there is a certain tension between the legitimacy of courts, which is derived from their professionalism, impartiality and independence from other branches of government as well as the public trust they enjoy, and the pressure they face (notably by political actors and members of the public) to be accountable and responsive to democratic values.[148] Moreover, courts are often well aware of their (relatively) precarious position – at least in some contexts – within the constitutional order. As such, it is somewhat unsurprising that some of these judges and courts have chosen – by necessity or otherwise – to engage, themselves, in what could be described as forms of populism, with a view to reducing the (metaphorical or actual) distance between themselves and the general public. Nevertheless, from a liberal-constitutionalist perspective, it could be argued that while judges may want to seek a certain balance between independence and responsiveness, their legitimacy ultimately rests on their ability to act (and be perceived) as neutral and impartial arbitrators and to decide independently from political pressures of different sorts, including institutional pressure from other branches of government.[149]

D. Populism and the Idea and Practice of Constitutionalism

It is clear, at this point, that populism is extremely wary of legal, constitutional and institutional constraints on the expression of the political power of 'the people'. As constituent power, it is argued, 'the people' cannot be constrained by institutional pre-commitments, given that they hold the authority to make and unmake institutional arrangements through which they are governed and thus, to institute a legal order in a given polity.[150] In other words, the authority to make and unmake constitutions and legal institutions is vested in 'the people' as a body that

[145] *SHIN Israeli Movement for Equal Representation of Women v Council for Cable TV and Satellite Broadcasting*, HCJ 5432/03 [2004] IsrLR 20, as cited in ibid 759.

[146] ibid.

[147] L Hilbink, 'Judicial Populism: A Conceptual and Normative Inquiry' (2024) *Law & Social Inquiry* 1, 10.

[148] See, eg, M Shapiro, *Courts* (Chicago, University of Chicago Press, 1981).

[149] This aspect is discussed in Part II of this book, particularly in ch 6 and in the conclusion.

[150] See Loughlin (n 56) 219.

exists prior to – and is independent from – a constitutional order. Constitutional constraints and liberal (or counter-majoritarian) institutions, such as courts, are thus depicted by populists as a hindrance to the implementation of the 'will of the people'. By contrast, liberal constitutionalists would retort that the liberal constitution does not merely serve to express the political will of the people as unity; it also purports to provide the institutional prearrangements and procedures that are essential for the democratic process itself. They would add that these institutional arrangements are not merely constraining devices; they are also enabling, insofar as they provide the very conditions for democratic deliberation, will-formation and compromise.[151]

As such, the populist conception of constitutionalism can appear to some as relatively limited or perhaps even as primitive. This is not to say, however, that populism does not, in fact, provide a useful and meaningful critique of liberal democracy and constitutionalism, at least from a liberal-constitutionalist perspective. In fact, populism arguably highlights some of the most important tensions within modern constitutionalism, namely the tension 'between individualism, universalism, and plurality on the one side and, on the other, the collectivism, particularism, and unitary structure of whose neglect the populist complains';[152] between 'voice' and 'rights';[153] between 'expediency' and 'design';[154] between 'politics of faith' and 'politics of scepticism'[155] or 'redemptive democracy' and 'pragmatic democracy';[156] between constituent ('revolutionary') and constituted ('electoral' and 'representative') powers; between 'democratic will' and 'constitutional reason';[157] between the 'democratic' and 'modernist' constitutional imaginaries;[158] between 'finality of legislation and judicial

[151] See, eg, J Habermas, *Between Facts and Norms: Contributions to a Discourse Theory of Law and Democracy* (Cambridge, MIT Press, 1996) 770. See also, generally, Holmes (n 114).

[152] Walker (n 76) 531.

[153] ibid.

[154] ibid 525.

[155] M Oakeshott, *The Politics of Faith and the Politics of Scepticism* (New Haven, Yale University Press, 1996) 21–38, as cited in Canovan (n 32) 8. For Oakeshott, under the 'politics of faith', the goal of politics is to achieve popular salvation through popular enthusiasm and mobilisation. As Canovan summarises, 'devotees of this political style are impatient of legalistic restrictions that may stand in the way of salvation'. By contrast, the 'politics of scepticism' is suspicious of the above traits of the politics of faith and, instead, places a greater emphasis on order, rights, institutions and the rule of law.

[156] Canovan (n 32). For Canovan, democracy has two faces: one 'pragmatic' face, based on multiparty systems, free elections and other institutional practices, and a 'redemptive' face, founded on a 'deep revulsion against institutions that come between the people and their actions, a craving for direct, unmediated expression of the people's will'. See ibid 9–13.

[157] See, eg, E Christodoulidis, 'The Aporia of Sovereignty: On the Representation of the People in Constitutional Discourse' (2001) 12 *The King's College Law Journal* 111, as mentioned in Corrias (n 59) 16–17.

[158] Blokker (n 7) 537–539. For Blokker, the 'modernist' constitutional imaginary 'understands constitutions as devices of order and stability that tame the human propensity to violence and unreason'; furthermore, it 'displays a distinctive emphasis on the rule of law, juridification, and the orderly limitation of power. Modernist constitutionalism is hence not necessarily about democracy, understood as popular self-rule and empowerment. It is about the preservation, stabilization, and careful management of an existing order, by means of a closed, independently operating legal system'. In contrast, the

supremacy';[159] and, finally, between *gubernaculum* ('government power, to control inordinate private interests to the benefit of a peaceful civil order') and *jurisdictio* ('civil control on government power').[160] If populism places a disproportionate emphasis on unity, constituent power, faith (or redemption) and *gubernaculum*, a similar but opposite critique could arguably be made of liberal constitutionalism, which focuses on individualism, constituted powers, scepticism (or pragmatism) and *jurisdictio*.

That said, it would probably be a mistake to perceive, as many populists do, the idea and practice of (liberal) constitutionalism merely as a limit on the political power of the people – and therefore as something to be discarded, limited and (or) subjugated to politics. The people, as a multitude, have different aspirations, which inevitably conflict.[161] As Martin Loughlin puts it, '[t]he aggregation of interests and opinions implicit in the concept of a democratic will can be recognized only when absorbed into some representative form', and therefore through certain institutional arrangements.[162] Arguably, these institutional arrangements established in a constitution serve to organise, and not simply constrain, political power. Seen that way, constitutions should not be viewed as a hindrance to the exercise of political power by the people; rather, their purpose is to generate and orchestrate the public power of a state[163] – including, I would argue, the people's ability to express their political will through their (elected) representatives.

V. Conclusion

An important part of the ideal-typical populist discourse, mainly for populists in power, is that they have dethroned the corrupt elites and restored power to 'the people'. Invoking the outcome of an election or a referendum, populists, as we have seen in the previous chapter, effectively imbue transient, temporal electoral majorities – that is, those who voted for them – with the characteristics of timeless unity and immutability.[164] In other words, populists take the outcome of an election or a referendum and elevate this outcome to the status of immutable and perpetual word: 'the people have spoken'.[165] In this second chapter,

'democratic' constitutional imaginary views 'constitutions as creative devices that push forward human liberty. The emphasis in the revolutionary understanding is the foundation of an entirely new order on the basis of emancipatory principles, such as equality, freedom, and self-rule'. Moreover, it 'finds its most distinctive expression in the idea of self-determination and self-government'.

159 See, eg, Walker (n 76) 531.

160 G Maddox, 'A Note on the Meaning of "Constitution"' (1982) 76 *American Political Science Review* 805, 809. See also CH McIlwain, *Constitutionalism: Ancient and Modern*, 2nd edn (Ithaca, Cornell University Press, 1958) 93–122, as mentioned in ibid, and Walker (n 76) 531.

161 M Loughlin, *The Idea of Public Law* (Oxford, Oxford University Press, 2003) 113.

162 ibid.

163 ibid.

164 Cahill (n 44), referring to Girard (n 44).

165 ibid.

I have added an extra layer to this elaboration of the ideal-typical populist discourse. I have argued that, through its discourse and actions, populism weakens the distinction between ordinary, day-to-day politics, on the one hand, and intemporal, timeless constitutional politics, on the other. This, of course, has important implications for constitutionalism, including a form of scepticism (if not outright hostility) vis-à-vis constitutional pre-commitments and independent and counter-majoritarian institutions, such as courts. In so doing, populists tend to emphasise the spaces of democratic self-rule and freedom from limitations of power, including institutional constraints.

Contemporary populism, it thus appears, is not just a critique of liberal democracy; it also comes with its own constitutional project – one that focuses on speedy and concentrated decision-making and, in doing so, challenges and redraws the spatiotemporal contours of liberal constitutional democracy. In the next chapter, I will argue that contemporary populism takes advantage of social acceleration and the abovementioned spatiotemporal contours of liberal democracy in order to put forward an alternative conception of democratic representation, one that populists (sometimes indirectly) claim to be better suited to the contemporary imperatives of temporal efficiency and rapidity. This alternative conception of democracy – based on speed and proximity (rather than process and institutional distance), as well as on the substitution of many minds for one – and its associated constitutional project will then be revealed, discussed and ultimately challenged.

3

Characterising Populism: Space, Time and 'Constitutional Impatience'

> L'impatience – finalement inefficiente – surimpose la temporalité de l'un aux rythmes de l'autre. [...] L'une des fonctions génératives du droit, civil et pénal, privé et public, interne et international, est au contraire de favoriser les inchronismes, les eurythmies; de permettre aux idées de se former, aux croyances de s'exprimer, pour faciliter les transitions et les aboutissements, plutôt que les jaculations verbales ou idéelles, et donc de prohiber les passages à l'acte, verbaux ou gestuels, et les cour[t]s-circuits de l'avidité ou de l'irascibilité toujours tentés par le paroxysme de la colère sur la pente du meurtre.[1]

I. Introduction

In the introductory chapter, I discussed how the main institutions of liberal constitutional democracy, which were designed – and which operate – following a distinctive spatiotemporal logic, are particularly vulnerable to social acceleration. In this chapter, I explain how contemporary populism takes advantage of this social acceleration and the spatiotemporal contours of liberal constitutional democracy, in order to put forward a different conception of democratic representation. More specifically, I argue that contemporary populism does not simply emerge in the context of this social acceleration; it acts in response to it, or even as a catalyst for it. As liberal institutions (particularly legislatures and courts) appear ill-equipped to adapt to and face this trend, populism manifests itself as a powerful and convincing critique of liberal constitutional democracy: it paints the latter as inefficient, slow-paced, elite-driven and opaque. However, populism is not just a critique of contemporary liberal democracy; it also comes with its own constitutional project – one that is, as populists would indirectly claim, better suited to the contemporary imperatives of temporal efficiency and rapidity. In fact, populism puts forward an alternative conception of representation, one that is based on spatial proximity, authenticity and temporal efficiency. Finally, taking a critical stance on the populist proposition, which I call 'constitutional impatience', my argument in the last part of this chapter is that this form of proximity

[1] R Draï, 'Éloge de la patience juridique' in P Gérard, F Ost and M van de Kerchove (eds), *L'accélération du temps juridique* (Bruxelles, Presses universitaires Saint-Louis Bruxelles, 2000) 170.

and acceleration, while appealing, runs the risk of transforming into immediacy, simultaneity and a form of occupation.

As mentioned earlier in this book, 'spatiotemporality' concerns time and space[2] – dimensions that have often been overlooked by constitutional theorists,[3] particularly in their study of populism.[4] Yet, they are inherent to the ideal-typical populist discourse. Indeed, I contend that considerations of both space and time – which should be studied together and relationally, rather than independently – are central to the populist constitutional narrative and imaginary. Moreover, and as discussed in more detail below, populism operates not only within the social spaces in which acceleration takes place, but also within the institutions it attempts to redesign and reshape.[5]

This chapter is divided into five sections. The second focuses on space, which is to be understood here (and elsewhere in this book) in a mostly metaphorical and discursive way, although it also sometimes refers to actual spaces. Put differently, I predominantly mean 'spatial scale', namely, how space is produced and mobilised discursively and politically, rather than 'jurisdiction', understood as a legal and administrative technology of governance.[6] In this second section, I discuss the populist critique of liberal-democratic distance, notably by analysing how populists attempt to respond to the abovementioned spatiotemporal distance by reorganising the political space in order to create an authenticity- and immediacy-based democracy of proximity. The third section of this chapter focuses on considerations of time. I argue that intrinsic to populism is a sense of urgency, expeditiousness and instantaneity that serves as a catalyst for social acceleration, discussed earlier in this monograph.[7] My argument in this regard can be divided into two sub-points. First, I suggest that populism is characterised by a sense of urgency and expeditiousness. Second, I assert that through their emphasis on a 'politics of instantaneity', populists often attempt to redraw the temporal contours

[2] See, generally, M Valverde, *Chronotopes of Law: Jurisdiction, Scale and Governance* (Abingdon, Routledge, 2015).

[3] For exceptions regarding time in particular, see, eg, S Ranchordás and Y Roznai (eds), *Time, Law, and Change: An Interdisciplinary Study* (Oxford, Hart Publishing, 2020); L Corrias and L Francot (eds), *Temporal Boundaries of Law and Politics: Time Out of Joint* (Abingdon, Routledge, 2018); T Poole, 'Time and Timelessness in Constitutional Thought' (2020) 27 *Res Publica* 255; L Barshack, 'Interpretation and the Legal Fabrication of Time' in S Ranchordás and Y Roznai (eds), *Time, Law, and Change: An Interdisciplinary Study* (Oxford, Hart, 2020); M Kumm, 'The Best of Times and the Worst of Times' in P Dobner and M Loughlin (eds), *The Twilight of Constitutionalism?* (Oxford, Oxford University Press, 2010); L Barshack, 'Time and the Constitution' (2009) 7 *International Journal of Constitutional Law* 553.

[4] For a (very) rare exception, see M Anastasiou, 'The Spatiotemporality of Nationalist Populism and the Production of Political Subjectivities' (2020) 13 *Subjectivity* 217. However, Anastasiou's approach focuses on nationalism and subjectivity. Moreover, it is deeply anchored in the Essex school of discourse analysis; as such, it is considerably different from mine.

[5] It should be noted that my attempt here is not to make any empirical claims about populism; rather, it is to make conceptual or interpretative claims about the *character* of populism – hence the title of this chapter.

[6] For a distinction between the two concepts, see Valverde (n 2) 56–57.

[7] Mainly in the introductory chapter.

of liberal constitutional democracy and to circumvent the delays built into it. In the fourth section, I make a more normative claim, namely that by focusing on immediacy and decisionism – what I call 'constitutional impatience' – at the expense of reflexivity and deliberation, populists tend to oversimplify and distort the constitutive features of constitutional democracy, including its important guardrails, ultimately collapsing what is worth protecting about the idea of constitutionalism. The fifth section concludes this chapter (and Part I of this book more broadly).

II. Space: From Distance to Proximity, Immediacy and Authenticity

Implicit in the ideal-typical populist discourse is the claim that contemporary liberal-democratic representation is spatiotemporally distant. Or rather, that it is perceived or depicted as physically distant, emotionally detached and generally unresponsive, insofar as the ruling elite is rarely publicly seen, except on a few rare, key (often televised or video-recorded) moments. Populists criticise political or economic actors – especially members of the economic elite and oligarchy – for being disconnected from the reality of the 'real' people and (or) for acting behind closed doors. The avowed aim of populism, therefore, is to put power back in the hands of the people, away from distant, technocratic and unaccountable institutions and other liberal intermediaries.

In the next two subsections, I will first discuss the populist critique of liberal-democratic distance and then explain how populists attempt to respond to this distance by reorganising the political space in order to create a democracy of proximity, based on immediacy and authenticity.

A. The Populist Critique of Liberal-Democratic Distance

Implicit to the ideal-typical populist discourse is a critique that political power is in the hands of a spatially distant and disconnected ruling elite. There are three main components to that alleged distance between the rulers and the ruled, between the elite and 'the people', namely: (1) a spatial, geographical or physical distance; (2) a symbolic distance; and (3) a cognitive, emotional or empirical distance.

First, there is a certain spatial, geographical or physical component to the contemporary populist critique of liberal-democratic distance. For example, in 1981 French sociologist Alain Touraine noted that populism 'resists stoutly against the dispossession of peoples and territories dominated from afar by a distant master'.[8] This is notably why several populist leaders emerged from

[8] A Touraine, *The Voice and the Eye: An Analysis of Social Movements* (trans A Duff) (Cambridge, Cambridge University Press, 1981) 20.

post-war, anti-colonial struggles, including in Asia.[9] More recently, populist movements have criticised urban and privileged elites, claiming that the latter are spatially, geographically and (or) physically separated from the people – both literally and figuratively. Shielded in their capital cities' ivory towers, it is alleged, the elites exercise economic and political power over the 'real' or 'ordinary' people living in rural areas or in post-industrial areas like the Rust Belt in the US or England's post-industrial North. Physically and geographically detached from the lives and concerns of 'ordinary' people, they are unable, it is said, to understand their concerns and preoccupations, thereby confirming the sense of alienation of the public from their rulers.[10] By contrast, populist leaders from Napoléon III in the mid-nineteenth century[11] to Hugo Chávez in the 2000s have long been noted for their spatial and physical proximity to the people, with their frequent trips across their respective countries to directly meet with the population (often using technological means stemming from what Hartmut Rosa calls 'technical acceleration'), and thereby establish high-speed and direct communication links with them.

Populism, therefore – through its discourse – contributes to the emergence of a new geography, map or scale, one of proximity between *gouvernants* and *gouvernés*. To borrow from Jacco Bomhoff, who wrote in a different context and referred to a different subject, populism arguably 'imagines – and contributes to the construction of – a world it purports merely to describe'.[12] This world is one in which liberal-democratic rulers are far removed from the realities of the 'true' people, due to their geographical distance vis-à-vis the latter, by contrast to populist leaders who are, in essence, physically and spatially present (and invested) in the life of their constituents. This represents a certain shift in scale, insofar as it suggests a different understanding of (spatial) proximity: its exact opposite – distance – thus becomes akin to a form of alienation.

Second, linked to that spatial, geographical or physical distance is an alleged symbolic distance, disconnection or separation between the elite and ordinary people, between the rulers and the ruled. Indeed, the acceleration of time, population growth, globalisation and the advancement of technology have, according

[9] See, eg, M Mietzer, 'Movement Leaders, Oligarchs, Technocrats and Autocratic Mavericks: Populists in Contemporary Asia' in C de la Torre (ed), *Routledge Handbook of Global Populism* (Abingdon, Routledge, 2019) 371.

[10] A similar argument has been made in relation to supranational institutions such as the EU. See, eg, M Tushnet and B Bugarič, *Power to the People: Constitutionalism in the Age of Populism* (Oxford, Oxford University Press, 2022) 231: '[T]he common thread is that technocracy in Brussels has displaced politics at national capitals'.

[11] See P Rosanvallon, *Le Siècle du populisme: Histoire, théorie, critique* (Paris, Seuil, 2020) 101; H Rosa, *Social Acceleration: A New Theory of Modernity* (New York, Columbia University Press, 2013) xv.

[12] See J Bomhoff, 'Back to *The Bremen* (1972): Forum Selection and Worldmaking' (2018) LSE Law, Society and Economy Working Papers (6/2018). In this piece, Bomhoff discusses the idea of scalar modulation and analyses the emergence of a new 'world'-scale thinking in economic law in the late 1960s, and notably how the US Supreme Court actively contributed to the emergence of this new scalar modulation through its acceptance of forum-selection clauses.

to some, led to a gradual transfer of power from national parliaments to 'bureaucratic agencies staffed with subject-matter experts' who have begun to undertake a 'quasi-legislative role'.[13] Members of the ruling elite – including judges, alongside (other) unelected 'technocrats' sitting in independent and (or) supranational institutions – are criticised for being disconnected or out of touch with the realities of the people.

Supranational institutions and experts are often a target of such rhetoric. Examples of this abound. For instance, the idea that the people have the willingness, knowledge and competence to make key political decisions by themselves, directly, without the need for experts and unnecessary supranational intermediaries, was arguably the central idea behind the 'Take back control' slogan in the campaign preceding the 2016 Brexit referendum. This was further illustrated by the words of then-Justice Secretary Michael Gove in June 2016. In a Sky News question and answer session, he made a case for Brexit based on the promise of national self-reliance. He said: 'I'm not asking the public to trust me; I'm asking the public to trust themselves.'[14] He added: 'I'm asking the British public to take back control of our destiny from those organisations which are distant, unaccountable, elitist and have their own interest at heart'.[15] International institutions, including international courts, have also been singled out, with populists like Benjamin Netanyahu describing the International Criminal Court (ICC) as a 'corrupt organisation' and Viktor Orbán criticising it as 'a political forum' (and announcing, in April 2025, Hungary's withdrawal from the Treaty of Rome and therefore the ICC's jurisdiction).[16]

However, 'faraway' supranational and (or) international organisations, institutions and experts are not the only targets of this type of discourse. A similar rhetoric has also been employed vis-à-vis domestic or national actors. Domestic courts and judges, for instance, have been singled out as 'disconnected' in Israel,[17] as 'out of touch' and even as 'enemies of the people' in British tabloids,[18]

[13] Y Mounk, *The People vs. Democracy: Why Our Freedom Is in Danger and How to Save it* (Cambridge, Harvard University Press, 2018) 60 (and 64).

[14] H Mance, 'Britain has had enough of experts, says Gove' (*Financial Times*, 3 June 2016): www.ft.com/content/3be49734-29cb-11e6-83e4-abc22d5d108c.

[15] ibid.

[16] S Crawshaw, 'Orbán quits the ICC, other nations have a choice to make: do we back the rule of law or not?' (*The Guardian*, 4 April 2025) www.theguardian.com/commentisfree/2025/apr/04/orban-quit-icc-rule-of-law.

[17] See, eg, then-Minister Miri Regev's statement that the High Court of Justice is 'disconnected from the people', discussed in A Harel and N Kolt, 'Populist Rhetoric, False Mirroring, and the Courts' (2020) 18 *International Journal of Constitutional Law* 756.

[18] J Slack, 'Enemies of the people: Fury over "out of touch" judges who have "declared war on democracy" by defying 17.4m Brexit voters and who could trigger constitutional crisis' (*Daily Mail*, November 2016) www.dailymail.co.uk/news/article-3903436/Enemies-people-Fury-touch-judges-defied-17-4m-Brexit-voters-trigger-constitutional-crisis.html. See also, eg, D Wilcock and J Maidment, 'Senior Scottish judge who ruled Boris Johnson's proroguing of Parliament illegal once called Brexit "a very onerous task … of mammoth proportions"' (*Daily Mail*, 11 September 2019) www.dailymail.co.uk/news/article-7452951/the-Scottish-judges-handed-Boris-Johnson-massive-Brexit-headache.html.

as 'hyenas' by then-President Jair Bolsonaro in Brazil[19] and as 'anti-democratic' (or 'undemocratic') by populist leaders in the US,[20] Poland (who added that the country is 'not a court-ocracy'),[21] Romania,[22] Armenia[23] and many other jurisdictions. To give a recent example from France, when Marine Le Pen – the populist leader of the right-wing party *Rassemblement National* – was found guilty in March 2025 of helping to embezzle 2.9 million euros of EU funds over 12 years for use by her party and banned from running for political office for five years, she denounced the judgment as a 'political decision' and a 'violation of the rule of law'.[24] She also organised a protest under the slogan 'Save democracy',[25] while Elon Musk, Viktor Orbán, Matteo Salvini, Geert Wilders and even the Kremlin – which described the judgment as a 'violation of democratic norms' – voiced their support for Le Pen.[26] The President of the *Rassemblement National*, Jordan Bardella, also criticised the decision – and the judiciary in general – in very strong terms. He said on television: 'Today, it is not [just] the Republic of Judges, it is now the *tyranny* of judges'.[27] Marion Maréchal, a former figure of the party (and Le Pen's niece), now Member of the European Parliament, also said – using words reminiscent of the ideal-typical populist discourse mentioned in the previous two chapters – that 'judges who view themselves above the sovereign people have decided to execute in a court of law the woman they were never able to force back at the ballot box'. These attacks on the legitimacy of the judiciary have led the French Superior Council of the Judiciary (*Conseil supérieur de la magistrature*) to make the unusual move of issuing a press statement in which it expressed its 'concern vis-à-vis the virulent reactions' provoked by the ruling, which 'are likely to seriously call into

[19] A Moreira Maués, 'Bolsonaro's First Year: Trying to Erode Democracy' (*International Journal of Constitutional Law Blog*, 1 February 2020) www.iconnectblog.com/bolsonaros-first-year-trying-to-erode-democracy.

[20] See ch 2.

[21] 'Poland MPs back controversial judiciary bill' (*BBC*, 15 July 2017) www.bbc.co.uk/news/world-europe-40617406.

[22] For example, right-wing populist candidate Călin Georgescu called Romania's central election authority's decision (later confirmed by the country's Constitutional Court) to bar him from running in the May 2025 presidential election as an 'anti-democratic putsch'. See Facebook post, 9 March 2025, www.perma.cc/ZBR7-9U4P. This decision sparked Elon Musk to ask, rhetorically, on X: 'How can a judge end democracy in Romania?' (*X*, 10 March 2025) x.com/elonmusk/status/1899079877283733997.

[23] See, eg, Prime Minister Nikol Pashinyan's 6 February 2020 speech in N Pashinyan, 'Speech at the Extraordinary Session of the National Assembly' (*The Prime Minister of Armenia*, 6 February 2020) www.primeminister.am/en/statements-and-messages/item/2020/02/06/Nikol-Pashinyan-Speech.

[24] See, eg, her 31 March 2025 interview on TF1: www.youtube.com/watch?v=ih7L20tUwG4&ab_channel=FRANCE24.

[25] See, eg, the Rassemblement national's call to 'support Marine Le Pen and save democracy!' (*X*, 31 March 2025) www.x.com/RNational_off/status/1906769205082419252.

[26] S Imseng, 'L'extrême droite s'offusque de la condemnation de Marine Le Pen' (*Tribune de Genève*, 31 March 2025) www.tdg.ch/marine-le-pen-lextreme-droite-soffusque-de-sa-condamnation-196458805608.

[27] 'Aujourd'hui, ce n'est plus la République des juges, c'est la tyrannie des juges'. See, eg, Julie Cloris, 'Marine Le Pen condamnée: Jordan Bardella dénonce une "decision disproportionnée" et la "tyrannie des juges"' (*Le Parisien*, 1 April 2025) www.leparisien.fr/politique/marine-le-pen-condamnee-jordan-bardella-denonce-une-decision-disproportionnee-et-la-tyrannie-des-juges-01-04-2025-VOB2BGRLABBDLMEYI4ZAK6RARE.php (emphasis added).

question the independence of the judiciary, the foundation of the rule of law'.[28] The Council warned that 'threats personally targeting the magistrates in charge of the case, just like statements by political leaders on the merits of the prosecution or the conviction, particularly during the deliberations, cannot be accepted in a democratic society' and called for 'moderation in the comments made with regard to the decision rendered'.[29]

The abovementioned populist critique of distance is, of course, not limited to judges per se; in fact, several other wielders of political power, including parliamentarians, have also been criticised as 'disconnected', 'undemocratic' and (or) 'unaccountable'. For instance, Geoffrey Cox, then UK Attorney General, said in February 2020 that there is now a palpable disconnect between 'ordinary people and their votes and what happens here in Westminster'.[30] He rhetorically asked: 'Throughout our constitutional arrangements, is there a sense that… there has been a move into areas which are properly for those who are elected to decide?', adding that

> [t]here is a real risk that those of us in Westminster or in the legal profession do not understand that out in the country there is a concern about whether or not decisions that ought to be taken by democratically accountable politicians are in fact being taken by those who are not elected.[31]

It is also in this context, arguably, that the ruling Conservative Party in the UK announced in 2020 its intention to move the House of Lords – whose members are also not elected – from London to York or Birmingham, with a view to 'reconnecting' politics with voters from outside the capital.[32] While this plan did not come to fruition, it nevertheless illustrates a certain sentiment that power wielders are too detached or disconnected from the ordinary people they are meant to represent.

More than a mere proposal for a reorganisation of the physical landscape, the populist critique of liberal-democratic distance is thus also, as it were, a metaphor for alienation. Interestingly, it is not just the ruling elite that have been criticised as symbolically distant and disconnected from the realities of the 'real' people: political parties in general and even mainstream news media have faced the same criticism. In fact, mainstream news media have suffered a dramatic loss of trust in recent years, especially since the 2008 crisis.[33] This, of course,

[28] Conseil supérieur de la magistrature (France), 'Communiqué de presse du 31 mars 2025: Défense de l'autorité judiciaire à la suite des réactions au délibéré rendu par le tribunal judiciaire de Paris le 31 mars 2025') www.conseil-superieur-magistrature.fr/actualites/communique-du-conseil-du-31-mars-2025.

[29] ibid.

[30] 'Concern about judges' powers must be heeded, says Attorney General' (*BBC*, 12 February 2020) www.bbc.co.uk/news/uk-politics-51474169.

[31] ibid.

[32] 'House of Lords "could move to York or Birmingham" – Tory chairman' (*BBC*, 19 January 2020) www.bbc.co.uk/news/uk-politics-51168744.

[33] See, eg, A Nicolaou and C Giles, 'Public trust in media at all time low, research shows' (*Financial Times*, 16 January 2017) www.ft.com/content/fa332f58-d9bf-11e6-944b-e7eb37a6aa8e, referring to the 2017 Edelman Trust Barometer.

has been further exacerbated by rhetoric such as Trump's characterisation of the news media as 'the enemy of the people'.[34] As discussed in more detail below, the proximity and simultaneity inherent to the ideal-typical populist discourse – and its corollary, the delegitimisation of mainstream media – must therefore be understood as part of a broader rejection of intermediary bodies as 'illegitimate disruptors of the expression of the general will', rather than as contributors necessary to its formation.[35]

It could be said in that regard that populist actors are proponents of what Michael Oakeshott calls the 'politics of faith', under which the goal of politics is to achieve popular salvation through popular enthusiasm and mobilisation.[36] As Margaret Canovan summarises, 'devotees of this political style are impatient of legalistic restrictions [and intermediary bodies in general] that may stand in the way of salvation'.[37] Focusing almost exclusively on what she calls the 'redemptive' face of democracy, with its 'strong anti-institutional impulse: the romantic impulse to directness, spontaneity and the overcoming of alienation',[38] they often harbour a 'deep revulsion against institutions that come between the people and their actions, a craving for direct, unmediated expression of the people's will'.[39] A clear example of this is the Five Stars Movement (M5S) in Italy, which depicted established political parties and mainstream media as 'obstructions to democracy that citizens can get rid of thanks to the [Internet]'.[40] The objective is thus to connect the citizens horizontally, through the Internet, without intermediary organisations – in other words, '[t]he Net does not want middlemen'.[41] The idea, again, is that these intermediaries are spatially distant and disconnected from the public. In some instances, this can lead some populists to seek more control over which media get to ask questions and engage with them. A recent example is the White House's decision, in February 2025, to block the Associated Press from the Oval Office and, a week later, to take control of the press pool covering the president. This decision was justified by Press Secretary Karoline Leavitt in these terms: '[F]or decades, a group of D.C.-based journalists, the White House Correspondents' Association, has long dictated which journalists get to ask questions of the president of the

[34] See, eg, MM Grynbaum, 'Trump Calls the News Media the "Enemy of the American People"' (*New York Times*, 17 February 2017) www.nytimes.com/2017/02/17/business/trump-calls-the-news-media-the-enemy-of-the-people.html.

[35] Rosanvallon (n 11) 45. See also N Urbinati, 'A Revolt Against Intermediary Bodies' (2015) 22 *Constellations* 477.

[36] M Oakeshott, *The Politics of Faith and the Politics of Scepticism* (New Haven, Yale University Press, 1996) 21–38.

[37] M Canovan, 'Trust the People! Populism and the Two Faces of Democracy' (1999) 47 *Political Studies* 8.

[38] ibid 10–11. For her, if there is not at least some degree of 'redemptive democracy's promise of salvation' (in 'pragmatic' democracy, defined mainly by institutions), then 'it may well reassert itself in the form of a populist challenge').

[39] ibid 13.

[40] N Urbinati, 'Antiestablishment and the Substitution of the Whole with One of its Parts' in de la Torre (ed) (n 9) 78.

[41] Cited in ibid.

United States in these most intimate spaces. Not anymore'.[42] Leavitt added: 'I am proud to announce that we are going to give the power back to the people who read your papers, who watch your television shows, and who listen to your radio stations.'[43]

Third, and finally, there is also an alleged cognitive, emotional or empirical distance between the elite and the people, namely a discrepancy between the 'statistical truth' put forward by elites and their technocrats to describe the current state of society, on the one hand, and the actual realities (including social conditions) felt and experienced by 'ordinary' people, on the other.[44] Populists criticise this alleged cognitive, emotional or empirical distance; and they attempt to remove or reduce it through the production of an alternative 'truth', in response to the 'fake news' disseminated by the elite, the technocrats and the journalists controlled by the oligarchy.[45] This is not too surprising, in and of itself, given that populism has long been associated with passion and emotions. To be clear, by 'passion', I do not imply excess; rather, like Rosanvallon, I refer to an arguably more neutral term, akin to 'affect' or 'emotion'.[46] Populist discourses, it appears, seek to channel the popular frustrations and social grievances of those who feel excluded from the political decision-making process. By doing so, populist politicians, movements and parties will often be successful in their attempts to mobilise passions and create collective forms of identification, which usually revolve around the notion of 'the people' and almost inevitably involve the creation of an 'us' versus a 'them', as discussed at length in chapter one.

In short, populists tend to criticise the spatial distance inherent to liberal-democratic representation. However, this is not a mere critique. Their aim, as discussed below, is to replace this distance with alternative forms of representation and political participation that are based upon elements of proximity and authenticity – and which, as discussed later, also act as catalysts for the acceleration of time.

B. The Populist Reorganisation of Space: Proximity, Immediacy and Authenticity

As we have seen so far, the avowed aim of populists is to put power back in the hands of the people, away from distant, technocratic and unaccountable institutions and other liberal-democratic intermediaries. Populists thus attempt

[42] 'Press Briefing by Press Secretary Karoline Leavitt' (*The American Presidency Project*, 25 February 2025,) www.presidency.ucsb.edu/documents/press-briefing-press-secretary-karoline-leavitt-1.

[43] ibid.

[44] Rosanvallon (n 11) 32–33. See also, generally, S Rosenfeld, *Democracy and Truth* (Philadelphia, University of Pennsylvania Press, 2018).

[45] This has led to the emergence of alternative media outlets, like Breibart News, or social media platforms, such as Truth Social.

[46] Rosanvallon (n 11) 63.

to remove the spatial distance – mainly metaphorical and discursive, but also actual, physical and geographical – between the leader (or party) and the people (or electorate) by reorganising the political space to put forward an alternative conception of representation, one that is first and foremost based on proximity. As Paul Blokker explains, populists endorse 'a program that promises to reduce the distance between ordinary citizens and the institutions'; their objective is to 'directly link the people to the institutions and to reenchant democracy, to make it meaningful to its citizens'.[47] This is done, I contend, through different means tied to a peculiar, 'populist' conception of representation, discussed in the first subsection below.

i. The Populist Conception of Representation

One important way in which populists aim to create this new conception of representation based on proximity is through identity- and similarity-based appeals to authenticity.[48] Indeed, a common hallmark of populism across the world is a certain form of identification between the populist leader and 'the people'.[49] The idea, here, is for populists to depict themselves as close to the people, as one of them – and even, in some cases, as the embodiment of the people.[50] In India, Prime Minister Narendra Modi has used his monthly radio programme, called *Mann Ki Baat* ('matters of the heart'), to claim that he is one of the people. He said: 'I am yours, I am one amongst you, I am with you, you elevated me in a way, and in this way I will continue to remain connected with you as a family member through Mann Ki Baat'.[51] In his study of Latin American populism, Carlos de la Torre noted how '[t]he populist leader is

[47] P Blokker, 'Populism as a Constitutional Project' (2019) 17 *International Journal of Constitutional Law* 536.

[48] Y Mény and Y Surel, *Par le peuple, pour le peuple: Le populisme et les démocraties* (Paris, Fayard, 2000) 75; C de la Torre, *Populist Seduction in Latin America*, 2nd edn (Athens, Ohio University Press, 2010) xix, 10, 66, 109; F Panizza, 'Introduction: Populism and the Mirror of Democracy' in F Panizza (ed), *Populism and the Mirror of Democracy* (London, Verso, 2005) 24–28; L Corrias, 'Populism in a Constitutional Key: Constituent Power, Popular Sovereignty and Constitutional Identity' (2016) 12 *European Constitutional Law Review* 23–24; E Peruzzotti, 'El populismo como ejercicio de poder gubernamental y la amenaza de hibradación de la democracia liberal' (2018) 11 *Revista SAAP* 213, 215–216; M Valverde, 'Forms of Veridiction in Politics and Culture: Avowal in Today's Jargon of Authenticity' (2018) 11 *Behemoth* 96; M-S Kuo, 'Against Instantaneous Democracy' (2019) 17 *International Journal of Constitutional Law* 558–559; N Walker, 'Populism and Constitutional Tension' (2019) 17 *International Journal of Constitutional Law* 523, 527–528; C Fieschi, *Populocracy: The Tyranny of Authenticity and the Rise of Populism* (New York, Columbia University Press, 2019) 35–39, 157–160; P Diehl, 'Twisting Representation' in de la Torre (ed) (n 9) 130, 137–139; Rosanvallon (n 11) 153–155; MS Kuo, 'Authenticity: The Ultimate Challenge in the Quest for Lasting Constitutional Legitimacy' (2021) 41 *OJLS* 265.

[49] Peruzzotti (n 48) 215–216.

[50] See, eg, de la Torre (n 48) 10, 66, 109, xix; Mény and Surel (n 48) 75.

[51] A Bajpai, '"Matters of the Heart": The Sentimental India Prime Minister on *All India Radio*' in C Kohl, B Christophe, H Liebau and A Saupe (eds), *The Politics of Authenticity and Populist Discourses: Media and Education in Brazil, India and Ukraine* (London, Palgrave McMillan, 2021) 109.

identified with the people – *el pueblo* – understood as the plebs in its struggle against the oligarchy'.[52] Some even claimed to be the embodiment of the people. Starting in the 1930s, for instance, Ecuadorean President José María Velasco Ibarra viewed and depicted himself as the incarnation of the people.[53] Another Ecuadorean President, Abdalá Bucaram, also often presented himself, as de la Torre observed, as a 'common man who had been unjustly persecuted by the oligarchy', a 'new Christ, the new messiah who would redeem the people from their suffering' and the 'embodiment of the people's will that stood above and beyond and any democratic institution or procedure'.[54] A perhaps more famous example is Hugo Chávez, in Venezuela, who frequently asserted that he *literally* was the people.[55]

In other cases, while populists will not go as far as to claim they incarnate the people, they will nonetheless convey the message that they are the only legitimate representative of the people, the (only) 'voice of the people', so to speak. A good example is Donald Trump, who frequently claimed in his 2016 presidential campaign speeches that he was the 'voice' of the 'forgotten men and women of [the] country' and that he was 'with you – the American people'.[56] In his January 2017 inaugural address, Trump even claimed that his election and inauguration meant that 'we are transferring power from Washington, D.C. and giving it back to you, the American People'.[57] He also clearly identified himself with the people – or at the very least as their sole legitimate representative – when he said: 'What truly matters is not which party controls our government, but whether our government is controlled by the people'.[58] He added: 'January 19, 2017 will be remembered as the day the people became the rulers of this nation again. The forgotten men and women of our country will be forgotten no longer.'[59] More recently, Trump used similar rhetoric in his 6 November 2024 victory speech, when he said: 'This is a magnificent victory for the American people that will allow us to make America great again'.[60] Similarly, in Britain, Boris Johnson – flanked with 'The People's Government' signs – said during his election victory speech in December 2019: 'You [the people of this country] voted for all these things, and it is now *this government, the people's government*, it is now our solemn duty to deliver on each

[52] de la Torre (n 48) 10.

[53] ibid 66.

[54] ibid 109, xix.

[55] See H Chávez, '¡Yo soy un pueblo, yo me siento encarnado en ustedes!' (*Bolivariana Televisión*, 2016 [2012]) www.youtube.com/watch?v=XPE4ymgVfT8.

[56] See, eg, Donald Trump's 2016 nomination acceptance speech in DJ Trump, 'Full text: Donald Trump 2016 RNC draft speech transcript' (*Politico*, 21 July 2016) www.politico.com/story/2016/07/full-transcript-donald-trump-nomination-acceptance-speech-at-rnc-225974.

[57] See Donald Trump's January 2017 inaugural address: DJ Trump, 'Full text: 2017 Donald Trump inauguration speech transcript' (*Politico*, 20 January 2017) www.politico.com/story/2017/01/full-text-donald-trump-inauguration-speech-transcript-233907.

[58] ibid.

[59] ibid.

[60] DJ Trump, 'Donald Trump's Victory Speech in Full: Transcript' (*Newsweek*, 6 November 2024) www.newsweek.com/donald-trump-victory-speech-full-transcript-1981234.

and every one of those commitments'.[61] Similar rhetoric can be found elsewhere, for example, in Narendra Modi's stress on his 'low-caste' origins in India and his 'self-portrayal as *pradhan sewak* (a servant of the masses)' or in Joko Widodo's (known as Jokowi) call, in Indonesia, 'for a government that serves the *orang kecil*, namely ordinary people'.[62]

In light of these appeals to authenticity and similarity, it is rather unsurprising that populists have been noted for what Pierre Ostiguy, a proponent of the socio-cultural approach to populism, has called a form of 'flaunting of the low'.[63] For Ostiguy, populism is 'characterized by a particular form of political relationship between political leaders and a social basis, one established and articulated through "low" appeals which resonate and receive positive reception within particular sectors of society for socio-cultural historical reasons'.[64] Through these means, the populist shows members of the public that he is 'more authentic than the "old" politicians'.[65] For instance, former Ecuadorean President Bucaram drew on 'popular culture and humor to attack the well-established "white" elites and champion the dignity and self-worth of his supporters', thereby establishing a dialogue with the public.[66] More recent examples of populist leaders 'flaunting of the low' can be found elsewhere. One may think of the late mayor of Toronto, Rob Ford, who publicly admitted to having 'smoked crack cocaine, probably in one of [his] drunken stupors'[67] – thereby making a spectacular demonstration of what Valverde describes as 'individual authenticity' and Foucauldian 'avowal' (truth-telling), in sharp contrast to the allegedly inauthentic, lie-ridden and dishonest liberal cosmopolitanism of what Ford called the 'downtown elites' (distinguished from the more suburban 'average people').[68]

This form of 'flaunting of the low' goes further – it also sometimes translates into other forms, including specific types of dress attire. For example, the populist President of El Salvador, Nayib Bukele, and the Prime Minister of Armenia, Nikol Pashinyan, were both noted for wearing informal attire at public events, including a (sometimes backward-facing) baseball cap, alongside their extensive

[61] See Johnson's victory speech in 'Election results 2019: Boris Johnson's victory speech in full' (*BBC*, 13 December 2019) www.bbc.co.uk/news/election-2019-50777071 (emphasis added).

[62] RJ Heydarian, 'Penal Populism in Emerging Markets: Human Rights and Democracy in the Age of Strongmen' in GL Neuman, *Human Rights in a Time of Populism: Challenges and Responses* (Cambridge, Cambridge University Press, 2020). 143.

[63] P Ostiguy, 'Populism: A Socio-Cultural Approach' in C Rovira Kaltwasser et al (eds), *The Oxford Handbook of Populism* (Oxford, Oxford University Press, 2017).

[64] ibid 73.

[65] A Masala, 'Populism as the Crisis of Political Trust' in A Fabris (ed), *Trust: A Philosophical Approach* (Cham, Springer, 2020) 193.

[66] de la Torre (n 48) xviii.

[67] 'Rob Ford's most unforgettable quotes' (*City News*, 22 March 2016) toronto.citynews.ca/2016/03/22/rob-fords-most-unforgettable-quotes.

[68] Valverde (n 48) 103–104; 109. Valverde raises the hypothesis that '[a]vowal, or rather the successful, felicitous utterances of personal flaws and faults could perhaps be acting – at least for white men – so as to create links between disparate political interests and projects and desires, such that groups with very different economic interests and collective biographies temporarily come together to support a single populist figure'.

use of social media.[69] In the same vein, populists often bring a certain element of linguistic proximity, in addition to the physical, geographical, symbolic and cognitive proximities described earlier. A good example is Trump's use of simple language in his speeches and on X (previously known as Twitter, before he was temporarily banned from that platform) and on his own social media platform, Truth Social. In the same vein, many have noted Trump's 'frequent misspellings, typos and other linguistic errors' in his tweets and posts.[70] Reports even claim that his aides purposively inserted grammatical and syntax errors in his tweets in order to mirror his style[71] and, arguably, to maintain an image of a president close to the 'real', ordinary people.[72] One may also think of former President Duterte's language and frequent invectives.[73]

By doing so, populists tend to put forward a conception of the relationship between the rulers and the ruled, between the representatives and the represented, that is constituted by a logic of proximity, immediacy and authenticity. In the ideal type of 'instantaneous democracy'[74] posited by populists, elected representatives are expected to 'instantiate' the authentic will of the people; the electorate, for its part, is persuaded to identify itself with the populist, notably through appeals to authenticity.[75] This view has garnered support in the academic literature on populism. For instance, in his book *Le Siècle du populisme : Histoire, théorie, critique*, Pierre Rosanvallon argues that populism introduces a form of 'immediate democracy' based on the idea of a substantial identity between the rulers and the ruled and a form of 'substantial representation' in which political representatives are not simply selected (or elected) representatives, but are the 'mirror', 'true image' or even 'other half' of the people.[76] This idea of elected representatives as 'mirroring' public sentiment is nicely captured by Miri Regev, then Israel's Minister of Culture and Sport, when she said: 'I did not come [here] in order to be loved [but] in order to voice the sentiments of the public.'[77] In other words, elected representatives – and even, in some cases, members of the judiciary[78] – are expected to not just be responsive to,

[69] See, eg, J Webber and M Stott, 'Election consolidates power of El Salvador's authoritarian president' (*Financial Times*, 1 March 2021) www.ft.com/content/f09c610a-ef51-495f-93cb-d952970757f1; A Roth, '"He's not a populist, he's popular': Nikol Pashinyan becomes Armenian PM' (*The Guardian*, 8 May 2018) www.theguardian.com/world/2018/may/08/hes-not-a-populist-hes-popular-nikol-pashinyan-becomes-armenian-pm; and ch 4.

[70] See, eg, M Oppenheim, 'Trump's aides deliberately "inserting grammatical errors into his tweets to mimic his style"' (*The Independent*, 22 May 2018) www.independent.co.uk/news/world/americas/trump-twitter-typos-aides-insert-white-house-a8363661.html.

[71] ibid.

[72] G Packer, 'The Left Needs a Language Potent Enough to Counter Trump' (*The Atlantic*, 6 August 2019) www.theatlantic.com/ideas/archive/2019/08/language-trump-era/595570.

[73] See, eg, Heydarian (n 62) 152.

[74] Kuo (n 48).

[75] ibid 558; D Vitale and R Girard, 'Public Trust and the Populist Leader: A Theoretical Argument' (2022) 11 *Global Constitutionalism*; Fieschi (n 48); Diehl (n 48).

[76] Rosanvallon (n 11) 153–155.

[77] Harel and Kolt (n 17) 746.

[78] See, eg, the warning by New Zealand's Justice Minister to 'take note of public sentiment and expectations when sentencing' in the early 2000s, an instance of penal populism discussed in J Pratt and M Clark, 'Penal Populism in New Zealand' (2005) 7 *Punishment and Society* 303, 306.

but also immediately 'instantiate' the authentic will of the people, thereby 'denying the good reasons of a longer time perspective of politics, and favouring the notion of representation as resemblance of the representative to the elector'.[79]

This concept of 'substantial' or 'instantaneous' representation is closely linked to the idea of imperative mandate, which is explicitly prohibited under a number of liberal-democratic constitutions.[80] As Giuseppe Martinico explains, an important feature of populism is 'the idea that representatives must respond immediately to the demands of the people with almost no autonomy in performing their public function, as though bound by a specific contract'.[81] It goes without saying that this conception of representation drastically reduces the autonomy of elected representatives. It is also closely tied to the Rousseauian idea that sovereignty cannot be represented nor alienated: '[t]he deputies of the people [...] neither are nor can be its representatives; they are merely its agents'.[82]

Of course, this idea of identity-identification between the rulers and the ruled inherent to contemporary populism is not entirely new; it has, in fact, underpinned self-government since the Enlightenment.[83] For instance, the idea of representation as sameness and as an instrument of selfhood was arguably a key element of Rousseau's discourse, notably when he wrote that laws are only laws 'when the whole people decrees for the whole people'.[84] It was also a key element of the Anti-Federalists' opposition to Hamilton and Madison.[85] The novelty of contemporary populism, however, lies in the fact that it takes this account of constitutional identity as both sameness and collective selfhood, and reduces it to a conception of representation as a specific form of *sameness* between representatives and represented.[86] By doing so, populists promote a deeply anti-institutional conception of democracy, with the need for a direct and unmediated relationship between the people and the populist leader, merged into a single entity or unity.[87] Moreover, as discussed in more detail below, this phenomenon seems to be exacerbated by

[79] C Pinelli, 'The Populist Challenge to Constitutional Democracy' (2011) 7 *European Constitutional Law Review* 5, 11.

[80] See, eg, Basic Law for the Federal Republic of Germany 1949, art 38(1); Constitution of the Italian Republic 1947, art 67; Spanish Constitution 1978, art 67(2); Constitution of the French Republic 1958, art 27; Weimar Constitution 1919, art 21.

[81] G Martinico, *Filtering Populist Claims to Fight Populism: The Italian Case in a Comparative Perspective* (Cambridge, Cambridge University Press, 2022) 150.

[82] J-J Rousseau, 'On the Social Contract, or Principles of Political Right' in J-J Rousseau (ed), *The Basic Political Writings* (Indianapolis, Hackett, 1986 [1762]) 198.

[83] Rosanvallon (n 11).

[84] JJ Rousseau, 'The Social Contract' [1762] in V Gourevitch (ed), *Rousseau: The Social Contract and Other Later Political Writings* (Cambridge, Cambridge University Press 1997 [1762]) 67, as cited in Corrias (n 48) 23.

[85] Rosanvallon (n 11) 154.

[86] See Corrias (n 48) 23–24. This idea builds upon what Hannah Pitkin calls 'descriptive representation', namely the idea that politicians should 'mirror' public sentiments, but the populist version goes further, in my view, insofar as it implies a form of sameness (or even fusion) between representatives and their constituents. See HF Pitkin, *The Concept of Representation* (Berkeley, University of California Press, 1972) particularly ch 4.

[87] Diehl (n 48), 136; S Issacharoff, 'The Corruption of Popular Sovereignty' (2020) 18 *International Journal of Constitutional Law*.

the rise of social media, which dispenses with the need for intermediary media and allows the populist to provide a means for the public to more directly identify itself with them – rather than through liberal-democratic institutions.

ii. Immediacy, Social Media and the Populist Constitutional Project

The populist appeals to authenticity and the populist conception of representation as sameness are not merely symbolic. They both also have a clear impact on social acceleration and the reorganisation of the spatiotemporal contours of liberal constitutional democracy. By emphasising the need for a direct, immediate and authentic democracy based on the idea of a substantial identity between the rulers and the ruled, they contribute to the current social acceleration discussed in the introductory chapter. Indeed, they put forward a conception of democracy and a constitutional project devoid (at least in part) of means of mediation, from institutional mediators to intermediary media, thereby favouring an immediate and direct communication (and indeed fusion) between rulers and the ruled, between representatives and the represented. Thus, the unmediated and spontaneous populist use of social spaces and the social acceleration to which it contributes are both seen as more 'authentic' than the ponderous, cumbersome and time-wasting processes of liberal democracy, from institutional deliberation and lengthy constitutional procedures to mainstream media filtering.

As briefly discussed earlier, populism is highly wary of intermediaries. Populists often distrust independent and unelected institutional intermediaries, such as courts and electoral commissions, for instance, but their distrust can also extend to mediators and mainstream news media – including broadcasters and journalists. For populists, the best (and most 'authentic') way of conveying their message – and to reduce the geographical, symbolic and cognitive distance between the rulers and the ruled – is through direct and spontaneous means of communication, without mediation. One of the key means to achieve this is through telecommunication channels. In fact, some scholars have gone as far as to claim that this use of the media is 'the *conditio sine qua non* of populism'.[88] This element, too, is far from new. As early as in the 1930s, Colombian populist leader Jorge Eliécer Gaitán was noted for his creative use of the radio to speak directly to the population: '[i]ncorporating popular music – *el porro* – Gaitán succeeded in entering the homes of his followers through his radio spots and transmitted speeches'.[89] He was not the only one.[90] In the US, President Franklin Delano Roosevelt – sometimes depicted as an 'economic populist'[91] – also

[88] M Anselmi, *Populism: An Introduction* (Abingdon, Routledge, 2018) 93.

[89] de la Torre (n 48) 18.

[90] Other populists, including President of Argentina Juan Domingo Perón, were also keen users of the radio, which they used to communicate directly with the people.

[91] Many of Roosevelt's economic policies were influenced by populists, such as William Jennings Bryan and the People's Party, including the progressive income tax. See D Rodrik, 'What Does a True

mastered the radio, 'speaking directly to ordinary Americans without journalistic intermediaries'.[92] More contemporary examples could also be mentioned. In India, for instance, Prime Minister Narendra Modi frequently uses the radio to directly communicate with the public, notably through the abovementioned monthly programme called *Mann Ki Baat*.[93]

Beyond the radio, many populist leaders have made use of the mass medium of television to cultivate their image, which some have called 'telepopulism'. For instance, many remember Hugo Chávez's own television programme, called *Aló Presidente*, in which he commented on recent news and answered phone calls from citizens, interacting with them directly.[94] Former Ecuadorean President Rafael Correa was also an avid user of both television and radio to communicate and interact directly with his constituents.[95] Beyond Latin America, the most emblematic figure of telepopulism is perhaps former Italian President Silvio Berlusconi, who owned three television channels and frequently used them to air television programmes as his main medium of communication, thereby developing a form of social and cultural hegemony.[96]

This phenomenon is, of course, exacerbated by the rise of the social web, particularly of social media platforms such as X (Twitter), Facebook and TikTok, which dispense with the need for intermediary media and provide the means for the public to directly identify itself with the populist leader.[97] Indeed, alongside appeals to authenticity, a key instrument that allows populists to reduce the distance between the elite and ordinary people is social media, with which they have a certain 'elective affinity'.[98] Linked to that use is an indirect claim that the current 'establishment is made of dinosaurs out-of-sync with the present technological era'.[99] Social media is particularly appealing to populists due to its lack of mediation – and therefore its inherent immediacy and direct connection with the people. The latter allows actors to 'speak their mind', without filters and intermediaries that would not only delay their message but also denaturalise their thoughts. By contrast, liberal-democratic elites are said to speak a 'slow' language,

Populism Look Like? It Looks Like the New Deal' (*New York Times*, 21 February 2018) www.nytimes.com/2018/02/21/opinion/populism-new-deal.html. On the influence of other populists – such as Huey Long – on Roosevelt's economic policies (and populist rhetoric), see JB Ludis, *The Populist Explosion: How the Great Recession Transformed American and European Politics* (New York, Columbia Global Reports, 2016) 28–32.

[92] T Frank, *People Without Power: The War on Populism and the Fight for Democracy* (London, Scribe, 2020) 89, referring to F Perkins, *The Roosevelt I Knew* (London, Penguin, 1946).

[93] Bajpai (n 51) and C Jaffrelot, 'Populism, remixed' (*The Indian Express*, 24 March 2017) indianexpress.com/article/opinion/columns/up-populism-narendra-modi-bjp-up-polls-remixed-4582699.

[94] Anselmi (n 88) 63.

[95] He notably had his own radio and television programme, entitled *Enlace Ciudadano* ('Citizen Link').

[96] Anselmi (n 88) 84. See also PA Taguieff, *L'illusion populiste: Essai sur les démagogies de l'âge démocratique* (Paris, Flammarion, 2007) 32–33 and generally.

[97] Kuo (n 48) 560.

[98] For an analysis of the 'elective affinity' between social media and populism, see P Gerbaudo, 'Social Media and Populism: An Elective Affinity?' (2018) 40 *Media, Culture and Society* 745.

[99] ibid 748.

one 'poised against unmediation and impulsivity, and confronting this language signals an impatience with those who do not or cannot speak a simple and readily understandable language'.[100]

These considerations are not merely stylistic or symbolic; they also have practical implications, notably in the way they promote a constitutional project and a form of democracy based on proximity and immediacy. Indeed, beyond language proximity, social media and other modern means of communication can also be useful for populists to directly speak to the people without having recourse to means of mediation (institutional mediation or otherwise) and with a level of immediacy that was previously unimaginable.[101] For example, Turkish President Recep Tayyip Erdoğan was noted for using FaceTime on a live news broadcast right in the middle of the failed 2016 coup d'état attempt, urging his supporters to take to the streets, in defiance of the curfew imposed by the military junta, to demonstrate their support for him.[102] In Brazil, before his election as president, Jair Bolsonaro used the WhatsApp messaging platform 'to distribute misleading information to his supporters'.[103] In the US, Trump used X (Twitter) to criticise the federal judges who had ruled against his 2018 'travel ban', referring to these judges as 'so-called judges'. He and other members of his administration have continued to do so on multiple occasions during his second presidential term.[104] In Armenia, Prime Minister Pashinyan was noticed for calling his supporters, in a Facebook Live address, to blockade the entrances outside courts in Armenia, describing judges as the 'puppets' of the previous regime.[105] Other populists, like former President of the Philippines Rodrigo Duterte, have also been noted for their use of social media like Facebook – including through the creation of fake profiles – to gain power,[106] before threatening to ban the platform after the latter took additional measures to identify and delete fake profiles.[107]

[100] H Bødker and C Anderson, 'Populist Time: Mediating Immediacy and Delay in Liberal Democracy' (2019) 13 *International Journal of Communication* 5960.

[101] L Russo 'Social Media and Democracy' in DJ Galligan (ed), *Constitution in Crisis: The New Putney Debates* (London, I.B. Tauris, 2017) 80.

[102] H Taş, 'The Chronopolitics of National Populism' (2020) *Identities* 1.

[103] Tushnet and Bugarič (n 10) 60.

[104] One can think, for example, of the attacks on District Judge James Boasberg, discussed in ch 2.

[105] 'Pashinyan instigates protests outside Armenian courts calling for transitional justice' (*OC Media*, 20 May 2019) oc-media.org/pashinyan-instigates-protests-outside-armenian-courts-calling-for-transitional-justice.

[106] L Etter, 'What Happens When the Government Uses Facebook as a Weapon?' (*Bloomberg Businessweek*, 7 December 2017) www.bloomberg.com/news/features/2017-12-07/how-rodrigo-duterte-turned-facebook-into-a-weapon-with-a-little-help-from-facebook. See also, generally, A Sinpeng, D Gueorguiev and AA Aruguay, 'Strong Fans, Weak Campaigns: Social Media and Duterte in the 2016 Philippine Election' (2020) 20 *Journal of East Asian Studies* 353.

[107] J Gutierrez and P Mozur, 'Duterte Lashes Out at Facebook After It Takes Down Fake Accounts' (*New York Times*, 29 September 2020) www.nytimes.com/2020/09/29/business/rodrigo-duterte-facebook-philippines.html; A Mendez, 'The Politics of Facebook: Is Duterte After the World's Social Media Giant?' (*ABS-CBS News*, 29 September 2020) news.abs-cbn.com/spotlight/09/29/20/the-politics-of-facebook-is-duterte-after-the-worlds-social-media-giant.

In other words, populists use social media to directly align themselves with the ordinary people, distancing themselves from the language of the elite while establishing direct, authentic and unmediated means of communication with their voters and supporters. In so doing, populists put forward a new conception of representation, one based on immediacy (and, one may add, ubiquity), which brings a certain physical (or virtual) presence and proximity between rulers and the ruled, both of which seem more appealing than a distant political platform or manifesto.[108]

While the focus thus far has mainly been on discursive space, it is worth adding that in some cases, populist discourses will even go beyond rhetoric and means of communication to associate (or link) 'the people' (and, therefore, the locus of power) with a specific spatial location or site, such as a city square, for example. This is precisely what Pashinyan did during the 2018 'Velvet Revolution' in Armenia, proclaiming the 'revolutionary Republic Square'[109] as the 'highest body of the people's power', the site where 'government has been formed', the location to which 'government is accountable' and the site in which 'the people's will' is voiced and expressed – a will that the government is 'bound to follow'.[110]

In short, from a spatial perspective, the populist constitutional project is one of proximity, authenticity and immediacy. Based on the idea of a substantial identity between the rulers and the ruled, populists put forward a conception of democracy that aims to remove means of mediation, from institutional mediators to mainstream media, thereby favouring fast-paced, immediate and direct communication (and indeed fusion) between *gouvernants* and *gouvernés*. Through their emphasis on the need for direct, authentic and immediate democratic means, they help reorganise and redraw the spatiotemporal contours of liberal constitutional democracy. Through their direct and personal connection to 'the people', populist leaders are able to both listen and respond to popular concerns free of mediation and, crucially, 'without having to negotiate the decision through constitutional structures'.[111] The populist project of proximity is thus perceived as more 'authentic' than the distant, ponderous processes of liberal democracy, including institutional deliberation and filtering by intermediaries, from political parties to mainstream media. For that reason, populists are keen users of the social web, which they view as a democratic space that allows them to speak freely, from the heart, immediately and directly to the population, free of unnecessary mediators and intermediaries.[112]

These spatial considerations, however, should not be understood in isolation. They are clearly linked to considerations of time as well. Indeed, for the

[108] Rosanvallon (n 11) 78.

[109] The square in Yerevan where many important gatherings took place during the Velvet Revolution.

[110] N Pashinyan, 'Speech at Rally Dedicated to 100 Days in Office' (*The Prime Minister of the Republic of Armenia*, 17 August 2018) www.primeminister.am/en/statements-and-messages/item/2018/08/17/Nikol-Pashinyan-100-day-rally.

[111] NW Barber, 'Populist Leaders and Political Parties' (2019) 20 *German Law Journal* 129, 130.

[112] Gerbaudo (n 98) 749; Valverde (n 48) 101.

abovementioned appeals to authentic representation to succeed, there appears to be the need for a certain form of timeless, unchanging conception of 'the people' active in the background. This means that populists draw strength both from the promise of the immediate (and proximate), on the one hand, and of 'time immemorial', on the other. Indeed, as we have seen earlier in this monograph,[113] there is a certain tendency amongst populists to aggregate the revolutionary, mystical and eternal 'sovereign people', understood as the unified People-as-One, with transient, temporal and inherently ephemeral electoral majorities at a given point in time – thereby imbuing the latter with the characteristics of timeless unity, permanency and immutability. These questions – and considerations of time more broadly – are addressed in more depth in the third section of this chapter, below.

III. Time: From Acceleration to Urgency, Expeditiousness and Instantaneity

Populists not only dislike intermediaries, viewed as spatially distant and (or) disconnected; they are also deeply impatient with liberal-democratic procedures and processes.[114] From a temporal perspective, they want to do things faster. With this aim in mind, they view the immediate expression of the political will of the People-as-One[115] as preferable to the slower, diluted and/or filtered expression that first passes through institutions, processes and procedures. In the same vein, intermediaries and other forms of mediation are seen as thwarting the 'will of the people' – or, at best, as slowing down its spontaneous and direct expression. At the very least, they are seen as susceptible to introducing a certain form of bias in the expression of the general will. Rejecting these forms of mediation, populists thus often put forward what some have called 'politics of instantaneity'[116] through the use of means of direct democracy and plebiscitary instruments, including referendums,[117] but also through prerogative powers.[118] Their claim is that, in this way, the voice of the people can be directly – and, I would add, instantly – heard.[119]

In this third section of the chapter, I argue that inherent to populism is a sense of urgency that not only emerges in response to social acceleration, discussed earlier in this monograph,[120] but that also serves as a catalyst for it. My argument

[113] Mainly in chs 1 and 2.
[114] See, eg, P Blokker, 'Populist Constitutionalism' in C de la Torre (ed), *Routledge Handbook of Global Populism* (Abingdon, Routledge, 2019) 114; N Urbinati, 'Democracy and Populism' (1998) *Constellations* 110, 110.
[115] Rosanvallon (n 11) 102. See also ch 1 of this monograph for a discussion on the concept of the People-as-One.
[116] See, eg, Corrias (n 48) 12.
[117] See ch 2.
[118] See ch 6.
[119] Corrias (n 48) 12, 19.
[120] Notably in the introductory chapter.

in that regard is twofold. First, I argue that the temporal contours of populist politics are characterised by urgency. Second, through their emphasis on a 'politics of instantaneity', populists often attempt to redraw the temporal contours of liberal constitutional democracy and to circumvent the delays built into it.

A. The Temporal Horizons of Populism: Urgency and Expeditiousness

While there is most often a clear sense of urgency and expeditiousness in the populist imaginary, the spatiotemporal orientation of the populist narrative tends to change slightly depending on whether populists are in opposition or in power.[121] Particularly (although not exclusively) when they are in opposition, populists tend to be both past- and future-oriented, often simultaneously. On the one hand, they often put forward a narrative of dispossession, alluding to a distant – yet still attainable – glorious and idealised past. This historical past is depicted in nostalgic, utopian and even, sometimes, mythical terms.[122] This orchestrated form of nostalgia can be seen, for instance, in the temporal references of Erdoğan's populism, which include nostalgia for the glory of the Ottoman era[123] or in Chávez's invocation of sacred anti-colonial and anti-imperialist figures such as Simon Bolívar.[124] Populists claim to have the willingness and power to bring the people back to this glorious, idealised past. This junction of past and present for a better future is contrasted with the new apparent, elite-driven (liberal) order of historicity, one in which 'the present and the future are seen from the perspective of the past'.[125] This new liberal order of historicity comes with a heavy burden, that of overhauling the injustices of the past, a 'past that does not pass', which is to be repaired with official apologies, criminal proceedings as well as truth and reconciliation commissions, for instance.[126] The populist depiction of the (distant) past is, by contrast, presented under a much more positive light, as an aspirational – and attainable – past. This 'accessible past', as it were, is depicted as spatially proximate – as directly or immediately within reach; and the quest for this attainable past informs both rhetoric and actions.[127] Another

[121] And, one may add, on the subject-matter. For instance, climate change is an emergency that many populists minimise or deny. It is rarely part of the future they envisage. I thank Catherine Dupré for this point.

[122] For an elaboration of (and nuances on) this view, see D Kenny, 'Back to the Populist Future? Understanding Nostalgia in Contemporary Political Discourse' (2017) 22 *Journal of Political Ideologies* 256.

[123] Taş (n 102) 5.

[124] Valverde (n 48) 101.

[125] Garapon, 'Judging the Past: Three Ways of Understanding Time' in Corrias and Francot (eds) (n 3) 17.

[126] ibid.

[127] To give an example, and as Conor Gearty has put it, '[Boris] Johnson's Brexit administration [was] in many ways an exercise in nostalgia, a search for a lost England'. See C Gearty, 'In the Shallow End' (*London Review of Books*, 27 January 2022) www.lrb.co.uk/the-paper/v44/n02/conor-gearty/in-the-shallow-end.

way in which time and space come together is the way in which some populists idealise a 'glorious' past, highlighting not only the 'greatness' of the nation at a given point in time, but also the spaces it occupied at that specific temporal point, including territories that have since then been 'lost'. An example of this is the way Orbán and his Fidesz party invoke the memory of Hungary prior to the 1920 Trianon Treaty, after which the country 'lost' approximately two-thirds of its territory. Both Orbán and Fidesz instrumentalise this memory to promote national unity, using the Treaty – presented as a 'great disaster' or 'national catastrophe' – as a scapegoat for the country's present-day problems and to foster a sense of historical injustice.[128]

On the other hand, and simultaneously, the populist narrative is also resolutely future-oriented. The avowed aim of populists is to restore the above-mentioned mythical, glorious past – as campaign slogans such as 'Make America Great Again' (used by Trump in his 2016 and 2024 presidential campaigns) illustrate. As such, the populist narrative arguably puts forward a non-linear and discontinuous[129] view of history: the past is presented as something to look forward to. In Europe, recent events such as the Euro crisis have also contributed, alongside the accelerated pace of change discussed above, to the blurring of the 'distinct temporalities of the constitutional past, present and future'.[130] Through their rhetoric, populists like Viktor Orbán not only refer to events of the past, they also, 'through marks and measures', shape and reshape that past – and, in so doing, also promise a shape for the future.[131] As Catherine Dupré has pointed out, '[t]he past, in its authoritarian and illiberal incarnations, is becoming increasingly attractive to a growing number of far right parties and may be seen as a future to aspire to for some governments'.[132] In the same vein, populists present the immediate future in a highly dichotomous, Manichean way. According to the populist narrative and discourse, voters must now choose between two options for the future. The first is what the 'elite' offers, namely an extension of the gloomy, dark and chaotic present. On the other is the bright future that populists currently in opposition offer, with its suspension of the present and the promise to restore the long-due grandeur and prosperity

[128] See, eg, L Rutai, 'Why Is Viktor Orban Keeping The 100-Year-Old Treaty Of Trianon Alive?' (*RadioFreeEurope/RadioLiberty*, 24 April 2024) www.rferl.org/a/hungary-treaty-of-trianon-orban-fidesz-ethnic-hungarians/32919124.html.

[129] By contrast, for example, to the Hegelian or Marxist view that history has an end. See Garapon (n 125) 19. For an example of a Hegelian-influenced view of time, see F Fukuyama, 'The End of History?' (1989) 16 *The National Interest* (Summer 1989). On that point, Catherine Dupré takes the view that the widespread or common 'belief in the linearity of time may well be one reason why the Hungarian constitutional developments since 2010 are not taken seriously by the EU'. C Dupré, *The Age of Dignity: Human Rights and Constitutionalism in Europe* (Oxford, Hart Publishing, 2015) 148, fn 41.

[130] Dupré (n 129) 148–150. For Dupré, the traditional temporal boundaries of constitutional time in the European context involve 'clear demarcations between the past, the present as a "never again" rejection of the past, and the future as the possibility of enhanced human rights protection as constructed by the European Court of Human Rights (ECtHR)'. See ibid 142.

[131] NC Lazar, *Out of Joint: Power, Crisis, and the Rhetoric of Time* (New Haven, Yale University Press, 2019) 1–4 (and ch 1).

[132] Dupré (n 129) 149.

(including lost spaces and territories) that were, in their view, unjustly taken away by the liberal elites and their acolytes.

As the elite-led present is depicted as 'the culmination of all wrongs', there is in the ideal-typical populist discourse a certain 'urgent need to interrupt the normal flow of time and accelerate towards the future'.[133] By doing so, populists tend to promote distrust in the current system of governance (broadly understood, including institutions, particularly courts, as well as the media, etc) and the ruling elite, while simultaneously distancing themselves from that system. In doing so, they project the image that they are not part of the elite, of that system of governance that has failed the people – while at the same time disguising, as some would point out, the fact that many populists are also part of the elite, at least the financial elite.[134] Drawing on the appeals to authenticity described in the second section of this chapter, the ideal-typical populist discourse is often expressed in 'highly emotional language', with a certain impatience towards reasoned arguments.[135] As Nick Barber explains, '[f]requently, the discourse of populism is framed in existential terms that seek to inspire fear and panic: The state faces a disaster that only the populist leader, through rapid, and sometimes unconstitutional action, can avert'.[136]

It is precisely in light of these existential threats, and in the context of the abovementioned attempts to distance themselves from the unresponsive elite and the system, that the populists' sense of urgency first becomes apparent. A classic example of populist urgency can be found in Roosevelt's constant speeches about 'the urgent need to take power away from economic elites and to return it to the average American'.[137] One may also think of Trump's presidential nomination acceptance speech in 2016, in which he said:

> Hillary Clinton's message is that things will never change. My message is that things have to change – and they have to change *right now*. Every day I wake up determined to deliver for the people I have met all across this nation that have been neglected, ignored, and abandoned.[138]

[133] FC da Silva and MB Vieira, 'Populism and the Politics of Redemption' (2018) 149 *Thesis Eleven* 1021.

[134] One may think, for instance, of Trump as 'an insider/outsider who mastered the insiders' game and beat them at it'. See R Howse, 'Epilogue: In Defense of Disruptive Democracy – A Critique of Anti-Populism' (2019) 17 *International Journal of Constitutional Law* 643. In a June 2016 speech in Pennsylvania, Trump even 'confessed' his status as a member of the financial elite. He said: 'Our politicians have aggressively pursued a policy of globalization, moving our jobs, our wealth and our factories to Mexico and overseas. Globalization has made the financial elite, who donate to politicians, very, very wealthy. I used to be one of them. I hate to say it, but I used to be one', as cited in L Cooper, *Authoritarian Contagion: The Global Threat to Democracy* (Bristol, Bristol University Press, 2021) 104. One may also think of Silvio Berlusconi, Pim Fortuyn and Jörg Haider, who 'were, already before their career took off, well connected with sections within the economic and political elites, without being truly part of them'. See C Mudde, 'The Populist Zeitgeist' (2004) 39 *Government and Opposition* 541, 560. Looking at a more recent example, the Argentinian president Javier Milei would also probably fit the description of an 'insider/outsider'. See, eg, G Silverman, '¡Che Milei! Argentina, the Far Right, and the Politics of anti-Peronism' (2024) 20 *IERES Occasional Papers* (February 2024).

[135] Barber (n 111) 131.

[136] ibid.

[137] Frank (n 92) 89.

[138] Trump, '2016 RNC Draft Speech Transcript' (emphasis added).

More recently, in his 2024 presidential campaign, Trump stressed the urgent need to wage war on drug cartels, warning that 'if we don't do something immediately, our country is gone!'[139] This element of urgency is also found in the rhetoric of many other contemporary populist leaders, including left-wing populist leaders such as Jean-Luc Mélenchon, leader of *La France insoumise*; in fact, this hastiness can even be found in the title of one of his books: *Qu'ils s'en aillent tous! Vite, la révolution citoyenne*.[140]

Once they attain power, however, the (spatio)temporal contours, horizons and ontology of populism tend to change slightly; populists become less past- (and future-)oriented and become more focused on the present – what some would call a form of 'presentism'.[141] Indeed, contemporary populism rejects the foundations of modern democratic governance, including its extended time horizon. As Samuel Issacharoff has noted, populists in power view the current moment with a certain distrust of the centrality of the institutional order of democracy and, perhaps more importantly, of 'the idea that there is a tomorrow and that the losers of today may unseat the victors in a new round of electoral challenge'.[142] As a result of populist impulses, politics is defined by existential issues, and everything is (often) turned into a binary choice:[143] the people or the elite; the virtuous and pious people or the immoral oligarchy; the hard-working people or the foreign, corrupt financial elite; Ahmet, Mehmet and Ayse or George and Hans.[144] Political disagreement is thus transformed into a more fundamental question of belonging – in short: us or them. By delegitimising the Other, or the enemy, populists imply that very little, if anything at all, can be gained from engaging with the said Other – from foreigners and supranational institutions to mere political adversaries. There can be no 'partial victory' or 'legitimate disagreement' in this binary world: the realm of politics is transformed from a 'challenge among adversaries to an unyielding battle against enemies'.[145] As such, there can only be a winner and a loser.

Populist temporality, therefore, collapses the (spatio)temporal distance between past, present and future: the imagined future of populists 'is not only immanent

[139] Trump, 'Full Election Victory Speech'.

[140] 'Let them all go! Hurry, the citizens' revolution' (emphasis added). See JL Mélenchon, *Qu'ils s'en aillent tous! Vite, la révolution citoyenne* (Paris, Flammarion, 2010).

[141] This is not to say that this focus on presentism (and/or immediacy) is also not a feature of liberal constitutionalism. On the contrary, one can think, for example, of the latter's focus on technocrats asked to quickly solve issues. I thank Massimo Fichera for raising this point.

[142] S Issacharoff, 'Democracy's Deficits' (2018) 85 *University of Chicago Law Review* 485, 486.

[143] ibid. See also Issacharoff (n 87) 1111.

[144] The formula is from the President of Türkiye Recep Tayyip Erdoğan, who put forward a distinctively Manichean worldview, dividing the world into two competing groups, namely the immoral, corrupt, greedy and foreign (mainly American and German) financial elite, on the one hand, and the morally pure, virtuous and resilient Turkish people, on the other. He notably said: 'We know that we are only responsible to our own people and our own righteousness. Our responsibility is to you, not to George or Hans but to Ahmet, Mehmet and Ayse'. See AJ Yackley, 'Erdogan calls on Turks to buy lira in "economic war"' (*Financial Times*, 10 August 2018) www.ft.com/content/f33b9b90-9c8c-11e8-9702-5946bae86e6d.

[145] Issacharoff (n 87) 1111, referring in part to M Ignatieff, 'Enemies vs. Adversaries' (*New York Times*, 16 October 2013) www.nytimes.com/2013/10/17/opinion/enemies-vs-adversaries.html.

to the present but also imminent; it is not positioned in some far-off future time that can only be dimly perceived in the present and, instead, it is about to arrive through promised rupture'.[146] This notion of temporal rupture is reminiscent of the Ancient Greek concept of *kairos*, understood as rupture or discontinuity, which is to be contrasted with the idea of continuous time (*chronos*).[147] In other words, populism can be understood, I would contend, as an attempt to break the *chronos*, the continuous flow of time. Joining time and space, 'the new age of populist fellowship, appearing in the near distance, represents a future that can almost be touched now'.[148]

Once they have obtained a clear mandate, populists put forward an agenda that is resolutely defined by immediacy and anti-institutionalism.[149] The latter can explain, at least in part, the populist recourse to plebiscitary instruments, described in more detail in chapter two. Indeed, from a temporal perspective, populism – as well as the plebiscitarianism it is sometimes associated with – is not particularly 'well suited to institutionalized politics that presume deliberation, procedural order, and compromise'.[150] Galvanised by the popular mandate they have received, populists in power are often impatient to implement their political promises to the people; and they will not hesitate to invoke or employ a wide range of means available to achieve this, including an increased resort to prerogative powers[151] and, in some cases, the replacement of (or significant amendments to) the existing constitutional and institutional framework, shown as the 'symbolic affirmation of the renewal of political unity'.[152]

B. Populism and the Politics of Instantaneity

It is precisely when they gain power that the sense of urgency of populists – and the populist acceleration of political time – becomes the most apparent. Indeed, once in power, populists often put forward a certain 'politics of instantaneity', notably through the establishment (and use) of plebiscitary instruments such as referendums,[153] as discussed in the previous chapter (and as also discussed later in Part II of this monograph), but also through an increased use of executive prerogatives, orders and decrees. Through this politics of instantaneity, populists attempt

[146] da Silva and Vieira (n 133) 21.
[147] Dupré (n 129) 157.
[148] da Silva and Vieira (n 133) 21.
[149] Issacharoff (n 87).
[150] ibid 1112.
[151] See, eg, ch 6. For the increased use of executive (including prerogative powers) in UK context, see, eg, D Lock and T Chowdhury, 'Expansions of Executive Power and Weakening of Democratic Safeguards in 2021' (*UKCLA Blog*, 17 January 2022) ukconstitutionallaw.org/2022/01/17/daniella-lock-and-tanzil-chowdhury-expansions-of-executive-powers-weakening-of-democratic-safeguards/?fbclid=IwAR0BgRWjeEg8Q2w1WktLQ3uw3yGnS1mK7OEawgBzdwPcrX__1hRBNbQKvJQ.
[152] Walker (n 48) 522.
[153] Corrias (n 48) 12, 19.

to redraw the temporal contours of liberal constitutional democracy – described in more detail in the introductory chapter – notably by favouring fast-paced, expeditious and present-oriented institutions and instruments over those that are more slow-paced, deliberative or future-oriented. In the same vein, and in the same way, populists also attempt to circumvent (or disrupt) the delays built into liberal democracy.[154]

One of the main constitutional instruments used by populists to implement this politics of instantaneity and to circumvent the delays built into liberal democracy is the executive prerogative, whose use is often justified on temporal grounds.[155] There are clear links between executive powers and urgency – links that are not always necessarily tied to authoritarian populism as such. For instance, Roosevelt invoked temporality on multiple occasions to justify the need for an 'undelayed executive power'.[156] He also used similar arguments when he threatened to pack the Supreme Court in response to the judicial activism of the Hughes court, which struck down elements of the New Deal in the 1930s. Interestingly, Roosevelt's justification for the use of executive powers in a situation of emergency was not only temporal or time-related, it was also spatial, as he drew analogies with a foreign invader: 'as great as the power that would be given to me if in fact invaded by a foreign foe'.[157] Similar parallels were also drawn by different leaders in the context of the Covid-19 pandemic.[158]

Of course, the Great Depression, World War II and the Covid-19 pandemic were all real and serious emergencies. Nevertheless, these emergencies were all depicted as inherently unpredictable and 'believed to unexpectedly disrupt the normal legal order and its regular temporality, putting the law out of joint'.[159] As such, the use of emergency powers was justified on the basis of unpredictability, with the underlying assumption that 'emergency responses cannot be subject to *ex ante* legal constraints'.[160] The latter assumption is itself based on Schmitt's belief that in situations of emergency, 'the regularity of law, i.e., the temporal continuity between *ex ante* legislation and *ex post* adjudication, has been interrupted and become dysfunctional' – this, in turn, justifies the state, in view of existential threats, to proclaim a 'state of exception'.[161] In that state of exception, when the

[154] Bødker and Anderson (n 100) 5961.

[155] See, eg, WE Scheuerman, 'President Trump's "Get it Done Faster" Emergency' (*Verfassungsblog*, 18 February 2019) www.verfassungsblog.de/president-trumps-get-it-done-faster-emergency.

[156] Scheuerman, *Liberal Democracy and the Social Acceleration of Time* (Baltimore, Johns Hopkins University Press, 2004) 66.

[157] Roosevelt's March 1933 inaugural address, as cited in ibid.

[158] On this, see generally R Girard, 'Accountability, Populism and Expertise: The United Kingdom Government's Response to Covid-19' (2021) *Public Law*.

[159] M de Wilde, 'Uncertain Futures and the Problem of Constraining Emergency Powers: Temporal Dimensions of Carl Schmitt's Theory of the State of Exception' in L Corrias and L Francot (eds), *Temporal Boundaries of Law and Politics: Time Out of Joint* (Abingdon, Routledge, 2018) 108.

[160] ibid 109. For instance, Eric A. Posner and Adrian Vermeule have expressed similar views in that regard. See, eg, EA Posner and A Vermeule, *The Executive Unbound: After the Madisonian Republic* (Oxford, Oxford University Press, 2010).

[161] de Wilde (n 159) 109, 113.

importance of the situation requires a swift and firm response, the sovereign 'is temporarily allowed to derogate from the "rule of law-provisions of the constitution" to protect the constitution itself'.[162]

However, emergency legislation (and sweeping executive authority) can also be used in non-emergency situations, for instance, in response to situations of legislative gridlock.[163] In some cases, however, populists can go (and have gone) further by using executive prerogatives to circumvent the delays (and slowness) of liberal constitutional democracy, even in normal times, sometimes through what Scheuerman calls a 'perversion of the traditional temporal justification for executive-centered emergency government'.[164] Indeed, originally designed to be used in truly extraordinary situations of emergency,[165] Lockean-type, executive-centred emergency powers have been used by populists in less-than-extraordinary situations. For instance, President Trump, after invoking the state of emergency in early 2019 in the context of the 'border crisis' between the US and Mexico, quickly conceded that this was legally unnecessary: 'I didn't need to do this, but I'd rather do it much faster. I just want to get it done faster, that's all'.[166] During his first presidential term, Trump signed a total of 220 executive orders, more than in any other presidential term since Roosevelt's New Deal reforms, which required 955 executive orders between 1933–1937. In 2024, promising to 'quickly save America from Joe Biden's economic disaster', Trump pledged to restore his executive order requiring that for every new regulation, two old regulations must be eliminated, asking Congress to make this requirement permanent.[167] Shortly after his January 2025 inauguration (for his second presidential term), Trump signed a slew of executive orders[168] – including 26 on his first day in office, a record, and 142 in

[162] ibid 118, referring to C Schmitt, 'The Liberal Rule of Law' in AJ Jacobson and B Schlink (eds), *Weimar: A Jurisprudence of Crisis* (Berkeley, University of California Press, 2000 [1928]) 156 and more specifically Schmitt's conception of 'the Constitution' (*die Verfassung*) as the fundamental political decision of the people upon which the constitutional laws (*Verfassungsgesetze*) are founded. On this, see C Schmitt, *Constitutional Theory* (trans Jeffrey Seitzer) (Durham, Duke University Press, 2008 [1928]) 76 and ch 2.

[163] M Tushnet, 'Varieties of Populism' (2019) 20 *German Law Journal* 384.

[164] Scheuerman (n 155).

[165] For the Lockean type of prerogative, see J Locke, *Second Treatise of Government* in *Second Treatise of Government* and *A Letter Concerning Toleration* (Oxford University Press, 2016 [1689]), ch XIV. That said, it is important to mention that some have raised the question as to whether the Lockean prerogative is actually an *emergency* power at all. See, eg, LC Feldman, 'Lockean Prerogative: Productive Tensions' in C Fatovic and BA Kleineman (eds), *Extra-Legal Power and Legitimacy: Perspectives on Prerogative* (Oxford, Oxford University Press, 2013) 78.

[166] 'Declaring a National Emergency Concerning the Southern Border of the United States' (Proclamation 9844, 15 February 2019) 84 Fed Reg 4949, mentioned in WE Scheuerman, 'Donald Trump meets Carl Schmitt' (2019) 45 *Philosophy and Social Criticism* 1170.

[167] DJ Trump, 'Agenda47: Liberating America from Biden's Regulatory Onslaught' (2024) *DonaldJTrump.com* www.rumble.com/embed/v2fmn6y/?rel=0.

[168] For an overview, see, eg, B Barrow, 'Everything Trump did in the first executive orders and actions of his presidency' (*AP News*, 23 January 2025) www.apnews.com/article/what-has-trump-done-trump-executive-orders-f061fbe7f08c08d81509a6af20ef8fc0.

his first 100 days, also a record[169] – and declared a number of emergencies, including a (symbolic) 'national energy emergency'[170] as well as a 'national emergency at the southern border' of the US.[171] Meanwhile, Trump has appeared uninterested in working with Congress on new legislation, having signed only five bills into law in his first 100 days, the smallest number at this stage in 70 years.[172]

In the name of 'efficiency', many populists advocate the primacy of executive powers over cumbersome and unnecessary constraints from legislatures, courts and independent agencies – such as the unitary executive theory in the US, which claims 'that the president is the only constitutionally authorized actor who can exercise executive power so that employee of every government agency must respond to his direct orders'.[173] The message is clear: populists sit above the law and legal constraints, as Trump put it in unambiguous terms when he echoed Napoléon Bonaparte and wrote on social media: 'He who saves his Country does not violate any law'.[174] Courts, for their part, are advised not to be in the way, as Vice-President JD Vance warned in a February 2025 tweet: 'Judges aren't allowed to control the executive's legitimate power'.[175] In short, populists view institutional constraints and 'artificial' delays to the implementation of the 'will of the people', especially those provoked and caused by unelected and unaccountable institutions such as administrative agencies and courts, as illegitimate and democratically unjustifiable.

From a (spatio)temporal perspective, an important element of the populist discourse (or chronotope, if you will) is the claim that distant, unaccountable institutions – from local or national mediators to supranational institutions – are not only far, detached and unresponsive to the needs of ordinary people, or 'undemocratic', as we have seen, but they are also inherently slow. The depiction of the EU amongst key members of the Conservative Party in Britain provides a ready example. One may think of the since-debunked[176] claim by Jacob Rees-Mogg,

[169] See, eg, 'Trump's first 100 days – in numbers' (*BBC*, 29 April 2025) www.bbc.co.uk/news/resources/idt-17e9c07b-93f4-45b3-9558-7590b9eaf3ad.

[170] 'Declaring a National Energy Emergency' (Executive Order 14156, 20 January 2025) 90 Fed Reg 8327.

[171] 'Declaring a National Emergency at the Southern Border of the United States' (Proclamation 10886, 20 January 2025) 90 Fed Reg 8327.

[172] 'Trump's first 100 days'.

[173] KL Scheppele, 'Trump's Counter-Constitution' (*Verfassungsblog*, 21 February 2025) www.verfassungsblog.de/trumps-counter-constitution. Scheppele gives as an example the executive order 'Ensuring Accountability for All Agencies' (Executive Order 14215, 18 February 2025) 90 Fed Reg 10447, which asserts that '[t]he Constitution vests all executive power in the President and charges him with faithfully executing the laws. […] [All] executive branch officials remain subject to the President's ongoing supervision and control'. On the unitary executive theory, see DM Driesen, 'The Unitary Executive Theory in Comparative Context' (2021) 72 *Hastings Law Journal* 1.

[174] (*X*, 15 February 2025) x.com/realDonaldTrump/status/1890831570535055759?lang=en.

[175] (*X*, 9 February 2025) x.com/JDVance/status/1888607143030391287?lang=en.

[176] C Morris, 'UK vaccine approval: Did Brexit speed up the process?' (*BBC*, 3 December 2020) www.bbc.co.uk/news/55163730?fbclid=IwAR0kzueumD2iEZg3nK-W_G3SUPKbbNwNy9pHfmNqofOJ1bXwgl51wnFMEhE.

the then-Leader of the House of Commons, that Brexit had allowed the UK to approve a vaccine against Covid-19 faster than EU countries. He wrote, in a tweet: 'We could only approve this vaccine so quickly because we have left the EU. Last month we changed the regulations so a vaccine did not need EU approval which is slower.'[177]

It is worth noting that the abovementioned anti-institutional considerations are not merely rhetorical or symbolic; they also have concrete, real-life and constitutional implications. First, they can lead to an increased use of the executive prerogative, as we have seen in the US, but also elsewhere, including in the UK.[178] In a similar fashion, they can also lead to the delegation of authority from Parliament (or the legislature) to the executive, sometimes in the form of secondary legislation (and/or so-called 'Henry VIII' clauses in the UK), an element discussed further in chapter six. To be sure, these delegations of authority are not, in and of themselves, unique to populists. For example, Henry VIII clauses have existed in the UK since at least 1888.[179] However, their use appears to have increased in recent years, notably under populist rule.[180]

Second, and in the same vein, the abovementioned increased use of prerogative powers is often accompanied by a drop in legislative activity. For example, in the US the number of legislative initiatives put forward by presidents has dropped steadily since Roosevelt's famous first 100 days (in which he presented the details of the New Deal).[181] Trump, for his part, 'had no significant legislative activity at all during his first hundred days in office [in his first term], and the number of substantial legislative initiatives amounted to zero'.[182] Yet, when they indeed choose to act by way of legislation, populists – impatient to implement what they view as the 'will of the people' – tend to 'favor fast-tracking bills and super-speedy legislative procedures'.[183] Examples of this abound. One may think, for example, of PiS in Poland, which used a fast-track procedure on some '40 percent of legislative acts' in its first full year in power, including 'the most important ones'.[184] In India, the Modi government passed important money bills under the 'guillotine',

[177] ibid. This claim was debunked by the head of the UK's medicines regulator and by the press. See, eg, ibid.

[178] Some commentators have expressed their concern over the 'increased' use of such powers. See, eg, R English, 'Henry VIII Powers v Parliament' (*Counsel*, 7 September 2021) www.counselmagazine.co.uk/articles/henry-viii-powers-v-parliament.

[179] P Seaward, 'Henry VIII Clauses' (*The History of* Parliament, 13 July 2017) www.historyofparliamentblog.wordpress.com/2017/07/13/henry-viii-clauses.

[180] For the increased use of delegated legislation and lessened forms of scrutiny under populist rule, see, eg, C Fasone, 'Catalysing Marginalisation? The Effect of Populist Governments on the Legislative and Scrutiny Functions of the Italian Parliament' (2021) 74 *Parliamentary Affairs* 802 (in the Italian context) and Girard (n 158) (in the UK context).

[181] More precisely, they dropped 'from seventy-six new statutes under Roosevelt, to seven and fourteen under Presidents George W. Bush and Barack Obama, respectively'. See Issacharoff (n 142) 499.

[182] ibid 500.

[183] Sadurski, *A Pandemic of Populists* (Cambridge, Cambridge University Press, 2022) 67.

[184] ibid.

an extraordinary legislative procedure which 'allows the Speaker of the House to put a bill to vote without any discussion'.[185] In all of these cases, the use of a fast-track procedure 'was not justified', Wojciech Sadurski contends, 'by any particular urgency at the time'.[186]

Third, the anti-institutionalism of populism and its impatience (or at least, its focus on speedy processes) also has important implications not just for parliament and the media, as we have seen, but also for the judiciary. As mentioned earlier – and as discussed in more depth in Part II of this monograph – courts have been noted by many for their inherent slowness.[187] Yet, populism puts pressure on courts to 'act fast' and against their very ingrained slowness. An example of this populist impatience vis-à-vis courts can be found in tweets by President Trump, including this one from 2017: 'The threat from radical Islamic terrorism is very real, just look at what is happening in Europe and the Middle-East. Courts must act fast!'[188] As Bødker and Anderson explain, '[w]hat is constructed here is a temporality of immediate action against the slowness of the judicial and legislative system'.[189] Indeed, populists align themselves 'with the immediacy of felt threats stemming from a broken system, threats that are seen as neglected by the judicial and legislative branches'.[190]

A fourth and final element of this politics of instantaneity is a strong willingness to engage in executive-driven constitutional change, whether through the enactment of a new constitution[191] or through a series of constitutional amendments.[192] To be clear, there is nothing inherently populist in favouring constitutional change over constitutional endurance. Nevertheless, there can sometimes be a clash between social acceleration, compounded by a populist focus on instantaneity and constituent (over constituted) power, and lengthy and burdensome amendment procedures. As William E Scheuerman explains, '[a] key desideratum of higher lawmaking is that it "proceed slowly and deliberately"'.[193] As such, at least in the US context, 'toilsome amendment procedures were clearly intended by the framers to decelerate popular debate and exchange in order to ensure its reasonable character'.[194] Yet, this focus on deceleration can sometimes lead to (possibly

[185] ibid. The bills in question include the Finance Bill and the Appropriation Bill. On this, see T Khaitan, 'Killing a Constitution with a Thousand Cuts: Executive Aggrandizement and Party-State Fusion in India' (2020) 14 *Law & Ethics of Human Rights* 49, 67.

[186] Sadurski (n 183) 67.

[187] See, eg, L Francot, 'Suspended in Gaffa: Legal Slowness in the Acceleration of Society' in L Francot and L Corrias (eds), *Temporal Boundaries of Law and Politics: Time Out of Joint* (Abingdon, Routledge, 2018). See also the introductory chapter.

[188] DJ Trump, 'The threat from radical Islamic terrorism is very real, just look at what is happening in Europe and the Middle-East. Courts must act fast!' (*Twitter/X*, 7 February 2017) x.com/realdonaldtrump/status/828797801630937089.

[189] Bødker and Anderson (n 100) 5956.

[190] ibid.

[191] See, eg, ch 5.

[192] See, eg, ch 4.

[193] Scheuerman (n 156) 82.

[194] ibid.

excessive) constitutional rigidity, if not even paralysis, and clash with the populist politics of instantaneity and its anti-institutional stance, thus leading to heightened (and often executive-driven) constitutional change.

In short, populism tends, through the means described above, to speed up political processes and to compress time horizons.[195] These new temporal horizons, which are grounded in political mobilisation and, sometimes, in a profound disregard of (or distrust vis-à-vis) the existing institutions and rules of constitutional governance,[196] can act as a catalyst for constitutional acceleration[197] and, more broadly, social acceleration.[198]

IV. The Populist Chronotope: From Proximity and Urgency to 'Constitutional Impatience'?

What we have seen, so far, is that contemporary populism emerges in a context of 'social acceleration'. The ideal-typical populist discourse (and imaginary) depicts liberal-constitutional democracy as 'distant', 'slow', 'inefficient', 'elite-driven' and 'opaque'. However, populism is not just a critique of liberal democracy; it also comes with its own constitutional project, one that not only aims to remove the distance between *gouvernants* and *gouvernés*, but that is also, as populists would (indirectly) claim, better suited to the contemporary imperatives of temporal efficiency and rapidity.

In this fourth section of the chapter, I take a more normative stance. I suggest, from a liberal-constitutionalist perspective, that while this emphasis on proximity and speed is appealing and has its advantages (and could plausibly be depicted as potentially consistent with constitutionalism), it is nonetheless driven and led by a form of what I call 'constitutional impatience', which can ultimately result in an oversimplification of constitutional democracy. To do this, I focus on what could be described as the 'populist chronotope'. My argument in that regard is twofold. First, through its emphasis on spatial proximity and immediacy, populism not only shortens the distance between the rulers and the ruled; it can also shrink the public sphere, possibly leading to a form of occupation. In the same vein, the emphasis on identity-based claims to authenticity can transform into a form of expulsion or othering. Second, from a temporal perspective, the populist focus on instantaneity and decisionism is often done at

[195] Issacharoff (n 87) 1111.

[196] ibid.

[197] In fact, Paul Blokker identifies populism as one of the main vectors of 'constitutional acceleration', understood as 'the increased propensity of different actors to engage in (formal) reform of the constitutional order'. See P Blokker, 'Introduction: Constitutional Challenges, Reform, and Acceleration' in P Blokker (ed), *Constitutional Acceleration within the European Union and Beyond* (Abingdon, Routledge, 2018) 3, 5–6.

[198] See introductory chapter.

the expense of reflexivity and deliberation. This compression of space and time, as it were, ultimately poses a risk that populists might distort not just the spatiotemporal contours (and separation of powers) of constitutional democracy, but also its constitutive features.

A. From Proximity, Immediacy and Authenticity to Occupation and Expulsion or Othering

It is hard, at first blush and as a matter of principle, to oppose any project aimed at reducing the distance between the rulers and the ruled – at 'closing the gap', as it were, between *gouvernants* and *gouvernés*. Why oppose the idea of (re)connecting the electorate with their elected representatives? Even from a liberal-constitutionalist perspective, there is nothing inherently wrong in politicians speaking directly to members of the public, without intermediaries, particularly in a context in which 'communication and information media [are] subject to powerful plutocratic interests'.[199] On the contrary, proximity is arguably an essential component of a representative democracy: citizens want to voice their opinion and to be heard by political decision-makers and, of course, they want the latter to be attentive to their demands.[200] Moreover, there are some indications in the literature that populism does indeed contribute to this form of spatial proximity. Laura Grattan, for instance, has drawn on Pierre Bourdieu[201] to assert that 'everyday populism' can help build parallel 'spaces of democratic practices and imagination'.[202] In a monograph published in 2016, Grattan further draws on the experience of the Occupy Wall Street movement (amongst other movements) to argue that populism can be the foundation for grassroots mobilisation and the creation of decentred spaces and horizontal powers that have the potential to renew and revitalise democracy in pluralistic and egalitarian ways, a theory of aspirational democratic populism that she calls 'populism's power'.[203] Others, like Robert S Jansen, have praised populism for its mobilisation effects.[204] In France, Federico Tarragoni has written a book in which he praises the 'democratic spirit'

[199] Scheuerman (n 156) 191.

[200] P Rosanvallon, *La Légitimité démocratique: Impartialité, réflexivité, proximité* (Paris, Seuil, 2008) 267. Rosanvallon argues that the legitimacy of proximity, which follows the generality of attention to the particular, is one of the three types of democratic legitimacy, alongside impartiality and reflexivity. See ibid 18.

[201] P Bourdieu, *Outline of a Theory of Practice* (trans Richard Nice) (Cambridge, Cambridge University Press, 1977) 170–171.

[202] L Grattan, 'Pierre Bourdieu and Populism: The Everyday Politics of Outrageous Resistance' (2012) 21 *The Good Society* 194.

[203] L Grattan, *Populism's Power: Radical Grassroots Democracy in America* (Oxford, Oxford University Press, 2016).

[204] RS Jansen, 'Populist Mobilization: A New Theoretical Approach to Populism' (2011) 29 *Sociological Theory* 82.

of populism (*l'esprit démocratique du populisme*).[205] Recent examples of more 'democratic' or 'revolutionary' populism, such as in Armenia in the context and direct aftermath of the 'Velvet Revolution' – discussed in more detail in the next chapter – initially appear to give weight to these arguments.

A closer analysis, however, reveals that the specific type of populist proximity, immediacy and authenticity described above can potentially, in certain circumstances, transform itself into a hegemonic system of simultaneity and occupation, which has the potential to ultimately affect or distort the constitutive elements of constitutional democracy. This appears to be the case particularly in more authoritarian – and right-wing, although not exclusively[206] – forms of populism. To make this argument, I draw on the work of French political theorist Claude Lefort. In his work on democracy and totalitarianism, Lefort elaborated on the concept of the 'empty place of power', which, for him, is an essential feature of democracy. In his view, there is a certain constitutive gap between the ideal of popular sovereignty – namely, the view that political power emanates from the people and that the legitimacy of power is ultimately based upon them – on the one hand, and the distribution of power at any given point in time, on the other.[207] This gap becomes more apparent through democratic representation, as the latter reveals a symbolically empty place between the people as the ultimate holder of political power, on one side, and those who exercise public authority at a specific moment in time, on the other.[208] This 'empty place of power', as Lefort calls it, is seemingly 'impossible to occupy, such that those who exercise public authority can never claim to appropriate it'.[209]

Yet, from a liberal-constitutionalist perspective, the populist focus on proximity and authenticity can sometimes transform into an attempt at occupying (or re-occupying) that very empty place of power.[210] This is done, notably, through appeals to personal authenticity dependent on the persistent (yet now debunked[211]) 'myth of wholly spontaneous and original speech',[212] but also, relatedly, through the creation of the fiction of the People-as-One, as we have seen earlier in this monograph.[213] This fiction is accompanied by an exclusive claim to representation, sometimes under the identity-identification between representatives and represented. As discussed earlier, the latter is a form of 'substantial representation' in

[205] F Tarragoni, *L'Esprit démocratique du populisme* (Paris, La Découverte, 2019).

[206] See, eg, ch 5.

[207] C Lefort, *The Political Forms of Modern Society: Bureaucracy, Democracy, Totalitarianism* (Cambridge, Polity, 1986) 279. See also M Loughlin, 'The Constitutional Imagination' (2015) 78 *Modern Law Review* 11.

[208] Corrias (n 48) 21.

[209] Lefort (n 207) 279.

[210] See also, eg, Corrias (n 48) 21.

[211] See the work of poststructuralists like Jacques Derrida and Judith Butler.

[212] Valverde (n 48) 101.

[213] Particularly in ch 1.

which political representatives are not simply selected (or elected) representatives, but the mirror or even the 'true image' of the people.[214] Yet, as Lefort explains,

> if the image of the people is actualized, if a party [or in this case, the leader] claims to identify with it and to appropriate power under the cover of this identification, then it is the very principle of the distinction between the state and society, the principle of the difference between the norms that govern the various types of relations between individuals, ways of life, beliefs and opinions, which is denied; and at a deeper level, it is the very principle of a distinction between what belongs to the order of power, to the order of law and to the order of knowledge which is negated. The economic, legal and cultural dimensions are, as it were, interwoven into the political.[215]

There is always a risk that the populist project of proximity and authenticity can, under certain circumstances, transform itself into a form of hegemony, simultaneity and occupation. The risk, in that case, and as Jan-Werner Müller explains, is that 'the pure people, or, in fact, the image of a pre-procedural people, as represented by a party or a single leader, will seek to occupy democracy's empty space of power'.[216]

This form of occupation, in my view, can be done in at least five different, albeit sometimes interrelated, ways. A first way in which a populist leader or regime can occupy the empty place of power is by seizing the democratic spaces: at a practical level, the leader becomes everywhere and here. This form of ubiquity of democratic representation leaves little room for cognitive dissidence and pluralism – especially when populists take power. By putting the emphasis on the idea of 'one people, one will', populism creates an environment in which the 'will of the people' can be distorted and used to silence opponents.[217] As Federico Finchelstein explains from a spatial perspective, under populism '[f]ewer spaces are left for political minorities to express themselves and they are presented as traitors to the "real" will of the nation or, worse, as mere puppets of foreign powers plotting against the country'.[218] A good example of this hegemonic occupation of the empty place of power can be found in Erdoğan's discourse. He, for instance, equated himself or his political party, AKP, with the whole Turkish nation, saying: 'If AKP loses, the whole of Turkey will lose, too.'[219] It should be highlighted that this is not mere rhetoric, especially when populists are in power. In the case of Türkiye, the populist project of proximity and authenticity has arguably led to a hegemonic occupation of democratic spaces, with various constitutional amendments tilting the democratic rules of the game in favour of the incumbents; dissidents and members of the press being muzzled or arrested; and various institutions of the state being captured by

[214] Rosanvallon (n 11) 154.

[215] Lefort (n 207) 279–280.

[216] J-W Müller, '"The People Must Be Extracted from Within the People": Reflections on Populism' (2014) 21 *Constellations* 488.

[217] A Weale, *The Will of the People: A Modern Myth* (Cambridge, Polity, 2018) 99.

[218] F Finchelstein, 'Fascism and Populism' in de la Torre (ed) (n 9) 315.

[219] Taş (n 102) 12.

Erdoğan, the AKP and their allies.[220] This hegemonic occupation of the empty place of power in Türkiye has recently become particularly evident, with the arrest and detention, in March 2025, of Ekrem İmamoğlu, Erdoğan's main political rival in Türkiye, a few days before he was poised to be selected as a candidate for the upcoming presidential elections.[221] A similar – but slightly less dramatic – analysis could be made in relation to Hungary and, until recently, Poland, amongst many others.[222]

A second way in which populists can occupy democratic spaces is through the concept of 'the people'. As discussed in more detail in chapter one, populism tends to re-establish the discursive frontiers of the people – and to re-articulate the political space into a highly dichotomised one – 'us' versus 'them'. Populism could thus be understood as a certain reorganisation of spatiality, of spatial boundaries – that is to say, a reorganisation of what is regarded as internal and external, and what is regarded as foreign and what is not.[223] Yet the boundaries of the people – as established or re-established by the populist leader – are not merely symbolic. They can also become real and concrete, as in the case of Trump's travel ban in his first term (and mass deportation of migrants in his second term), or even become physical barriers, as in the cases of Trump's Mexico Wall or Orbán's border barrier (or fence) constructed in Hungary along its border with Serbia and Croatia, combined with anti-migrant rhetoric.[224] The establishment of boundaries – symbolic or real and physical – is thus an important part of the ideal-typical populist discourse, imaginary and political project. As Orbán himself puts it, '[b]orders, after all, are fundamental aspects of life: without borders, existence is impossible. Something which has no borders, no contours, does not exist'.[225]

[220] See, eg, OO Varol, 'Stealth Authoritarianism' (2015) 100 *Iowa Law Review* 1673; OO Varol, 'Stealth Authoritarianism in Turkey' in MA Graber, S Levinson and M Tushnet (eds), *Constiutional Democracy in Crisis?* (Oxford, Oxford University Press, 2018).

[221] S Girit, T Luckhurst and H Khalil, 'Protests erupt in Turkey after Erdogan rival arrested' (*BBC*, 19 March 2025) www.bbc.co.uk/news/articles/c5yren8mxp8o.

[222] For Hungary, see, eg, G Halmai, 'A Coup Against Constitutional Democracy: The Case of Hungary' in Graber, Levinson and Tushnet (eds) (n 220). For Poland, see, eg, W Sadurski, *Poland's Constitutional Breakdown* (Oxford, Oxford University Press, 2019).

[223] See, eg, the *Daily Mail* comment depicting the European Convention on Human Rights as a 'charter for criminals and parasites': 'the "human rights" of the indigenous population must be considered. Do these rights not safeguard them from having dangerous rapists placed in their midst? If they do not, then they are not worth having, and we would be better off without them': 'Human rights is a charter for criminals and parasites our anger is no longer enough' (*Daily Mail*, 15 July 2012) www.dailymail.co.uk/debate/article-2173666/Human-rights-charter-criminals-parasites-anger-longer-enough.html, discussed in J Waldron, 'Rule-of-Law Rights and Populist Impatience' in GL Neuman (ed), *Human Rights in a Time of Populism* (Cambridge, Cambridge University Press, 2020) 46–54.

[224] For a discussion on how states go beyond fixed, state borders and use different bordering techniques and legal tools to exclude migrants through a manipulation of the functional location of border control practices, see A Shachar, *The Shifting Border: Legal Cartographies of Migration and Mobility* (Manchester, Manchester University Press, 2020).

[225] V Orbán, 'Prime Minister Viktor Orbán's speech at a conference held in memory of Helmut Kohl' (*About Hungary*, 16 June 2018) www.abouthungary.hu/speeches-and-remarks/prime-minister-viktor-orbans-speech-at-a-conference-held-in-memory-of-helmut-kohl.

This is not to say, of course, that boundaries are not part of other discourses and imaginaries as well, including liberal-democratic discourses and imaginaries.[226] On the contrary, liberal-democratic discourses – and their institutions – also provide for various forms of othering.[227] In the same vein, the determination of what is (or is not) foreign is not, of course, unique to populism as such. It can be seen in many constitutional orders, for instance, in relation to immigration law[228] and private international law,[229] to name a few. Indeed, as Jacco Bomhoff points out, the 'people – their lives, injuries, and grievances – are really only "foreign" to [any given] constitutional order when that order makes them so'.[230] Yet this phenomenon appears to be even more prominent in certain populist discourses and, in instances of populism in power, in the populist constitutional orders. Put differently, authoritarian populists, especially when in power, go further by excluding and delegitimising opponents – and, as in the case of Türkiye, arresting them and simply removing them from the political sphere.[231] This way, populism can thus lead not just to a form of enclosure of space, but also to a form of expulsion or othering.

A third way of occupying the state for populists is through a shift of focus from the main, traditional institutions of constitutional democracy and modern democratic governance – including legislatures, but also political parties – to individual leaders and politicians, who claim to offer a better, and more direct, link with the people.[232] Through a form of identification between the leader and the people, horizontal accountability and the role of mediators such as political parties are neglected. By suggesting a unity between the leader and the people, horizontal spaces of critique and accountability – including within political parties – are reduced.[233] To be sure, the decline of political parties precedes, to a certain extent, the contemporary rise of populism.[234] The effects of that decline,

[226] On borders, fences and other walls, more broadly, see, generally, E Vallet (ed), *Borders, Fences and Walls: State of Insecurity?* (Abingdon, Routledge, 2016).

[227] See, eg, H van Houtum and T Van Naerssen, 'Bordering, Ordering and Othering' (2002) 93 *Tijdschrift voor economische en sociale geografie* 125.

[228] In this regard, see, eg, L Volpp, 'Imaginings of Space in Immigration Law' (2012) 9 *Law, Culture & the Humanities* 456.

[229] J Bomhoff, 'Immanence and Irreconcilability: On the Character of Public Law as Political Jurisprudence' in M Wilkinson and M Dowdle (eds), *Questioning the Foundations of Public Law* (Oxford, Hart Publishing, 2018).

[230] J Bomhoff, 'Constitutionalism and Mobility: Expulsion and Escape among Partial Constitutional Orders' in J Bomhoff, D Dyzenhaus and T Poole (eds), *The Double Facing Constitution* (Cambridge, Cambridge University Press, 2020) 222.

[231] H Kribbe, *The Strongmen: European Encounters with Sovereign Power* (Newcastle, Agenda, 2020) 146–148.

[232] Issacharoff (n 142) 491; Issacharoff (n 87).

[233] Diehl (n 48) 138.

[234] See, eg, P Mair, *Ruling the Void: The Hollowing Out of Western Democracy* (London, Verso, 2013). In fact, populism may be caused (or exacerbated) by the decline of political parties, possibly forming a feedback loop between the weakness of parties and the rise of populism. See, eg, Barber (n 111). On the decline of political parties, see also M Loughlin, 'The Contemporary Crisis of Constitutional Democracy' (2019) 39 *Oxford Journal of Legal Studies* 443. On the 'incompleteness' of this theory and

however, are compounded by the shift of focus of responsible and productive governance from political parties to individuals. What results is 'the decline of the parties as the locus of democratic politics and the rise of the individual-centered definition of politics'.[235] The cumulative outcome is the collapse of deliberative structures (which require compromise) and their replacement with a personalistic and decisionist leader (who decides in the name of 'the people').[236]

A fourth way populists occupy the empty place of power, as alluded to previously in this monograph, is through the use of plebiscitary instruments, typically referendums. For Lefort, democracy not only involves consent from the people; it must also be understood in terms which make it impossible for political actors to monopolise it and to claim to embody the entire *societas*.[237] Yet, as we have seen in chapter one, what populists sometimes do is instrumentally take the outcome of a referendum – which they have often initiated themselves, after carefully selecting the issue (and, sometimes, the question) – to claim to speak on behalf of the entire people, the People-as-One, understood as unity.[238]

Finally, a fifth interrelated way in which populists can occupy the empty place of power is by 'occupying the state', notably by replacing existing office holders with friends and allies of the regime.[239] A key to achieving this is through legalistic means, including through the enactment of new constitutions, often (but not always[240]) legitimised by constituent assemblies,[241] whose function tends to focus on limiting the power of opponents and dissidents.[242] By doing so, populism not only occupies the state, but also, and perhaps more crucially, the autonomy of public law as a whole. Indeed, public law can be understood as a 'form of discourse through which a range of enduring central dilemmas "over matters of common existence" can be expressed and negotiated, but through which also, crucially, their reconciliation or elimination can be forever deferred'.[243] Yet, the inherent impatience of populism attacks the very openness, open-endedness and 'unresolvability' inherent to public law's functioning and logic.[244] Indeed, constitutional

a more sociological approach to populism, however, see P Rosanvallon, *Counter-Democracy: Politics in an Age of Distrust* (trans Arthur Goldhammer) (Cambridge, Cambridge University Press, 2018) 267-ss.

[235] Issacharoff (n 142) 491.

[236] See, eg, J Scholtes, 'The Complacency of Legality: Constitutionalist Vulnerabilities to Populist Constituent Power' (2019) 20 *German Law Journal*. See also ch 2 of this monograph.

[237] C Lefort, 'Le Pouvoir' in C Lefort, *Le Temps présent: Écrits (1945–2005)* (Paris, Belin, 2007) 981–982, as mentioned in Rosanvallon (n 11) 209.

[238] This possibility is discussed in more depth in ch 6.

[239] D Landau, 'Abusive Constitutionalism' (2013) 47 *University of California Davis Law Review* 213. See also J-W Müller, *What is Populism*? (London, Penguin, 2017) 66–68.

[240] The case of the Fundamental Law of Hungary (2011), adopted by Fidesz (who had then won a two-thirds parliamentary majority) provides a counterexample.

[241] See, eg, Venezuela (1999), Bolivia (2006–2007) and Ecuador (2007–2008), discussed in ch 5. See also, generally, ch 2.

[242] This is discussed in more detail in chs 2 and 5 of this monograph.

[243] Bomhoff (n 229) 64, referring to M Loughlin, *Foundations of Public Law* (Oxford, Oxford University Press, 2010) 157.

[244] Bomhoff (n 229) 64–65.

impatience rejects the multistage process[245] of constitutional democracy, which itself is based on social division, contestation, pluralism and heterogeneity. This multistage process calls for the diffusion of political power across different institutions, spaces and channels, allowing for various and perennial forms of questioning and contestation. Yet, constitutional impatience rejects the multistage nature of this process; instead, it aims for a sort of substantial unity, unanimity and acclamation that eliminates democratic dilemmas and closes or puts an end to the 'perpetual conflict' and 'unresolvability' inherent to both public law and constitutional democracy.

From a spatial perspective, therefore, more authoritarian forms of populism can arguably not only shorten the distance between the rulers and the ruled, but they can also – and perhaps more importantly – shrink the public sphere.[246] By doing so, (authoritarian) populists tend to follow a certain Caesarist conception of the political, one under which the public is not understood as the space of interaction and reflection between individuals and groups (including, possibly, political parties), but is, rather, 'only apprehended under the fixed institutions legitimized by the election' – as espoused, for example, by Napoléon III in France.[247] When seen in this light, some of the ideas embraced by populists appear as not entirely new. Carl Schmitt, for instance, once wrote that

> [c]ompared to democracy that is direct, not only in the technical sense but also in a vital sense, parliament appears [to be] an artificial machinery, produced by liberal reasoning, while dictatorial and Caesaristic methods not only can produce the acclamation of the people but can also be a direct expression of democratic substance and power.[248]

However, these ideas are re-actualised by contemporary, authoritarian populists in a way that is sometimes reminiscent of totalitarianism, especially fascism, albeit ultimately different from them.[249] In the same vein, populism, despite its mobilisation potential,[250] can potentially shrink the democratic spaces by reducing – rather than multiplying – political competition and claims to representation.[251] As Lefort once wrote, '[d]emocracy inaugurates the experience of an ungraspable, uncontrollable society in which the people will be said to be sovereign, of course, but whose identity will constantly be open to question, whose identity will remain

[245] See, eg, Kuo (n 48).

[246] Rosanvallon (n 11) 110.

[247] ibid 113.

[248] C Schmitt, *The Crisis of Parliamentary Democracy* (Cambridge, MIT Press, 2000 [1923]) 16–17.

[249] For instance, populism, contrary to totalitarianism, does not require total subservience to the state. On the connections (and differences) between populism and fascism, in particular, see, generally, F Finchelstein, *From Fascism to Populism in History* (Oakland, University of California Press, 2019). For an analysis of the shared historical background between fascism and populism (but also the differences between the two concepts), see also S Skinner, 'Identifying Dangers to Democracy: Fascism, the Rule of Law and the Relevance of History' in D Giannoulopoulos and Y McDermott (eds), *Judicial Independence Under Threat* (Oxford, Oxford University Press, 2022).

[250] See, eg, Jansen (n 204) 82.

[251] Müller (n 239) 70 and D Prendergast, 'The Judicial Role in Protecting Democracy from Populism' (2019) 20 *German Law Journal* 248. This is not to deny, however, that technocracy also, in its own way, '[shrinks] the space for democratic decision-making'. See Tushnet and Bugarič (n 10) 231.

forever latent'.[252] Yet, this very identity is revealed by populism, which ultimately tends to close it – rather than multiply it.

In short, the spatial perspective reveals a certain gap, or a symbolically 'empty place', between the distribution of power at any given point in time and the ideal of popular sovereignty.[253] This gap is inherent to constitutional democracy. As Slavoj Žižek puts it in clear spatiotemporal terms, 'the emptiness of the place of power is a distance that makes every empirical bearer of power deficient, contingent, and temporary'.[254] Authoritarian forms of populism, however, attempt to close this divide through appeals to proximity, authenticity and, one may add, permanence. Yet, as I have argued in this section, populism's attempt to (re)occupy the place of power can potentially lead to a hegemonic occupation, monopolisation or closure of this very empty place of power. It can do so by 'occupying' democratic spaces – through the entrustment of power to a single figure, the leader, and through the loss or weakening of intermediate structures[255] – thereby leaving little room for pluralism, dissidence and differences of opinion, and possibly leading to forms of expulsion or othering. This raises questions as to whether the populist proximity described above is real or whether it is, rather, a proximity *de façade* – or, as Jan-Werner Müller put it, an 'aesthetic production of "proximity to the people"'.[256]

B. 'Constitutional Impatience', Space-Time Compression and the Oversimplification of Constitutional Democracy?

As we have seen above, populism is impatient with institutions, procedures and intermediaries, which are often perceived or depicted as 'thwarting the will of the people'. More specifically, many populists allege that democratic intermediaries, such as political parties, mass media and other mediating institutions, tend to 'filter out the authentic choices from the people, turning democracy into the instrumentality of the privileged sectors of society'.[257] These institutions – sometimes portrayed by populists as instruments of 'legal impossibilism'[258] – are said to fail to 'give voice to the authentic opinions of the people'.[259] The avowed aim of populists, therefore, is to (re-)create a form of 'true', 'authentic' or 'substantive' democracy based on spatial proximity, immediacy and temporal efficiency, in replacement for the distant, unresponsive, slow-paced and mediated nature of the 'procedural' conception of contemporary liberal constitutional democracy. This

[252] Lefort (n 207) 303–304.
[253] Corrias (n 48) 21.
[254] S Žižek, 'Against the Populist Temptation' (2006) 32 *Critical Inquiry* 559. Žižek therefore appears to adopt a certain spatial understanding of Lefort's 'empty place of power', in contrast to Laclau, for instance, who views such 'emptiness as a type of identity, not a structural location'. See E Laclau, *On Populist Reason* (London, Verso, 2005) 166.
[255] Barber (n 111) 133.
[256] Müller (n 239) 43.
[257] Kuo (n 48) 557.
[258] This neologism was created by the leader of the PiS in Poland, Jarosław Kaczyński. See ch 2.
[259] Kuo (n 48) 558.

form of space-time compression, as it were, is partly the result of social acceleration; the latter accelerates technological and social change and innovation, in a way that sometimes overcomes and collapses existing spatial barriers, as discussed at more length in the introductory chapter.[260] However, it is exacerbated, I would argue, by contemporary populism, which, in its more authoritarian forms, tends to substitute process for speed and, in some cases, institutions for personalisation.[261]

Yet, I contend that this instantaneous[262] and deeply anti-institutional[263] conception of 'democracy' put forward by (authoritarian-leaning) populists ultimately amounts to an oversimplification of constitutional democracy. Indeed, the latter is premised on a complex constellation of different components, all interacting and interplaying together. These elements, in my view and building on Issacharoff, Rosanvallon and others, include popular sovereignty (and political participation more broadly), free elections, political parties and competition, political intermediaries, stable institutions of state and a vibrant civil society, amongst other components.[264] These components are linked and interact with each other through a complex, multistage (and sometimes lengthy) process of constitutional governance.[265]

Yet, and as Ming-Sung Kuo argues forcefully, populism tends to transform the complex multistage decision-making process of constitutional democracy into a simple, instantaneous process that affects constitutional democracy's structure of articulated politics.[266] Populism's 'constitutional impatience', instantaneousness and proximity thus leave little room for deliberation and what Rosanvallon calls 'reflexive democracy'.[267] In other words, the populists' 'immediate' conception of democracy goes beyond the populist call for a more 'direct' form of democracy. If the latter rejects the delegation of political power to representatives, the former goes even further insofar as it rejects not only the delegation of power, but also the interface of representative democracy, that is to say, 'the institution or procedure which contributes functionally to the formation of collective expression'.[268] As a result, the immediate democracy of populism rejects all reflexivity of the social.[269] It rejects, in other words, the 'openness, learning and self-correction, inherent in

[260] See, eg, Rosa (n 11); H Rosa, 'Social Acceleration: Ethical and Political Consequences of a Desynchronized High-Speed Society' (2003) 10 *Constellations*; WE Scheuerman, 'Liberal Democracy and the Empire of Speed' (2001) 34 *Polity* 41.

[261] On the latter point, see D Landau, 'Personalism and the Trajectories of Populist Constitutions' (2020) 16 *Annual Review of Law and Social Science*.

[262] Kuo (n 48).

[263] Issacharoff (n 87) 31.

[264] ibid. See also S Issacharoff, 'Safeguarding Democratic Institutions' (*Verfassungsblog*, 29 April 2017) www.verfassungsblog.de/safeguarding-democratic-institutions.

[265] Kuo (n 48).

[266] ibid, 556.

[267] See Rosanvallon (n 200) 195–215; in English, see P Rosanvallon, *Democratic Legitimacy: Impartiality, Reflexivity, Proximity* (trans Arthur Goldhammer) (Princeton, Princeton University Press, 2011) 137–147.

[268] Rosanvallon (n 11) 178 (my translation).

[269] ibid.

the right of the opposition and ordinary citizens to contest decisions, goals, and norm interpretations'.[270]

This emphasis on expeditiousness and immediacy – as expressed mainly by (and through) the executive – thus often comes at the expense of process, contestation and deliberation. Yet, deliberation is not a mere aspiration; it is ingrained not only in the ideal of constitutional democracy, but also in its institutions. As Issacharoff puts it, '[t]he central claim to superior competence of democracies is not the process of governance but the outputs that result; deliberation is necessarily slower and more complicated than decree'.[271] In that regard, legislatures have an important deliberative function, which goes back in part to Montesquieu, John Stuart Mill and Alexander Hamilton. Locke makes it clear that the supreme power is the legislative power, and that the executive power is subordinate to it.[272] Yet, what we are currently witnessing is the authoritarian-populist 'instantaneisation' and 'executivisation' of political power, namely a gradual transfer of political power to the executive. As discussed earlier, the populist reliance on executive rule has strong Schmittian overtones. In constitutional terms, populists follow Carl Schmitt's main argument that the chief executive (be it a president or a prime minister) is the real 'guardian of the constitution' and, therefore, the ultimate legal authority.[273] Liberal institutions like legislatures and courts, in particular, are left to a secondary role – when they are not captured.

It could be added, from a liberal-constitutionalist perspective, that these anti-institutionalist attacks on courts are not necessarily limited to courts as institutions (or political actors); they can also have clear implications for constitutional and fundamental rights.[274] As Jeremy Waldron has pointed out, these rights usually seek 'to maintain procedural Rule-of-Law values in the face of pressure brought by an impatient public for quick action on law-and-order issues and swift punishment for those accused of offenses'.[275] Populist leaders are unlikely to get in the way of these 'impatient demands for more expedited forms of justice'.[276] On the contrary, they tend to support (and perhaps even catalyse) these demands for swifter (and sometimes harsher) action against those accused of violent crimes, for instance.[277] Examples of this abound, from Duterte in the Philippines to Trump in the US. One may think, for instance, of

[270] A Arato and JL Cohen, *Populism and Civil Society: The Challenge to Constitutional Democracy* (Oxford, Oxford University Press, 2022) 122.

[271] Issacharoff (n 142) 514.

[272] Locke (n 165) 75. See also introductory chapter.

[273] C Schmitt, *Political Theology: Four Chapters on the Concept of Sovereignty (trans George Schwab)* (Chicago, University of Chicago Press, 2006 [1922]). See also D Dyzenhaus, 'Lawyer for the Strongman' (*Aeon*, 12 June 2020) www.aeon.co/essays/carl-schmitts-legal-theory-legitimises-the-rule-of-the-strongman.

[274] See, eg, Blokker (n 47) 549. See also, generally, Neuman (ed) (n 62). For a completely different approach, namely how populist actors increasingly and deliberately deploy human rights discourses, see F Mégret, 'Human Rights Populism' (2022) 13 *Humanity* 240.

[275] Waldron (n 223) 47.

[276] ibid 53.

[277] See also the discussion on penal populism in ch 2.

Trump's comments in November 2017 about the speed of US terrorism trials. He said: 'We have come up with punishment that's far quicker and far greater than the punishment these animals are getting now. They'll go through court for years.'[278] He added: 'We need quick justice and we need strong justice, much quicker and much stronger than we have right now. Because what we have right now is a joke and it's a laughingstock.'[279] Waldron points out that this expression of impatience by populist leaders is not insignificant, because 'patience and long drawn-out procedures are exactly what the procedural aspect of the Rule of Law seems to require'.[280] One may also add, drawing on Lefort, that rights are not merely liberal hindrances on democracy; they are also 'one of the generative principles of democracy'.[281] To be sure, it is not only populist leaders who put forward these anti-rights views; they are also shared by some voters, who – as Yascha Mounk has noted – 'are growing impatient with independent institutions and less and less willing to tolerate the rights of ethnic and religious minorities'.[282] Nevertheless, populist leaders are keen to capitalise on – and perhaps even instrumentalise – this popular impatience and transform it into a form of 'constitutional impatience'.

Indeed, the temporal perspective shows that populists often favour quick, efficient executive decision-making over long and tedious legislative processes, as well as new constitutions over long and burdensome constitutional amendment processes. For populists, if liberal-democratic procedures and intermediaries were perhaps justified in an era in which direct democracy had obvious spatial and temporal impracticalities (especially in geographically large states), as Montesquieu and Madison pointed out more than two centuries ago,[283] this justification no longer stands today, with the advent of technology. Yet, the new, 'instantaneous' conception of democracy put forward by populists, which is mainly based on a 'pursuit of unmediated politics at the expense of democratic representation and deliberation'[284] – notably through decisionism (if not acclamation) and the extensive use of plebiscitary instruments – is arguably based on a rather primitive concept of democracy, without prior rules or preconditions, and with little (if any) deliberation. Yet, politics requires plural voices,[285] not consensus

[278] Waldron (n 223) 47, referring to G Kessler, 'President Trump's statement that the speed of U.S. terrorism trials "is a laughingstock"' (*The Washington Post*, 6 November 2017) www.washingtonpost.com/news/fact-checker/wp/2017/11/06/president-trumps-statement-that-the-speed-of-u-s-terror-cases-is-a-laughingstock.

[279] ibid.

[280] ibid.

[281] Arato and Cohen (n 270), drawing on Lefort (n 207) 256–260.

[282] Mounk (n 13) 13.

[283] Scheuerman (n 156) 44, referring to J Madison [Publius], 'Federalist No 10: The Utility of the Union as a Safeguard Against Domestic Faction and Insurrection' (22 November 1787) and Montesquieu, *De l'Esprit des lois* (Paris, Barillot, 1748).

[284] Kuo (n 48).

[285] J Rawls, *Political Realism* (New York, Columbia University Press, 1996). Albert Weale takes from John Rawls 'the idea that plural voices are the predictable consequence of human reasoning working under free institutions'. See Weale (n 217) 100, 121.

or acclamation. Through its focus on expeditiousness and decisionism, populism thus tends to substitute process for speed – and, in doing so, to close off debate. The result, I contend, is a spatiotemporal compression – a chronotope that risks oversimplifying constitutionalism and, more broadly, constitutional democracy, which is premised on 'slowing down': keeping every position open to revision, indefinitely deferring any final decision, and thus maintaining the 'empty place' of democracy.[286]

V. Conclusion

In this chapter, I have introduced and elaborated on the concept of 'constitutional impatience', namely the way in which populists take advantage of the existing social acceleration and the (spatio)temporal contours of liberal constitutional democracy in order to put forward an alternative conception of democratic representation and a constitutional project based on spatial proximity, as well as temporal efficiency and rapidity. I have argued, more specifically, that populists tend to be impatient with liberal-democratic procedures and processes, which are perceived and depicted as slow-paced, passive and unresponsive.

From a spatial perspective, populism is based upon proximity, similarity and authenticity. Following the idea of a substantial identity between the rulers and the ruled, populists put forward a conception of democracy and a constitutional project that aims to remove means of mediation, from institutional mediators to mainstream media, thereby favouring fast-paced, immediate and direct communication (and indeed fusion) between *gouvernants* and *gouvernés*. Through their emphasis on the need for direct, authentic, spontaneous and immediate democratic means, they help reorganise and redraw the spatiotemporal contours of liberal democracy.

From a temporal perspective, populists want to do things faster: the temporal orientation of populist politics is characterised by a sense of urgency and expeditiousness, which acts as a catalyst for the social acceleration of time. Rejecting liberal-democratic forms of mediation, populists often put forward a 'politics of instantaneity', which focuses on means of direct democracy and the (re-)politicisation of liberal-democratic institutions, including courts, but also constitutions and other legal instruments. Their claim is that by redrawing the temporal contours of liberal constitutional democracy and circumventing the delays built into it, the voice of the people can be directly and immediately heard.[287]

However, from a more normative perspective, this populist chronotope – or this form of what I have called 'constitutional impatience' – runs the risk of

[286] See Bomhoff (n 229) 81.
[287] Corrias (n 48) 12, 19.

oversimplifying constitutional democracy. First, through its emphasis on spatial proximity, immediacy and authenticity, populism not only shortens the distance between the rulers and the ruled; it can also shrink the public, discursive space between the state and the private sphere, possibly leading to a form of occupation. In the same vein, the emphasis on identity-based claims to authenticity can lead to forms of expulsion or othering. Second, from a temporal perspective, the populist focus on expeditiousness, instantaneity and decisionism is often done at the expense of reflexivity, deliberation and exchange of ideas, substituting process for speed.

In the end, to reemploy the Bakhtinian concept of the chronotope mentioned in the introductory chapter,[288] what this analysis ultimately reveals is that populist time shapes populist space, and vice versa. The dynamics of populist impatience tend to shrink, as it were, the spatial distance between *gouvernants* and *gouvernés*, between the leader and the ruled. Yet, the proximity and authenticity of the populist space also, in turn, shapes and contributes to the existing acceleration of political time by removing the need for institutional and political intermediaries, from the media to legislatures and courts. The result is a compression of space and time, a 'constitutional impatience' that can potentially lead to spatiotemporal occupation and, perhaps most importantly, distort not just the temporal contours of constitutional democracy, but also some of its constitutive features. This 'constitutional impatience', I contend – with its focus on immediacy, proximity, speedy and concentrated decision-making in both space and time – not only challenges the spatiotemporal contours of liberal constitutional democracy; it is also likely to collapse what is worth protecting about the very idea of constitutionalism.

[288] Namely, 'the intrinsic connectedness of spatial and temporal relationships that are artistically expressed in literature'. See M Bakhtin, *The Dialogic Imagination: Four Essays* (Austin, University of Texas Press, 1981) 84, as cited in Valverde (n 2) 9–10.

PART II

Responding to Populism: Questioning the Role of the Judiciary against the 'Constitutional Impatience' of Populism

4

Revolution, Democratisation and Judicial Obstruction in Armenia

I. Introduction

In the first part of this monograph, particularly in chapter three, I discussed how populism can sometimes involve a form of 'constitutional impatience', namely the way in which some populists take advantage of the existing social acceleration and the (spatio)temporal contours of liberal democracy in order to put forward an alternative conception of democratic representation based on spatial proximity as well as temporal efficiency and rapidity. In this second part of the book, I examine, through three different case studies, how courts have responded to this form of constitutional impatience and its inherent focus on speed, proximity and, in some cases, occupation. As mentioned in the introductory chapter, the purpose of this second part is to test, question and ultimately challenge the optimistic view of constitutional courts as potential bulwarks against authoritarian, self-aggrandising populists, broadly speaking, and, more specifically, Ming-Sung Kuo's claim that courts can play the role of institutional decelerators in response to the 'instantaneous' conception of democracy put forward and defended by populists.[1] As we will see in this part of the monograph, populism's relationship with the judiciary – and with constitutionalism more broadly – yields divergent tensions and impacts, which challenge assumptions regarding both the institutional role of courts and the nature of constitutionalism itself.

In this first case study, I examine an understudied example, namely that of Armenia in the months that followed the popular uprising that took place there in April–May 2018, often referred to as the 'Velvet Revolution'.[2] The aftermath of the uprising can be viewed as a prototypical and (or) paroxysmal example of a clash between a popular and newly elected prime minister and a hostile and defiant constitutional court with strong ties to a previous regime. In doing so, I suggest that courts can potentially become institutional obstructors by blocking the reforms of a newly elected, democratic government replacing a semi-authoritarian

[1] M-S Kuo, 'Against Instantaneous Democracy' (2019) 17 *International Journal of Constitutional Law*. See also discussion in introductory chapter.

[2] See, eg, L Broers and A Ohanyan (eds), *Armenia's Velvet Revolution: Authoritarian Decline and Civil Resistance in a Multipolar World* (London, IB Tauris, 2021).

regime. The analysis is divided into six sections. In the next section (section II), I begin by discussing the factual background, with a focus on the 2018 Velvet Revolution. I then – in the third section – analyse Nikol Pashinyan's 'constitutional impatience', both while in opposition and in power. Section IV focuses on Pashinyan's proposed reforms to the judiciary – and the ensuing standoff between his government and the Constitutional Court. Then, in the fifth section, I address the possibility that Pashinyan's populism may in fact be an instance of 'revolutionary' or 'democratic' populism, which is rarely accounted for in the legal literature on populism, and that the judicial response to Pashinyan's populism is more akin to a form of 'institutional obstruction' than an instance of what Kuo calls 'judicial deceleration'. These elements, I suggest, highlight the possibility of a more 'positive' relationship between populism and constitutionalism than is generally believed. Section IV, finally, concludes and briefly introduces the next case study.

II. Background: The 2018 'Velvet Revolution'

It all began with a march. On 31 March 2018, a man began a two-week, 120-km 'Take a step' (*K'ayl ara*) protest march across Armenia.[3] The man in question, 42-year-old Nikol Pashinyan, was protesting against strong signs that members of the ruling party, the Republican Party of Armenia (RPA), were planning to nominate then-President Serzh Sargsyan as Prime Minister, despite the fact that Sargsyan was legally barred, under the Constitution, from running for a third presidential term. However, a series of constitutional amendments – drafted by the ruling party between 2013 and 2015 in a process that featured minimal public consultation[4] – had recently transformed Armenia from a presidential to a parliamentary republic, with the transfer of several executive powers from the President to the Prime Minister, the latter being appointed by a parliamentary majority.[5] These constitutional amendments were approved in a referendum in December 2015 by 63 per cent of Armenian voters, but with a minimal turnout (51 per cent) and amid claims of widespread fraud, including bribery, coercion and ballot box stuffing.[6]

[3] L Broers, 'Introduction: An Unlikely Transition?' in Broers and Ohanyan (eds) (n 2) 4.

[4] ibid 2.

[5] M Lanskoy and E Suthers, 'Armenia's Velvet Revolution' (2019) 30 *Journal of Democracy* 85, 91. See also Venice Commission, *First Opinion on the Draft Amendments to the Constitution (Chapters 1 to 7 and 10) of the Republic of Armenia* (Opinion No 757/2014, 29 October 2015) CDL-AD(2015)037; Venice Commission, *Second Opinion on the Draft Amendments to the Constitution (In Particular to Chapters 8, 9, 11 to 16) of the Republic of Armenia* (Opinion No 757/2014, 28 October 2015) CDL-AD(2015)038.

[6] See ODIHR Election Observation Mission, 'Republic of Armenia: Constitutional Referendum, 6 December 2015 – Final Report' (*OSCE/ODIHR*, 5 February 2016) www.osce.org/files/f/documents/7/9/220656.pdf 2. See also A Iskandaryan, 'The Velvet Revolution in Armenia: How to Lose Power in Two Weeks' (2018) 26 *Demokratizatsiya* 465, 473; Z Weise, 'Armenia's disputed move toward true democracy' (*Politico*, 6 April 2018) www.politico.eu/article/armenia-true-democracy-disputed-move-eu-agreement-turkey; AFP, 'Armenia votes to curb presidential powers in disputed referendum' (*The Guardian*, 7 December 2015) www.theguardian.com/world/2015/dec/07/armenia-vote-disputed-referendum-president-powers.

Crucially, Sargsyan had pledged, shortly before this referendum, not to run for office again, whether as President or Prime Minister.[7] However, by the end of March 2018 – that is, a year after parliamentary elections which had seen Sargsyan's RPA win an absolute majority in Parliament amid fresh claims of vote-buying and intimidation of voters[8] – there were growing signs that Sargsyan was, in fact, planning to sidestep the two-term limit and seek the RPA's nomination as Prime Minister.[9] At the time, Sargsyan, the executive, and the RPA-controlled Parliament were experiencing abysmal levels of support and trust amongst the general population. For instance, a late 2017 Caucasus Barometer poll revealed that only 17 per cent of the respondents reported they trusted then-President Sargsyan; while 65 per cent said they distrusted him.[10] Similarly, 59 per cent of respondents said they distrusted the executive government.[11] For its part, the RPA-dominated Parliament was also experiencing record low levels of trust, with only 12 per cent of respondents reporting they 'fully' or 'rather' trusted Parliament in October 2017.[12]

It is in that context that Pashinyan, a former journalist, a critic of the regime and the leader of a small opposition party in Parliament, began his two-week 'Take a step' march from Gyumri, Armenia's second city, to Yerevan, the country's capital, accompanied by a handful of supporters. Initially prompted by 'widespread disillusionment with socioeconomic decline, persistent insecurity and authoritarian encroachment',[13] the protests – until then carried out on a relatively small scale – gradually intensified after 11 April 2018, when Sargsyan announced that he would, after all, accept the RPA's nomination as Prime Minister despite his earlier promise not to run for office again. Sargsyan's decision sparked popular outrage: in the following days, after Pashinyan's march had finally reached Yerevan, peaceful protests intensified across the capital, under the slogan 'Take a step, reject Serzh!' (*K'ayl ara, Merzhir Serzhin!*).[14] The aim of the protests, coordinated by Pashinyan through daily Facebook livestreams but carried out in a decentralised

[7] A Grigoryan, 'Armenia's Path to Democratization by Recursive Mass Protests' (2019) 7 *Caucasus Survey* 157, 165; Weise (n 6).

[8] See ODIHR Election Observation Mission, 'Republic of Armenia: Parliamentary Elections, 2 April 2017 – Final Report' (*OSCE/ODIHR*, 10 July 2017) www.osce.org/files/f/documents/6/7/328226.pdf, 2. See also, eg, 'Transparency International: 45 cases of Armenia election bribe distribution, promise were recorded in 10 days' (*NEWS.am*, 29 March 2017) www.news.am/eng/news/381523.html.

[9] For a discussion of presidential term limit evasion, see, generally, M Versteeg et al, 'The Law and Politics of Presidential Term Limit Evasion' (2020) 120 *Columbia Law Review* 173.

[10] 'Caucasus Barometer 2017 (Armenia) – TRUPRES: Trust towards President' (Caucasus Research Resource Center) www.caucasusbarometer.org/en/cb-am/TRUPRES.

[11] 'Caucasus Barometer 2017 (Armenia) – TRUEXEC: Trust towards Executive government' (Caucasus Research Resource Center) www.caucasusbarometer.org/en/cb-am/TRUEXEC.

[12] 'Caucasus Barometer 2017 (Armenia) – TRUPARL: Trust towards Parliament' (Caucasus Research Resource Center) www.caucasusbarometer.org/en/cb2017/TRUPARL.

[13] Broers (n 3) 1.

[14] L Abrahamian and G Shagoyan, 'Velvet Revolution, Armenian Style' (2018) 26 *Demokratizatsiya* 509, 521. This slogan comes from the melding of Pashinyan's 'K'ayl ara' march with local protests that had begun on 12 April 2018 under the slogan 'Merzhir Serzhin'. See Broers (n 3) 4.

manner,[15] was very clear: it was to stop Sargsyan from being installed as Prime Minister of Armenia on 17 April 2018. And the strategy in that regard was based on civil disobedience: the plan, for that day, was to block the streets surrounding Parliament to prevent Members of Parliament from voting and confirming Sargsyan's nomination.[16]

While Sargasyan was eventually appointed Prime Minister on that day, it was a short-lived victory for the RPA; it had become clear, by then, that what was originally a marginal, small-scale protest led by Pashinyan had gradually given way to a country-wide popular uprising which quickly came to be known as the Velvet Revolution.[17] The revolution was dubbed 'velvet' by reference to the bloodless 1989 revolution in Czechoslovakia.[18] The use of the 'velvet' adjective was seen as a call to both the authorities and the protestors to remain peaceful and to abstain from using violence, a call that was for the most part respected by both sides.[19]

The Velvet Revolution was carried out successfully: protests continued to grow in the capital in the following days. Over 100,000 people (some estimate between 150,000 and 200,000 people)[20] – in a country with a total population of less than three million – gathered in peaceful protests in and around Republic Square, in Yerevan.[21] On 23 April 2018, as soldiers began to join protests, Sargsyan admitted he had 'got it wrong'[22] and resigned – that is, just over three weeks after the beginning of Pashinyan's 'My Step' protest march and just 11 days after the beginning of the large-scale protests and civil disobedience.[23] Karen Karapetyan, a former Prime Minister, initially replaced Sargsyan in the post, but the mass protests continued. On 1 May 2018, a special session took place in Parliament to elect a new Prime Minister, but Pashinyan failed to secure the necessary number of votes.[24] However, on 8 May 2018, as nonviolent protests and acts of civil disobedience were

[15] A Ishkanian, 'Armenia's Unfinished Revolution' (2018) 117 *Current History* 271, 272; Abrahamian and Shagoyan (n 14) 523–525.

[16] Abrahamian and Shagoyan (n 14) 521.

[17] The term 'revolution' is widely used to describe the events that took place between 17 April 2018, the beginning of Serzh Sargsyan's term (as Prime Minister), and 8 May 2018, the date Nikol Pashinyan was appointed Prime Minister.

[18] The use of this adjective should not be confused with the 'colour revolutions' which took place in certain countries of the post-Soviet space, including the 'Rose Revolution' in neighbouring Georgia under the leadership of Mikhail Saakashvili or the 'Orange Revolution' in Ukraine. Anna Ohanyan argues that the uprising in Armenia differs from the events that took place in these countries given its 'decentralised' and 'socially rooted' nature, as opposed to the 'elite-driven' colour revolutions. See A Ohanyan, 'Velvet Is Not a Colour' in Broers and Ohanyan (eds) (n 2) 25. See also A Ohanyan, 'Armenia's Democratic Dreams' (*Foreign Policy*, 7 November 2018) www.foreignpolicy.com/2018/11/07/armenias-democratic-dreams.

[19] Abrahamian and Shagoyan (n 14) 513–514. That said, it should be noted that almost 200 protesters were arrested on 20 April 2018. Pashinyan himself (and some of associates) were also arrested on or around 22 April 2018. See Broers (n 3) 4.

[20] Abrahamian and Shagoyan (n 14) 521; Ishkanian (n 15) 272.

[21] Abrahamian and Shagoyan (n 14) 521.

[22] R Demytrie, 'Why Armenia 'Velvet Revolution' won without a bullet fired' (*BBC*, 1 May 2018) www.bbc.co.uk/news/world-europe-43948181.

[23] Ohanyan (n 18).

[24] Grigoryan (n 7) 171.

still paralysing the country, Pashinyan was finally elected as Prime Minister by a parliamentary vote of 59 to 42, marking the success and end of the initial stage of the Revolution.[25] In December 2018, early elections – widely seen as the first free and fair elections in Armenia in decades[26] – were called, and Pashinyan's My Step Alliance received 70.42 per cent of the vote and 88 of the 132 seats in the unicameral Parliament,[27] bringing to a dramatic end to the 20-year rule of the RPA.[28]

The success of the Velvet Revolution was somewhat surprising to many observers, especially considering that some earlier protests, like the 1 March 2008 protests, had ended in a bloodbath.[29] For Armine Ishkanian, Pashinyan's My Step movement succeeded where others had failed for three main, interconnected reasons: 'First, the presence of a charismatic leader; second, the existence of a politically active constituency; and third, the seizing of a key window of opportunity.'[30] Many factors can be suggested to explain Pashinyan's charisma in particular. His populist style and performance, discussed in the section below, surely made him appealing to the public. The fact that he was convicted on a charge of inciting 'mass disorder' in the context of the 1 March 2008 protests – in which 10 people were killed and nearly 200 were injured while demanding a recount of the presidential election's vote – and spent nearly two years in prison (he was released in a general amnesty in 2011)[31] could also explain the people's sympathy towards him. His relentless criticism of Sargsyan and the RPA – often targeting the oligarchy and sprawling corruption and cronyism – in his six-year stint as a National Assembly member (and fierce opponent of the regime)[32] was also a potential factor.[33]

III. Pashinyan's 'Constitutional Impatience'

To make his revolution successful, Nikol Pashinyan used rhetoric and actions which closely align with many of the key elements of the ideal-typical populist discourse – as elaborated and discussed in the first two chapters of this monograph – both before and after taking power. Mirroring the 'constitutional impatience' expressed by other populists and elaborated in chapter three, Pashinyan put forward an

[25] Ishkanian (n 15).

[26] See, eg, ODIHR Election Observation Mission, 'Republic of Armenia: Early Parliamentary Elections, 9 December 2018 – Final Report' (*OSCE/ODIHR*, 7 March 2018) www.osce.org/files/f/documents/b/7/413555.pdf. See also, eg, Broers (n 3) 5.

[27] Grigoryan (n 7) 172.

[28] The RPA failed to obtain 5% of the vote, the threshold for representation in the National Assembly. See Lanskoy and Suthers (n 5) 86.

[29] See, eg, Iskandaryan (n 6) 468.

[30] Ishkanian (n 15) 271.

[31] Grigoryan (n 7) 162.

[32] Iskandaryan (n 6) 475.

[33] Ishkanian (n 15) 271.

alternative conception of democratic representation based on proximity, authenticity, promptness and, to a certain extent, impulsivity. The first subsection will focus on Pashinyan's populist discourse – rhetoric and actions – prior to taking power, while the second will analyse his discourse after taking power.

A. Populist Impatience While in Opposition

First, Pashinyan and his supporters, following the populist ideal type, shortened the time frame and discursively divided the political space in Armenia into a clear 'us-against-them' logic, turning all aspects of political life into a binary choice.[34] More specifically, they put forward a personified and Manichean worldview in their standoff against Sargsyan: they pitted a unified, young and virtuous people, led and embodied by Pashinyan, the symbol of change, on one side, against an evil and immoral 'Other' or enemy, namely the corrupt, entrenched, disconnected[35] and middle-aged ruling elite, personified by Sargsyan, 'the man who had lied to the nation',[36] on the other. By doing so, Pashinyan and his supporters attracted emotional investment and made the protests chiefly about moral values, broadly defined: protestors gathered across the country and in the diaspora, from Paris to Glendale, California, to voice their 'anger and discontent with the morally bankrupt and kleptocratic, oligarchic RPA regime' which had been in power for two decades.[37] While resolutely anchored in the specific context of a transition from a robust and entrenched semi-authoritarian (or hybrid) regime[38] to a constitutional democracy, this type of discourse – with its focus on the anger vis-à-vis the corrupt oligarchy and (or) ruling elites – nevertheless shares many similarities with left-wing populist discourses, from Latin America to Europe, including that of members of Syriza (in Greece) and Podemos (in Spain), amongst others.

Second, Pashinyan often identified himself (or the protest movement he was leading) discursively with 'the people' or 'the nation'. For instance, in a brief

[34] S Issacharoff, 'Democracy's Deficits' (2018) 85 *University of Chicago Law Review* 486; S Issacharoff, 'The Corruption of Popular Sovereignty' (2020) 18 *International Journal of Constitutional Law* 1111.

[35] A Ishkanian, 'A Revolution of Values: Freedom, Responsibility, and Courage in the Armenian Velvet Revolution' (*LSE EUROPP Blog*, 3 May 2018) blogs.lse.ac.uk/europpblog/2018/05/03/a-revolution-of-values-freedom-responsibility-and-courage-in-the-armenian-velvet-revolution.

[36] Iskandaryan (n 6) 479.

[37] Ishkanian (n 35).

[38] Most analysts and commentators described Armenia under the rule of the RPA (ie, until 2018) as a 'semi-authoritarian' ('hybrid', 'competitive authoritarian' or 'semi-consolidated authoritarian') regime. See, eg, E Aghekyan, 'Nations in Transit: Armenia' (*Freedom House*, 2018) freedomhouse.org/country/armenia/nations-transit/2018. See also Broers (n 3) 7; P Stronski, 'Armenia's Democratic Triumph' (*The Atlantic*, 24 April 2018) www.theatlantic.com/international/archive/2018/04/armenia-president-populism/558773; and S Levitsky and L Way, *Competitive Authoritarianism: Hybrid Regimes After the Cold War* (Cambridge, Cambridge University Press, 2010) 207–213. In their seminal work, Levitsky and Way define 'competitive authoritarian' regimes as political systems that are 'competitive in that opposition parties use democratic institutions to contest seriously for power, but they are not democratic because the playing field is heavily skewed in favour of incumbents'. See ibid 5.

televised meeting with Sargsyan on 22 April 2018, Pashinyan asked the former to resign. Sargsyan refused and warned Pashinyan to remember 'the lesson of March 2008', referring to the violent repression of the 1 March 2008 protests, which led to the death of 10 people, to which Pashinyan responded: 'You cannot threaten the Armenian nation.'[39] This is not to say, of course, that Pashinyan's views did not represent the belief of significant parts of (and quite possibly an overwhelming majority of) the Armenian population at the time. Indeed, some commentators, while recognising that the events of the Revolution 'seemed to tap into the rising tide of populism around the globe', have argued that the events of the Revolution were indeed 'a genuine expression of the will of the people'[40] – if, of course, such a thing does in fact exist.[41] Nevertheless, the identification of the leader with 'the people' – or 'the nation' in this instance[42] – remains one of the most important hallmarks of populism and a key element of the ideal-typical populist discourse.[43] In this particular instance, it also shows the mobilising and unifying character (or potential) of anti-establishment populism.

Third, Pashinyan's language, political style, performance and appearance during the early stages of the Velvet Revolution were distinctly theatrical and anti-establishment, as well as based on proximity, shared identity and similarity-based appeals to authenticity.[44] With a view to distinguishing himself from the ruling elite, Pashinyan – a 'media-savvy and charismatic' political leader[45] – chose to establish a typical proximity-based, populist connection between the leader and the public, appearing in his communications as 'a person, often with habits and tastes similar to those of the people'.[46] For instance, on several occasions – including on the day Sargsyan was appointed Prime Minister, as well as on the day of the abovementioned television meeting with Sargsyan – Pashinyan wore distinctive revolutionary attire, including a camouflage t-shirt, backpack and black baseball cap, together with growing a beard.[47] This was in sharp contrast to his pre-Revolution 'suited and booted bourgeois intellectual chic' accoutrements.[48]

[39] Lanskoy and Suthers (n 5) 93.

[40] See, eg, Stronski (n 38).

[41] See, eg, *ch 1*; J Waldron, 'Bicameralism and the Separation of Powers' in Jeremy Waldron (ed), *Political Political Theory: Essays on Institutions* (Cambridge, Harvard University Press, 2016) 77; and, generally, A Weale, *The Will of the People: A Modern Myth* (Cambridge, Polity, 2018).

[42] Another example is when Pashinyan discursively presented himself as the 'people's candidate'. See Abrahamian and Shagoyan (n 14) 518.

[43] See ch 1.

[44] See ch 3.

[45] Broers (n 3) 4.

[46] A Masala, 'Populism as the Crisis of Political Trust' in Adriano Fabris (ed), *Trust: A Philosophical Approach* (Cham, Springer, 2020) 193. It should be noted that Masala, here, does not refer to Pashinyan specifically.

[47] A Roth, '"He's not a populist, he's popular': Nikol Pashinyan becomes Armenian PM' (*The Guardian*, 8 May 2018) www.theguardian.com/world/2018/may/08/hes-not-a-populist-hes-popular-nikol-pashinyan-becomes-armenian-pm. See also Abrahamian and Shagoyan (n 14) 522.

[48] F Light, 'Armenia's surprising populist uprising' (*UnHerd*, 10 May 2018) www.unherd.com/2018/05/armenias-surprising-populist-uprising.

In doing so, he also engaged in what Pierre Ostiguy has called the 'flaunting of the low',[49] showing the public that he was 'more authentic than the "old" politicians'.[50] Interestingly, there was even a sort of 'redemptive' aspect to Pashinyan's 'revolutionary' populism, akin to Latin American versions.[51] Indeed, he toured 'Armenia's small towns and cities, receiving the sort of response usually reserved for an evangelical preacher'[52] and even allegedly identified himself, later on, with Christ.[53] When he became Prime Minister, Pashinyan quickly discarded his revolutionary vogue and stored away his camouflage t-shirt and backpack, replacing them with a suit and a tie. Nevertheless, he maintained his distinctive populist style and rhetoric, notably in his speeches, as discussed in the next subsection.

Fourth, and in the same vein, Pashinyan claimed to have established a high-speed and direct spatiotemporal connection between himself and 'the people' (or 'the nation'), notably through the use of information technology – and, in particular, social media. Indeed, he 'skillfully used social media, particularly Facebook and live-streaming technology, to establish a direct connection with the public'.[54] This allowed him to bypass the engrained slowness of intermediaries: through social media and other means, 'Pashinyan managed to react immediately to some virtual messages. This eliminated any sense of distance between him and ordinary Facebook users/protesters, as did his regular livestreams.'[55]

This form of 'revolutionary' (or perhaps 'democratic') populism,[56] combined with widespread disenchantment vis-à-vis the ruling elite, can provide an insight into why the Velvet Revolution was successful – and why it succeeded so quickly.[57] In fact, the Revolution was possibly a response to a certain form of what Jack M Balkin calls (in the American context) 'constitutional rot', understood as a problem of representation, in which the existing political system (and the party that runs it) is seen as insufficiently democratic and republican, that is to say, insufficiently responsive to popular will and popular opinion and

[49] P Ostiguy, 'Populism: A Socio-Cultural Approach' in C Rovira Kaltwasser, P Ochoa Espejo, P Taggart and P Ostiguy (eds), *The Oxford Handbook of Populism* (Oxford, Oxford University Press, 2017).

[50] Masala (n 46) 193.

[51] See, generally, C de la Torre, *Populist Seduction in Latin America*, 2nd edn (Athens, Ohio University Press, 2010).

[52] Light (n 48).

[53] 'Analyst: Armenia PM Pashinyan has started identifying himself with Christ' (*NEWS.am*, 22 November 2019) www.news.am/eng/news/545866.html.

[54] Ishkanian (n 15) 273.

[55] Abrahamian and Shagoyan (n 14) 522–523. Pashinyan, seven years after the Revolution, continues to do regular livestreams.

[56] See section V below.

[57] That said, some argue that although the Velvet Revolution may have seemed sudden, it nevertheless built on decades of protest movements, democratic precursors to the Velvet Revolution, notably in the late 1980s, in 2008 and in 2013. See, eg, Lanskoy and Suthers (n 5) 86–87. See also Grigoryan (n 7) and, generally, M Zolyan, 'Thirty Years of Protest: How Armenia's Legacy of Political and Civic Protests Prepared the Velvet Revolution' in Broers and Ohanyan (eds) (n 2).

insufficiently devoted to the public good (being focused, instead, on a small number of individuals and groups – namely, the 'oligarchy' or, at least, the wealthy elite).[58]

B. Populist Impatience While in Power

Even after taking power, Pashinyan maintained his distinctive populist rhetoric. In a public speech marking his first 100 days in office in August 2018, the newly appointed Prime Minister (whose party did not yet enjoy a parliamentary majority at the time) said, referring to the 'people's rule': '[T]here is no coalition government in Armenia, there is no parliamentary majority in Armenia'.[59] He added: 'There is [only] the citizen of Armenia: the highest power belongs to the people, and people have direct control of everything in Armenia. This is the crucial point of our revolution.'[60]

In words that clearly reveal the spatial dimension of populism (with the people and the locus of power being located in, or associated with, a physical space – namely, a city square), Pashinyan went on to say:

> And now I want to say what it means; in practice, it means that the revolutionary Republic Square[61] is proclaimed as the highest body of the people's power. This means that the government has been formed here, the government is accountable to this square and the government is bound to comply with the people's will voiced in this square. This means that when we make the most important decisions in Armenia's political life, we must come together in this square and authorize the government to carry out this or that action or prohibit the government from doing this or that act. So, you are the highest and sole government in the Republic of Armenia. The power in the Republic of Armenia belongs to you.[62]

Employing the ideal-typical populist discourse described in chapter one, notably the focus on the people as 'unity',[63] the 'direct rule' of the people,[64] the critique of

[58] JM Balkin, 'Constitutional Rot' in CR Sunstein (ed), *Can It Happen Here? Authoritarianism in America* (New York, Dey St, 2018) 19–20.

[59] N Pashinyan, 'Speech at Rally Dedicated to 100 Days in Office' (*The Prime Minister of the Republic of Armenia*, 17 August 2018) www.primeminister.am/en/statements-and-messages/item/2018/08/17/Nikol-Pashinyan-100-day-rally.

[60] ibid.

[61] The square in Yerevan where many important gatherings took place during the Velvet Revolution.

[62] Pashinyan (n 59).

[63] ibid. Pashinyan notably said: '[T]oday is the day of unity and unity of the Armenian people. [...] This is the rally of the victory of the Armenian people, this is the rally of the unity of the Armenian people'.

[64] ibid. Later in the same speech, he said: 'I also want to applaud Armenia's proud dignified and victorious citizens, that is, all of you, the entire Armenian nation, who eventually, despite all doubts, proved that we are an exceptional nation with an exclusive mission. You ushered in a historic era of people's direct rule in the 21st century. Then, long live the highest bearer of the power in the Republic of Armenia, the citizen of the Republic of Armenia, the Armenian people!'

the oligarchy[65] and the emphasis on his role as the 'direct and immediate representative of the people of Armenia',[66] Pashinyan also highlighted the need to resort to direct democracy and plebiscitary instruments as the (true) expression of the 'will of the people'. Referring to the (revolutionary) people of Armenia, he said:

> [Y]ou are the highest and sole government in the Republic of Armenia. The power in the Republic of Armenia belongs to you. But this is not the only novelty of our political life. In the near future, together with joint efforts, we have to strengthen the referendum institut[ion], and many decisions should be made by people in referendums. It refers to both local and national referendums. Therefore, such critical changes should be made in the near future as would allow the government and the people to decide together on issues of municipal, regional, national importance, and even the most important international events in referendums. This is the fundamental change that will usher in the second [stage] of our revolution.[67]

Pashinyan's distinctive populism was not just a mere political style; it also transposed into concrete political and legal actions, particularly after he took power. Impatient to move to the 'second stage' of the Velvet Revolution, Pashinyan quickly announced he would tackle two primordial and seemingly interrelated priorities, that is, the issue of corruption and that of the independence of the judiciary.[68] The country was, at that time, widely perceived as one of the nations with the most widespread corruption problems in the world, particularly amongst high-ranked government officials.[69] One of the first steps to counter this was the high-profile and spectacular arrest of General Manvel Grigoryan, an influential former military commander and high-senior RPA politician charged with 'embezzlement and illegal possession of ammunition'.[70]

Another, related priority was the implementation and safeguarding of the rule of law more broadly. Shortly upon taking office, Pashinyan used strong words to criticise – notably in a live Facebook interview – the 'paralysis' of judges and state prosecutors, 'lamenting their inability to carry out their duties without receiving

[65] ibid. He said: '[W]ithin 40 minutes after I became Prime Minister, I eliminated the banana and sugar monopolies. I declare that there is no monopoly in Armenia today, there is no petrol monopoly, no monopoly of anything, there is only the monopoly of power, and you are the owner of that power, the citizens of Armenia, the people of the Republic of Armenia'.

[66] ibid.

[67] ibid.

[68] ibid. See also Ishkanian (n 15) 274; DL Feldman and H Albasic, 'The Remarkable "Velvet Revolution": Armenia's Experiment Against Government Corruption' (2019) 21 *Public Integrity* 420, 422–423.

[69] See, eg, 'Corruption Perceptions Index – Armenia' (*Transparency International*, 2018) www.transparency.org/en/cpi/2018/index/arm. See also GRECO, 'Compliance Report for Armenia – Fourth Evaluation Round: Corruption Prevention in Respect of Members of Parliament, Judges and Prosecutors' (*GRECO*, 21 December 2017) rm.coe.int/fourth-evaluation-round-corruption-prevention-in-respect-of-members-of/1680775f12.

[70] M Edwards, 'Armenia's Post-Revolution Party is Over' (*Foreign Policy*, 15 October 2018) www.foreignpolicy.com/2018/10/15/the-counterrevolution-is-coming-to-armenia. See also Lanskoy and Suthers (n 5).

functions from above'.[71] Alluding to the idea that a considerable number of judges might have been serving the country's 'corrupt' political and economic system, he also issued a clear warning to them: 'I want to tell the representatives of previous authorities and the judges who keep receiving instructions from them: "Come to your senses and don't mess with the people!"'[72]

IV. Judicial Reform: The Populist against *Ancien Régime* Judges

Pashinyan stayed true to his words. On the issue of the rule of law, Pashinyan quickly ordered the arrest of several high-ranking officials, including Sargsyan's brother and bodyguard, often on corruption grounds.[73] However, the most powerful, spectacular and highly symbolic arrest was that of former President Robert Kocharyan for his presumed role in the 1 March 2008 events – during which popular protests against the outcome of the 2008 presidential election were violently crushed by the regime, allegedly on the order of then-President Kocharyan himself.[74] While some saw the arrest as politically motivated or as a vendetta, others saw it as a move towards restorative and (or) transitional justice, especially considering that these events are still viewed by many in Armenia as a social and collective wound.[75] Kocharyan, however, was quickly released by order of a Yerevan district court judge, which led Pashinyan to announce plans for a radical judicial reform on the basis that '[c]ourts are remnants of the former corrupt authorities' and that the '[p]eople have no trust in the judiciary and therefore it lacks legitimacy'.[76] The following subsection will analyse Pashinyan's judicial reform – and its outcome.

[71] Ishkanian (n 15) 274.

[72] Pashinyan (n 59).

[73] Former President (and Prime Minister) Serzh Sargsyan himself was arrested, later, in December 2019, that is less than two weeks after criticising the new authorities at a conference in Zagreb, Croatia. Sargsyan was indicted on charges of corruption. See A Mejlumyan, 'Armenian ex-president charged with "theft of state money"' (*Eurasianet*, 4 December 2019) www.eurasianet.org/armenian-ex-president-charged-with-theft-of-state-money. Sargsyan allegedly embezzled the equivalent of more than one million US dollars from the state budget. See 'Update – criminal case against ex Armenian president Sargsyan to be taken to trial' (*JAMnews*, 10 January 2020) www.jam-news.net/former-ousted-armenian-president-charged-with-embezzling-more-than-1-mln. At the time of writing, in October 2025, Sargsyan's fate was still uncertain: he was acquitted in May 2024, but his acquittal was overturned by the Anti-Corruption Court of Appeals, which sent the matter back to the lower court. See, eg, N Bulghadarian, 'Court Overturns Acquittal of Serzh Sargsyan' (18 April 2025, *Azatutyun*) www.azatutyun.am/a/33389570.html [in Armenian]. New corruption charges were also laid against him in May 2025. See A Barseghyan, 'New charges against ex-Armenian President Serzh Sargsyan' (26 May 2025, *OC Media*) oc-media.org/new-charges-against-ex-armenian-president-serzh-sargsyan.

[74] Edwards (n 70).

[75] See, eg, Broers (n 3) 3.

[76] AFP, 'Armenian PM announces clean-up of judiciary' (*France24*, 20 May 2019) www.france24.com/en/20190520-armenian-pm-announces-clean-judiciary.

A. From Judicial Intervention to Judicial Vetting and Transitional Justice

On 18 May 2019, just over a year after Nikol Pashinyan was appointed Prime Minister, a Yerevan district court judge ordered the release from pre-trial detention of former President Robert Kocharyan.[77] The decision of Judge Davit Grigoryan, a figure of the previous regime,[78] to release Kocharyan – and, three days later, to formally suspend his trial, suggesting that the former president should enjoy immunity from prosecution[79] – was seen by many as politically motivated and sparked widespread outrage in the country.[80] The day after Kocharyan's release from detention, Pashinyan himself called his supporters on Facebook to literally and physically block the courts, before backtracking later on the same day, writing on his Facebook page that 'the demonstration [had] achieved its goal'.[81]

The next day, on 20 May 2019, Nikol Pashinyan announced, in a televised address, his plans for a radical reform of the Armenian judiciary, which he dubbed as the 'second and most important phase'[82] of the Velvet Revolution. Arguing that courts 'have lost their legitimacy' and that 'too many judges are beholden to the country's former authorities',[83] Pashinyan contended that '[t]he people of Armenia still view the judicial authorities as a remnant of the former corrupt system where conspiracy is constantly being planned and implemented against the people'.[84] Pashinyan did question in part the truthfulness of this public perception, but nevertheless added that '[t]he fact that the judiciary doesn't have the trust of the people means that it also doesn't have [...] enough legitimacy to operate'.[85] He added: 'Unfortunately, I can't conclude that the judicial system is not subjected to shadowy and illegal influences mainly coming from the former corrupt system

[77] The decision was later overturned by the Court of Appeals, but was ultimately confirmed by an RPA-friendly Constitutional Court in Constitutional Court of Armenia, *On the Case of Conformity of Article 35 and Part 2 of Article 135 of the Criminal Procedure Code of the Republic of Armenia with the Constitution on the Basis of the Application of Robert Kocharyan* (DCC-1476, 4 September 2019) [unofficial translation]. This is discussed further below.

[78] A Ohanyan, 'How Old Courts Derail New Democracies' (*Foreign Policy*, 14 August 2019) www.foreignpolicy.com/2019/08/14/how-old-courts-derail-new-democracies. Interestingly, Grigoryan was himself arrested a year later with charges of document forgery. See 'Former Judge in Kocharian Case to Stand Trial' (*Azatutyun*, 20 May 2020) www.azatutyun.am/a/30624263.html [in Armenian].

[79] N Bulghadarian, 'Kocharian's Trial Suspended' (*Azatutyun*, 21 May 2019) www.azatutyun.am/a/29955039.html [in Armenian].

[80] AFP (n 76).

[81] ibid.

[82] ibid.

[83] 'Armenian PM Calls for Radical Justice Reforms as "Second Phase of Revolution"' (*RFE/RL*, 20 May 2019) www.rferl.org/a/armenians-heed-call-to-block-courts-pashinian-to-speak-on-second-phase-of-revolution/29952220.html.

[84] ibid.

[85] ibid.

because these two systems are connected to each other through human, political and other ties.'[86]

Pashinyan's plans for judicial reform, for which he said he counted on the assistance and support of international partners,[87] initially included a controversial 'vetting process' of all of the country's 231 judges, which would take place during a transitional period.[88] The claimed objective of this 'vetting process' was to allow the public to have 'full information about the judges' political ties, origin, property status and activities as judges and in their previous capacity, and their individual and professional traits', a process which would, he said, reveal whether the judges could continue to serve as independent members of the judiciary.[89] It was announced a few weeks later that this 'vetting' would be carried out by the Supreme Judicial Council[90] and the Corruption Prevention Commission.[91] An additional criterion for judges, Pashinyan said in his initial speech, would be whether judges had had a ruling found unlawful or overturned by the European Court of Human Rights (ECtHR), in which case they would be asked to resign, leave or be dismissed.[92] As one commentator pointed out, this was arguably a very strong measure, given that 'a different finding by the ECtHR does not necessarily imply corruption or incompetence', especially 'in cases where there is room for more subjective judicial interpretation'.[93]

Nonetheless, both transitional justice and the proposed vetting process received the implicit or explicit support of several influential international and supranational actors, including the Council of Europe's European Commission for

[86] RFE/RL, 'Pashinyan Tells Supporters to Block Courts, Asks Judges to Resign' (*The Armenian Mirror-Spectator*, 21 May 2019) www.mirrorspectator.com/2019/05/21/pashinyan-tells-supporters-to-block-courts-asks-judges-to-resign.

[87] AFP (n 76).

[88] S Vasilyan, 'Completing Armenia's Revolution: Transitional Justice and Judicial Vetting' (*ConstitutionNet*, 3 July 2019) www.constitutionnet.org/news/completing-armenias-revolution-transitional-justice-and-judicial-vetting.

[89] RFE/RL (n 86).

[90] This body was 'effectively paralysed' at the time by the recent resignation of five of its nine members, including its head, Gagik Harutyunyan. Two of these members were quickly replaced by members nominated by the ruling My Step Alliance and elected by parliament. See R Stepanian, 'Parliament Majority Leader Sheds Light on Judicial "Vetting"' (*Azatutyun*, 24 June 2019) www.azatutyun.am/a/30017085.html [in Armenian] and Vasilyan (n 88).

[91] Stepanian (n 90).

[92] RFE/RL (n 86). A measure along these lines was introduced in 2020, with Draft Laws which aimed to amend the Judicial Code and the Law on the Constitutional Court. The terminology employed in the Draft Laws, including the '*deliberate* violation by a judge of a fundamental human right' (emphasis added), was however criticised by the Venice Commission, the latter raising concerns about legal certainty and described this 'incompatibility requirement' as 'in effect a disciplinary measure disguised as an incompatibility requirement', among other concerns. See Venice Commission, *Joint Opinion of the Venice Commission and the Directorate General of Human Rights and Rule of Law (DGI) of the Council of Europe on the draft laws on making amendments to the Constitutional Law on the Judicial Code and to the Constitutional Law on the Constitutional Court* (Opinion No 1074/2021, 21 March 2022) CDL-AD(2022)002, [20], [43]-ss, [89].

[93] Vasilyan (n 88).

Democracy through Law ('Venice Commission') as well as the EU, in addition to several think tanks, actors from the finance sector and credit rating agencies.[94] The Venice Commission in particular endorsed the vetting process, under certain conditions. In a letter that was made available to the public, the Venice Commission's then-President, Gianni Buquicchio, expressed his general support for the measures – provided that they are 'devised and carried out by legal means, in compliance with the Constitution and taking into account European standards concerning the rule of law and respect for human rights'.[95]

However, on 4 September 2019, the My Step parliamentary bloc suffered another major blow from the judiciary when the RPA-friendly Constitutional Court of Armenia ruled that the criminal prosecution of former President Robert Kocharyan might lead to an 'unjustified restriction' to his 'right to personal freedom', protected under Article 27 of the Constitution, thus effectively calling into question the legality of the state's prosecution of Kocharyan.[96] The matter had been referred to the Constitutional Court following a controversial decision from Yerevan district court Judge Davit Grigoryan, which was later overturned by the Court of Appeals, leading to the re-arrest of the former President.[97] By the end of that year, it had become clear that the focus of the government was the overhaul of the Constitutional Court: on 30 December 2019, a new Expert Commission on Constitutional Reform was set up by a prime ministerial executive order,[98] precisely with a view to leading this judicial reform.[99]

B. From Judicial Vetting and Transitional Justice to 'Early Retirement Incentives'

The first step for the overhaul of the Constitutional Court was to introduce a 'package' mainly comprising a toned-down version of judicial vetting, including amendments to the procedures under which the financial declarations of judges would be verified and details of the disciplinary process for judges and

[94] ibid.

[95] 'Venice Commission on judiciary reforms, vetting in Armenia' (*NEWS.am*, 27 May 2019) www.news.am/eng/news/515010.html; 'Official transcript and copy of Venice Commission President Buquicchio's letter to PM Pashinyan' (*Armenpress*, 28 May 2019) www.armenpress.am/eng/news/976413.html; J Keay, 'Making the "Velvet Revolution" Work' (2019) 33 *Global Finance* 144.

[96] Constitutional Court of Armenia, Decision DCC-1476. See also 'Armenian Constitutional Court rules "right to freedom" violated in case against ex president Kocharyan' (*JAMnews*, 5 September 2019) www.jam-news.net/armenian-constitutional-court-rules-right-to-freedom-violated-in-case-against-ex-president-kocharyan.

[97] 'Constitutional Court to examine applications of Robert Kocharyan and judge David Grigoryan in August' (*Armenpress*, 10 July 2019) www.armenpress.am/eng/news/981294.html; ibid.

[98] Prime Ministerial Executive Order No 1986 of 30 December 2019 (Armenia), establishing a new Expert Commission on Constitutional Reform.

[99] L Sargsyan and H Manougian, 'The Armenian Government's Plan to Change the Constitution' (*EVN Report*, 4 February 2020) www.evnreport.com/politics/the-armenian-government-s-plan-to-change-the-constitution.

their liability, as well as periodic evaluations. However, what was arguably the most radical and controversial measure contained in the package was a proposed amendment to the Law on the Constitutional Court,[100] which was meant to incentivise Constitutional Court justices (those appointed before the 2015 constitutional amendments took effect) to resign before the end of their mandate while maintaining several financial advantages. The intentions of the Armenian government were clear, as the Venice Commission pointed out: the My Step alliance wished 'to offer certain judges whom they associate with the "old regime" a "dignified exit", as an alternative to more radical modalities which were considered earlier [that] year'.[101] The Armenian authorities also made clear references to the 'revolutionary context', which, according to them, 'necessitate[d] the renewal of the composition of the [Constitutional Court] appointed largely under the previous regime, and by the public distrust in the current composition' of the Court.[102]

The My Step alliance questioned the legitimacy of several of the current Constitutional Court justices and accused them of 'being linked to the "former corrupt regime" and of "impeding judicial reforms"'.[103] Notably, they questioned the legitimacy of the Chairperson of the Constitutional Court, Hrayr Tovmasyan – a former member of the RPA who had held a number of key positions within the previous regime, including that of Minister of Justice – contending that he was elected as Chairperson under 'false pretences'.[104] The My Step parliamentary bloc had even introduced a bill in Parliament in September 2019 to remove him, arguing that, as a key member of the RPA until shortly before his election as Chairperson, he was still constrained by his ties with the previous regime. In particular, the bill questioned his handling of the case against former President Kocharyan, noting that he did not recuse himself from the case despite having family ties with one of Kocharyan's lawyers involved in the case.[105] While the bill was successfully approved by Parliament, a motion to dismiss Justice Tovmasyan was rejected in October 2019 by the Constitutional Court itself, which has the final say on matters involving the dismissal of Constitutional Court justices.[106] Justice Tovmasyan's legitimacy was also challenged from within the Constitutional Court, with newly appointed Justice Vahe Grigoryan – best known as one of the lawyers who had represented the victims

[100] Law on the Constitutional Court, adopted by the National Assembly on 9 December 1997, signed by President Levon Ter-Petrossian on 30 December 1997.

[101] Venice Commission, *Joint Opinion of the Venice Commission and the Directorate of Human Rights (DHR) of the Directorate General of Human Rights and Rule of Law (DGI) of the Council of Europe on the Amendments to the Judicial Code and Some Other Laws* (Opinion No 963/2019, 14 October 2019) CDL-AD(2019)024 [57].

[102] ibid.

[103] Gayane Saribekian, 'Armenian High Court Judges Spurn Early Retirement Offered by Government' (*Azatutyun*, 27 February 2020) www.azatutyun.am/a/30458221.html [in Armenian].

[104] Sargsyan and Manougian (n 99).

[105] ibid.

[106] ibid.

of the 1 March 2008 shootings – symbolically calling himself Chairperson of the Constitutional Court.[107]

The Venice Commission largely supported the measures proposed by the Armenian government, despite certain concerns as to whether the retirement schedule would be truly voluntary. For the Venice Commission, the proposed mechanisms 'increase the accountability of judges and are more efficient to prevent corruption, without, at the same time, disproportionately encroaching on the judges' independence'.[108] As for the early retirement scheme, the Commission emphasised the importance of Constitutional Court judges' security of tenure and of 'irremovability' as 'an essential guarantee' of judicial independence.[109] The Commission also noted that 'it is not acceptable to change the composition of the Constitutional Court every time a Government comes to power',[110] but nevertheless concluded that 'in principle, provided that such a scheme remains strictly voluntary and does not hamper the effective functioning of this Court, there are no standards that would lead the Venice Commission to oppose it'.[111] The early retirement incentive was adopted by Parliament in late December 2019.[112] Constitutional Court justices were ultimately offered a monthly compensation equivalent to their current salary until the foreseen end of their term, provided that they voluntarily stepped down by 27 February 2020.[113]

C. From 'Early Retirement Incentives' to Mass Removal

Yet, the 'early retirement incentives' did not prove successful; they were rejected en masse by all the Constitutional Court justices, which led Pashinyan to call for a referendum on a constitutional amendment on the mass removal of these

[107] Justice Grigoryan challenged Justice Tovmasyan's legitimacy as Chairperson of the Constitutional Court by arguing that because the Constitution 'refers to the "judges" of the Constitutional Court rather than "members" of the Court, which was the terminology used previously [before the 2015 constitutional amendments], only he and Arman Dilanyan (who was confirmed as a "judge" in 2018) are authorised to serve' on the Court. See ibid.

[108] Venice Commission (n 101) [14].

[109] ibid [58].

[110] ibid [63].

[111] ibid. Regarding the scope and the 'truly voluntary nature' of early retirement schemes, the Commission referred, at [60], to two of its previous opinions (regarding Poland and Hungary, respectively), namely: Venice Commission, *Opinion on the Draft Act amending the Act on the National Council of the Judiciary; on the Draft Act amending the Act on the Supreme Court, proposed by the President of Poland, and on the Act on the Organisation of Ordinary Courts* (Opinion No 904/2017, 11 December 2017) CDL-AD(2017)031, [44]-[52], [130]; and Venice Commission, *Opinion on Act CLXII of 2011 on the Legal Status and Remuneration of Judges and Act CLXI of 2011 on the Organisation and Administration of Courts of Hungary* (Opinion No 663/2012, 19 March 2012) CDL-AD(2012)001, [102]–[110].

[112] Sargsyan and Manougian (n 99).

[113] ibid.

recalcitrant judges. Indeed, as none of the Constitutional Court justices seemed to have any interest in the early retirement proposal, the My Step parliamentary bloc did not even wait until the expiry of the deadline and, on 6 February 2020, swiftly introduced in Parliament a constitutional amendment modifying transitional Article 213 of the Constitution of Armenia (as amended in 2015) regarding the tenure of the Chairperson and members (justices) of the Constitutional Court. This new amendment, if approved by referendum, would dismiss seven of the nine Constitutional Court justices – namely, the seven judges who were appointed prior to the entry into force in 2018 of a constitutional amendment limiting their term to 12 years – as well as the Court's Chairperson, who had been appointed for 17 years just three weeks prior to the entry into force of the amendment limiting the Chairperson's term to six years.[114]

To justify this new, drastic move, Pashinyan claimed, in a speech in Parliament with strong populist overtones, that the Constitutional Court 'ha[d] become an advocate of electoral fraud and illegal power' and had, through 'constitutional manipulations' and with the help of its chairperson, Hrayr Tovmasyan, 'appropriated the power of the people'.[115] In the words of Pashinyan, the Armenian Constitution cannot, legally and in practice, 'be amended without the permission of the Constitutional Court';[116] this lacuna, combined with a lack of checks and restraints over the Court's powers, 'restrict[s] the highest holder of power – the people's authority', thereby constituting a 'direct and terrible threat to democracy' and a form of 'usurpation of powers'.[117] On that basis, Pashinyan called for a constitutional amendment which, if approved by referendum, would ultimately lead to a 'new' Constitutional Court. This new court, in Pashinyan's own words, would 'not be under the banner of any political force or grouping or official, but [...] before the people'; it would be 'the supreme constitutional court, but no higher than the people'.[118]

Given the judges' refusal to step down, Pashinyan argued that a constitutional amendment approved by referendum was the only means to reform a constitutional court too closely tied with a corrupt and semi-authoritarian (former) regime. Without waiting for the Expert Commission on Constitutional Reform's

[114] Sargsyan and Manougian (n 99); L Sargsyan, 'Understanding Armenia's Constitutional Court' (*EVN Report*, 23 February 2020) www.evnreport.com/politics/understanding-armenia-s-constitutional-court. See art 166(1) of the Constitution of Armenia. See also art 166(2) of the Constitution of Armenia regarding the (new) term of the Chairperson. It should be noted that the early retirement offer nonetheless remained valid until 27 February 2020, but none of the Constitutional Court members accepted it, with some judges calling the offer 'immoral' and 'dishonourable', and some commentators calling it a 'bribe'. See 'Constitutional Court Judges Reject Government's Early Retirement Offer' (*Asbarez*, 27 February 2020) www.asbarez.com/constitutional-court-judges-reject-governments-early-retirement-offer.

[115] Pashinyan's 6 February 2020 speech in Pashinyan, 'Speech at the Extraordinary Session of the National Assembly'.

[116] As per the Constitution of the Republic of Armenia (adopted 5 July 1995, as amended 6 December 2015), arts 168 and 169(2).

[117] Pashinyan, 'Speech at the Extraordinary Session of the National Assembly'.

[118] ibid.

recommendations, a referendum was scheduled to take place on 5 April 2020 but was postponed in March 2020 and ultimately cancelled as a result of the Covid-19 pandemic.[119]

D. The Replacement of the Chairperson and the End of the Clash with the Constitutional Court

The clash between Pashinyan's ruling party and the Constitutional Court ultimately came to an end in the summer of 2020. As a result of the impossibility of holding a referendum on the issue of the Constitutional Court judges as initially planned due to the Covid-19 pandemic, there appeared to be a constitutional conundrum: given that the Constitution (as amended in 2015) allows Constitutional Court judges to rule on the constitutionality of any legislation, decision or constitutional amendment, any member of Parliament could ask the Constitutional Court to rule on any (individual or group) dismissal of the Court's justices, who in turn could decide on the constitutionality of their own dismissal.[120]

In late June 2020, Pashinyan used his My Step party majority (which held two-thirds of the seats in Parliament) to circumvent the court's apparent 'conflict of interest' and unilaterally pass a constitutional amendment that immediately removed three (rather than seven, as originally planned) of the Constitutional Court's nine judges.[121] The hastily-adopted constitutional amendment, which came into force on 26 June 2020, amended Article 213 of the Constitution in a way that effectively removed the three justices of the Constitutional Court who had served a 12-year term – the maximum term for judges appointed after the entry into force of the 2015 constitutional amendments.[122] In addition, the six-year non-renewable term limit of the Chairperson of the Constitutional Court was applied regardless of the year of appointment, as a result of which Justice Tovmasyan was removed as Chairperson, although he kept his position as a justice of the Court.[123] Pashinyan justified the move by arguing that the

[119] 'Constitutional Referendum Postponed as Armenia Declares State of Emergency' (*Asbarez*, 16 March 2020) www.asbarez.com/constitutional-referendum-postponed-as-armenia-declares-state-of-emergency; 'Constitutional Referendum Indefinitely Delayed' (*Asbarez*, 18 May 2020) www.asbarez.com/constitutional-referendum-indefinitely-delayed.

[120] See arts 168 and 169(2) of the Constitution of Armenia. See also the Law on the Constitutional Court.

[121] A Mejlumyan, 'Armenia moves again to remove old judges' (*Eurasianet*, 23 June 2020) www.eurasianet.org/armenia-moves-again-to-remove-old-judges.

[122] Amendment to the Constitution of the Republic of Armenia (adopted 22 June 2020). The justices affected were Hrant Nazaryan, Felix Tokhyan, and Alvina Gyulumyan.

[123] 'End of an epic: Armenian authorities renew Constitutional Court, head of court replaced' (*JAMnews*, 15 September 2020) www.jam-news.net/new-judges-constitutional-court; N Nalbandian, 'New Members of Armenian Constitutional Court Appointed' (*Azatutyun*, 15 September 2020) www.azatutyun.am/a/29897125.html [in Armenian]. He was, however, indicted in December 2019 on counts of abuse of power related to an alleged real estate fraud (namely, an illegal privatisation), charges he rejected as 'politically motivated'. In September 2024, a Yerevan first instance

Constitutional Court 'represents the corrupt regime of Serzh Sargsyan, rather than the people, and it must go'.[124]

This law amending the Constitution was passed in an extraordinary session in Parliament – which was boycotted by the opposition – on the very same day the Venice Commission issued an opinion on the mandate of Constitutional Court justices.[125] In this opinion, the Commission generally 'recognise[d] the legitimacy of the authorities' wish to ensure that the composition of the Constitutional Court reflects within a reasonable time-frame the provisions of the current Constitution', but expressed its strong preference for a 'transitional period which would allow for a gradual change in the composition in order to avoid any abrupt and immediate change endangering the independence of this institution'.[126] Apprehensive that an immediate dismissal might create a 'dangerous precedent for future governments', the Commission stressed the importance of 'allow[ing] a gradual change over a certain period and to ensure that this measure remains an exception'.[127]

Impatient to implement his reform, however, Pashinyan and his parliamentary faction disregarded the Commission's 'transitional' period recommendation and followed through with the dismissals, which had already been approved by Parliament. They also rejected the proposal to seek an *ex ante* constitutional review of the draft amendments, conspicuously on the basis of the affected judges' conflict of interest in the matter.[128] The decision by the President of the National Assembly (Parliament) to adopt the constitutional amendment on second reading – without requesting a prior review from the Constitutional Court – generated some controversy, as a textual interpretation of Articles 168 and 169(2) of the Constitution clearly required an *ex ante* review in the event of a constitutional amendment.

The four justices affected by the measure – namely, the three dismissed judges and former Chairperson Tovmasyan – unsuccessfully challenged the validity of the constitutional amendments before the ECtHR.[129] Two months later, in September 2020, three new Constitutional Court judges were elected in a process that was boycotted by both opposition factions in Parliament: Bright Armenia

court found him guilty, but he was released from criminal liability due to the statute of limitations having expired. If the guilty verdict is upheld by higher courts, he will 'likely be ousted from the court'. See, eg, S Galstian, 'Former Constitutional Court Head Convicted in "Political Trial"' (*The Armenian Mirror-Spectator*, 22 September 2024) www.mirrorspectator.com/2024/09/22/former-constitutional-court-head-convicted-in-political-trial.

[124] Mejlumyan (n 121).

[125] ibid.

[126] Venice Commission, Opinion No 988/2020, CDL-AD(2020)016 [77]–[78].

[127] ibid [78].

[128] See parliamentary debates in the extraordinary sitting of 22 June 2020 (first and second reading).

[129] The Court refused to apply an interim measure to freeze the enforcement of the constitutional amendments and preserve the concerned justices' offices, on the basis that it does 'not involve a risk of serious and irreparable harm of a core right under the [European] Convention [on Human Rights]'. See *Gyulumyan and Others v Armenia* App no 25240/20 (ECtHR, 8 July 2020). In late 2023, the First Section of the ECtHR ultimately rejected the applicant's claims that the amendments violated arts 6(1) and 8 of the Convention. See *Gyulumyan and Others v Armenia* App no 25240/20 (ECtHR, 21 November 2023).

and Prosperous Armenia.[130] After one failed attempt,[131] the Constitutional Court judges finally elected their new chairperson on 12 October 2020, following the procedure prescribed by Article 166 of the Constitution.[132] This marked the end of an era, particularly given the symbolic and practical importance of the chairperson for the Constitutional Court and the Armenian constitutional order more broadly.

The validity of the amendment was confirmed in an April 2021 ruling by the Constitutional Court. The latter – now without its expunged judges – first recognised that 'draft amendments to the Constitution are subject to mandatory preliminary review'.[133] However, in a somewhat teleological (or perhaps 'creative' or 'flexible') way, it also created a rule of 'reasonable exception' for situations in which 'it is impossible for the Constitutional Court to check the constitutionality of the draft in compliance with the principles of the key procedural guarantees and principles of constitutional justice'.[134] The Court added that '[n]eglecting [this] reasonable exception' could amount to 'prioritizing the subjective interests of the justices of the Constitutional Court before the high public interest of expression of the sovereign will of the constituent power', a reality that would be 'intolerable from the viewpoint of the supremacy of the Constitution'.[135] It concluded that the decision to adopt the amendment without prior review did not violate the Constitution, as it met conditions 'set by the Constitutional Court as a reasonable exception to the rule of mandatory preliminary review of draft amendments to the Constitution'.[136] This ruling marked the definitive victory of the populist over a defiant judiciary, although additional (including disciplinary) measures were also taken against lower court judges in the months and years that followed.[137]

V. Judicial Deceleration … Or Obstruction?

Let us take stock of where we are. In the introductory chapter, I discussed the literature on populism and the courts, including the common view according to which courts have a key role to play in defending constitutionalism and liberal constitutional democracy, as well as Kuo's argument that courts can act as

[130] JAMnews (n 123).

[131] N Nalbandian and S Harutyunyan, 'Armenian Constitutional Court Fails to Elect New Chair' (*Azatutyun*, 25 September 2020) https://www.azatutyun.am/a/30858200.html [in Armenian].

[132] G Balasyan, 'Armenia's Constitutional Court Gets New President' (*HETQ.am*, 12 October 2020) www.hetq.am/en/article/122989.

[133] Constitutional Court of Armenia, *On the Case of Conformity of Clause 4.2 of Part 2 of Articles 5, Parts 2 and 7 of Article 86 of the Constitutional Law Rules of Procedure of the National Assembly on the Basis of the Application of a least One Fifth of the Total Number of the Deputies of the National Assembly of the Republic of Armenia* (DCC-1590, 13 April 2021) [unofficial translation] [5.4].

[134] ibid [5.8].

[135] ibid.

[136] ibid [5.13].

[137] Notably by the Supreme Judicial Council. This is discussed in section V(B) of this chapter, below.

institutional decelerators against the 'instantaneous' conception of democracy that contemporary (or 'new') populism puts forward. In sections II and III of this chapter, I discussed Pashinyan's populism and impatience in the context (and in the aftermath) of the Velvet Revolution. Having discussed aspects of transitional justice and Pashinyan's reforms to the judiciary in the previous section, I will now analyse Pashinyan's populism and the Armenian courts' response to judicial reforms, notably in light of Kuo's theory of judicial deceleration, described in the introductory chapter. First, I will suggest that Pashinyan's rhetoric and actions were largely part of a 'revolutionary' (or perhaps 'democratic') form of populism – rather than the more authoritarian forms of populism described in the first part of this monograph and in the mainstream legal literature on populism. Second, in relation to judicial response to populism and taking into account the Constitutional Court's judgments, its composition (before the amendment) and its hostility vis-à-vis the judicial reforms, I will discuss the alternative possibility that courts may in fact, in certain circumstances, act as institutional *obstructors* – rather than decelerators – by impeding democratic reforms and constitutional changes.[138]

When using the existing framework in the mainstream literature on populism, constitutionalism and the courts, it is hard to see the constitutional amendment to dismiss constitutional court justices as anything else than another populist form of 'abusive constitutionalism', a term coined by David Landau and referring to the use (and abuse) of mechanisms of constitutional change with a view to undermining or eroding the democratic order.[139] Indeed, it would be easy to depict Pashinyan as a would-be autocrat or authoritarian-leaning leader who uses (and abuses) mechanisms of constitutional change, including constitutional amendments, to reduce checks on his power and erode the democratic order. Moreover, the Constitutional Court, for its part, could be portrayed – following the same existing framework in the literature – as a 'victim' of populist attacks on its legitimacy, or perhaps even as a heroic court, standing in the way of these constitutional changes, a rampart of the democratic order against abusive constitutionalism, attempting to slow down the populist impatience of Pashinyan and his acolytes.

In all fairness, this framework in the existing literature does indeed fit very well with many instances of authoritarian populism, where a populist leader, impatient with procedures and liberal-democratic constraints, quickly moves to remove checks and balances and curb hostile judiciaries – notably, but not always exclusively, by removing Constitutional Court judges and replacing them

[138] In a similar fashion, Costas Douzinas pointed out, in a comment during the 1st Populist Constitutionalism (PopCon) International Conference at the Aristotle University of Thessaloniki Law School on 7 May 2021, that Greek courts have obstructed or blocked several social democratic reforms put forward by Syriza during its stay in power. Douzinas himself is a former Syriza Member of Parliament in Greece.

[139] D Landau, 'Abusive Constitutionalism' (2013) 47 *University of California Davis Law Review* 189.

with friendlier and less hostile individuals. Examples of this type of behaviour abound, but a particular contemporary example comes to mind in that regard: that of El Salvador. In this Central American state, a newly elected and highly popular president, Nayib Bukele, first elected in 2019, swiftly moved to consolidate his authoritarian grip on power after winning the February 2021 legislative elections by a wide margin.[140] One of his most spectacular moves to extend his authority, shortly after getting a two-thirds supermajority in the Salvadorean legislature, was to seize control of the Supreme Court's Constitutional Chamber. President Bukele's party, *Nuevas Ideas*, did so by removing, through a congressional vote,[141] the Constitutional Chamber's five justices (as well as Attorney General Raúl Melara).[142] In pure populist fashion, Bukele depicted the move as a 'decision of the Salvadorean people'.[143] After the Court ruled that the congressional vote ousting the five judges was unconstitutional,[144] Bukele, who has a history of criticising and disobeying Supreme Court rulings[145] – including an order from the Constitutional Chamber to comply with previous Supreme Court decisions[146] – responded by firing the attorney-general and replacing him with an ally of the regime.[147] A few months later, in August 2021, Bukele and his party even went as far as to pass two laws allowing authorities to dismiss all of the country's judges and prosecutors who are 60 years and older or with over 30 years of service (that is to say, approximately 35 per cent of all Salvadorean judges), a move viewed by many organisations and commentators as a threat to judicial independence.[148] Unsurprisingly, and notwithstanding the fact that, from a strictly formalistic perspective, the legislative assembly had the constitutional authority to remove Constitutional Chamber judges by a two-thirds vote,[149] the mass removal

[140] J Webber, 'El Salvador's president seizes control of top court with firing of judges' (*Financial Times*, 2 May 2021) www.ft.com/content/e59496a6-a844-425c-85ed-98341a26093e.

[141] El Salvador, Legislative Assembly, Decree No 2, *Official Gazette*, vol 431, no 81 (1 May 2021).

[142] El Salvador, Legislative Assembly, Decree No 4, *Official Gazette*, vol 431, no 81 (1 May 2021).

[143] He wrote on X (Twitter): 'Y el pueblo salvadoreño, a través de sus representantes, dijo: "¡DESTITUIDOS!", a sentence which could be translated in English as: 'And the Salvadorean people, through its representatives, said: "DISMISSED!"' (X/Twitter, 2 May 2021) x.com/nayibbukele/status/1388678337447534601.

[144] El Salvador, Constitutional Chamber of the Supreme Court of Justice, Judicial Review 1-2021 (1 May 2021).

[145] Just like other many other populists, including Modi, Bolsonaro and, more recently, Trump.

[146] El Salvador, Constitutional Chamber of the Supreme Court of Justice, Habeas Corpus 148-2020 (16 April 2020). See also, generally, Human Rights Watch, 'El Salvador: President Defies Supreme Court' (*Human Rights Watch*, 17 April 2020) www.hrw.org/news/2020/04/17/el-salvador-president-defies-supreme-court. Other ignored judgments include El Salvador, Constitutional Chamber of the Supreme Court of Justice, Judicial Review 6-2016/2-2016 (9 February 2018).

[147] Webber (n 140).

[148] See, eg, Human Rights Watch, 'El Salvador' and G Labrador', 'Asamblea de Bukele reforma la ley para purgar a un tercio de los jueces' (*Elfaro*, 1 September 2021) www.elfaro.net/es/202109/el_salvador/25681/Asamblea-de-Bukele-reforma-la-ley-para-purgar-a-un-tercio-de-los-jueces.htm.

[149] Under art 186 of the Constitution of the Republic of El Salvador (adopted 15 December 1983). See also JI Hernández G, 'The Mass Removal of Constitutional Judges in El Salvador: A New Case of Constitutional Authoritarian-Populism' (*International Journal of Constitutional Law Blog*, 14 May 2021) www.iconnectblog.com/the-mass-removal-of-constitutional-judges-in-el-salvador-a-new-case-of-constitutional-authoritarian-populism.

(or 'purge') of judges has been described in the academic literature as a 'new case of constitutional authoritarian-populism'.[150] Similarly, several historical cases of mass removal of judges, such as Juan Perón's impeachment and trial of four of the five sitting Supreme Court judges in Argentina in 1947, have also been seen under a critical lens in the academic literature, for example, as a way to remove checks on the power of the executive.[151]

Following the existing analytical framework in the literature, it may be tempting to associate the removal of Constitutional Court justices in Armenia in a similar fashion. Yet, as we have seen earlier in this chapter, in the case of Armenia the situation is arguably not as simple as it seems at first blush. Rather than acting as the guardian of democracy, engaging in what Kuo has dubbed 'judicial deceleration' in the face of instantaneous democracy and (or) of an impatient populist leader, it might very well be that the Constitutional Court of Armenia had truly become, instead, an institutional 'obstructor', a sort of 'authoritarian enclave' hindering democratisation processes following a democratic revolution. This hypothesis is further explored below. However, I first want to suggest preliminary lines for a potential distinction between more 'revolutionary' (or 'democratic') forms of populism, on the one hand, and more 'authoritarian' forms of the same phenomenon, on the other; as well as for a potential distinction between democracy-enhancing judicial deceleration, on the one hand, and anti-democratic judicial obstruction, on the other.

A. Distinguishing Revolutionary or Democratic Populism from Authoritarian Populism

The line between democracy-enhancing, 'revolutionary' (or 'democratic') and 'authoritarian' forms of populism, and similarly between judicial deceleration and judicial obstruction, can be thin. For this reason, it is important to distinguish between these different phenomena. Bojan Bugarič, for example, points out that populism is 'Janus-faced', 'simultaneously facing different directions'.[152] He argues that 'despite the current hegemony of authoritarian populism, a much different sort of populism is also possible: Democratic and anti-establishment populism, which combines elements of liberal and democratic convictions.'[153] While he does not provide a clear definition of 'democratic populism', Bugarič suggests that

[150] See, eg, Hernández (n 149). For Hernández, the mass removal of constitutional judges violates, from a substantive perspective, 'the core components of constitutional democracy embedded [in the] 2001 Inter-American Democratic Charter'.

[151] See, eg, G Helmke, *Courts under Constraints: Judges, Generals, and Presidents in Argentina* (Cambridge, Cambridge University Press, 2012) 63–65, as mentioned in A Arato, 'Populism, Constitutional Courts, and Civil Society' in C Landfried (ed), *Judicial Power: How Constitutional Courts Affect Political Transformations* (Cambridge, Cambridge University Press, 2019) 319.

[152] Bugarič, 'The Two Faces of Populism: Between Authoritarian and Democratic Populism' (2019) 20 *German Law Journal* 391.

[153] ibid.

'democratic populists' generally 'seek to protect and defend democracy by making it more responsive, equitable and inclusive'.[154] Robert Howse goes further: he strongly criticises the use of the term 'populism' by 'anti-populist elites'; taking issue with the latter, he associates some forms of (democratic) populism with radical democracy, democratic reforms and what he calls 'disruptive politics', generally referring to 'efforts against establishment or elite politics that are consistent with protecting minority rights, constitutional democracy and pluralism'.[155] As examples of 'progressive and inclusive populism', Howse refers to Syriza in Greece, the Bernie Sanders movement and the 'disruptive democratic politics' of Congresswoman Alexandria Ocasio-Cortez in the US.[156] For his part, Gábor Halmai, building on Isaiah Berlin, differentiates between 'good' (or 'true') and 'bad' (or 'false') populism; he argues that authoritarian populism is 'bad' (or 'false') populism, as it uses populism as a rhetorical device to hide autocratic aims, by contrast to the 'good' (or 'true') populism, which aims for equality and can be democratic.[157] Douglas Johnson distinguishes more clearly between 'democratic' and 'authoritarian' populism(s). He views democratic populism as 'a focus on the needs of the common people, both the poor and the middle classes', a concept that 'involves the notion of building the support of these constituencies to counterbalance and, if necessary, to politically defeat the powerful special interests of the elites, especially the economic elites'.[158] Johnson argues that 'often-ascribed characteristics of populism […] lie on a spectrum in which one end is authoritarian and the other is action legitimately appropriate to the role of social movements in a democratic society'.[159]

In the specific context of post-Velvet Revolution Armenia, four elements in particular, in my view, give weight to the argument that Pashinyan's reforms to the judiciary can be understood as a part of a form of democratic or revolutionary populism – rather than as an instance of authoritarian populism – and that Armenian courts were acting more as anti-democratic judicial obstructors than democracy-enhancing institutional decelerators. These are the following: (1) Pashinyan's decision to operate largely within the existing institutional-constitutional framework; (2) the lack of neutrality and independence of the Armenian courts; (3) the judiciary's decision to engage in a head-on confrontation with the newly elected regime; and (4) the impossibility, in practice, of amending the provisions of the Constitution pertaining to the composition of the Constitutional Court.

[154] ibid 395.

[155] R Howse, 'Epilogue: In Defense of Disruptive Democracy – A Critique of Anti-Populism' (2019) 17 *International Journal of Constitutional Law* 645.

[156] ibid.

[157] G Halmai, 'Populism, Authoritarianism and Constitutionalism' (2019) 20 *German Law Journal* 296, 298, referring (in part) to I Berlin et al, 'To Define Populism' (1968) 3 *Government and Opposition*. See also D Rodrik, 'What Does a True Populism Look Like? It Looks Like the New Deal' (*New York Times*, 21 February 2018) www.nytimes.com/2018/02/21/opinion/populism-new-deal.html.

[158] DA Johnson, 'In Defense of Democratic Populism' in GL Neuman (ed), *Human Rights in a Time of Populism: Challenges and Responses* (Cambridge, Cambridge University Press, 2020) 215.

[159] ibid 195.

These elements are also indicative, in my view, of a more 'positive' relationship between populism and constitutionalism than commonly assumed – at least in these specific circumstances.

A first important element to take into account in that regard, particularly in a transitional context, is whether the populist leader decides to act within the existing constitutional framework or whether they choose, instead, to either bypass this framework or replace it with a new constitution, with its own specific constitutional-legal institutions. Indeed, as Bruce Ackerman notes, in the context of a transition from a semi-authoritarian regime to a more established democracy, the newly elected president or prime minister ('charismatic leader') often faces two options, especially when an apex court vetoes key initiatives put forward by the elected branches: they can choose to operate within the existing constitutional framework; or they can repudiate it as an instrument for the entrenchment of power by the old regime, entirely devoid of any legitimacy.[160] In that latter case, the populist leader can then move on to create a constituent assembly tasked with drafting a new constitution, as it happened in recent decades in Peru, Venezuela or Ecuador, for instance. As we have seen in Part I (and in the next chapter), the enactment of a new constitution, in such circumstances, can go beyond mere symbolism: it can be used by the populist, charismatic leader as a tool to tilt power in their favour.

Pashinyan, for his part, chose to follow the first path: he chose to operate, in the aftermath of the Velvet Revolution, largely within the existing constitutional and legal framework, however flawed, without repudiating it entirely from the outset, but, rather, by reforming it from the inside, most notably through legislative measures and reforms – and ultimately through a constitutional amendment leading to the removal of three Constitutional Court justices.[161] This is not to say, of course, that choosing not to (fully) replace the previous constitution is the only

[160] See, generally, B Ackerman, *Revolutionary Constitutions: Charismatic Leadership and the Rule of Law* (Cambridge, Harvard University Press, 2019).

[161] There have been attempts to reform the Constitution since Pashinyan took power. The above-mentioned Expert Commission on Constitutional Reform (sometimes also translated as 'Specialised Commission for Constitutional Reforms') was dissolved in December 2021 after a series of emergencies, including the Covid-19 pandemic and the 2020 Nagorno-Karabakh war, had thwarted its work. It was replaced in January 2022 with a new Constitutional Reform Council, chaired by the Minister of Justice. One of the main elements that the Council is expected to consider is whether Armenia should move from a parliamentary system to a presidential or semi-presidential one. However, while seats had been allocated to the two main parliamentary opposition parties, these parties announced that they would boycott the constitutional reform process, arguing that the latter is 'an attempt by the current government to entrench its incumbency'. See H Manougian, 'Armenia's Constitutional Journey Continues' (*ConstitutionNet*, 31 January 2022) www.constitutionnet.org/news/armenias-constitutional-journey-continues; 'Armenia to Create Constitutional Reforms Council' (*Armenpress*, 20 December 2021) www.armenpress.am/eng/news/1071166. Moreover, in May 2024, Pashinyan changed the Council's mandate to request the drafting of a completely new constitution, although there are strong indications that this is perhaps driven more by geopolitical pressure than by a genuine desire to entirely repudiate the existing constitutional framework, as discussed below and in S Galstian, 'New Armenian Constitution Still Not Discussed by Government Panel' (*Azatutyun*, 22 November 2024) www.azatutyun.am/a/33212473.html [in Armenian].

factor to take into consideration in assessing whether a specific type of populism is a form of authoritarian populism (engaging in 'abusive constitutionalism', for instance) or if it is, on the contrary, an instance of what could be described as 'revolutionary' or 'democratic' populism. Indeed, there might very well be instances in which a complete overhaul of the constitutional and legal framework is necessary to achieve democratisation. In the case of Armenia, while some have initially applauded Pashinyan for his decision to operate mainly within the existing constitutional framework and avoid 'constitutional re-engineering',[162] others have warned that this strategy may become a 'liability', as an 'unreformed holdover judiciary has the capacity to derail substantially all reforms and anti-corruption initiatives formulated by parliament'.[163] This possibility – which has arguably materialised in the present case, at least to an extent and particularly until the 2020 reforms – is discussed in more detail below.

A second element to take into consideration in assessing if a populist assault on a constitutional court is a form of authoritarian populism or, rather, a kind of 'revolutionary' or 'democratic' populism is whether the existing judiciary is truly neutral and independent. This is all the more important in a context of democratisation. As Ulrich Preuß explains,

> [w]hile in established constitutional democracies there is normally no dispute as to the impartiality and neutrality of the constitutional court, in post-authoritarian countries in transition towards constitutional democracy, the court's impartiality is either openly challenged or subject to a widespread diffuse distrust'.[164]

The latter situation arguably applies to the case of post-Velvet Revolution Armenia: the Constitutional Court (and the judiciary in general) was subject to widespread distrust, as the Venice Commission recognised,[165] and there were 'undoubtedly questions about the neutrality of Armenia's Constitutional Court judges'.[166] The neutrality of Constitutional Court justices was questioned in part due to the fact that, of the nine justices, seven had been appointed by Pashinyan's predecessors (and current political opponents) – and, perhaps more importantly, some of these justices had even held influential political posts within the previous regime.[167] The most striking example is probably that of the former chairperson of the Court,

[162] See, eg, S Vasilyan, 'Armenia's (R)Evolutionary Breakthrough: Constitutionalism at Work?' (*ConstitutionNet*, 28 June 2018) www.constitutionnet.org/news/armenias-revolutionary-breakthrough-constitutionalism-work.

[163] Ohanyan (n 78).

[164] UK Preuß, 'Judicial Power in Processes of Transformation' in C Landfried (ed), *Judicial Power: How Constitutional Courts Affect Political Transformations* (Cambridge, Cambridge University Press, 2019) 353.

[165] Venice Commission (n 92) CDL-AD(2022)002 [7].

[166] T de Waal, 'Armenia's Fight Over the Rule of Law Has Echoes Across the Region' (*World Politics Review*, 3 March 2020) www.worldpoliticsreview.com/articles/28574/armenia-s-fight-over-the-rule-of-law-has-echoes-across-the-region.

[167] 'Armenia to hold referendum on Constitutional Court in April' (*Reuters*, 9 February 2020) www.reuters.com/article/us-armenia-referendum/armenia-to-hold-referendum-on-constitutional-court-in-april-idUSKBN2030O1.

Hrayr Tovmasyan. As briefly mentioned earlier, this highly influential justice, a former Minister of Justice under the RPA government, was appointed by an RPA-led Parliament in 2018 for a mandate of 17 years. However, his appointment allegedly came about following a subterfuge (and an alleged falsification),[168] just a few days before the entry into force of a constitutional amendment that would limit the term of the chairperson to six years (and of the individual judges for 12 years).[169]

Yet, the issue with a judiciary that is too strongly linked to a former regime is that it may very well give way to a system in which 'old' courts legitimise previous authoritarian regimes, thereby hindering ongoing democratisation processes.[170] Indeed, constitutional courts with deep ties to a former regime can use their judicial review powers (either in their weak or strong forms) to engage in what David Landau and Rosalind Dixon have described as 'abusive judicial review'.[171] Through this process, courts use their review powers to actively undermine (rather than protect) liberal democratic constitutionalism – not necessarily just to legitimise abusive constitutional changes enacted by a would-be autocrat, as is often the case, but also, I would add, to impede democratic reforms and democratisation processes more broadly. This is precisely what happened, or at least what Pashinyan claims to have happened, in the case of Armenia, with the Constitutional Court blocking several reforms, including reforms to the judiciary supported by a wide range of international actors, including the Venice Commission.

The fact that a constitutional court has strong ties to an existing (or, in this case, a previous) regime is not exactly a new phenomenon. In fact, there is some evidence that judicial intervention in post-Soviet courts, including the Constitutional Court of Armenia, is 'more often than not the product of direct political instruction or manipulation'.[172] As Armen Mazmanyan convincingly argues in a 2015 survey of judicial politics in the post-Soviet countries, behind almost 'every instance of apparently brave judicial decision-making in politically sensitive situations' hides a form of 'political partisanship, affiliation, or manipulation'.[173] In many of these politically-sensitive decisions, in which we could probably include the Kocharyan ruling and the Court's unwillingness to amend the Constitution to allow changes to the composition of the Court, 'the judiciary's political empowerment is more likely than not a false impression: in reality, it is a substitute or a deceptive cover for

[168] See S Vasilyan, 'Armenia's Constitutional Referendum: Denting the Constitutional Court?' (*ConstitutionNet*, 18 March 2020) www.constitutionnet.org/news/armenias-constitutional-referendum-denting-constitutional-court and the discussion above. See also Pashinyan, 'Speech at the Extraordinary Session of the National Assembly'.

[169] ibid.

[170] Ohanyan (n 78).

[171] D Landau and R Dixon, 'Abusive Judicial Review: Courts Against Democracy' (2020) 53 *University of California, Davis Law Review*.

[172] A Mazmanyan, 'Judicialization of Politics: The Post-Soviet Way' (2015) 13 *International Journal of Constitutional Law* 208.

[173] ibid.

direct political action by the dominant political power-holder'.[174] Arguably, in this case, the dominant power-holder remained the former RPA regime, which, despite having lost power, nevertheless continued to maintain a strong grip on Armenia's political-institutional sphere.

A third element to take into account, linked to the previous point, is whether this 'impartial' judiciary chooses to engage in a head-on confrontation with the new regime. To borrow Ackerman's framework, in the first stage of a constitutional revolution ('Time One'), revolutionary insurgents denounce the existing regime as 'illegitimate'. This is a moment of 'high-energy politics'.[175] Once the old regime has been replaced with a new, revolutionary (and, on their own account, 'legitimate') one, the political branches of government 'will predictably accuse the judiciary of playing politics if it tries to use its old-style legalisms to veto key initiatives advanced by the movement party in power'.[176] This risk of confrontation can lead to two outcomes. Either the courts embark on a direct clash with the political branches, risking institutional humiliation, or they take a step back and build up 'an increasingly elaborate body of authoritative opinions that will serve as the basis for greater professional self-confidence as the years go by'.[177]

Interestingly, in the case of post-revolution Armenia, the courts chose the first option – to clash head-on with Pashinyan and his parliamentary faction. In doing so, the Court ran counter to the tradition, in the post-Soviet world, of constitutional courts seeking integration into the dominant power rather than resisting it, largely for considerations of self-preservation and survival.[178] The most striking example is probably the Constitutional Court's decision,[179] in April 2019, to side with the previous regime and validate a 'counterrevolutionary' bill[180] that had been introduced by the RPA parliamentary faction after Pashinyan's appointment as Prime Minister but before the December 2018 parliamentary elections – and therefore at a time when RPA still held a parliamentary majority. This bill, adopted by Parliament on 2 October 2018, was meant to impede Pashinyan's plan to dissolve the RPA-led Parliament and to hold elections in December of the same year.[181] As the President of the Republic had refused to sign the bill, the latter had not yet

[174] ibid.

[175] Ackerman (n 160) 4.

[176] ibid 9.

[177] ibid.

[178] Mazmanyan (n 172).

[179] Constitutional Court of Armenia, *On the Case of Conformity of Clauses 2 and 3 of Part 6 of Article 50 Prescribed by Part 1 of Article 2 of the Constitutional Law Adopted by the National [Assembly] on Making Supplements and Amendments to the RA Constitutional Law on Rules of Procedure of the National Assembly with the Constitution of the Republic of Armenia on the Basis of the Application of the President of the Republic* (DCC-1454, 19 April 2019) [unofficial translation].

[180] Law on Making Amendments and Addenda to the RA Constitutional Law Rules of Procedure of the National Assembly, adopted by the National Assembly on 2 October 2018 (but not signed by the President of the Republic).

[181] N Nalbandian, 'Armenian Court Validates "Counterrevolutionary" Bill' (*Azatutyun*, 22 April 2019) www.azatutyun.am/a/29897125.html [in Armenian].

entered into force, and the President had referred the matter to the Constitutional Court. The latter, in an *in abstracto* decision rendered by Chairperson Tovmasyan, wrote that, notwithstanding the recent events that had led to Pashinyan's appointment as Prime Minister and the low level of support for the RPA at the time, the (then RPA-led) Parliament held 'a direct [form of] democratic legitimacy' as the 'highest representative body of the people', and that the mechanisms ensuring the proper functioning of the legislative functions 'did not allow the [dissolution of Parliament], which is directly formed by the people, by virtue of law, if the deputies [are] unable to demonstrate their will for objective reasons'.[182] The Court added that the 'constitutional requirement of openness of the meetings of the National Assembly [Parliament] [had not been] violated' in this case and that it was 'impossible to reliably determine the true will of the legislator'.[183] As a result, the Court held that the disputed bill (preventing the dissolution of the RPA-led Parliament) was in full compliance with the Constitution.[184] Interestingly, the Court emphasised 'the key role of the National Assembly [Parliament] in shaping the will of the people',[185] but did not seem to give any weight to the appointment of Pashinyan as Prime Minister, nor to the recent political events (namely, the Velvet Revolution) which had led to the latter.

The Court's decision to side with the previous RPA regime and engage in a clash with a newly appointed Prime Minister, Pashinyan, was all the more surprising given that the case had become largely moot by the time it was delivered in April 2019: the December 2018 elections had already taken place and had been won, by a wide margin, by Pashinyan's My Step alliance. Nevertheless, the Court's decision to validate a 'counterrevolutionary' bill and throw some sand into the works of the newly elected regime is in line with Palomar Aguilar's suggestion (in a different context) that 'the degree of judicial complicity in authoritarian repression may have significant implications for the ability and willingness of courts to facilitate transitional justice following regime transition'.[186] This lack of judicial restraint indeed may be seen as an attempt, by the Court, to 'gain time' (and to delay the election of a new, 'revolutionary' parliamentary majority) by using the 'notorious slowness of the legal process'.[187] Of course, this particular attempt was ultimately unsuccessful in this specific instance, as new parliamentary elections took place in December 2018 regardless of the bill and its disputed constitutional validity.

[182] Constitutional Court of Armenia, Decision DCC-1454 (19 April 2019) 9.

[183] ibid 17.

[184] ibid 18.

[185] ibid 6.

[186] P Aguilar, 'Judiciary Involvement in Authoritarian Repression and Transitional Justice: The Spanish Case in Comparative Perspective' (2013) 7 *International Journal of Transitional Justice* 245, as summarised by Tamir Moustafa in T Moustafa, 'Law and Courts in Authoritarian Regimes' (2014) 10 *Annual Review of Law and Social Science* 281, 291–292.

[187] ML Volcansek, 'Judicialization of Politics or Politicization of Courts in New Democracies?' in Landfried (ed) (n 164) 81.

Other examples of Armenian courts siding with the previous regime could also be mentioned, including the two Kocharyan cases, briefly mentioned above – particularly the Constitutional Court's 2019 decision.[188] In an opinion written by Chairperson Tovmasyan, the Court ruled that the provision of the Code of Criminal Procedure[189] that allegedly removed the immunity of officials contradicted parts[190] of the Constitution and was thus invalid.[191] This controversial ruling led critics to accuse the Court – and more specifically then-Chairperson Tovmasyan – of 'abusing the power of [their] office to shield figures linked to the previous regime from prosecution – most notably former presidents Kocharyan and Sargsyan – in addition to repeatedly obstructing key reform packages passed by Parliament'.[192] However, it should be noted that the Constitutional Court ultimately ruled, in March 2021 – that is to say, *after* the three controversial justices with ties to the previous regime had been removed from office (with former Chairperson Tovmasyan nevertheless remaining as justice) – that the provision of the Criminal Code under which Kocharyan was charged was indeed unconstitutional,[193] which led, two weeks later, to his acquittal and his return to politics.[194]

Finally, regarding the abovementioned use of constitutional amendment procedures to remove the Constitutional Court justices appointed by (and/or with ties to) the previous regime,[195] the decision to bypass the Court could be justified, at least in part, by the fact that the Constitution could not legally be amended without the mandatory *ex ante* approval of the Constitutional Court itself. Indeed, under Articles 168 and 169(2) of the Constitution of Armenia

[188] Constitutional Court of Armenia, Decision DCC-1476.

[189] Code of Criminal Procedure of the Republic of Armenia (adopted 1 July 1998), art 35.

[190] Namely, art 27(1), para 4 (on personal liberty); art 61(1) (on the right to judicial protection); art 63(1) (on the right to a fair trial); and art 75 (on the organisational structures and procedures for the exercise of fundamental rights and freedoms) of the Constitution of Armenia.

[191] Constitutional Court of Armenia, Decision DCC-1476 16. Interestingly, the judgment was accompanied by two dissenting opinions, one by Justice Arman Dilanyan and another by Justice Felix Tokhyan. See ibid 17–32 [1–16] and 33–41 [1–9], respectively.

[192] R Elliott, 'Armenia to Hold Fifth Constitutional Referendum in the Spring' (*The Armenian Weekly*, 12 February 2020) www.armenianweekly.com/2020/02/12/armenia-to-hold-fifth-constitutional-referendum-in-the-spring/.

[193] Constitutional Court of Armenia, *On the Case of Conformity of Article 300.1 of the Criminal Code of the Republic of Armenia with the Constitution on the Basis of the Applications of Robert Kocharyan and the First Instance Court of General Jurisdiction of Yerevan* (DCC-1586, 26 March 2021) [unofficial translation]. See also 'Armenia's top court dismisses Kocharyan case as "unconstitutional"' (*OC Media*, 26 March 2021) www.oc-media.org/armenias-top-court-dismisses-kocharyan-case-as-unconstitutional.

[194] A Mejlumyan, 'Armenian ex-president acquitted' (Eurasia.net, 6 April 2021) www.eurasianet.org/armenian-ex-president-acquitted. However, in September 2024 the Court of Cassation overturned the acquittal and allowed a reclassification of the charges. At the time of writing, in October 2025, Kocharyan's new trial appears to be ongoing. See, eg, A Khulian, 'Judge Bans Reporter From Covering Kocharian's Trial' (*Azatutyun*, 21 April 2025) www.azatutyun.am/a/33391780.html. Another trial on separate bribery charges ended in 2024 due to the expiry of the statute of limitations. See more on this below.

[195] That is to say, appointed before the entry into force of ch 7 of the Constitution of Armenia (as amended in 2015).

(as amended in 2015), the Constitutional Court must perform a preliminary review of the constitutionality of draft constitutional amendments.[196] Yet, in this instance, the Court would have had to rule, essentially, on the effective dismissal of its own justices – something it was clearly not prepared to do.[197] This 'conflict of interest',[198] combined with the possible impartiality of certain Constitutional Court justices, as discussed above, gave rise to a form of constitutional strait-jacket, what Pashinyan called a 'cruel example of the usurpation of power'.[199] This can thus explain the decision by Pashinyan and his parliamentary faction to remove three judges and the Chairperson by way of a constitutional amendment in June 2020. It is worth mentioning that without going as far in their analyses, both the Venice Commission and the ECtHR have recognised the legitimacy of the aim pursued by the constitutional amendment, despite the fact that Pashinyan's parliamentary faction chose to ignore the Venice Commission's suggestion for a 'transitional period' in which the contested judges could have maintained their role within the Constitutional Court.[200] In its 2023 *Gyulumyan* ruling (in response to an action brought forward by the three dismissed justices and the then-Chairperson of the Constitutional Court, whose mandate was also terminated), the ECtHR notably mentioned that the June 2020 constitutional amendment

> had a legitimate aim, since [its] objective was to ensure that the high democratic standards concerning the independence of the Constitutional Court […] produced their effects as soon as possible, and that all judges of the Constitutional Court would enjoy the same status irrespective of the time of their appointment […]. [H]ad the June 2020 amendment not taken effect, the full implementation of the 2015 reform would have been excessively protracted as it would have taken the authorities up to the next twenty years to achieve all the objectives sought. For instance, [Justice Tovmasyan] would have remained [chairperson] of the Constitutional Court until 2035.[201]

The dismissal of the three Constitutional Court justices and the termination of the tenure of its then-Chairperson (who was appointed by an RPA-led Parliament with a life mandate) by way of a constitutional amendment, as well as the reduction of all of the other justices' terms of office to 12 years, also appears to have

[196] Art 168(2) of the Constitution of Armenia.

[197] As evidenced by the Constitutional Court's decision to reject Parliament's motion on the dismissal of Tovmasyan as Chairperson. See 'Constitutional Court rejects parliament's motion on ousting Hrayr Tovmasyan' (*Armenpress*, 14 October 2019) www.armenpress.am/eng/news/991611.

[198] In that regard, art 14(2) of the Law on the Constitutional Court of Armenia provides that members of the Constitutional Court may not use the authority of their position as a judge to favour their own interests. See also Venice Commission, *Opinion on Three Legal Questions in the Context of Draft Constitutional Amendments Concerning the Mandate of the Judges of the Constitutional Court* (Opinion No 988/2020, 22 June 2020) CDL-AD(2020)016 [71]: 'the Constitutional Court should use extensive self-restraint in order to avoid any impression of favouring the personal interest of the judges when reviewing amendments concerning the Court itself'.

[199] See Pashinyan, 'Speech at the Extraordinary Session of the National Assembly'.

[200] Venice Commission (n 198) CDL-AD(2020)016.

[201] *Gyulumyan and Others v Armenia* (2023) [77], referring also to ibid.

some level of support within the Court itself. In an April 2024 interview with me in Yerevan, Justice Vahe Grigoryan, then Vice-Chairperson of the Constitutional Court (and now ECtHR judge), conveyed his satisfaction with the ECtHR decision, saying that the Strasbourg Court had assessed the constitutional-legal context of post-Revolution Armenia with 'surgical accuracy'. He took the view that the value of the transitional period proposed by the Venice Commission had to be assessed against the risks of delaying fundamental reforms in a transitional democracy. To support this position, Justice Grigoryan mentioned that Armenia by that time was already in a state of emergency, declared by the government to fight the spread of Covid-19. He explained that the Constitutional Court, as the main institution ensuring the checks-and-balances in a constitutional democracy, could not itself be in a transitional mode. Justice Grigoryan also mentioned the broader political context, which included the political crisis in the aftermath of the 2020 Nagorno-Karabakh War, juxtaposed with the request, by almost the entirety of the General Staff of the Armed Forces, for the resignation of the democratically elected government. In Justice Grigoryan's view, the Constitutional Court 'remained unshattered in its allegiance to the fundamentals of constitutional democracy', mentioning in support of this view the Court's decision on the unequivocal support of the principle of democratic control over the armed forces,[202] which stemmed from the same context. In summarising his opinion, he stated that 'any potential lack of resolve in a country's transition to democracy, especially in relation to reforms to the judiciary and the broader justice system, is likely to seriously hinder this transition, if not end in tragedy for that democracy'.[203]

To summarise, four elements illustrate (or at least give weight to the argument), in my view, that Pashinyan's actions in the wake and immediate aftermath of the Velvet Revolution were more akin to 'revolutionary' or 'democratic' populism than authoritarian forms of populism. These elements are: Pashinyan's decision to (at least initially) operate largely within the existing constitutional framework; the strong ties of the Constitutional Court (and its Chairperson) with the previous regime; the Court's decision to engage in a head-on confrontation with the new government; and the Court's apparent conflict of interest and visible unwillingness to rule on the legality of the dismissal of its own judges. In the same vein, and for the reasons mentioned above, a strong case could be made that Armenian courts, particularly the Constitutional Court, had acted in the aftermath of the Velvet Revolution as an institutionally co-opted and insulated 'semi-authoritarian haven', and ultimately as 'judicial obstructors' rather than institutional decelerators against Pashinyan's 'constitutional impatience'.

[202] Constitutional Court of Armenia, *On the Case of Conformity of Part 3 of Article 40 of the Law on Military Service and the Status of a Serviceman with the Constitution on the Basis of the Application of the President of the Republic* (DCC-1616, 2 November 2021).

[203] Author's interview with Justice Vahe Grigoryan, Yerevan, 30 April 2024.

B. The 'Final Stage' of the Revolution: Democratisation in the Long Term?

Given that many of Pashinyan's reforms are still ongoing, the long-term effects of the Velvet Revolution on the state of democracy in Armenia remain to be seen. Indeed, it is still unclear, at the time of writing, whether Pashinyan will be (or has been) successful in effectively increasing, in the long term, the degree of political freedom and political competition in Armenia. It is possible that, as has often happened in the past, the revolution fades away or, even, that freedom vanishes into quasi-authoritarianism.[204] The situation in Armenia remains complicated, partly due to events such as the Second Nagorno-Karabakh War in late 2020 and Azerbaijan's 2023 offensive, which has led to the displacement of over 100,000 ethnic Armenians from Nagorno-Karabakh to Armenia.[205] While his Civil Contract party comfortably won snap elections in 2021 in the aftermath of a clash with the country's then-top military officer who had called for his resignation as Prime Minister,[206] Pashinyan's personal popularity ratings have declined significantly in recent years, partly due to his handling of the abovementioned events.[207] Many have also voiced their concerns over what they perceive as a lack of effective checks and balances in the country and a concentration of power in the hands of the ruling party as a result of the institutional changes put forward since 2019 – which might jeopardise democratisation efforts in the long term.[208] Some recent events appear to give weight to these concerns, including the controversial arrest, in June 2025, of Russian-Armenian billionaire Samvel Karapetyan and, a few days later, of prominent Archbishop Bagrat Galstanyan, charged with orchestrating a plot to overthrow the government following a standoff with the Armenian Apostolic

[204] This is precisely what Vahram Abadjian suggests in V Abadjian, 'Pashinyan's Gambit or Armenia's Failed Revolution' (2020) 5 *Acta Via Serica* 121. It is also what arguably happened in Tunisia under Kais Saied's governance, nearly a decade after the Jasmine Revolution. See, eg, T Desrues and E Gobe, 'Kais Saied's Governance: The Tunisian President's Drift from Inclusive Populist Constitutionalism to "Caesarism"' (2025) *Journal of North African Studies* (advance access). Interestingly, Said has 'given himself the right to dismiss judges', on the mere basis of a police report alleging corruption. See 'Tunisian President Saied: "A populist criticising representative democracy" standing for re-election' (*France24.com*, 29 August 2024) www.france24.com/en/africa/20240829-tunisia-president-kais-saied-a-populist-who-criticises-representative-democracy-election.

[205] See, eg, G Wright, 'Nagorno-Karabakh: Armenia says 100,000 refugees flee region' (*BBC*, 30 September 2023) www.bbc.co.uk/news/world-europe-66969845.

[206] With 53.9% of the vote and a comfortable majority of 71 seats (out of 107 – the total number of seats in Parliament fluctuates due to additional and levelling (adjustment) seats.

[207] As of June 2025, Pashinyan and Civil Contract continue to lead in the polls, but with only 17% of respondents expressing their intention to vote for the party. Similarly, while Pashinyan remains the most trusted politician in Armenia (13%), a vast majority (61%) of respondents said they do not trust any politician. See 16–26 June 2025 poll conducted by Breavis on behalf of the International Republic Institute's Center for Insights on Survey Research, www.iri.org/resources/public-opinion-survey-residents-of-armenia-june-2025.

[208] See, eg, H Nikoghosyan and V Ter-Matevosyan, 'From "Revolution" to War: Deciphering Armenia's Populist Foreign Policy-Making Process' (2023) 23 *Southeast European and Black Sea Studies* 207.

Church.[209] It is in this broader context of polarisation and cleavage that scholar and commentator Armen Mazmanyan has suggested that Pashinyan's 'populist zero-sum game' may have transformed political competition in Armenia into an 'existential struggle', where tomorrow's loser risks facing the same treatment endured by yesterday's, which could revert all institutional changes enacted by Pashinyan's forces since taking power.[210] This casts doubt over the long-term success of democratisation efforts in the country. Moreover, on many levels Armenia remains at this point a deeply imperfect democracy, a 'partly free' country with significant rule of law concerns, including courts that 'face systemic political influence' as well as 'judicial institutions [that] are undermined by corruption'.[211]

Yet, there are reasons to believe that Armenia has made strong progress since 2018 and is likely to continue its process of democratic consolidation, at least in the short-to-medium term. First, there have been two cycles of free and fair parliamentary elections since the beginning of the Velvet Revolution – one in 2018 and another in 2021, with a third one nearing in 2026.[212] Second, while indicators generally have to be interpreted with caution,[213] it is nonetheless interesting to note that Freedom House gave Armenia a score of 55/100 in its Freedom in the World 2021 report, a major, 10-point jump between 2018 and 2021.[214] According to Freedom House, the increase is due, in part, to the strengthening of the legal framework for anticorruption measures and the prosecution of former government officials, as well as the reduction of undue influence in business activities by affiliates of the previous regime.[215] Similarly, Freedom House's Nations in Transit Report score for Armenia made a major jump from 26/100 ('semi-consolidated

[209] See, eg, R Demytrie, 'Armenia's PM offers to expose himself in escalating Church row' (*BBC*, 26 June 2025) www.bbc.co.uk/news/articles/c4gk0nw2nn0o.

[210] A Mazmanyan, 'Constitutional Choices After a (Democratic) Revolution: Lessons from Armenia, and elsewhere' (paper presented at the 'Building Institutional Resilience' international workshop, Malyi Center, University of Chicago Law School, 26–27 September 2024; unpublished manuscript; on file with author).

[211] 'Freedom in the World 2025 – Armenia' (*Freedom House*, 2025) www.freedomhouse.org/country/armenia/freedom-world/2025.

[212] Beyond the 2018 parliamentary elections discussed above, the 2021 parliamentary election was also viewed as free and fair by international observers, despite some shortcomings. See, eg, 'Freedom in the World 2022 – Armenia' and ODIHR Election Observation Mission, 'Republic of Armenia: Early Parliamentary Elections, 20 June 2021 – Final Report' (*OSCE/ODIHR*, 27 October 2021) www.osce.org/files/f/documents/5/4/502386.pdf.

[213] For instance, the American anthropologist Sally Engle Merry has warned against the reliance on 'simplified numerical representations' in the field of global governance, arguing that this turn to indicators 'introduces a new form of knowledge production with implications for relations of power between rich and poor nations and between governments and civil society'. According to Merry, '[t]he deployment of statistical measures tends to replace political debate with technical expertise', and '[t]he growing reliance on indicators provides an example of the dissemination of the corporate form of thinking and governance into broader social spheres'. See SE Merry, 'Measuring the World: Indicators, Human Rights, and Global Governance' (2011) 52 *Current Anthropology* S83, S83.

[214] 'Freedom in the World 2021 – Armenia' (*Freedom House*, 2021) www.freedomhouse.org/country/armenia/freedom-world/2021.

[215] ibid.

authoritarian regime') in 2018 to 34/100 ('transitional or hybrid regime') in 2022 – and increased to 35/100 in 2023, a score it maintained in 2024.[216] The Economist Intelligence Unit's Democracy Index for Armenia has also risen sharply, from 4.11 in 2017 to 5.54 in 2019 (but 5.35 in 2020, a score it currently maintains).[217]

More specialised indicators paint a similar picture. For example, the corruption perceptions index in Armenia increased significantly in the years that followed the Velvet Revolution, from 35/100 in 2018 (rank: 105/180 in the world) to 49/100 (rank: 58/180 in the world) in 2021, a major, 14-point jump – by far the highest increase amongst Eastern European and Central Asian countries.[218] In 2022, Transparency International noted that '[s]ince the 2018 Velvet Revolution, Armenia has made significant progress in its measures to counter corruption'.[219] In a region marred with '[w]idespread democratic backsliding and weakening justice systems [that] are undermining [the] control of corruption',[220] such a significant improvement is noteworthy. These elements indicate a certain level of democratic development in Armenia since the Velvet Revolution, which, combined with the abovementioned reform to the judiciary, could in the long term lead to more judicial independence, a higher degree of effective judicialisation and more efficient checks on the executive in the country.

That said, some recent developments have perhaps cast some shadow over Pashinyan's democratisation efforts, showing potential signs of stagnation. To give an example, there has been a relatively small regression in the abovementioned indicators since the end of the clash with the Constitutional Court in 2021. For example, the corruption perception index has dropped slightly, from 49/100 (rank: 58/180) in 2021 to 46/100 (rank: 63/180) in 2022, before moving back up to 47/100 (rank: 62/180) in 2023, a rating it retained in 2024.[221] Similarly, Armenia's score in the Freedom in the World index dropped by one per cent in 2023, from 55/100 to 54/100, a score it kept in 2024 and 2025.[222] Concerns remain about potential political interference in the judiciary, as evidenced by the controversial suspension and replacement of the Chairperson of the Supreme Judicial Council (the body in charge of appointing, disciplining and dismissing judges) with Karen Andreasyan, a former Justice Minister under Pashinyan's government who had sought, as minister,

[216] 'Nations in Transit 2024 – Armenia' (*Freedom House*, 2024) www.freedomhouse.org/country/armenia/nations-transit/2024.

[217] Economist Intelligence Unit, 'Democracy Index: Armenia' (*Our World in Data*, 5 March 2025) www.ourworldindata.org/grapher/democracy-index-eiu?tab=chart&country=~ARM#explore-the-data.

[218] 'Corruption Perceptions Index: Armenia' (*Transparency International*, 2021) www.transparency.org/en/cpi/2021/index/arm.

[219] M Bak, 'U4 Helpdesk Answer 2022: Overview of corruption and anti-corruption' (*Transparency International*, 18 April 2022) knowledgehub.transparency.org/assets/uploads/kproducts/Overview-of-corruption-and-anti-corruption-in-Armenia_2022-final.pdf.

[220] 'Corruption Perceptions Index 2023' (*Transparency International*, 2024) images.transparencycdn.org/images/Report_CPI2023_Eng.pdf 16.

[221] 'Corruption Perceptions Index: Armenia' (*Transparency International*, 2024) www.transparency.org/en/cpi/2024/index/arm.

[222] 'Freedom in the World 2025 – Armenia' (*Freedom House*, 2025) www.freedomhouse.org/country/armenia/freedom-world/2025.

to revive the idea of judicial vetting and had called for the Judicial Council to engage in a mass removal of 'corrupt' judges.[223] In late 2023, the same Judicial Council suspended no less than seven judges on the basis of alleged 'serious disciplinary violations'.[224] In July 2024, the Judicial Council terminated the powers of the judge in charge of the bribery trial of former President Robert Kocharyan (whose case had been dismissed due to the expiry of the statute of limitations).[225] In November of the same year, Andreasyan resigned – at Pashinyan's request – as Chairperson of the Judicial Council, along with the Chairperson of the Anti-Corruption Committee and four other high-ranking officials, due to the 'poor performance' of the relevant bodies and the slow pace of the reforms and corruption trials, with Pashinyan saying that his 'patience is running out'.[226]

Moreover, there have also been recent talks to draft a new constitution that would be put to a referendum in 2026 or 2027, though these initiatives appear to be driven more by geopolitical and external pressure than by a genuine desire to break with the existing constitutional framework.[227] Nevertheless, these initiatives appear to be marked by a certain lack of transparency (in relation to who would draft the new constitution, when and how) and limited public consultation and deliberation.[228] In terms of his political style, Pashinyan continues to follow the ideal-typical populist discourse and to view himself as the 'representative of the people's power', as evidenced by a March 2025 Facebook post in which he wrote: 'No one brought me to power. In 2018, the People's, non-violent, Velvet Revolution brough the People to power. I am just a representative of the People's power and the People will replace me with someone else whenever they want.'[229]

In relation to his judicial reforms (including the removal of judges), was Pashinyan's intention really to make the judicial system 'truly independent', as

[223] See ibid and 'Member Quits Armenian Judicial Watchdog in Protest' (10 October 2022) www.azatutyun.am/a/32074294.html [in Armenian]. On judicial vetting, see section III(A) and (B) above.

[224] G Balasanyan, 'Armenia's Judicial Council Suspends Seven Judges in 2023' (*Hetq.am*, 13 December 2023) www.hetq.am/en/article/162760; N Sahakian, 'Ruling Party Installs New Members of Armenian Judicial Watchdog' (*Azatutyun*, 6 October 2022) www.azatutyun.am/a/32068538.html [in Armenian].

[225] 'Judge Danibekyan has discredited the Judiciary: Karen Andreasyan' (*Iravaban.net*, 16 July 2024) www.iravaban.net/en/485923.html.

[226] A Barseghyan, 'Armenian cabinet members resign following Pashinyan's criticism' (*OC-Media*, 18 November 2024) oc-media.org/armenian-cabinet-members-resign-following-pashinyans-criticism.

[227] As Gayane Saribekian explains, Azerbaijan 'continue[s] to make the signing of a peace treaty with Armenia conditional on a change of its constitution which they say contains territorial claims to Azerbaijan. Baku specifically wants Yerevan to remove a constitutional preamble that mentions Armenia's 1990 declaration of independence, which in turn cites a 1989 unification act adopted by the legislative bodies of Soviet Armenia and the Nagorno-Karabakh Autonomous Oblast. The only legal way to do that is to enact an entirely new constitution through a referendum'. See G Saribekian, 'Minister Pledges to Meet Pashinian's Deadline For New Constitution' (*Azatutyun*, 5 December 2024), www.azatutyun.am/a/33227929.html [in Armenian].

[228] T Mughnetsian and A Mazmanyan, 'Behind the Gridlock: The Hidden Politics of Armenia's Constitutional Impasse' (*ConstitutionNet*, 26 May 2025) www.constitutionnet.org/news/voices/behind-gridlock-hidden-politics-armenias-constitutional-impasse.

[229] N Pashinyan (*Facebook*, 10 March 2025) www.facebook.com/nikol.pashinyan.

he then claimed, or was it rather to gain control over the courts, as his critics have argued?[230] Perhaps there is some level of truth in both. Pashinyan's actions nevertheless raise interesting and important questions, particularly in the context of a transition from an authoritarian regime to a more established constitutional democracy. As Anna Ohanyan highlighted in a piece written before Pashinyan's overhaul of the judiciary,

> [e]stablishing judicial independence after democratic transitions has proved challenging in the post-Soviet world. Courts have either become conduits for reformers to consolidate their newfound power – sometimes to the detriment of democracy – as in Georgia and Ukraine, or they have become a final garrison for authoritarian forces, as it appears to be the case in Armenia. In both cases, judicial independence [seems] unattainable.[231]

Yet, the importance of judicial independence in a context of a transition towards liberal constitutional democracy cannot be overstated. For instance, there appears to be a strong correlation between the rise of judicial independence and political competition.[232] Put differently, judicial independence is essential to the long-term success of the Velvet Revolution.

In the end, while some may view actions such as the immediate dismissal of Constitutional Court justices in June 2020 as a (temporary) setback for liberal constitutional democracy in Armenia and just another form of populist impatience, Pashinyan's efforts may very well prove to have, in fact, durable beneficial impacts on the degree of political freedom and the scale of political competition in Armenia and, by extension, the degree of judicial independence and effective judicialisation in the country – although this may be difficult to assess. While the long-term success of the Velvet Revolution remains to be seen, this case study illustrates how a populist-led democratic regime can potentially contribute to democratisation efforts and strengthen liberal-democratic institutions, including its judiciary, at least in the short-to-medium term and in a way that is rarely acknowledged in the mainstream legal literature on populism.[233]

VI. Conclusion

In the spring of 2018, Armenia experienced a bloodless and democratic revolution, dubbed the 'Velvet Revolution', which saw the overthrow of a corrupt, hybrid or semi-authoritarian regime. Immediately upon taking power, newly elected

[230] See, eg, Abadjian (n 204) 130. See also Stepanian (n 90); S Vasilyan, 'Armenia's overlapping constitutional reforms: Wither the Constitutional Court?' (*ConstitutionNet*, 30 July 2020) www.constitutionnet.org/news/armenias-overlapping-constitutional-reforms-wither-constitutional-court.

[231] Ohanyan (n 78).

[232] Mazmanyan (n 172) 209.

[233] In fact, Armenia is considered to be one of the few countries in recent years that went the opposite way of the democratic 'degradation', 'backsliding' or 'decay' noted elsewhere in the world.

Prime Minister Nikol Pashinyan and his government began to tackle the issue of corruption[234] and announced their plan for an ambitious legal and judicial programme of reform. Yet, Pashinyan quickly found the courts in his way, particularly the country's Constitutional Court, whose neutrality had been questioned by several actors due to its ties to the previous regime. Using rhetoric and actions which share many of the key features of the ideal-typical populist discourse,[235] Pashinyan went on to call upon his supporters to blockade the courts and, in February 2020, accused the Constitutional Court of having 'appropriated the power of the people' and of being a 'direct and terrible threat to democracy'.[236] The same day, he announced his plan for the mass removal, by way of a constitutional amendment, of all Constitutional Court justices appointed by the previous regime. In the end, constitutional amendments passed by Parliament in June 2020 led to the dismissal of three Constitutional Court justices and the appointment of a new Chairperson.

When analysing the actions and the judicial reforms proposed by Pashinyan in light of the contemporary literature on populism and (or) democratic erosion, these changes may, at first glance, appear to be another authoritarian-populist attempt to undermine the existing framework of constitutional governance, more specifically the independence of the judiciary and the separation of powers. Pashinyan is certainly not the first populist leader to forcefully remove apex court judges.[237] Yet, what I have suggested in this chapter is that things in the case of post-Velvet Revolution Armenia are far more complicated than they may initially appear: in fact, Pashinyan may have had 'valid' or 'democratic' reasons to do so, at least from a liberal-constitutionalist perspective, given the Constitutional Court's strong ties to the previous, semi-authoritarian regime that had been entrenched in Armenia for most of the previous two decades and its unwillingness to implement reforms marking a clear break with the previous era. This finding is significant, I contend, as this case study thus reveals a possibly more 'positive' relationship between populism and constitutionalism than the conventional wisdom suggests.

Indeed, the existing liberal-constitutionalist literature – which often views revolutions with a potentially misplaced suspicion[238] – appears to be ill-equipped or ill-adapted to analyse and view constitutional changes and judicial reforms

[234] Tushnet and Bojan Bugarič identify corruption as one of the 'two common failures by political elites that populists have focused on'. See M Tushnet and B Bugarič, *Power to the People: Constitutionalism in the Age of Populism* (Oxford, Oxford University Press, 2022) 59.

[235] See Part I of this book, especially ch 1.

[236] Pashinyan, 'Speech at the Extraordinary Session of the National Assembly'.

[237] One may think, for example, of the example of Justice Maria Lourdes Sereno, removed during President Rodrigo Duterte's presidency in the Philippines. Other examples would include the El Salvador example discussed in this chapter, or more historical examples such as former Argentinian President Juan Perón's famous decision, in 1947, to impeach and try four of the five Supreme Court judges.

[238] M Hailbronner, 'Introduction: Defending "Democratic Populism"?' (2019) 17 *International Journal of Constitutional Law* 681, 681. See also, generally, Ackerman (n 160).

through a more 'democratic' lens, given that a non-contextual, element-by-element analysis would surely lead to the conclusion that Pashinyan's reforms to the judiciary amount to a frontal assault on some of the main precepts of constitutional democracy. At the very least – and from a spatiotemporal perspective – the existing literature on populism seems to be focused on (or imply) conditions of 'normal constitutionality'.[239] As such, it lacks the necessary tools to discuss situations of what László Sólyom, the President of the post-communist Constitutional Court of Hungary between 1989 and 1998, has called 'transitional constitutionality': namely, the 'inevitable agenda of transition' from authoritarianism to constitutional democracy.[240]

To be sure, one may have important normative objections regarding the rhetoric used to justify the abovementioned constitutional changes and, perhaps more importantly, the means used by Pashinyan and his government to achieve them – initially through a referendum, and later via a constitutional amendment passed unilaterally through Parliament. These concerns also extend to the scope of the changes, which first involved the immediate removal of *all* Constitutional Court justices appointed before 2019 and were later revised to a more limited version: the immediate dismissal of three justices (without a transitional period) and the removal of Justice Tovmasyan as Chairperson of the Court. One may add to this list a number of politically charged trials and the recent suspension, by the Supreme Judicial Council, of several lower court judges involved in high-profile cases. Nevertheless, it would be difficult or perhaps unfair at this point to depict these actions as a clear and unequivocal instance of what comparative constitutional law scholars have called 'abusive constitutionalism'[241] (or as a form of 'stealth authoritarianism'[242] or 'autocratic legalism'[243]).

In the same vein, while Pashinyan's rhetoric and actions can clearly be identified with the ideal-typical populist discourse analysed and described in chapter one, they do not necessarily sit well with the more negative depictions of (authoritarian) populism in power, seen in analyses relating to Fidesz's Hungary, PiS's Poland or Chávez's Venezuela, for instance. Indeed, while future developments

[239] The expression is from Ulrich Preuß, in Preuß (n 164), discussing L Sólyom, 'The Role of Constitutional Courts in the Transition to Democracy: With Special Reference to Hungary' (2003) 18 *International Sociology* 133.

[240] Sólyom refers here to elements such as, inter alia, 'the issues of punishing the political crimes of the past, which raises the problem of retroactive criminal legislation; the issue of "lustration", ie the unveiling of the activities and identification of agents of the Communist secret services, and probably their temporary exclusion from key public offices'. See ibid 137-ss. While different in nature, given the spatiotemporal differences between Hungary in the 1990s and Armenia in the 2020s, these issues nevertheless share certain important similarities with the context of 'transitional justice' in Armenia in the aftermath of the 2018 Velvet Revolution.

[241] Landau (n 139).

[242] OO Varol, 'Stealth Authoritarianism' (2015) 100 *Iowa Law Review*.

[243] KL Scheppele, 'Autocratic Legalism' (2018) 85 *University of Chicago Law Review* 545. This concept is discussed further in ch 5.

may shed a different light upon the situation in Armenia, the instance of 'revolutionary' (or 'democratic') populism described in this chapter seems to give weight to the argument put forward by certain scholars that there are, in fact, different forms of populism – some of which have a more 'democratic' character than others.[244] In fact, it may well be an example of what Mark Tushnet, drawing on Hannah Arendt,[245] calls 'transformative populism', that is to say, the transformation of subjects into citizens which could, in a second step, lead to the replacement of populism by ordinary politics.[246] At the very least, there seems to be a continuum at play here, from 'revolutionary', 'democratic' (or perhaps 'transformative') populism on one end of the spectrum, to (purely) authoritarian forms of populism on the other end of the spectrum.[247] In addition, while it remains too early to call in a more definitive way in the specific case of post-Velvet Revolution Armenia, Pashinyan's populism may very well lead to (or at least contribute to) a long-term 'reduction in the effective political power of existing elites'.[248]

* * *

This case study has, I would contend, implications that go beyond Armenia. First, it points in the direction of a potentially more 'positive' relationship between (democratic) populism and constitutionalism than is commonly assumed. Second, it suggests that deviations from the principle of constitutionalism may in extraordinary circumstances be legitimate – and may even sometimes be necessary to (re)establish liberal constitutional democracy – provided that these deviations are tailored and of an exceptional nature. This may equally be relevant to other contemporary cases, potentially including the PiS-packed Constitutional Tribunal in post-2023 Poland, in relation to which some commentators have argued that deviations from certain rule of law principles – including the irremovability of judges – may be appropriate if they are 'exceptional, temporary and proportionally tailored'.[249]

[244] See, eg, Tushnet and Bugarič (n 234); M Tushnet, 'Varieties of Populism' (2019) 20 *German Law Journal*; Bugarič (n 152); D Fontana, 'Unbundling Populism' (2018) 65 *UCLA Law Review*.

[245] H Arendt, *On Revolution* (New York, Viking, 1963).

[246] That is to say, the transformation of subjects into citizens which could, in a second step, lead to the replacement of populism by ordinary politics. See Tushnet (n 244) 383.

[247] See, eg, Johnson (n 158) 215.

[248] Tushnet (n 244) 383.

[249] See, eg, G Halmai, 'Can the Rule of Law Be Restored by Violating Its Principles? The Current Polish Debate' (*Verfassungsblog*, 3 January 2025) www.verfassungsblog.de/can-the-rule-of-law-be-restored-by-violating-its-principles. See Venice Commission, *Joint Opinion of the Venice Commission and the Directorate General Human Rights and Rule of Law on European standards regulating the status of judges* (Opinion 1206/2024, 14 October 14 2024) CDL-AD(2024)029 and Venice Commission, *Opinion on the draft constitutional amendments concerning the Constitutional Tribunal and two draft laws on the Constitutional Tribunal* (Opinion No 1293/2024, 7 December 2024) CDL-AD(2024)035. See also OSCE, *Opinion on Two Bills of the Republic of Poland on the Constitutional Tribunal (Sejm Prints No 253 and 254, as of 24 July 2024)* (JUD-OIK/592/2024 [TN], 24 August 2024), which expressly refers to the situation in Armenia on multiple occasions.

Moreover, the complexity of Pashinyan as a political figure suggests that analyses of populism that distinguish between 'good' or 'true' (usually left-wing) and 'bad' or 'false' (usually right-wing) populism could sometimes be more nuanced. Pashinyan's populism straddles left- and centre-right positions. If his political style – namely, the way he mobilised mass protests and cast himself as the voice of the people against a corrupt elite and the oligarchy – might sometimes be associated with left-wing (or 'true') forms of populism, his ideological positioning is based on ideas that are not necessarily and (or) inherently left-wing, including anti-corruption, the rule of law, democratic reform, institutional transparency and the reduction of monopolies, as well as policies that could be viewed as centrist or centre-right, such as seeking foreign investment and reducing taxes for small businesses.[250]

Finally, from a spatiotemporal perspective – and from the specific angle of the 'judicial deceleration' lauded by Kuo and discussed in the introductory chapter – what this first case study illustrates is that courts can indeed decelerate the populist impatience to promote and implement constitutional change, but they can do so to such an extent that it may, in fact, become a form of institutional obstruction – particularly in a context of 'transitional constitutionality'. Instead of securing democratic spaces, as strong and independent courts are often expected to do, the judiciary can potentially act as a constraint on political liberalisation[251] and, even, become an 'authoritarian enclave'.[252] It is possible, indeed, that the judiciary could eventually transform into the last rampart or bastion of an illegitimate *ancien régime* and (or) into a major hurdle in the transition from semi-authoritarianism to constitutional democracy. In such circumstances, populist attacks on the judiciary can, perhaps counterintuitively, be seen as indicative of a 'positive' relationship between two concepts that are often seen as oxymorons, namely populism and constitutionalism. In any event, while it is too early to make a final determination in that regard, the situation in Armenia in the immediate aftermath of the Velvet Revolution appears, on its face, to give weight to Tushnet's argument that '[t]reating efforts to transform the courts as a strong point against populism', for instance, by 'criticizing populists for assaulting judicial independence' as well as other 'similar criticisms of other populist-supported constitutional changes may often be a defense of a failed status quo rather than a politically neutral defense of a central component of constitutionalism as such'.[253]

[250] In fact, Pashinyan has even claimed that Armenian politics are in a 'post-ideological landscape'. He said: 'There are no clear lines between political ideologies anymore […] in the 21st century, those lines disappeared. It's not acceptable for me to call our party "liberal," "centrist," or "social democrat," because the goals we have to achieve are beyond "-isms"'. See M Edwards, 'Armenia's Revolution Will Not Be Monopolized' (*Foreign Policy*, 13 December 2018) www.foreignpolicy.com/2018/12/13/armenias-revolution-will-not-be-monopolized.

[251] AU Bali, 'The Perils of Judicial Independence: Constitutional Transition and the Turkish Example' (2012) 52 *Virginia Journal of International Law* 235, 235, as cited in Moustafa (n 186) 286.

[252] Moustafa (n 186) 286.

[253] Tushnet (n 244) 385.

In the next case study, which focuses on Ecuador under the presidency of Rafael Correa (2007–2017), I will discuss a further, quite different possibility, namely that courts can even, in certain circumstances, accelerate (rather than decelerate) the populist flow of time by becoming active agents of executive consolidation, executive aggrandisement and authoritarian-leaning constitutional change.

5

'Constitutional Impatience', Judicial Capture and Executive Aggrandisement in Ecuador

I. Introduction

In the previous chapter, I questioned the optimistic view of constitutional courts as potential bulwarks against authoritarian, self-aggrandising populists, broadly speaking, and, more specifically, Ming-Sung Kuo's claim that courts can play the role of institutional decelerators in response to the 'instantaneous' conception of democracy put forward and defended by populists – or what I have called 'constitutional impatience' earlier in this monograph. By reference to the case of Armenia in the immediate aftermath of the Velvet Revolution (2018–2020), I argued that instead of being an impetus for the deceleration of the populist flow of time and for the re-establishment of democratic channels and processes, courts can sometimes become judicial obstructors in the face of democratic changes. In doing so, I challenged usual assumptions about the relationship between populism and constitutionalism, as well as about the institutional role of courts against populist constitutional impatience. In this second chapter of Part II of the book, I now turn my attention to another case study, namely Ecuador under the presidency of Rafael Correa (2007–2017). In this example, I wish to discuss an alternative possibility, namely that courts can, in certain circumstances, not only decelerate or obstruct democratisation, but even contribute to the *acceleration* of the populist flow of time by becoming active agents of executive consolidation and authoritarian-leaning constitutional change, potentially contributing to the aggrandisement of an impatient and omnipotent executive.

The situation in Ecuador from 2007 to 2017 shares several affinities with the previous case study on post-Velvet Revolution Armenia. Perhaps the most striking similarity is the existence, in both cases, of a particular post-revolutionary context fuelled by a certain form of 'revolutionary' (or possibly 'democratic') populism, alongside a repudiation of the previous regime (amid a background of deep socio-economic inequalities and exclusion)[1] and the rejection of many institutions associated with the latter.

[1] This was particularly the case in Ecuador. See, eg, D Landau, 'Populist Constitutions' (2018) 85 *University of Chicago Law Review* 529. A similar pattern was also observed in other countries of the Andes, including Venezuela and Bolivia.

Nevertheless, and as will become clearer in this chapter, Correa's populist project is ultimately different from that of Nikol Pashinyan on at least two major levels and is possibly indicative of a more 'negative' relationship between populism and constitutionalism than what was discussed in the previous chapter. First, while Pashinyan operated largely within the existing constitutional and institutional framework, Correa chose to entirely repudiate the former system, replacing it with a new constitution containing a new assortment of rights – including socio-economic and environmental rights – but also with its own set of legal institutions that he wished to control, from electoral commissions to judicial councils. Second, and perhaps most importantly for the purposes of this monograph, Correa's new constitutional-legal order arguably came as part of a broader project of executive consolidation, involving the subtle capture and subversion of several counter-majoritarian institutions (including independent courts, but also key 'fourth-branch'[2] institutions of the state) from within, all while maintaining a façade of democracy and legitimacy. The result, as I argue in this chapter, is that courts can simply refuse to act as institutional decelerators against an impatient and omnipotent executive. This refusal casts doubt on their general ability, in the long term, to perform their democratic functions, particularly in a context of executive dominance and consolidation. However, beyond simply refusing to act as decelerators, I further argue that courts can even *accelerate* the populist acceleration of time by becoming agents, enablers (or instruments) of executive consolidation and authoritarian-leaning constitutional change.[3]

This chapter is divided into six main sections. In the second section, I discuss Correa's 'Citizens' Revolution', which involved a dynamic engagement with the idea of the constitution, and, as I argue, was the product of a form of 'constitutional impatience'. In the third section, I analyse an underexamined aspect of Correa's populist presidency, namely the way he captured the judiciary and other key institutions of the state. I then turn my attention, in the fourth section, to three judgments of the Constitutional Court of Ecuador in which the Court refused to act as an institutional decelerator against an impatient executive and chose, instead, to accelerate Correa's populist 'constitutional impatience' by acting as a wilful agent of executive consolidation and enabling authoritarian-leaning constitutional change. In the fifth section, I discuss how Correa's populist project of judicial capture is linked to – or even a key part of – a broader project of executive aggrandisement. Finally, section VI concludes and briefly introduces the next (and final) case study.

[2] See T Khaitan, 'Guarantor Institutions' (2021) 16 *Asian Journal of Comparative Law* S40.

[3] D Landau and R Dixon, 'Abusive Judicial Review: Courts Against Democracy' (2020) 53 *University of California, Davis Law Review* 1322.

II. Constitutions, 'Constitutional Impatience' and Legal Symbolism: Rafael Correa's Citizens' Revolution

As we have seen in Part I of this monograph, a key component of the populist politics of immediacy[4] is a certain dynamic engagement with the constitution, which is perceived as a 'necessary response to the rapid changes of 'post-modern' society (in which politics needs to respond rapidly to societal change)'[5] or, similarly, as an 'urgent answer to imminent threats to the political community'.[6] As discussed in more detail in chapter two, this means, in practice, that populists often conduct a certain re-politicisation of constitutions, the latter being understood and depicted as mere 'vehicles *of* the popular will, rather than as significant constraints *on* that will'.[7] To do so, they invoke the eternal 'People-as-One', as above and beyond transient constitutions – which, as discussed earlier, are inevitably momentary and sometimes even ephemeral.[8]

In the case of Correa, this became apparent in the context of his Citizens' Revolution, more particularly with the complete repudiation of the existing constitutional and legal-institutional framework, following a nationwide plebiscite (and a new constituent assembly), and its replacement with a new constitution in 2008. This form of 'constitutional impatience' in action is discussed in the following subsection.

A. The Citizens' Revolution and the Enactment of the 2008 Constitution

The abovementioned politics of immediacy and its inherent dynamic engagement with the constitution were particularly obvious during Correa's first term as president, between 2007 and 2009. Correa, a charismatic, US-trained economist who campaigned on a progressive political platform,[9] was elected president in November 2006 with 56.7 per cent of the vote in a runoff election.[10] As an

[4] See ch 3.

[5] P Blokker, 'Populist Constitutionalism' in C de la Torre (ed), *Routledge Handbook of Global Populism* (Abingdon, Routledge, 2019) 124. See also R Prandini, 'The Future of Societal Constitutionalism in the Age of Acceleration' (2013) 20 *Indiana Journal of Global Legal Studies*.

[6] Blokker (n 5) 124.

[7] ibid.

[8] See ch 2.

[9] C Silva-Portero, 'Chronicle of an Amendment Foretold: Eliminating Presidential Term Limits in Ecuador' (*ConstitutionNet*, 20 January 2016) www.constitutionnet.org/news/chronicle-amendment-foretold-eliminating-presidential-term-limits-ecuador. See also CM Conaghan, 'Ecuador: Correa's Plebiscitary Presidency' (2008) 19 *Journal of Democracy* 46, 46.

[10] ibid 50.

anti-system outsider, Correa's campaign was based on several key elements of the ideal-typical populist discourse elaborated in the first two chapters of this monograph – particularly its left-wing variant. For instance, he depicted his main adversary, the banana tycoon Álvaro Noboa, as an 'exploitative oligarch'.[11] He also notably openly aligned himself with two contemporary populist presidents, Hugo Chávez of Venezuela and Evo Morales of Bolivia.[12]

Soon after being sworn in as president in January 2007, Correa launched his Citizens' Revolution, which had been a key element of his 2006 electoral campaign. Through anti-establishment appeals, Correa – just like Chávez and Morales had done before him – successfully mobilised mass constituencies[13] against the 'oligarchy' and the 'neoliberal exclusionary system'.[14] Facing a hostile yet fragile[15] legislative branch, he famously said, at the time, that he had 'won the election, but not power'.[16] Impatient with the institutional constraints imposed by Congress, courts and other agencies of 'horizontal accountability',[17] Correa claimed that power was still 'controlled by economic interests, the banks, the *partidocracia* [party dominance or *partyarchy*] and the media connected to the banks'.[18] The aim of the Citizens' Revolution, therefore, was to remedy this and to 'give power back to the people', as it were. This would be done through extraordinary means, marking a clear rupture with the past legal-institutional order, and first and foremost through the election of a new Constituent Assembly (a hallmark of many forms of left-wing populism[19]). This Constituent Assembly would be tasked with the complete revamp of the state's institutions, notably to 'mark a definitive break with neoliberalism' and 'end poverty'.[20]

The ultimate goal, Correa said, was to reject the 'bourgeois state' and replace it with a form of 'substantial democracy', in contrast to the liberal, bourgeois and superficial 'procedural democracy'; in other words, Correa promised to deliver a 'true democracy' (*una democracia verdadera*) which, as Catherine M Conaghan summarised, 'would deliver not procedural niceties, but substantial

[11] See, eg, CM Conaghan and C de la Torre, 'The Permanent Campaign of Rafael Correa: Making Ecuador's Plebiscitary Democracy' (2008) 13 *Press/Politics* 267, 273.

[12] Conaghan (n 9) 46.

[13] On anti-establishment appeals, mobilisation and competitive authoritarianism, see S Levitsky and J Loxton, 'Populism and Competitive Authoritarianism in the Andes' (2013) 20 *Democratization* 107 108.

[14] M Becker, 'Correa, Indigenous Movements, and the Writing of a New Constitution in Ecuador' (2011) 38 *Latin American Perspectives* 60.

[15] According to Levitsky and Loxton, 'competitive authoritarianism is more likely to emerge where political parties are weak'. See Levitsky and Loxton (n 13) 109.

[16] Conaghan (n 9) 47. Here again, there are some similarities with Pashinyan's Armenia, particularly in the period that immediately followed Pashinyan's appointment as Prime Minister, but before he gained a parliamentary majority. See ch 4.

[17] CM Conaghan, 'Delegative Democracy Revisited: Ecuador Under Correa' (2016) 27 *Journal of Democracy* 109, 109. See also, generally, G O'Donnell, 'Delegative Democracy' (1994) 5 *Journal of Democracy* 55.

[18] Conaghan (n 9) 47; Conaghan and de la Torre (n 11) 278.

[19] See ch 2.

[20] Conaghan (n 9) 49; Conaghan (n 17) 110.

improvements in people's lives'.[21] Correa made it clear that the bourgeois institutions and actors would not be allowed to get in the way of this historic social transformation.[22] To achieve this, the Constituent Assembly would be endowed with legal and extralegal (or extraconstitutional) powers: not only would it be charged with the writing of a new constitution to replace the 1998 Constitution, but it would also be vested with '"full powers" to overrule or dissolve and replace all existing institutions'.[23] This was in line with what members of Correa's movement depicted as 'deliberative radical democracy', understood as an 'alternative to liberal democracy', with the overt goal of dismantling the previous bourgeois-liberal order and replacing it with a brand new institutional framework, starting from scratch.[24]

The first step of the Citizens' Revolution was to hold a plebiscite or referendum (*consulta popular*) on whether Ecuador should establish a new constitution. The plebiscite was launched through an executive decree, which was contested by opponents as 'unconstitutional'.[25] The 'Yes' side, led by Correa, won by a landslide, with 82 per cent of the vote, in April 2007.[26] The second, related step involved winning the elections for a Constituent Assembly tasked with the drafting of a new constitution. In September 2007, Correa's party, Alianza PAIS (*País*),[27] won 80 of the Constituent Assembly's 130 seats, allowing him a prominent role in the drafting of the new constitution.[28] The third step was to draft the constitution. Again, Correa showed clear signs of impatience during that process. In fact, Alianza País's project of deliberative radical democracy clashed with Correa's populist-charismatic leadership – and his tendency for (plebiscitary) acclamation – in the Constituent Assembly.[29] As Carlos de la Torre explains, 'Correa became impatient with debates in the assembly that might cost votes in the referendum to approve the constitution. The president prioritized what opinion polls were telling him over demands of social movement organizations and some of his assemblymen.'[30] Impatient with what he saw as 'signs of an overly democratic, naive, and inefficient leadership in the assembly', he requested and obtained the resignation of the President of the Constituent Assembly and replaced him with a man more in tune with his own fast-paced ambitions and wishes.[31] The fourth and final (preliminary)

[21] Conaghan (n 17).
[22] ibid.
[23] Conaghan (n 9) 49.
[24] C de la Torre, *Populist Seduction in Latin America*, 2nd edn (Athens, Ohio University Press, 2010) 193.
[25] Conaghan (n 9) 51.
[26] Conaghan and de la Torre (n 11) 274; de la Torre (n 24) 188.
[27] Also known in English as the PAIS Alliance. The acronym PAIS (*País* means 'country' in Spanish) stands for *Patria Altiva I Soberana*, which can be translated as the 'Proud and Sovereign Homeland'.
[28] Conaghan (n 9) 46.
[29] de la Torre (n 24) 194.
[30] ibid 194. See also C de la Torre, 'Latin America's Authoritarian Drift: Technocratic Populism in Ecuador' (2013) 24 *Journal of Democracy* 33.
[31] de la Torre (n 24) 194.

step was to have the new constitution approved via plebiscite. In September 2008, it was endorsed by almost two-thirds (64 per cent) of the electorate, but at the cost, as one commentator pointed out, of 'limiting deliberation on its content and of not following its own institutional procedures'.[32]

That said, the new constitution was lauded by many for its 'socially transformative' components[33] and for its expanded list of rights, including rights to food, water, health, social security, cultural identity, collective indigenous rights[34] and, even, 'rights of nature'.[35] In fact, the 2008 Constitution was seen by some as containing 'one of the most extensive and creative sets of rights in the world',[36] with a tiered constitutional amendment system that makes it very difficult for a (present or future) legislature or executive to restrict or remove these constitutional rights and guarantees.[37] With a view to expanding and promoting the rights to participation and setting up various mechanisms of social control and transparency, the new constitution also established a new branch of government, the Transparency and Social Control branch (*Función de Transparencia y Control Social*), also known as the 'fifth power' of the Republic.[38] This citizen's branch is formally organised around the Council for Citizen Participation and Social Control (*Consejo de Participación Ciudadana y Control Social*).[39]

In terms of policy, Correa and his Alianza País movement generally followed a progressive agenda, with high-speed societal changes. However, he was opposed to abortion and even threatened to resign if the National Assembly decriminalised abortion as part of a reform of the Penal Code.[40] He also implemented land policies viewed by some as unfavourable to the country's indigenous population, and he opposed proposals to make Kichwa, the Ecuadorian variant of the pan-Andean Quechua language, an official language at the national level.[41] In fact, several Ecuadorian indigenous groups viewed the 2008 Constitution and the new constitutional order it established as a 'mixed bag', with some aspects seen as 'significant and dramatic gains' for indigenous aspirations and others as a 'jump backward'.[42]

From an institutional perspective, the new constitution was viewed by many commentators as establishing a form of hyperpresidentialism,[43] concentrating

[32] ibid.

[33] R Martínez Dalmau, 'Democratic Constitutionalism and Constitutional Innovation in Ecuador: The 2008 Constitution' (2016) 43 *Latin American Perspectives* 158, 159; 161.

[34] See, eg, Constitution of the Republic of Ecuador 2008 [*Constitución de la República del Ecuador 2008*] (RO 449, 20 October 2008), art 56.

[35] See, eg, ibid, title II, ch 7 (arts 74–78).

[36] Landau and Dixon, 'Tiered Constitutional Change' (2018) 86 *George Washington Law Review* 438, 486.

[37] ibid. This 'tiered' amendment system is discussed in more detail below.

[38] See 2008 Constitution of Ecuador, title IV, ch 5, particularly art 204.

[39] See, eg, ibid, arts 204, para 3; 207–210.

[40] See, eg, 'Ecuador abortion: President Correa threatens to resign' (*BBC*, 11 October 2013) www.bbc.co.uk/news/world-latin-america-24499248.

[41] de la Torre (n 30) 36. Kichwa is, however, an 'official language for intercultural relationships', alongside Spanish. See Becker (n 14) 56. See also de la Torre (n 24) 194.

[42] Becker (n 14) 57–58.

[43] de la Torre (n 30) 35.

powers and loosening institutional checks and balances.[44] It was also widely seen as contributing to the consolidation and crystallisation of Correa's discretionary or executive powers to the detriment of other branches of government, including legislative authority.[45] This concentration of power led a number of commentators to accuse Correa of eroding democracy.[46] Yet, it should nevertheless be highlighted that, to employ Giovanni Sartori's framework as applied by Martin Loughlin, the main goal of the 2008 Ecuadorian Constitution was not necessarily to restrict arbitrary power and limit government – what Sartori calls the *garantiste* function of the constitution – but, rather, to implement a more ideological project, namely, to transform or revolutionise society to achieve greater equality.[47] In that sense, Correa's engagement with the constitution (and constitutionalism more broadly) is somewhat reminiscent of Sartori's 'façade' constitution.[48] As Loughlin explains, drawing on Sartori, 'façade constitutions not only obscure the ways in which political power is actually exercised, but also replace the *garantiste* constitution's educative *purpose* – an education in liberty – with an educative *effect*, which has a more explicitly ideological character'.[49] In the case of Correa's Ecuador, the objective (and effect) of the new constitution clearly appeared to be more ideological, more specifically to 'help transform society in order to realise equal liberty', rather than 'to restrain government for the better protection of individual liberties'.[50]

B. Space, Time and Legal Symbolism

The enactment of the 2008 Constitution – and the circumstances surrounding its drafting and adoption – are also in line with Correa's approach to governance, which some have described as a 'plebiscitary presidency', that is to say, a presidency that aims to 'connect the president directly to voters, with minimal interference or "filtering" by parties, civil society groups, or the media'.[51] The plebiscitary component of Correa's presidency is particularly striking when one examines the frequency at which Ecuadorians were asked to vote to confirm aspects of the Citizens' Revolution: that is, more than five times in just eight years.[52]

In terms of space, and to use the framework developed in the first part of this monograph, Correa's political strategy involved mass rallies in which Correa

[44] M Loughlin, 'The Contemporary Crisis of Constitutional Democracy' (2019) 39 *Oxford Journal of Legal Studies* 440.

[45] See, eg, ibid; D Landau, 'Abusive Constitutionalism' (2013) 47 *University of California Davis Law Review* 206; de la Torre (n 24) 35.

[46] See, eg, T Ginsburg and AH Huq, *How to Save a Constitutional Democracy* (Chicago, University of Chicago Press, 2018) 94.

[47] Loughlin (n 44) 441–442; G Sartori, 'Constitutionalism: A Preliminary Discussion' (1962) 56 *American Political Science Review* 853, 855.

[48] Sartori (n 47) 861.

[49] Loughlin (n 44) 441.

[50] ibid 441–442.

[51] See, eg, Conaghan (n 9) 53.

[52] Silva-Portero (n 9). See also de la Torre (n 24) 175.

himself (and many of his candidates and allies) were in 'close proximity' to the public.[53] He often presented himself as the 'incarnation of common people's dreams of social mobility'.[54] Moreover, his presidency was marked by a ubiquitous presence in the media, in which he frequently emphasised the importance of restoring the dignity of the Ecuadorian people.[55] To do so, he sought to establish a direct, immediate, authentic and unfiltered link with his voters, notably by launching a weekly broadcast to his constituents.[56]

In terms of time, Correa's approach to governance was marked by speed; one could even say a sense of urgency. Like many populists, he issued an important number of executive decrees (some of which were based on the loose declaration of 'emergencies'), particularly in the period that followed his accession to power.[57] His untrammelled use of executive powers (allegedly to 'give back power to the downtrodden people', as it were) was effectively cemented by the enactment of the 2008 Constitution. Regarding the latter, Correa seemingly perceived the constitution as a short-term political and instrumental tool. As we have seen in chapter two, this approach is relatively common amongst populists – and it is far from unique to Correa in the Ecuadorian context. This may be due, in part, to Ecuador's long history of populism.[58] As Conaghan has pointed out, under the Ecuadorian *partidocracia*, '[t]he party elites' short-term and instrumental approach turned the constitution and laws into malleable contraptions, easily manipulated in the face of this or that shifting exigency'.[59] A striking illustration (or consequence) of this is the spectacular frequency with which constitutions have been enacted (and repealed) in the country. In fact, the 2008 Constitution was Ecuador's twentieth since it became an independent republic in 1830, in 178 years of existence.[60] As such, the average lifespan of an Ecuadorian constitution at the time of the adoption of the 2008 Constitution was therefore just under nine years.[61]

[53] de la Torre (n 24) 182.
[54] ibid 184.
[55] Conaghan (n 9) 53–54. See also de la Torre (n 24) 189–190.
[56] Conaghan (n 9) 53.
[57] ibid 55.
[58] In that regard, see generally de la Torre (n 24).
[59] Conaghan (n 9) 48.
[60] That is to say, a republic separate from Simón Bolívar's Republic of Gran Colombia. Ecuador declared its independence from Spain on 10 August 1809 and joined the Republic of Gran Colombia on 24 May 1822 before becoming a separate republic on 13 May 1830.
[61] [(2008–1830) / 20 = 8.9]. It is worth noting that at the time of writing (in October 2025), however, the 2008 Constitution has entered its 18th year of existence, which means that the average lifespan of an Ecuadorian constitution has slightly increased, but it remains just under ten years. In any event, the average lifespan of Ecuadorian constitutions remains considerably lower than the average lifespan of a constitution, which is 17 years. See, in that regard, NC Lazar, 'Constitutional Preambles and the Uncertain Future' in L Corrias and L Francot (eds), *Temporal Boundaries of Law and Politics: Time Out of Joint* (Abingdon, Routledge, 2018) 127. That said, the 2008 Constitution appears to show signs of endurance, given current President Daniel Noboa's recent – but unsuccessful – attempt to set up a new constituent assembly tasked with the drafting of a new constitution. This attempt was rejected by voters in a referendum held in November 2025. See, eg, Andrés Martínez-Moscoso, 'The People's Verdict: Why did Ecuador's Constitutional Referendum Fail?' (2 December 2025, *ConstitutionNet*) https://constitutionnet.org/news/voices/peoples-verdict-why-did-ecuadors-constitutional-referendum-fail.

In any event, this understanding of the constitution as a short-term political and instrumental tool was not only apparent in the way the 2008 Constitution was enacted (and in the frequency in which constitutions are generally adopted in Ecuador), but also in Correa's peculiar understanding of the constitution and constitutionalism more broadly. In general, and as alluded to above in the discussion on the 2008 Constitution, he seemed to view institutional checks and balances as illegitimate hurdles thwarting the realisation of his promised project of social transformation. Probably because of Correa's constitutional impatience, there was often very little room for disagreement, deliberation and (or) compromise – not just in the drafting of the Constitution, but also in the way he governed. This is a relatively common characteristic of populist governance: as Samuel Issacharoff has highlighted:

> [p]opulist impulses shorten the time frame and turn everything into a binary choice, a political life at the knife's edge. Us or them, success or perfidy, the people or the oligarchs, Americans or foreigners. There can be no spirit of partial victory, of legitimate disagreement, or even of mutual gain through engagement.[62]

This was apparent on several occasions during Correa's presidency, notably in the way he implemented changes – including constitutional and institutional ones – that he viewed as essential to his project of social transformation.

Finally, from the perspective of legal symbolism, Correa's Citizens' Revolution masked some major alterations to the Ecuadorian politico-legal order by reproducing, adapting and manipulating established legal symbols – including existing institutions and independent courts – through the new constitution that he enacted, giving the latter a certain appearance of stability and legitimation, but in a way that favoured the new regime.[63] These legal-institutional changes, implemented in a subtle but systemic way, targeted the main constitutional actors of the state, especially those in charge of scrutinising the actions of the executive, such as courts and electoral bodies. These major changes are discussed in the following section.

III. From 'Constitutional Impatience' to Judicial (and Institutional) Capture

One underexamined aspect of Correa's populist presidency is the specific way in which he took control of the Ecuadorian judiciary (as well as key 'fourth-branch'[64] institutions of the state) – and how this capture had a profound impact

[62] S Issacharoff, 'Democracy's Deficits' (2018) 85 *University of Chicago Law Review* 486.

[63] On the question of legal symbolism, see J Přibáň, *Legal Symbolism: On Law, Time and European Identity* (Abingdon, Routledge, 2007) 54, as summarised in B van Klink, 'Law at the Right Time: A Plea for Slow Law in Hasty Times' in Luigi Corrias and Lyana Francot, *Temporal Boundaries of Law and Politics: Time Out of Joint* (Abingdon, Routledge, 2018) 41, 50.

[64] See Khaitan (n 2).

on Ecuadorian democracy. A closer look at the latter reveals a surprising number of similarities with contemporary instances of *right*-wing populism, notably in Eastern and Central Europe. Indeed, Correa followed a common (authoritarian) populist playbook, namely maintaining a façade of (liberal) democracy through the presence of institutions that could formally stand in the way of the presidency, but by capturing them from within. This form of institutional (or state) capture was achieved in at least four steps, some of which are relatively similar to the steps taken to carry out the capture of state institutions in Hungary (and, to a certain extent, in Poland) since 2010.[65]

A. First and Second Steps: Court-Packing and Judicial Reform

The first step was the removal of judges, particularly constitutional and apex court judges. In 2007, after Correa issued a decree calling for a plebiscite on the convening of a Constituent Assembly, a clash occurred between Congress and the Supreme Electoral Tribunal (*Tribunal Supremo Electoral*) – which was controlled by Correa.[66] This clash led to the dismissal, by the Supreme Electoral Tribunal, of 57 members of Congress.[67] The latter were replaced with an equal number of new legislators, who, while officially independent, largely supported the new Correa administration.[68] The dismissed legislators brought their case to what was then the country's Constitutional Court, the *Tribunal Constitucional* ('TC'). Soon after the latter ruled that the dismissal of the 57 Congressmen and Congresswomen was unconstitutional, Correa rejected the ruling and suggested that TC justices should be 'prosecuted'.[69] The new Correa-led majority in Congress then voted to remove nine of the TC's justices, claiming that their terms had expired.[70] The TC itself was officially disbanded in 2008, with the enactment of the new constitution, which created a new constitutional court, the Constitutional Court of Ecuador (*Corte Constitucional del Ecuador*).

[65] Of course, many of Correa's changes predate those in Hungary (and Poland), which has led Kim Lane Scheppele to wonder if Correa (alongside Hugo Chávez in Venezuela) 'may well have given [Hungarian Prime Minister Viktor] Orbán the idea that a new constitution would give him the opportunity to sweep away the power of the opposition, if he could control the drafting process, which he then did to produce a constitution that was supported only by his own party'. See KL Scheppele, 'Autocratic Legalism' (2018) 85 *University of Chicago Law Review* 545, 554–555.

[66] Landau (n 45) 207.

[67] These legislators were stripped out of their seats in Congress after unsuccessfully trying to remove the head of the TSE, Jorge Acosta. The TSE argued that by doing so, these 57 legislators had attempted to obstruct the electoral process. See Conaghan (n 9) 52. See also Landau (n 45) 207; Ginsburg and Huq (n 46) 94; and K Weyland, 'Latin America's Authoritarian Drift: The Threat from the Populist Left' (2013) 24 *Journal of Democracy* 18, 22.

[68] Conaghan (n 9) 52.

[69] ibid.

[70] ibid.

The second step was packing the courts – including lower courts – with judges loyal to the regime. This was done in two main ways. The first mechanism used to pack the courts was through the nomination of members of the newly established Constitutional Court. Indeed, under the 2008 Constitution, members of the Constitutional Court are appointed by a tripartite commission comprising two persons nominated by each of the following branches of government: the legislature, the executive and the abovementioned Transparency and Social Control branch.[71] Yet, in addition to his control over the executive branch, Correa benefited from a legislative coalition supporting his government, which also influenced the Transparency and Social Control branch.[72] The latter, packed with loyalists of Correa's government, was widely viewed as 'a de facto extension of the executive'.[73] As a result, Correa and his allies got themselves into a position in which they could easily influence the appointment of Constitutional Court judges, particularly from 2012 onwards.[74]

Another, related mechanism used to pack existing (including ordinary) courts was through a 'judicial reform' in 2011 that gave the executive branch even more control over the appointment of judges.[75] In line with Correa's abovementioned 'plebiscitary' style of democracy, the latter reform was legitimised through a referendum which comprised ten questions, including two questions regarding the judiciary.[76] The aim of the judicial reform was to give the executive branch control over a transitional body, the Council of the Transitional Judiciary (*Consejo de la Judicatura de Transición*), which, over a period of 18 months, would replace the Judicial Council (*Consejo de la Judicatura*) and be given the power to appoint judges.[77] In a typical populist fashion, Correa justified his reform on the basis that the sitting 'judges [were] as destructive and dangerous as criminals'.[78] The referendum also contained a question on the extension of the period of detention without trial – a reform that Nicola Lacey (and others) would probably define as an instance of 'penal populism'[79] – as well as questions on media ownership and

[71] 2008 Constitution of Ecuador, art 434.

[72] J Castro-Montero and G van Dijck, 'Judicial Politics in Unconsolidated Democracies: An Empirical Analysis of the Ecuadorian Constitutional Court (2008–2016)' (2017) 38 *Justice System Journal* 380, 384. See also Basabe-Serrano 'Ecuador: Reforma constitucional, nuevos actores políticos y viejas prácticas partidistas' (2009) 29 *Revista de Ciencia Política* 381.

[73] See, eg, Conaghan (n 17) 112.

[74] 'El oficialismo se filtra en Corte Constitucional, el más poderoso ente de Ecuador' (*El Universo*, 11 November 2012) www.eluniverso.com/2012/11/11/1/1355/oficialismo-filtra-mas-poderoso-ente-pais.html.

[75] de la Torre (n 30) 38.

[76] 'El referéndum, anexos y consulta popular estarán en una sola papeleta' (*El Universo*, 24 February 2011) www.eluniverso.com/2011/02/24/1/1355/referendum-anexos-consulta-popular-estaran-sola-papeleta.html.

[77] 'Universal Periodic Review of Ecuador: Human Rights Watch's Submission to the Human Rights Council' (*Human Rights Watch*, 21 November 2011) www.hrw.org/node/244577/printable/print.

[78] I Caselli, 'Ecuador referendum tackles judges, media and bull-fights' (*BBC*, 6 May 2011) www.bbc.co.uk/news/world-latin-america-13280795.

[79] See, eg, N Lacey, 'Populism and the Rule of Law' (2019) 15 *Annual Review of Law and Social Science*. See also ch 2 of this monograph.

state control over published content, which were justified by the government on the basis that 'Ecuadorean media have historically been in the hands of the country's wealthy elite'.[80] All questions were approved by voters in the referendum by majorities ranging from 51 to 57 per cent.[81]

B. Third and Fourth Steps: *Error Inexcusable* and Judicial Discipline

However, Correa did not limit himself to the appointment of judges.[82] To ensure the long-lasting loyalty of judges (many of whom were appointed by the executive), Correa implemented an efficient system of sanctioning of recalcitrant or uncooperative judges. The third – and perhaps most important – step of the populist capture of the judiciary was therefore the politicisation (and 'executivisation') of judicial conduct and discipline. The main mechanism employed, in that regard, was the doctrine of the 'inexcusable error' (*error inexcusable*), which was implemented in 2012 in the context of amendments to the Organic Code of the Judicial Function (*Código Orgánico de la Función Judicial*).[83] The latter empowered the Judicial Council to suspend or remove justice officials, including judges, if they acted with 'criminal intent, evident negligence or inexcusable error'.[84] However, the concept of inexcusable error was not defined in the law, nor were its constitutive elements clarified in any official document.[85] The lack of definition made the concept prone to manipulation and improper uses by the political branches of government, including for the purpose of influencing the decision of judges, thereby violating their independence.[86] And this is exactly what happened. After 2012 (and especially following the appointment

[80] Caselli (n 78).

[81] 'Ecuador President Rafael Correa "wins referendum"' (*BBC*, 8 May 2011) www.bbc.co.uk/news/world-latin-america-13325112.

[82] In fact, the appointment of judges is in and of itself (often) insufficient to ensure that they will be loyal to the actors that have appointed them. The example of former Colombian President Álvaro Uribe, discussed in the introductory ch, provides an example: the Court blocked his second effort at a term-limit extension despite the fact that he had appointed four of its nine members.

[83] Organic Code of the Judicial Function (*Código Orgánico de la Función Judicial*) (Ley 0) RO Supl 544 (9 March 2009).

[84] ibid, particularly art 109.

[85] DM Yamunaque Parra, 'El error inexcusable y la independencia judicial interna' (2016) (unpublished Master's thesis, Universidad Andina Simón Bolívar), repositorio.uasb.edu.ec/bitstream/10644/5625/1/T2278-MDE-Yamunaque-El%20error.pdf, 9–10; 40. The concept was later defined – and its scope of application clarified – in a post-Correan ruling by the Constitutional Court, Ruling (*Sentencia*) No 3-19-CN/20 (29 July 2020) and in a December 2020 statute, the *Organic Law Amending the Organic Code of the Judiciary (Ley Orgánica Reformatoria del Código Orgánico de la Función Judicial), Law w/n (Ley s/n), Official Register, RO 345-S (8 December 2020)*, which amended the Organic Code of the Judicial Function (see, particularly, arts 109(7), 109.1–109.4, 114, 114.1 and 131 of the latter) to include, for example, the obligation to hold a public hearing to allow affected judges to defend themselves and present their arguments.

[86] Yamunaque Parra (n 85) 9–10; 40.

of Gustavo Jalkh as President of the Judicial Council in 2013[87]), the somewhat vague and opaque concept of inexcusable error was indeed used as a tool by the Judicial Council to sanction and dismiss judges, particularly judges who had rendered decisions against (or unfavourable to) the Ecuadorian state.[88] In fact, it is reported that 145 Ecuadorian judges were suspended or removed by the Judicial Council for having committed 'inexcusable errors' in the period between 2013 and August 2017.[89]

In Ecuador, the politicisation of judicial discipline was even sometimes accompanied with what Kim Lane Scheppele and other scholars have called 'autocratic legalism', that is to say electoral mandates and legal-constitutional change 'used in the service of an illiberal agenda',[90] as well as thinly veiled threats and coercion. For example, there is evidence that Correa directly interfered with the independence of the judiciary in a 2010 memo that was circulated amongst judges of the then National Judiciary Secretary on behalf of President Correa.[91] This memo allegedly presented instructions from Correa that any judge issuing a ruling that effectively prevented public works projects – including mining projects – from taking place would *personally* have to reimburse the Ecuadorian state for the 'damage and harm' incurred as a result of the project's cancellation.[92] This example is in line with what Kurt Weyland calls 'discriminatory legalism', that is to say, the formal use of 'legal authority in discretionary ways to promote cronies and allies while punishing or intimidating critics and opponents in politics and society'[93] – a concept perhaps better understood by the maxim 'for my friends, everything; for my enemies, the law!'[94] While the focus of the discussion here is on courts, it should be added that this form of discriminatory legalism was also used against other key actors, including members of the mainstream media, for instance, in the case of the editor and three board members of the country's largest privately owned newspaper, *El Universo*, who were held liable for defamation and each sentenced to a three-year

[87] 'Ecuador: Political Interference in the Judiciary: Strong Evidence of Intimidation, Retaliatory Firings of Judges Under Correa' (*Human Rights Watch*, 20 April 2018) www.hrw.org/news/2018/04/20/ecuador-political-interference-judiciary.

[88] J Soza Meza, 'Error inexcusable' (*Derecho Ecuador*, 22 May 2018) www.derechoecuador.com/error-inexcusable.

[89] Human Rights Watch (n 77).

[90] See Scheppele (n 65) 548. For an earlier use of the term 'autocratic legalism', see J Corrales, 'The Authoritarian Resurgence: Autocratic Legalism in Venezuela' (2015) 26 *Journal of Democracy* 37, 38: Corrales defines 'autocratic legalism' as the '*use*, *abuse*, and *non-use* (in Spanish, *desuso*) of the law in service of the executive branch'.

[91] Landau and Dixon (n 3) 1339. See also Dixon, 'Constitutional Rights as Bribes' (2018) 50 *Connecticut Law Review* 767, 800.

[92] CM Kauffman and PL Martin, 'Testing Ecuador's Rights of Nature: Why Some Lawsuits Succeed and Others Fail' (18 March 2016), paper presented at the International Studies Association Annual Convention, Atlanta, GA, static1.squarespace.com/static/55914fd1e4b01fb0b851a814/t/5748568c8259b5e5a34ae6bf/1464358541319/Kauffman++Martin+16+Testing+Ecuadors+RoN+Laws.pdf 11.

[93] Weyland (n 67) 23.

[94] ibid. This expression is sometimes attributed to Getúlio Vargas, former President of Brazil (1930–1945 and 1950–1954). See, eg, O'Donnell (n 17) 40.

custodial sentence for an editorial; as well as a number of indigenous activists accused of 'terrorism' for resisting mining extraction.[95]

The fourth and arguably final step was to capture the National Electoral Council (*Consejo Nacional Electoral*), which allowed Correa's party to gain a majority in the National Assembly, notably through gerrymandering: the cities of Quito and Guayaquil, the two largest cities of Ecuador – and, perhaps not so coincidentally, two Correa strongholds – being given extra seats.[96] In the context of elections, the National Electoral Council allowed programming favourable to Correa to air unimpeded on state-run media, while forcing political opponents to withdraw some television advertisements characterised as 'offensive to the president'.[97] This was particularly helpful to Correa in the context of the 2013 election. Beyond the National Electoral Council, other state institutions, such as the Secretariat of Presidential Communications (*Secretaría General de Comunicación de la Presidencia*), also played an instrumental role in maintaining Correa's power and influence, notably through state-run media – particularly through a live radio and television show run by Correa himself, as well as 'through advertisements that private media [were] required to broadcast'.[98]

C. Outcome: Judicial and Institutional Capture

In carrying out the abovementioned changes, and by (at least partially) capturing the judiciary and other institutions of the state, Correa applied parts of the (authoritarian) populist playbook written and followed in Türkiye,[99] Venezuela[100] and, more recently, in Hungary,[101] Poland,[102] the Philippines[103] and

[95] See, eg, C de la Torre, 'The People, Democracy, and Authoritarianism in Rafael Correa's Ecuador' (2014) 21 *Constellations* 457, 459; 461. It should be noted that the convicted editor and board members were later pardoned by the president. Nevertheless, Correa and 'other state officials [continued to] use libel laws in order to intimidate and to try to silence critical journalists'. See, eg, ibid 459. Libel laws have similarly been used in other populist regimes such as Recep Tayyip Erdoğan's Türkiye. For the latter, see, eg, OO Varol, 'Stealth Authoritarianism' (2015) 100 *Iowa Law Review*.

[96] de la Torre (n 30) 37.

[97] ibid 38.

[98] Conaghan (n 17) 113.

[99] See, eg, Varol (n 95); OO Varol, 'Stealth Authoritarianism in Turkey' in MA Graber, S Levinson and M Tushnet (eds), *Constitutional Democracy in Crisis?* (Oxford, Oxford University Press, 2018).

[100] See, eg, Levitsky and Loxton (n 13); KL Scheppele, 'The Party's Over' in Graber, Levinson and Tushnet (eds) (n 99) 499–503.

[101] See, eg, G Halmai, 'A Coup Against Constitutional Democracy: The Case of Hungary' in Graber, Levinson and Tushnet (eds) (n 99) and Scheppele (n 100) 503–505.

[102] See, eg, W Sadurski, *Poland's Constitutional Breakdown* (Oxford, Oxford University Press, 2019); W Sadurski, 'How Democracy Dies (in Poland): A Case Study of Anti-Constitutional Populist Backsliding' (2018) Sydney Law School Research Paper No 18/01; W Sadurski, 'Constitutional Crisis in Poland' in Levinson and Tushnet (eds) (n 99).

[103] See, eg, D Gatmaytan, The Case of the Philippine Judiciary – Guardian of Democracy or Enabler of Populism?' in S Hardt, AW Heringa and H-T Nguyen (eds), *Populism and Democracy* (The Hague, Eleven International Publishing, 2020).

elsewhere. For instance, the first aspect of Correa's capture of the judiciary – namely, the launch of a judicial reform legitimised by referendum in 2011 – is somewhat reminiscent of then-Prime Minister Recep Tayyip Erdoğan's reform of the judicial system in Türkiye, implemented just a year earlier, in 2010. That year, Erdoğan passed important constitutional changes, also legitimised by a national referendum, that gave the president the power to name the vast majority (namely, 14 out of 17) of the country's Constitutional Court judges.[104] Erdoğan, like Correa, did not stop there. He also passed legislation, in 2014, that empowered the Minister of Justice 'to directly appoint members to the High Council of Judges and to control the inspection board that disciplines judges'.[105] The result of the latter change was not significantly different from what happened in Ecuador: in fact, within a mere six months, more than 3,000 judges were removed by the High Council.[106] Erdoğan also went even further by shifting the power to decide which political parties are legal (and therefore allowed to put forward candidates for election) from the judiciary to the legislature.

Erdoğan's Türkiye, of course, is not the only relevant point of comparison here. The wide powers granted to discipline and sanction judges are also reminiscent of a statute in Poland adopted in December 2019 and signed into law in Poland in February 2020, dubbed the 'muzzle law', that gave the PiS-led government the power to fine, suspend and even dismiss judges whose decisions (and actions) they considered 'harmful'.[107] The capture of the National Electoral Council, for its part, brings to mind that of the Electoral Commission in Hungary by the ruling party Fidesz.[108] This executive strengthening and correlative weakening of independent branches of power drastically eroded constitutionalism – pointing out, as mentioned above, in the direction of a negative relationship between populism and constitutionalism. Indeed, this executive consolidation had a dramatic impact on the ability of courts, in particular – but also other institutions, such as fourth-branch institutions like the National Electoral Council – to perform their constitutional functions and to act as a bulwark against hyperpresidentialism and the concentration of presidential or executive powers. This is discussed in the section below.

[104] N Bermeo, 'On Democratic Backsliding' (2016) 27 *Journal of Democracy* 11.

[105] ibid.

[106] ibid, referring to Y Arat, 'The Decline of Democracy in Turkey: Popular Support, Institutional Decay', unpublished manuscript, Princeton University, March 2015.

[107] Law amending the Law relating to the organisation of the ordinary courts, the Law on the Supreme Court and certain other laws (*Ustawa o zmianie ustawy – Prawo o ustroju sądów powszechnych, ustawy o Sądzie Najwyższym oraz niektórych innych ustaw*) U of 2020, item 190 (20 December 2019). See also L Pech, P Wachiowiec and D Mazur, 'Poland's Rule of Law Breakdown: A Five-Year Assessment of EU's (In)Action' (2021) 13 *Hague Journal on the Rule of Law* 1.

[108] See, eg, M Tushnet and B Bugarič, *Power to the People: Constitutionalism in the Age of Populism* (Oxford, Oxford University Press, 2022) 83, 89–90.

IV. The Constitutional Court and the Refusal of Institutional Deceleration: Captured Courts as Active Agents of Executive Consolidation?

Despite (or perhaps because of) the aforementioned strains on constitutionalism, Ecuadorian courts under Correa were unwilling or unable to intervene and act as efficient institutional decelerators against an impatient and omnipotent executive. On the contrary, they can be said to have succumbed to raw executive power and to have transformed into Rosalind Dixon and David Landau refer to as 'agents, rather than opponents, of antidemocratic constitutional change'.[109] As these two scholars explain,

> [b]eyond coercion, regimes have a range of formal legal tools to influence the composition and powers of the judiciary. Most of these changes fall into one of two buckets: attempts to 'pack' a court by influencing its composition and attempts to 'curb' a court by threatening its institutional powers or resources.[110]

As we have seen in the previous section, Correa arguably did both: he first packed the courts by removing judges and replacing them with friends of the regime; and then he curbed the courts through threats to their independence, particularly with the instrumental use of the inexcusable error doctrine. As a result, Ecuadorian courts arguably transformed into 'illiberal courts' which, instead of providing a check on the power of the executive, became instrumental in helping the executive circumvent constitutional and institutional constraints and concentrate power into its hands.[111] While maintaining the trappings of an independent judiciary, Ecuadorian courts were arguably weaponised to legitimise unconstitutional actions and policies and, similar to what happened recently in Hungary, Poland, Türkiye and elsewhere, to 'alter the meaning of the constitution through constitutional interpretation'.[112]

In that context, it is rather unsurprising that courts under Correa were unable to exercise their role as institutional decelerators in the face of populist constitutional impatience. Yet, this was not due to a lack of opportunity: Ecuadorian courts, most particularly the Constitutional Court, had several chances to fulfil this role, opportunities that they did not seize. In fact, at least three landmark cases from the Constitutional Court in which the latter refused to act as

[109] Dixon and Landau (n 3) 1322. Something very similar occurred in Bolivia, where the Plurinational Constitutional Tribunal confirmed the constitutionality of the amendment allowing Morales to put his candidacy forward for a third presidential term. See Plurinational Constitutional Tribunal of Bolivia (*Tribunal Constitucional Plurinacional de Bolivia*), Decision No 84 of 2017 (28 November 2017), as mentioned in ibid 1362.

[110] ibid 1339.

[111] P Castillo-Ortiz, 'The Illiberal Abuse of Constitutional Courts in Europe' (2019) 15 *European Constitutional Law Review* 48, 48; 62.

[112] ibid 62.

institutional decelerators against an impatient and self-aggrandising populist executive further indicate that the Court did in fact succumb to executive power. These three cases, discussed in the next three subsections, are the 2011 judgment on the qualification of the referendum questions,[113] the 2011 judgment on the state of exception in the judicial branch[114] and the 2014 judgment on presidential term limits.[115]

A. The 2011 Judgment on the 'Qualification of the Referendum Questions'

The first decision, rendered by the 'interim'[116] Constitutional Court on 15 February 2011, stems from the background of the May 2011 referendum on the reform of the judiciary. As discussed earlier in section III of this chapter, the proposed reform involved changes to the functions of the Judicial Council[117] as well as the length of preventive detention,[118] amongst other aspects. As mentioned above, the main aim of the reform was to give the executive branch control over a transitional body, the Transitory Judicial Council, which, over a period of 18 months, would replace the Judicial Council and be given the power to appoint judges.[119] In this case, the Court had to examine the wording of the questions that the executive was planning to put to the people via referendum and assess whether they complied with the 2008 Constitution. One of the main elements to be assessed by the Court was the type of procedural vehicle required for each proposed change to the Constitution.

The 2008 Constitution provides for three procedural vehicles in relation to constitutional change – what some would call a 'tiered' model of constitutional change, with different rules (or procedural vehicles) of constitutional amendment for different aspects and parts of the constitution, for example.[120] The first procedural vehicle in the Ecuadorian Constitution is the *enmienda constitucional* ('constitutional amendment'), understood as an ordinary constitutional amendment, more specifically as an amendment which does *not* alter the fundamental structure or the constitutive nature and elements of the state, which does *not* entail any limitations on constitutional rights and guarantees, and which does *not*

[113] Constitutional Court of Ecuador (*Corte constitucional del Ecuador*), Decision (*Dictamen*) No 001-11-DRC-CC, Case No 0001-11-RC (15 February 2011).

[114] Constitutional Court of Ecuador (*Corte constitucional del Ecuador*), Decision (*Dictamen*) No 008-11-DEE-CC, Case No 0000-10-EE (29 September 2011).

[115] Constitutional Court of Ecuador (*Corte constitucional del Ecuador*), Decision (*Dictamen*) No 001-14-DRC-CC, Case No 0001-14-RC (31 October 2014).

[116] As its members came from the defunct Constitutional Tribunal, in the context of the 'transition regime'. See Castro-Montero and van Dijck (n 72) 384; El Universo (n 74).

[117] 2008 Constitution of Ecuador, arts 179 and 181.

[118] ibid art 77(1), (9) and (11).

[119] Human Rights Watch (n 77).

[120] See Landau and Dixon (n 36).

modify the procedure for amending the 2008 Constitution. Under Article 441 of the Constitution, the first option for carrying out an *enmienda* is by referendum, at the initiative of the President of the Republic (or of a private citizen with the support of at least eight per cent of all registered voters). A second way to enact an *enmienda* is at the initiative of at least one-third of all members of the National Assembly, provided it is approved by a two-thirds majority of all of its members.[121] This second option means that *enmiendas* may, in practice, be initiated and approved by mere legislative process, without the need for a referendum.

The second procedural vehicle for constitutional change is the more substantive *reforma parcial* ('partial reform'), a higher tier of constitutional change which requires a more burdensome procedure, notably approval in a referendum. Under Article 442(1) of the Constitution, *reformas parciales* may *not* entail any limitations on constitutional rights and guarantees, nor may they modify the procedure for amending the 2008 Constitution – hence why they are referred to in the 2008 Constitution as 'partial' reforms, in contrast to a third procedural vehicle, 'constitutional replacement', described below. Such *reformas parciales* may be initiated by the President of the Republic (or by a private citizen with the support of at least one per cent of registered voters),[122] but the draft *reforma parcial*, once approved by a majority of National Assembly members, must then be approved by a majority (at least 50 per cent +1) of votes in a referendum.[123]

Finally, a third means of constitutional change under the 2008 Constitution is a more complete 'constitutional replacement'. This third procedural vehicle, found in Article 444 of the Constitution, provides for the establishment, through referendum, of a constituent assembly, which may establish and ordain a new constitution. To enter into force, the constitution written by the constituent assembly must be approved by a majority (at least 50 per cent +1) of votes in a referendum. This obviously more demanding procedural vehicle would be necessary in the case of a fundamental change to the structure and (or) a major substantive change to the constitution, such as one involving a restriction to constitutional rights and guarantees, for example.

In this case, the Court took the view that the wording of the questions, particularly those related to the length of detention without trial, could potentially infringe constitutional rights and guarantees.[124] In the event of such infringement, as explained in the previous paragraphs, the third (and most demanding) procedural vehicle would be required to carry on these changes, namely a 'constitutional replacement' – through the establishment of a new constitution written by a new constituent assembly. However, in an unusual and possibly 'anti-technical'[125]

[121] Alternatively, it can be approved by a simple majority in a referendum.
[122] 2008 Constitution of Ecuador, art 442(1).
[123] ibid, art 442(2) and (3).
[124] See Decision No 001-11-DRC-CC [50/55].
[125] C Castro Montero, 'Rigidez de la constitución y reforma constitucional: Estudio analítico de la actuación de los jueces constitucionales durante el período 2008–2019' (2020) Universidad Internacional SEK, Facultad de ciencias sociales y jurídicas, thesis: repositorio.uisek.edu.ec/bitstream/123456789/3734/1/CRISTINA%20CASTRO%20MONTERO.pdf 40.

decision, the Court decided to change – of their own accord – the wording of the referendum questions[126] proposed by the executive, in order to make them compliant with the less burdensome *enmienda constitucional* procedural vehicle. The Court also downplayed the constitutional changes, including the replacement of the Judicial Council, stating that 'the purpose of this constitutional amendment is to seek confirmation, by the people, of the proposed change which, in the opinion of this Court, would directly legitimise the new formation of the [judicial] body'.[127]

A minority of judges, however, disagreed with the ruling, arguing in an extensive, 87-page dissenting opinion written by Justice Dr Nina Pacari Vega[128] that the constitutional changes proposed in the referendum questions would alter the fundamental structure of the Ecuadorian state[129] and (or) entail restrictions to constitutional rights.[130] As a result, she wrote, such changes could only be carried out following the most burdensome procedural vehicle, that is to say, through a new constituent assembly.[131] Later, Justice Pacari Vega even described the majority opinion as a 'political decision, more than a legal one'.[132] The majority opinion was also criticised by a number of actors and scholars, who argued that the proposed changes to the constitution did in fact entail limitations on constitutional rights and guarantees, particularly the presumption of innocence, and negatively impacted judicial independence.[133]

It could be argued that the outcome of this judgment, and perhaps also the decision to change the wording of the referendum questions,[134] not only illustrates the Constitutional Court's refusal to act as an institutional decelerator in the face of an impatient executive; it also shows a certain willingness on the part of the Court to actually *help* the executive by becoming an agent of what some would

[126] Namely, questions 1, 2, 3, 4, 5. See Decision No 001-11-DRC-CC, [36/55], [39/55], [41/55], [43/55], [47/55].

[127] ibid [46/55].

[128] Another, 9-page separate dissenting opinion was written by Justices Dr Hernando Morales Vinueza and Dr Alfonso Luz Yune in relation to the first proposed question, on preventive detention. The two justices wrote that such constitutional change would infringe upon rights and, therefore, could only be carried following the establishment of a constituent assembly. See p [9/9] of such dissenting opinion.

[129] Questions 4 and 5. See Decision No 001-11-DRC-CC, dissenting opinion of Justices Dr Nina Pacari Vega, with which Dr Hernando Morales Vinueza and Dr Alfonso Luz Yune agree (on aspects relating to questions 2 to 5), [87/87].

[130] Questions 1, 2, 3, 4 and 5. See ibid [86/87], [87/87].

[131] As per 2008 Constitution of Ecuador, art 444. See ibid.

[132] PM Erazo, 'Ecuador: Luz verde para referendo de Correa' (*BBC News Mundo*, 16 February 2011) www.bbc.com/mundo/noticias/2011/02/110216_ecuador_referendo_ao.

[133] See, eg, Castro Montero (n 125) 40, referring to A Grijalva, 'La consulta: Una violación infraganti de la Constitución' (2011), Repositorio Facultad Latinoamericana de Ciencias Sociales.

[134] That said, a counterargument could be made that the Constitutional Court's initiative to modify the wording of the referendum questions is, in fact, similar to the judicial practice (or remedy) of 'reading in' (and/or 'reading down'), which allows courts in certain jurisdictions to ensure the constitutional validity of a statute by inserting (or removing, in the case of 'reading down') a few words into the statute. See, eg, s 3 of the Human Rights Act 1998 (c 42) and *Ghaidan v Godin-Mendoza* [2004] UKHL 30 in the UK context; or *Trial Lawyers Association of British Columbia v British Columbia (AG)*, [2014] 3 SCR 31 and *Schachter v Canada*, [1992] 2 SCR 679 in the Canadian context.

call 'antidemocratic constitutional change'[135] – or, at the very least, of executive consolidation and authoritarian-leaning constitutional change. In any event, the Court showed some signs of institutional capture by the executive. This, I contend, became even more apparent in the other judgments discussed in the two sections below.

B. The 2011 'State of Exception in the Judicial Branch' Judgment

The second case, rendered by the Constitutional Court on 29 September 2011, stems from the aftermath of the abovementioned May 2011 referendum on the reform of the judiciary. On 5 September 2011, at the request of the newly created Council of the Transitional Judiciary,[136] President Correa issued an executive decree that declared a 60-day[137] state of exception (emergency) in the judicial branch.[138] Impatient to execute his controversial overhaul of Ecuador's judiciary and seemingly galvanised by the outcome of the 2011 referendum, which had given some sense of legitimacy to his proposed overhaul, Correa wanted to expedite and facilitate the judicial reform – and, arguably, to circumvent the apparently slow existing processes.[139] Correa's executive decree notably pointed out the lack of 'adequate computer systems' in the judicial system, apparently preventing the 'generation of accurate information for institutional strategic planning', as well as a 40 per cent rise in the number of judicial cases in 2008 compared with 2002.[140] As discussed in Part I of this monograph, an important part of the ideal-typical populist discourse and imaginary is that issues of various sorts need to be dealt with immediately. Indeed, not only do many populists seek quick solutions – as the abovementioned executive order illustrates – but they also take the view that the most important issues for the state or society are immediate dangers requiring an immediate response. In this particular case, the state of exception in the judicial branch decree, upon approval by the Constitutional Court, would empower the executive to reassign judges and make budget appropriations without the consent of the National Assembly.[141]

According to the text of the executive order, the state of exception decree was necessary to 'guarantee the right to justice provided under the Republic's Constitution' and to 'prevent an *imminent* internal upheaval [*conmoción*]'.[142] The executive decree was worded in broad (and, arguably, relatively vague) terms. For

[135] Landau and Dixon (n 3) 1322.
[136] See section II.A of this chapter, above.
[137] The maximum duration permitted under the 2008 Constitution of Ecuador, art 166(2).
[138] Executive Decree (*Decreto ejecutivo*) No 872 (No T6102-SNJ-11-1124) (5 September 2011), art 1.
[139] R Planas, 'Ecuador: Correa Declares Courts in State of Exception' (*Americas Society/Council of the Americas* (*AS/COA*), 8 September 2011) www.as-coa.org/articles/ecuador-correa-declares-courts-state-exception.
[140] Executive Decree No 872, as reproduced in Decision (*Dictamen*) no 008-11-DEE-CC [3/17].
[141] ibid. See also Planas (n 139).
[142] Executive Decree No 872, art 1 (emphasis added).

instance, the second element of the executive order declared the 'national mobilisation' of the 'personnel of the Judicial Function'[143] – which raised concerns that this could be invoked to threaten and possibly remove undesirable judges.[144] In fact, many members of the opposition and commentators questioned the legality of the decree.[145] They pointed out that Article 164 of the 2008 Constitution provides that the President of the Republic may declare a state of exception 'in the event of aggression, international armed conflict or internal, serious internal upheaval, public calamity or natural disaster'[146] – and that no such event applied in the current case.[147]

Yet, in a comparatively short judgment, the Constitutional Court ruled that the executive decree issued by Correa was justified and 'adequately motivated'.[148] For the Court, the 'imminent internal upheaval' invoked in the executive order was 'serious' (*grave*) and 'based on facts that are real and of public knowledge'.[149] The Court notably treated as facts the alleged technological insufficiencies in the administration of justice, the accumulation of cases and the 'inaction of the administrative bodies which have conspired against the citizens' right to an efficient and timely administration of justice' contained in the executive order.[150] Invoking the outcome of the 2011 referendum which approved the creation of the Council of the Transitional Judiciary, the Court wrote that the operationalisation of plans and programmes through the ordinary (namely, non-exceptional) legal regime would be 'ineffective', as the ordinary legal regime currently 'hinders [*obstaculiza*] the speed of the action of the leaders of the popular will: the Council of the Transitional Judiciary'.[151] It dismissed the idea that the content and effects of the executive order infringe upon the principle of separation of powers or the system of checks and balances.[152] Regarding the 'imminent internal upheaval' invoked in the executive decree, the Court made little of the fact that the upheaval was presented in the latter as 'imminent' (as in forthcoming) rather than present and, more importantly, 'serious' (*grave*), as per the wording of Article 164 of the 2008 Constitution.[153] Instead, it simply rubberstamped Correa's executive decree, treating its content and the allegations upon which it was based as accepted facts.[154]

[143] ibid, art 2.
[144] See, eg, Human Rights Watch (n 77).
[145] See, eg, L Roldós Aguilera, 'El estado de excepción' (*El Comercio*, 7 September 2011) www.elcomercio.com/opinion/excepcion-1.html.
[146] (My translation). See 2008 Constitution of Ecuador, art 164.
[147] Planas (n 139).
[148] Decision No 008-11-DEE-CC [9/17].
[149] ibid.
[150] ibid [8/17]. The Court here used the exact same wording as the one contained in the executive order.
[151] ibid [12/17].
[152] ibid [14/17], [15/17], [16/17].
[153] See 2008 Constitution of Ecuador, art 164: '*grave* conmoción interna, calamadidad pública o desastre natural' (emphasis added).
[154] Decision No 008-11-DEE-CC [8/17], [11/17].

Interestingly, in this case, the Court appears to have adopted the above-mentioned part of the populist discourse and imaginary, namely that issues of various sorts need to be dealt with immediately. In doing so, the Court legitimised Correa's sense of urgency and decisively came down on the side of his 'constitutional impatience'. Yet, it did have the opportunity to reject Correa's hastiness in implementing constitutional change – an opportunity it did not seize. It notably had the opportunity to reject Correa's re-politicisation of liberal institutions – particularly the judiciary – and to secure (or re-establish) the traditional spatiotemporal contours of liberal democracy.[155] Perhaps even more importantly, it had the power to protect democratic channels and debate; as Samuel Issacharoff has pointed out, 'deliberation is necessarily slower and more complicated than decree'.[156] Instead, it chose to endorse Correa's project of anti-mediation and hyperpresidentialism. It opted to become, in other words, a wilful agent of an increasingly impatient and authoritarian regime – rather than a check on the powers of the latter – thereby contributing to the existing acceleration of political time and the consolidation of executive powers. This turned out to be even more apparent less than three years later, in 2014, when it became clear that the Constitutional Court had become an instrument – instead of an opponent – of executive consolidation and authoritarian-leaning constitutional change, as discussed in the following subsection.

C. The 2014 'Term Limits' Judgment

A third case, the so-called 2014 'term limits' judgment, further illustrates the Constitutional Court's refusal to act as an institutional decelerator against an impatient and omnipotent executive; going even further this time, I contend, the Court instead chose to be an agent (or instrument) of the executive, by authorising (if not possibly even facilitating) and legitimising what could accurately be described as an authoritarian-leaning constitutional change.[157] In 2014, Correa, then serving his second term as president since the enactment of the 2008 Constitution (and third term overall since he was first elected president in 2007), sought to abolish term limits for presidents. Under Article 144(2) of the 2008 Constitution, a President of the Republic is barred from running for a third term: she or he holds power for a term of four years and can only be re-elected once.[158] Yet Correa, wishing to run as a candidate in the 2017 presidential election, called upon members of the National Assembly – then dominated by members of his

[155] See introductory ch.

[156] Issacharoff (n 62) 514.

[157] Landau and Dixon would go further and call this 'antidemocratic constitutional change'. See Landau and Dixon (n 3) 1322.

[158] 'La Presidenta o Presidente de la República permanecerá cuatro años en sus funciones y podrá ser reelecto por una sola vez'.

own political movement, Alianza País – to amend this provision of the 2008 Constitution and to allow the potential re-election of a president beyond his or her second term.[159]

Many in the political opposition and some commentators took the view that the removal of term limits would constitute a constitutional change altering the fundamental structure and (or) the constitutive nature and elements of the state.[160] For example, Carlos Bernal Pulido argued that a constitutional change of this kind 'would de-naturalize the system of powers' by allowing indefinite presidential re-election.[161] He took the view that the possibility of indefinite re-election violates five essential components of the 2008 Constitution, namely: 'the constitutional right to equality, constitutional rights concerning political participation of minority parties, the principles of the rule of law and separation of powers, and the institutionalization of deliberative democracy'.[162] As such, the opposition and these commentators argued that the proposed constitutional change should be treated as a *reforma parcial*, a higher tier of constitutional change which, as discussed above, requires approval in a referendum.[163]

Correa and members of his Alianza País, however, disagreed. Possibly wary that they might lose a referendum on that question, they argued that presidential term limits are not a constitutive element of the state structure (in contrast to elections, for instance) and that, as such, the removal of the term limits requires a simple and less burdensome *enmienda*. Under Article 443 of the 2008 Constitution, the Constitutional Court has jurisdiction to rule on which of these procedural vehicles is to be used in each circumstance. As such, the matter was referred by the President of the National Assembly to the Constitutional Court of Ecuador on 26 June 2014.

On 31 October 2014, the Constitutional Court of Ecuador delivered its judgment. In a landmark, 140-page decision,[164] it ruled that the proposed amendment to Article 144 of the 2008 Constitution to remove presidential term limits could be processed via *enmienda*, that is to say, via ordinary constitutional amendment. To justify its decision, the Court ruled that the removal of presidential term limits did *not* alter or affect any constitutional rights and guarantees. The Court took the view that, on the contrary, the proposed constitutional change sought to 'ensure' or 'guarantee' the constitutional principle of democratic participation for all citizens,

[159] El Comercio, 'Oficialismo plantea reforma constitucional para nueva reelección de Rafael Correa en 2017' (*El Comercio*, 28 February 2014) www.elcomercio.com/actualidad/politica/oficialismo-plantea-reforma-constitucional-nueva.html. See also C Bernal Pulido, 'There are Still Judges in Berlin: On the Proposal to Amend the Ecuadorian Constitution to Allow Indefinite Presidential Reelection' (*International Journal of Constitutional Law Blog*, 10 September 2014) www.iconnectblog.com/there-are-still-judges-in-berlin-on-the-proposal-to-amend-the-ecuadorian-constitution-to-allow-indefinite-presidential-reelection.

[160] See, eg, Silva-Portero (n 9).

[161] Bernal Pulido (n 159).

[162] ibid.

[163] ibid. See 2008 Constitution of Ecuador, art 442(2).

[164] Decision No 001-14-DRC-CC.

protected under Article 95 of the 2008 Constitution, as well as individual rights of participation, protected under Article 62, paragraphs (1) and (2) of the 2008 Constitution.[165]

The Court first stated that the 2008 Constitution does not recognise the alternation principle (*alternancia*, according to which there should be regular changes in the composition of the political representatives of a given polity) as a constitutive element of the state, in contrast to the previous (1998) Constitution of Ecuador, for example, which clearly listed this element in its Article 1.[166] Second, and perhaps more importantly, the Court stressed the importance of ensuring that individual citizens can exercise their right of participation 'without institutional limitations', a responsibility that is vested in the state.[167] In this particular instance, the Court stated that preventing candidates who have already held a public office (and who have been re-elected once) – such as Correa – from running for office again 'entails an unjustified limitation to the constitutional rights of participation' of these candidates, as well as to the people's right to vote and ability to select their democratic representatives.[168] As such, the Court took the view that the proposed constitutional change sought to 'ensure a full and integral exercise of the constitutional right of participation' – both for electors and those office holders who wished to be re-elected 'without discrimination'.[169] In light of the above, the Court concluded that the proposed changes to the 2008 Constitution did not seek to alter the democratic character of the Ecuadorian state, nor did they seek to modify the constitutive elements of the state or its fundamental structure. On the contrary, the Court wrote, these changes 'reaffirmed the new decision-making role of the Ecuadorean citizens in the political life of their country, in democratically selecting and allowing (or not) their elected representatives or rulers from staying in power', adding, with words reminiscing the ideal-typical populist discourse on popular sovereignty discussed in chapter one (as well as the populist emphasis on constituent power discussed in chapter two), that 'it is known that only the will of the people constitutes the foundation of authority'.[170] As such, the Court ruled that the amendment could be carried under the less stringent procedural vehicle provided for under Article 441(2) of the 2008 Constitution, namely the *enmienda constitucional* vehicle, which does not require a referendum to be held.[171]

With the clearance of the Constitutional Court, the National Assembly approved the constitutional amendment allowing unlimited presidential terms

[165] ibid [65/140].
[166] ibid [59/140], [60/140], referring to the Constitution of the Republic of Ecuador 1998 (RO 151, 5 June 1998), art 1. The Court also referred to the Constitution of the Republic of Ecuador (RO 995, 28 August 1979), art 1, which also contained this principle of alternation.
[167] Decision No 001-14-DRC-CC [61/140].
[168] ibid [63/140].
[169] ibid.
[170] ibid [65/140].
[171] ibid [66/140].

on 3 December 2015, with 100 members of the National Assembly voting in favour of the wider package of 16 constitutional amendments[172] amid protests and demonstrations in Quito, Guayaquil and Cuenca.[173] At the time of the vote, Correa's Alianza País held two-thirds of the 137-seat National Assembly.[174]

By delivering the judgment in this case, the Court once again refused to act as an institutional decelerator; on the contrary, I contend, it chose to act as a wilful enabler of executive consolidation by facilitating – and even accelerating, in the sense that it closed off additional political debate on the question – a possibly authoritarian-leaning constitutional change. A similar pattern, following similar judgments from their respective Constitutional Court, was later followed in other Latin American countries, including Evo Morales' Bolivia[175] and, more recently, Nayib Bukele's El Salvador.[176] For example, a few months after the mass removal of constitutional judges and their replacement with allies of the regime, briefly discussed in the previous chapter, the Constitutional Chamber of the Supreme Court of El Salvador rendered a controversial judgment allowing the immediate presidential re-election of President Bukele despite explicit constitutional prohibitions, including an unamendability provision[177] – a judgment which was portrayed as an instance of 'constitutional authoritarian populism'.[178]

It should be noted, however, that this was not the end of the story, at least not in Ecuador.[179] Indeed, protests continued to emerge across the country, and Correa eventually backed down and decided not to run again for President in the 2017 election, choosing instead to support his handpicked political heir, Lenín Moreno, as his successor, possibly with a view to reclaiming power again in the 2021 election.[180] Yet, Moreno himself quickly broke with Correa after winning the February 2017 election and, in a referendum that took place only a few months

[172] See Letter to Mrs Gabriela Rivadeneira Burbano, President of the National Assembly (*Presidenta de la Asamblea Nacional*) (25 June 2014) www.asambleanacional.gob.ec/sites/default/files/private/asambleanacional/filesasambleanacionalnameuid-28/PEDIDO%20A%20CORTE%20ENMIENDA.pdf.

[173] D Collins, 'Protests in Ecuador as lawmakers approve unlimited presidential terms' (*The Guardian*, 4 December 2015) www.theguardian.com/world/2015/dec/04/protests-in-ecuador-as-lawmakers-approve-unlimited-presidential-terms.

[174] ibid.

[175] Plurinational Constitutional Tribunal of Bolivia (*Tribunal Constitucional Plurinacional de Bolivia*), Decision No 84 of 2017 (28 November 2017).

[176] See, eg, Constitutional Chamber of the Supreme Court of Justice (*Sala de lo Constitucional de la Corte Suprema de Justicia*) 1-2021 (3 September 2021).

[177] Constitution of El Salvador, art 248(4). See also art 88.

[178] JI Hernández G, 'The Constitutional Chamber in El Salvador and Presidential Reelection: Another Case of Constitutional Authoritarian-Populism' (*International Journal of Constitutional Law Blog*, 10 September 2021) www.iconnectblog.com/the-constitutional-chamber-in-el-salvador-and-presidential-reelection-another-case-of-constitutional-authoritarian-populism.

[179] Evo Morales was ousted from office in November 2019, amid popular protests disputing the outcome of the 2019 Bolivian general election and pressure from the army. He officially resigned on 10 November 2019, after nearly 14 years in power and a few weeks after (officially) winning a fourth presidential term.

[180] C de la Torre, 'Latin America's Shifting Politics: Ecuador After Correa' (2018) 29 *Journal of Democracy* 77, 78.

later, convinced Ecuadorians to bring back presidential term limits – thereby barring the way for Correa to eventually return as President.[181] One could thus interpret this as an instance of political constitutionalism stepping in to fill the gap left by the absence of well-functioning, genuinely independent mechanisms of legal constitutionalism. Indeed, this experience reveals that courts can refuse – as the Constitutional Court of Ecuador did on at least two separate occasions or judgments – to act as institutional decelerators against an impatient populist executive. However, and perhaps more importantly, this case study further reveals that courts can go further by not only failing to exercise their constitutional functions amid political and executive pressures, but also opting to act as *agents* of executive consolidation rather than as bulwarks against authoritarian-leaning constitutional change. The 2014 'Term Limits' ruling, in particular, illustrates that the Ecuadorian Constitutional Court yielded to executive power – at least during the Correa presidency – thus acting as a facilitator of democratic erosion, executive consolidation and authoritarian-leaning constitutional change, primarily through means that could accurately be described as 'abusive judicial review'.[182]

D. Judicial Review in Ecuador: From Revolutionary Populism to Authoritarian Legalism?

Finally, and to employ Theunis Roux's typology of judicial review regimes, the combination of partial capture of the judiciary and a form of abusive judicial review in Ecuador can be seen as clear indications of a move towards a relatively light form of 'authoritarian legalism'.[183] The latter is defined as a judicial review regime 'in which political authority is in part legitimated by the autonomy given to judges in defined areas of social life'; that said, '[i]n areas more sensitive to the power holder's interests, however, judges routinely defer to political prerogatives'.[184] Under this regime, Roux explains, 'judicial review continues to operate, and may in fact flourish in certain areas, but is ineffective in the crucial sense that it provides few resources for proponents of a more open and competitive democratic system to challenge authoritarian power holders'.[185] In the case

[181] M Ayala and M Rochabrún, 'Ecuador Votes to Bring Back Presidential Term Limits' (*New York Times*, 4 February 2018) www.nytimes.com/2018/02/04/world/americas/ecuador-presidential-term-limits.html. See also ibid. On how populist constitutions sometimes 'outlive' the regimes that created them, see D Landau, 'Personalism and the Trajectories of Populist Constitutions' (2020) 16 *Annual Review of Law and Social Science*, especially 294: 'Over the long run, the experimental potential of these [populist] constitutions may be higher, and the democratic threat lower, than is apparent around the time they are written.'

[182] See, generally, Landau and Dixon (n 3); S Issacharoff, 'The Corruption of Popular Sovereignty' (2020) 18 *International Journal of Constitutional Law* 1115.

[183] T Roux, *The Politico-Legal Dynamics of Judicial Review: A Comparative Analysis* (Cambridge, Cambridge University Press, 2018) 257.

[184] ibid.

[185] ibid 81.

of Ecuador, the overarching societal interests to which judges were subordinate were arguably the interests of social justice (as defined and understood by Correa), including the achievement of greater equality, and the completion of the Citizens' Revolution.

In fact, there is some evidence that, at least from 2011 onwards, the Constitutional Court of Ecuador showed extreme deference to executive prerogatives and 'effectively declined to review politically sensitive cases'.[186] This is in line with an argument, put forward by José Luis Castro-Montero and Gijs van Dijck, that the Ecuadorian Constitutional Court (a formally unfettered court) still had – at least during Correa's era – in reality strong 'incentives to favor the government when ruling politically salient cases, that is to say, those cases in which high importance is attributed by the government and public opinion to a case' despite the existence of 'strong *de jure* protections and almost unfettered powers'.[187] Using quantitative analysis, they found that the Court was more likely to use its (*in abstracto*) judicial review powers to strike down laws when declarations of unconstitutionality were sought by public officials compared to non-public parties; and when cases were reported in the media.[188] In that regard, it is particularly telling that, in ten years, the Constitutional Court did not declare unconstitutional a single declaration of emergency, despite the fact that many such declarations arguably did not comply with all constitutional standards.[189]

These elements indicate a certain move towards a form of authoritarian legalism – if not even, quite possibly, a particularly 'light' form of authoritarian instrumentalism. The latter is understood as a judicial review regime under which 'law's subordination to politics is complete', with law being fully 'instrumentalized in service to a single, overarching conception of the just society that brooks no alternatives'.[190] In such a regime, Roux explains, 'there is no conception of law as an autonomous source of authority that is capable of constraining political power'; it is, rather, a mere 'projection of political authority, and its sole role is to define the just society, promote its achievement and discipline citizens into conforming to its prescriptions'.[191] While law in Ecuador under Correa probably did not go as far as to become completely subordinate to politics, there are nonetheless some indications, as explained above, that judicial review was travelling in a particular authoritarian direction, with a diminished understanding of law as a (less) autonomous source of authority, less capable of constraining political power – at

[186] ibid 260. Roux here refers to Chile's Supreme Court under the rule of General Augusto Pinochet, but some of these principles – particularly the extreme deference to executive prerogatives – also apply in the cases discussed in this chapter. After the departure of the military junta and the reestablishment of democracy in 1990, 'the Chilean judiciary stuck to its self-presentation as a politically impartial actor, thereby inhibiting the development of the more robust, judicially led style of constitutionalism seen in Colombia and Costa Rica'. See ibid.

[187] Castro-Montero and van Dijck (n 72) 382.

[188] ibid 381–382.

[189] C Castro Montero (n 125) 37–38.

[190] Roux (n 183) 261–262.

[191] ibid, 262.

least compared to other typologies of judicial review such as democratic legalism and democratic instrumentalism. In any event, there is clear evidence that the Constitutional Court used (and possibly abused) its judicial review powers to routinely side with the Correa government and help the latter consolidate its grip over the Ecuadorian institutional and legal-political sphere. As discussed in the next section, this form of authoritarian legalism (or even, maybe, authoritarian instrumentalism), combined with the abovementioned institutional capture, is quite possibly linked to a broader project of executive consolidation, more specifically what Nancy Bermeo, Tarunabh Khaitan and others have called 'executive aggrandisement'.[192]

V. Judicial Capture as Part of a Project of Executive Aggrandisement?

In an article[193] published in 2016, Nancy Bermeo defined executive aggrandisement as a 'common form of backsliding [that] occurs when elected executives weaken checks on executive power one by one, undertaking a series of institutional changes that hamper the power of opposition forces to challenge executive preferences'.[194] This is usually done gradually and incrementally through formal and legal channels, for instance, via constitutional amendments or profound changes to the institutions of democracy, including the legal and judicial systems.[195] Often undertaken by populists (although not necessarily just by them),[196] executive aggrandisement has become more widespread in recent years and now occurs in various countries. It is often carried out and justified by populists in the name of 'the people'. As mentioned in Part I of this monograph, political opponents are discredited as 'special interests', as 'not belonging to the nation' or even as 'enemies'. From a temporal perspective, this leads to a certain paradox. On the one hand, processes of de-democratisation under executive aggrandisement tend to be 'slower', more piecemeal and more incremental than the more dramatic and sudden breakdowns seen in the past.[197] On the other hand, the result of these

[192] See Bermeo (n 104); T Khaitan, 'Killing a Constitution with a Thousand Cuts: Executive Aggrandizement and Party-State Fusion in India' (2020) 14 *Law & Ethics of Human Rights*.

[193] Bermeo (n 104).

[194] ibid 10.

[195] Notably through court-packing and changes to legislation, including changes to defamation laws. An example of court-packing is Recep Tayyip Erdoğan's decision to pass multiple constitutional changes via referendum, which allowed him to appoint fourteen of the seventeen Constitutional Court judges. See ibid 11–12. See also Varol (n 95). On court-packing, see D Kosař and K Šipulová, 'Comparative Court-Packing' (2023) 21 *International Journal of Constitutional Law* 80.

[196] ibid. Bermeo mentions the examples of populist leaders Erdoğan's in Türkiye and Correa in Ecuador (2007–2017), but adds that many others non-populist political actors, from former Senegal President Abdoulaye Wade to former Ukraine President Viktor Yanukovych, have also engaged in similar activities. See ibid 12–13.

[197] Bermeo (n 104) 14.

changes can be seen as a form of acceleration of political time and processes. Indeed, the ultimate aim of these populists is arguably to remove as many barriers and means of mediation as possible in the long term, in order to facilitate and accelerate their project, while retaining a façade of democracy.[198]

In fact, while this chapter focuses on Ecuador, there are now several empirical studies that highlight the 'striking similarities' regarding how some authoritarian populists arguably 'undermine democracy'[199] through mechanisms that could be associated with executive aggrandisement. A common element seems to be how some populists in power circumvent, weaken or erode checks on their power, including judicial checks, thereby causing serious damage to constitutionalism. For example, a 2018 study using data pertaining to 19 countries in Latin America between 1982 and 2012 identified frequent and common populist attacks on four essential elements of constitutional democracy.[200] The first, and arguably most important, is the way populists circumvent or simply override essential checks on executive power, particularly the courts. By way of example, the authors' analysis of relevant data shows that 'after four years of populist rule, courts have 34% less independence than they would have under a typical democratic government'.[201] The same study shows that free media and civil rights and liberties, as well as the quality of elections, also suffer under populist rule.

This is not to say, of course, that populism should only be understood as a dangerous and uniquely and unequivocally illiberal phenomenon; as we have seen in the previous chapter on Armenia in the aftermath of the Velvet Revolution, the relationship between populism and constitutionalism can be 'positive', at least to an extent. The case of Ecuador under Correa additionally shows that populism – particularly its left-wing variant – can also be accompanied by an increase in constitutionally protected rights,[202] political participation[203] (although the latter appears to be mainly focused on means of direct democracy), as well as a sharp decline in the levels of poverty[204] and inequality.[205] For instance, a 2019 study has revealed that the social transformation experienced in Ecuador has led to an 'important reduction in vertical and horizontal inequality during the last 15 years, and particularly during the last decade', although questions remain regarding the

[198] See ch 2.

[199] B Bugarič, 'Could Populism Be Good for Constitutional Democracy?' (2019) 15 *Annual Review of Law and Social Science* 47.

[200] C Houle and PD Kenny, 'The Political and Economic Consequences of Populist Rule in Latin America' (2018) 53(2) *Government and Opposition* 256.

[201] Bugarič (n 199) 47, referring to ibid.

[202] See section II.A of this ch, above.

[203] C Mudde and C Rovira Kaltwasser, *Populism: A Very Short Introduction* (Oxford, Oxford University Press, 2017) 83. See also RS Jansen, 'Populist Mobilization: A New Theoretical Approach to Populism' (2011) 29 *Sociological Theory*.

[204] World Bank numbers show that the proportion of Ecuadorians living in poverty fell from 37.6% to 24.5% between 2006 and 2014, as mentioned in Conaghan (n 17) 114.

[205] I Gachet, DF Grijalva, PA Ponce and D Rodríguez, 'Vertical and Horizontal Inequality in Ecuador: The Lack of Sustainability' (2019) 145 *Social Indicators Research* 861, 895.

long-term sustainability of such a reduction.[206] Moreover, and as illustrated in the previous case study on Armenia, a contextual analysis is thus necessary to assess the current and long-term implications of populism for liberal constitutional democracy in a given country. While important, indicators are not always sufficient to paint a complete picture. To summarise – and as Mark Tushnet has put it, referring to Andean populism – sometimes the populist-led social and institutional 'transformation might be accompanied by a reduction in the formal power – and freedom – of existing elites', but this reduction 'is not in itself enough to condemn the populist transformation as illiberal'.[207]

Nevertheless, in the specific case of Ecuador under the presidency of Correa, the executive's constitutional impatience – and more particularly the capture of the judiciary and other key institutions of the state – arguably diminished checks and balances on the executive branch, to such an extent that it would be difficult to depict this transformation as anything but an illiberal form of executive aggrandisement and dominance. Through the use of the 'instrumentalities of governance',[208] the capture of the Ecuadorian judiciary was a key step in achieving this form of executive dominance, effectively wearing down the opposition. This was done following steps that share important similarities with other countries that have also seen their judiciary captured by the executive, including Poland. The main specificity in the case of Ecuador, however, was the significant role of the inexcusable error doctrine, described in the third part of this chapter. Although formally there was no change in the constitutional guarantee legislation in Ecuador, in practice the Judicial Council, through the inexcusable error doctrine, had a chilling effect by sanctioning and even removing judges who had rendered a decision unfavourable to the government. As a result of the above, remaining independent judges were simply unable to perform their 'deceleration' function lauded by Kuo and to re-establish democracy's empty place of power. On the contrary, and as we have seen, captured courts – particularly the Constitutional Court – even acted as *accelerators* (rather than decelerators) of the populist flow of time by becoming active enablers and agents of executive aggrandisement and consolidation.

VI. Conclusion

For Martin Loughlin, the case of Ecuador under the presidency of Correa (2007–2017) reveals an inherent ambiguity in the understanding of both populism and the concept of constitutional democracy.[209] Loughlin first highlights the innovative character of the 2008 Constitution of Ecuador, notably the 'vast array

[206] ibid.

[207] M Tushnet, 'Varieties of Populism' (2019) 20 *German Law Journal* 383.

[208] Samuel Issacharoff in M Orey, 'The Undoing of Democracy?' (*NYU Law – The Magazine*, 11 September 2020) www.law.nyu.edu/news/ideas/undoing-democracy-richard-pildes-samuel-issacharoff.

[209] See, eg, Loughlin (n 44) 438, 440–442.

of social rights' it protects and the way it aims to promote real equality for rights-bearers in a situation of inequality.[210] As he notes, this is a 'far cry' from the classic understanding of the constitution as an instrument 'designed to bolster the established order through the protection of life, liberty and property'.[211] Moreover, there are strong indications that the 2008 Constitution of Ecuador was indeed (at least partially) successful in establishing a progressive and less unequal socio-institutional order, as many indicators show that poverty and economic inequality drastically declined during Correa's presidency.[212] These elements illustrate the democratic and transformative potential of populism, and allude to an understanding of the phenomenon as a relatively coherent political and constitutional theory and project.[213]

Yet, as discussed in this chapter and as Loughlin himself recognises, the 2008 Constitution was also, simultaneously, a key part of a large-scale 'reform that loosens institutional checks and balances'.[214] This was done mainly through legal-institutional channels; and the result was a form of engrained executive dominance or aggrandisement, as well as the gradual erosion of constitutionalism in Ecuador. One may also question the truly participative character of this form of populism, especially considering the relative 'one-man show' nature of Ecuadorian politics under Correa's presidency – with its focus on substantial unity, unanimity and acclamation, arguably to the detriment of deliberation and compromise – and the relative weakness of the institutional checks on his discretionary powers. In light of these potentially conflicting assessments of Correa's populism, the question remains, therefore, for Loughlin, 'whether constitutional democracy is designed to restrain government for the better protection of individual liberties or whether it should aim to help transform society in order to realize equal liberty'?[215]

It would be beyond the scope of this chapter and monograph to attempt to answer this question about the fundamental aim of constitutional democracy (and, indirectly, about the fundamental character of populism) in a definitive way. From a legal-institutional perspective, however, four clear conclusions emerge from the analysis conducted in this chapter. First, a key component of the populist politics of immediacy is a particular dynamic, instrumental and short-term engagement with the constitution. Indeed, and despite his progressive, egalitarian and inclusive agenda, Correa, from a legal-institutional perspective, ultimately followed the typical authoritarian-populist playbook. He did so by invoking the constituent power in a first step and discretionary political power in a second step

[210] ibid 440.
[211] ibid.
[212] Conaghan (n 17) 114. Regarding economic inequalities, see, eg, Federal Reserve Bank of St. Louis, 'GINI Index for Ecuador' (*FRED Economic Data*, 2019) fred.stlouisfed.org/series/SIPOVGINIECU. This data shows that the Gini (inequality) index for Ecuador fell dramatically between 2017 (53.4) and 2018 (45.4), indicating a drop in inequalities in the country during Correa's presidency.
[213] See, eg, F Tarragoni, *L'esprit démocratique du populisme* (Paris, La Découverte, 2019).
[214] Loughlin (n 44) 440.
[215] ibid 441–442.

to disable institutional checks on his power. In doing so, he showed his preference for short-term benefits over the long term.[216] Second, and in the same vein, this case study reveals that populist immediacy and dynamic engagement with the constitution come with a form of politicisation and instrumentalisation of the legal-institutional order, which, in the case of Ecuador, was accompanied by an extended use of executive powers. Third, formally independent institutions such as courts (and electoral commissions) simply do not have the ability, in a context in which they are captured or controlled by the executive, to act as efficient institutional decelerators against an impatient and omnipotent executive, nor can they act as a bulwark against hyperpresidentialism and the concentration of presidential or executive powers. On the contrary, they can quickly succumb to the overwhelming forces of populist politics and become active agents of democratic erosion and executive consolidation.[217] The fourth and final conclusion is that the process of judicial (and state) capture described in this chapter is (often) part of a broader project of executive aggrandisement, aimed at reducing and weakening curbs on the powers of an omnipotent executive.

As mentioned previously, this case study is indicative of a potential tension between the promotion of democratic change and the protection of liberal values. This is important, because as we have seen in chapter four, the relationship between populism and constitutionalism is context-specific and can possibly yield 'positive' outcomes. Nevertheless, in the specific case of Correa's Ecuador, the four conclusions mentioned above point towards a possibly more 'negative' relationship between populism and constitutionalism. Of course, nothing is ever completely black or white, particularly in the case of a major overhaul of the social order. As David Landau summarises in relation to Ecuador, Correa's presidency showed 'little patience with constitutionalism as a constraint on power, but the program of action [he embodied] perhaps did help to galvanize changes in the social structure'.[218] However, despite their progressive ambitions and their focus on democratic participation, the political and constitutional transformations conducted in Ecuador over the ten years of Correa's populist presidency appear to have ultimately resulted in eroded electoral accountability and, even, possibly, weakened forms of democratic participation and deliberation. This was done, notably, through judicial and institutional capture, following incremental steps that were rather similar to the ways in which more authoritarian, *right*-wing (or fundamentalist religious) populist movements – such as Erdoğan's AKP in Türkiye,[219] Jarosław Kaczyński's PiS in Poland[220] and Narendra Modi's BJP in India,[221] amongst others – recently managed to capture (at least in part) key

[216] Issacharoff (n 182) 1115.
[217] Landau and Dixon (n 45); ibid.
[218] Landau (n 181) 302.
[219] See, eg, Varol (n 95).
[220] See, eg, Sadurski, *Poland's Constitutional Breakdown* (n 102).
[221] See, eg, Khaitan (n 192).

institutions of the state and weaken restraints on their own power. These elements thus point in the direction of a difficult relationship between populism and constitutionalism, at least in such contexts.

In the end, one may wonder if the two potentially conflicting aims of modern constitutional democracy discussed by Loughlin – that is to say, to restrain government to better protect individual liberties *or* to transform society to achieve better equal liberty – are really, in fact, antithetical or perhaps, alternatively, complementary and both necessary to achieve constitutional democracy. As for the role of courts in that regard, the analysis conducted in this chapter is a further illustration that courts are not necessarily a panacea in a context of populist 'constitutional impatience': indeed, their ability (and willingness) to decelerate political time and re-establish democracy's empty place of power appears to be contingent on their institutional independence.[222] In fact, once pressured or even captured, courts can even *accelerate* (rather than decelerate) the populist flow of time by becoming active agents and enablers of executive aggrandisement and consolidation. In doing so, courts can establish themselves as (sometimes long-term) allies of a regime – even when the latter is repudiated by a vast majority of voters.[223] That said, in the right institutional setting and context, courts can nevertheless be more successful in decelerating the populist tempo and re-establishing democratic channels and processes. This will be the object of the next and final chapter of this monograph.

[222] See ch 6. And, perhaps, on the existence of a deeply engrained democratic (and *garantiste*) culture. On this, see conclusion.

[223] See, eg, ch 4.

6

Executive Power(s), 'Constitutional Impatience' and the Role of Courts as Institutional Stabilisers in the United Kingdom

I. Introduction

As discussed in Part I of this monograph, contemporary populism does not operate in a vacuum; it emerges and functions in the context of what political and social theorists have called 'social acceleration'.[1] While liberal institutions – particularly legislatures and courts – appear ill-equipped to adapt to this trend, populism manifests itself as a powerful critique of liberal democracy: it depicts the latter as distant, lethargic, opaque and elite-driven. Taking advantage of the spatiotemporal contours of liberal democracy, populism puts forward an alternative conception of democratic representation: one that not only aims to reduce the distance between *gouvernants* and *gouvernés*, but that is also, as populists would indirectly claim, better suited to the contemporary imperatives of temporal efficiency and rapidity. Indeed, populists are typically impatient with intermediaries, institutions (including legislatures and courts) and liberal-democratic procedures, which are seen as illegitimately thwarting the direct expression of the authentic 'will of the people'.[2]

To achieve their objectives as quickly as possible, populists are often eager to invoke executive powers, including prerogative powers – from the executive prerogative in its US meaning to the Royal Prerogative in the context of the UK. As William E Scheuerman notes, this is often done through a 'perversion of the traditional temporal justification for executive-centered emergency government'.[3] For

[1] See, eg, H Rosa, Social Acceleration: Ethical and Political Consequences of a Desynchronized High-Speed Society' (2003) 10 *Constellations* 71–80.

[2] See Part I of this monograph.

[3] WE Scheuerman, 'President Trump's "Get it Done Faster" Emergency' (*Verfassungsblog*, 18 February 2019) www.verfassungsblog.de/president-trumps-get-it-done-faster-emergency. For a discussion of the traditional liberal-democratic temporal separation of powers, see WE Scheuerman, *Liberal Democracy and the Social Acceleration of Time* (Baltimore, Johns Hopkins University Press, 2004) and the introductory ch.

example, Lockean-type emergency powers – initially designed for truly extraordinary situations of emergency[4] – have recently been used in less-than-extraordinary situations.[5] In the UK, while no emergency powers were invoked in the context of Brexit,[6] prominent politicians from Nigel Farage to Boris Johnson have nonetheless invoked on multiple occasions the urgency of 'getting Brexit done', notably 'in the face of [an] unrelenting parliamentary obstructionism' and of an 'endless refusal', by Parliament, 'to deliver on the mandate of the people'.[7] In fact, it was arguably the key element of the Conservative manifesto in the 2019 general election,[8] which they won by a large margin. In these politicians' view, 'artificial' delays to the implementation of the 'will of the people', provoked either by courts or Parliament, were democratically unjustified. From the perspective of space and time, the idea was for 'the people', understood as a unity and under the auspices of the executive, to 'take back control' over political time and to 'seize' the agenda, both literally and figuratively.

Through its distrust of and impatience with liberal institutions and other intermediaries, populism can serve as a catalyst (or, as some would say, a pretext) for the acceleration of political time and democratic processes – and for the shrinking of the distance between rulers and the ruled. In so doing, it favours proximity, simultaneity, and immediacy – the result of which is a form of what I have called in chapter three 'constitutional impatience'. Yet, it is precisely in this context that courts can arguably provide a judicial response to populism, notably by playing the role of institutional decelerators and (or) stabilisers. As Ming-Sung Kuo remarks, judicial proceedings have been noted – and sometimes criticised – for their slow pace, which, perhaps counterintuitively, 'can be a structural asset of the multistage process of constitutional governance in its pushback against new populism'.[9]

Of course, in reply to populist claims of proximity, simultaneity and immediacy, many liberal constitutionalists would respond that while sound decision-making (whether judicial or not) can indeed be lengthy, the relatively slow pace of the

[4] For the Lockean type of prerogative, see J Locke, *Second Treatise of Government* in *Second Treatise of Government* and *A Letter Concerning Toleration* (Oxford University Press, 2016 [1689]), ch XIV.

[5] For example, and as briefly mentioned in ch 3, Donald Trump, after declaring a national emergency in 2019 in the context of the 'border crisis' between the US and Mexico, quickly conceded that it was not temporally justified: 'I didn't need to do this, but I'd rather do it much faster. I just want to get it done faster, that's all.' Cited in Scheuerman (n 3).

[6] However, they were – of course – used in different contexts. One may think, for example, of the use of discretionary (statutory) powers of governance during Covid.

[7] HC Deb, vol 667, col 236 (29 October 2019). Boris Johnson said, in the House of Commons: 'There is only one way now to move this country forward and to have that debate, and that is to get Brexit done. There is only one way to get Brexit done, in the face of this unrelenting parliamentary obstructionism – this endless, wilful, fingers crossed, "Not me, guv!" refusal to deliver on the mandate of the people – and that is to refresh this Parliament and to give the people a choice.'

[8] The Conservative and Unionist Party, 'Manifesto 2019 – Get Brexit Done: Unleash Britain's Potential (2019) assets-global.website-files.com/5da42e2cae7ebd3f8bde353c/5dda924905da587992a064ba_Conservative%202019%20Manifesto.pdf.

[9] M-S Kuo, 'Against Instantaneous Democracy' (2019) 17 *International Journal of Constitutional Law* 571.

judiciary can sometimes be a virtue, particularly in a context of social acceleration and populist impatience. For example, and as Bart van Klink notes, slowness 'is a coping strategy that enables us to deal with our fast-changing world. It gives us time to reflect and react in a prudent way to new situations, building practical knowledge and experience acquired in the past.'[10] He, in the same vein, adds that '[b]y developing a "sense of slowness", we learn to discover the changes that are both desirable and feasible.'[11] From an institutional perspective, it could also be argued that the distinctive temporal regime of the judiciary is an essential part of its autonomy and authority.[12] However, and as we have seen in the previous two chapters, the 'engrained slowness'[13] of the judiciary is not exactly, in and of itself, a panacea for populist constitutional impatience and other pressures for executive consolidation. Under certain circumstances, courts can in fact become institutional obstructors by blocking the reforms of a democratic, newly elected government led by a populist leader replacing a semi-authoritarian regime (chapter four). Moreover, once captured, courts can even accelerate (rather than decelerate) the populist flow of time by becoming active agents and enablers of executive aggrandisement and consolidation (chapter five).

This chapter, which focuses on the UK in the period that followed the Brexit referendum, paints a slightly more positive picture for courts as potential institutional decelerators and reveals a 'mixed' relationship between populism and constitutionalism (by contrast to the possibility of a 'positive' relationship discussed in chapter four and the more 'negative' one discussed in chapter five). In this chapter, I argue that courts can act – and have indeed acted, in at least two recent high-profile cases – as institutional decelerators *and* stabilisers in the face of an impatient executive. More specifically, courts have reacted and responded to the executive-led acceleration of time: in so doing, they have calmed populist impatience as well as pressures for executive aggrandisement, while acting in defence of the constitutional order. I make this argument by reference to two Supreme Court rulings, namely *Miller (no 1)*[14] and *Miller (no 2)/Cherry*.[15] Nevertheless, as I assert in the third section of this chapter, the effects of institutional deceleration and stabilisation are subject to important constraints; furthermore, the more substantive virtues of judicial (or institutional) deceleration praised by its proponents – including its alleged contributions to democratic learning as part of the multistage process of constitutional-democratic governance[16] – are grounded in empirical claims that remain, ultimately, difficult to verify.

[10] B van Klink, 'Law at the Right Time: A Plea for Slow Law in Hasty Times' in L Corrias and L Francot, *Temporal Boundaries of Law and Politics: Time Out of Joint* (Abingdon, Routledge, 2018) 44.

[11] ibid.

[12] L Francot, 'Suspended in Gaffa: Legal Slowness in the Acceleration of Society' in Francot and Corrias (eds) (n 10) 99.

[13] See introductory ch.

[14] *R (Miller) v Secretary of State for Exiting the European Union* [2017] UKSC 5.

[15] *R (Miller) v The Prime Minister /Cherry v Advocate General for Scotland* [2019] UKSC 41.

[16] Kuo (n 9) 564.

This chapter proceeds in four sections. In section II, I examine how UK courts have managed to slow down the populist acceleration of political time and the executive-led constitutional impatience. I do so by reference to the political and legal context of each case, analysing the Brexit referendum and the Royal Prerogative (*Miller (no 1)*), as well as the prorogation of Parliament (*Miller (no 2)/Cherry*). In section III, I discuss the limits of institutional deceleration and stabilisation in the UK context (and beyond), notably by reference to the public reception of judgments, the forces of politics or political pressure, institutional independence and the alleged role of courts as 'democratic educators'. Section IV, finally, concludes.

II. UK Courts as Institutional *Stabilisers*

The main claim of this chapter is that in the UK, courts have shown – at least in two high-profile Supreme Court cases, *Miller (no 1)* and *Miller (no 2)/Cherry* – that they have the power and willingness to act as institutional decelerators or stabilisers and to respond to constitutional impatience by slowing down the populist tempo and acceleration of political time – and counteracting the populist tendency to avoid and bypass institutional intermediaries such as Parliament and the courts. However, before discussing these two judgments in more depth, it is important to provide some conceptual clarifications.

Earlier in this monograph, I have used the term '*institutional* deceleration' instead of Kuo's preferred term '*judicial* deceleration'.[17] I did so because the adjective 'institutional' is, in my view, more precise than 'judicial', given that the reference point of deceleration is actually the proper constitutional decision-making process, which involves different institutions, rather than the judicial process per se. In this chapter, I want to add a second conceptual clarification, which I believe more accurately describes the role of courts in the face of social and political acceleration, particularly in the UK context. Instead of using the term 'deceleration', I employ the concept of 'stabilisation', understood as 'the process of becoming or being made unlikely to change, fail or decline'.[18] This is so because I believe the term 'institutional stabiliser'[19] more accurately reflects or describes the role of courts, particularly UK courts, in the face of

[17] Kuo actually uses the terms 'institutional decelerator' or 'institutional deceleration' twice in his article, compared to the 15 instances of 'judicial deceleration' or 'institutional deceleration'. See ibid.

[18] 'Stabilization', *Cambridge Dictionary*, www.dictionary.cambridge.org/dictionary/english/stabilization (earlier definition from 2022; the closest current definition would perhaps be 'the fact of something such as an economy or system becoming able to continue in a regular and successful way without unexpected changes').

[19] On the 'stabilising' role of the judiciary, see, eg, S Issacharoff, 'Constitutional Courts and Democratic Hedging' (2011) 99 *Georgetown Law Journal*. In this article, Issacharoff frequently uses the term in reference to the 'stabilising' function of new constitutional courts in a broader context of democratic governance and transition towards democracy. While I take inspiration from Issacharoff's work, my understanding in this chapter is more spatiotemporally oriented and perhaps broader in scope, in that it is less focused on new constitutional courts and (or) emerging democracies.

the constitutional impatience described in chapter three. Indeed, in my view, what courts are trying to do in response to populist constitutional impatience is not necessarily just to slow down (as such) the constitutional decision-making process. While judicial responses may indeed have the effect of putting the brakes on the populist acceleration of time, they can also, at times, have the opposite effect: they can even contribute to this said acceleration and (or) constitutional impatience, as we have seen in the previous case study on Ecuador under the presidency of Rafael Correa (chapter five). One may even point out, in the UK context, that the two *Miller* decisions – which are discussed in more detail later in this chapter – were handed down very fast, even possibly in record time.[20] Rather, what courts are actually attempting, in my view, is more accurately described as endeavouring to *stabilise* the constitutional decision-making process: their aim is to ensure that the institutional mechanics of the system of constitutional governance are followed, and, in so doing, they contribute to preventing this system from changing, failing or declining, particularly in the face of populist constitutional impatience.

This is not to say, of course, that this stabilising function is necessarily or always, in and of itself, democracy-enhancing. A more contextual analysis is required to make such a determination. There certainly are circumstances in which courts can become institutional obstructors (rather than stabilisers or decelerators) by blocking and (or) impeding the reforms of a democratic-leaning, newly elected government replacing a semi-authoritarian regime, as we have seen in chapter four. In such instances, this 'stabilising' (or more accurately, in this case, obstructing) function could become a major hurdle in the transition towards consolidated democracy. Nevertheless, in the right circumstances, courts can play the role of democracy-enhancing institutional stabilisers by re-establishing democratic channels and ensuring that the proper constitutional-institutional procedures and processes are duly followed. This is precisely what they have done in the UK context, as I argue in the following two subsections. Far from being a panacea, however, the stabilising and democracy-enhancing function of courts remains subject to important constraints and (or) limitations, which is the subject of the section III of this chapter.

[20] For example, with regard to *Miller (no 2)/Cherry*, the legal challenge was launched pre-emptively (that is, before the Prorogation Order was issued) in Scotland on 30 July 2019. The Prorogation Order was made on 28 August 2019 and, two days later, the Outer House of the Court of Session issued a procedural decision – see *Cherry v Advocate General for Scotland* [2019] CSOH 68 – as well as, on 4 September 2019 a substantive judgment – see *Cherry v Advocate General for Scotland* [2019] CSOH 70. In England, the Divisional Court issued its judgment on 11 September 2019 – see *R (Miller) v The Prime Minister* [2019] EWHC 2381 (QB). The matter was then sent directly to the UK Supreme Court (as a 'leap-frog' appeal, made under s 13 of the Administration of Justice Act 1969 (c 58), which was granted by the Divisional Court for reasons of urgency). The Supreme Court heard the appeals less than a week later, ie, between 17-19 September 2019 and issued its final ruling on 24 September 2019, that is, less than two weeks after the Divisional Court ruling and less than a month after the Prorogation Order was announced. See *R (Miller) v The Prime Minister /Cherry v Advocate General for Scotland* [2019] UKSC 41.

A. The Brexit Referendum, the Royal Prerogative and the *Miller (no 1)* Case

i. Brexit and the Place of Referendums in the UK Constitution

On 23 June 2016, a majority of British voters cast their vote in favour of the UK leaving the EU in a countrywide referendum (the 'Brexit referendum'). Following the ideal-typical populist discourse discussed in chapter one, the outcome of the Brexit referendum was depicted by many politicians and tabloids as a clear and unequivocal expression of the 'will of the people', namely the unassailable *decision* of the British people to leave the EU.[21]

Yet, notwithstanding its apparent democratic credentials, the constitutional status (or the legal value) of a referendum in the UK legal order was – and remains, to a certain extent – relatively poorly understood and uncertain.[22] First, the concept of referendum remains a bit of a 'novelty' (or even an 'anomaly', as some commentators put it)[23] in the British constitutional framework. While the Victorian jurist Albert Venn Dicey argued in favour of introducing referendums in Britain as early as in 1890,[24] the referendum as a legal instrument has

[21] See, eg, M Freeden, 'After the Brexit Referendum: Revisiting Populism as an Ideology' (2017) 22 *Journal of Political Ideologies* 1. On the 'will of the people', see, eg, A Weale, *The Will of the People: A Modern Myth* (Cambridge, Polity, 2018).

[22] See, eg, G Marshall, 'The Constitution: Its Theory and Interpretation' in V Bogdanor (ed), *The British Constitution and the Twentieth Century* (Oxford, Oxford University Press, 2003) 62. Certain measures for the procedural regulation have been introduced, including the Political Parties, Elections and Referendums Act 2000 (c 41). Nevertheless, many questions remain, for instance on the issue as to whether referendums can be binding in the UK despite the principle of parliamentary sovereignty and, more broadly, whether the advisory character of referendums is congruent with the idea of parliamentary sovereignty. On this, see House of Lords Select Committee on the Constitution, *Referendums in the United Kingdom: Report with Evidence* (12th Report of Session 2009–10, HL Paper 99, 2010) www.publications.parliament.uk/pa/ld200910/ldselect/ldconst/99/99.pdf [192]–[197]. That said, the alternative vote referendum in 2011 would have introduced a new voting system without the need for further legislation. See Parliamentary Voting System and Constituencies Act 2011 (c 1). The latter was a nationwide referendum to replace the first-past-the-post system with the AV system. It was rejected by a majority of voters.

[23] A Deighton, 'Referendums for EU Politics?' in DJ Galligan (ed), *Constitution in Crisis: The New Putney Debates* (London, I.B. Tauris, 2017) 71. See also EF Delaney 'Brexit Optimism and British Constitutional Renewal' in MA Graber, S Levinson and M Tushnet (eds), *Constitutional Democracy in Crisis?* (Oxford, Oxford University Press, 2018) 200. In 1945, Clement Attlee, leader of the Labour party, objecting to a poll on the continuation of the wartime coalition, went as far as to say that: 'I could not consent to the introduction into our national life of a device so alien to all our traditions as the referendum, which has only too often been the instrument of Nazism and Fascism. Hitler's practices in the field of referenda and plebiscites can hardly have endeared these expedients to the British people', as cited in V Bogdanor, *Power and the People: A Guide to Constitutional Reform* (London, Victor Gollancz, 1997) 120. Similarly, Margaret Thatcher was opposed to the concept of referendum, which she regarded as 'a device of dictators and demagogues'. See P Kay, 'Is Representative Democracy Ripe for Review and Modification in Favour of More Direct Democracy?' in Galligan (ed), ibid 58.

[24] AV Dicey, 'Ought the Referendum to Be Introduced into England?' (1890) 57 *Contemporary Review* 489.

seldom been used in the UK, at least until recently.[25] The first time it was used nationwide[26] was in the mid-1970s, when Prime Minister Harold Wilson called a referendum, conducted in June 1975, on whether the UK should remain in the European Community (the Common Market), and, even then, it was portrayed as a consultation exercise whose result was not binding.[27] Since then, it has been used in certain limited circumstances, mostly at the regional level,[28] notably on issues pertaining to devolution,[29] the creation of regional elected assemblies,[30] confirmation of a peace process,[31] change to the voting system[32] and independence.[33] The referendum thus remains, as it were, an ad hoc instrument,[34] often used as a means to mediate internal party divisions;[35] and frequently employed more as a 'tactical device rather than on the basis of a constitutional principle'.[36]

Second, and in relation to the previous point, it is relatively unclear what the constitutional and legal effects of a referendum are in a context in which Parliament dominates, at least in theory, the constitutional and legal order.[37] If, historically, the British Constitution has tended to favour parliamentary sovereignty over popular sovereignty, the recent rise of referendum politics has indeed 'complicated and undermined that consensus, shining a bright light onto certain insufficiencies of the British system'.[38] In other words, the outcome of a referendum – often depicted as the 'will of the people' – may potentially clash with the will of Parliament, which, at least before the Brexit vote, was overwhelmingly

[25] See House of Lords Select Committee on the Constitution, *Referendums in the United Kingdom* [1].

[26] There was, however, some prior uses of the referendum in the UK, for example, in the case of the 1920 Scottish referendum on prohibition, local polls in Wales in the 1960s as to whether pubs should be opened on Sundays as well as the 'Border Poll' of Northern Ireland in March 1973, which was boycotted by the Nationalist side. See ibid 9–10 (Box 1) ([2], [6]).

[27] B Ackerman, *Revolutionary Constitutions: Charismatic Leadership and the Rule of Law* (Cambridge, Harvard University Press, 2019) 13.

[28] With the exception of the Brexit referendum, of course, and the AV referendum of May 2011.

[29] See, eg, the devolution referendums in Scotland and in Wales in March 1979 and in September 1997.

[30] See, eg, the referendums regarding the creation of a Greater London Authority in May 1998 and of an elected regional assembly for North East England in November 2004 (the latter was rejected by voters).

[31] See the referendum on the Belfast Agreement in Northern Ireland in May 1998.

[32] See the (failed) AV referendum in May 2011.

[33] See the independence referendum in Scotland in September 2014, which was won by the 'No' side.

[34] See Eoin Daly's criticism of that depiction in E Daly, 'Constitutionalism and Crisis Narratives in Post-Brexit Politics' (2020) 68 *Political Studies* 895.

[35] Delaney (n 23) 192.

[36] House of Lords Select Committee on the Constitution, *Referendums in the United Kingdom* [205]. See also Bogdanor (n 23) 121, 128–129.

[37] See, eg, AV Dicey, *Introduction to the Law of the Constitution*, 8th edn (London, Macmillan, 1915 [1885]) 3–4; 37. Of course, some more recent developments have questioned this constitutional orthodoxy (in its pure and absolute form) or its future. See, eg, Lord Steyn and Lord Hope's respective dicta in *Jackson v Attorney General* [2005] UKHL 56 [102], [104], [107]. See also Laws LJ's introduction of the idea of 'constitutional statutes' in *Thoburn v Sunderland City Council* [2002] EWHC 195 (Admin).

[38] Delaney (n 23) 192, 200–205.

in favour of 'Remain'.[39] This can create obvious legitimacy issues, particularly in a country where political power is said to lie, historically and constitutionally, in the hands of Parliament. As Vernon Bogdanor put it in 1997, the British Constitution, as it currently stands, 'knows nothing of the people. If Parliament is sovereign, then the people cannot be. If the people are to become sovereign, then Parliament can no longer be sovereign'.[40] In any event, the case of Brexit – and the apparent hesitation of Members of Parliament (MPs), in the months that followed the vote, to 'implement' the outcome of the referendum[41] – reveals the possibility of a fundamental clash between popular sovereignty (as expressed through one of its specific forms, direct democracy), on the one hand, and parliamentary sovereignty, on the other.

This is not to say, of course, that referendums in the UK take place in a context of complete legal vacuum. For example, the 2016 Brexit referendum was authorised by a statute, the European Union Referendum Act 2015, that was approved by a vast majority of MPs.[42] This statute *required* a referendum to be held on whether the UK should remain a member of the EU and provided the specific wording of the referendum question,[43] amongst other aspects. It did not, however, provide that the outcome of the referendum would be legally binding, nor did it provide for any specific consequences in the event of a majority of voters voting for 'Leave'. Therefore, while the statute did in fact legally force the organisation of a referendum on the issue of EU membership, following certain parameters, it left MPs, the executive and other political actors with the task of deciding what to do with the outcome of the vote, whatever the outcome would be.

To be clear, the fact that the outcome of a referendum is usually not legally binding does not necessarily mean that political actors do not feel bound by it. It is precisely what happened in the aftermath of both the 1975 and 2016 referendums in the UK: both were considered as definitive and politically binding even though they were, from a purely legal perspective, only advisory.[44] Yet, this apparent gap between law and politics – between what law requires and what political incentives are – blurs and complicates the overall picture. The fundamental question remains: in the event of a clash between the electorate and their elected representatives, who, in practice, shall prevail? In other words, who is the sovereign? As discussed in chapter one, the locus of sovereignty arguably does not reside in the elusive concept of 'the people', nor in one specific institution (namely, Parliament – as Dicey would argue). Rather, sovereignty should be understood as a juristic concept

[39] According to Philip Kay, a poll conducted a day before the Brexit referendum revealed that approximately 75% of the 650 MPs supported Remain. Yet, as a result of the vote, 'about 365 of those original 479 Remainers supported the government's EU motion, the so-called "Brexit Bill"'. See Kay (n 23) 59.

[40] Bogdanor (n 23) 15.

[41] See next subsection of this chapter.

[42] European Union Referendum Act 2015 (c 36).

[43] ibid s 1(1) and 1(4).

[44] See, in that regard, A Deighton, 'Referendums for EU Politics?' in DJ Galligan (ed), *Constitution in Crisis: The New Putney Debates* (London, I.B. Tauris, 2017) 72.

tied to the state; as such, sovereignty arguably resides in the political relationship between the people and the state.[45]

ii. Populism, 'Constitutional Impatience' and the Royal Prerogative

As we have seen, the outcome of the Brexit referendum, irrespective of its consultative nature, was immediately translated by politicians and tabloids into a clear, formal and untouchable expression of the 'will of the people', namely the unassailable *decision* of the British people to leave the EU. To employ the framework of Part I of this monograph, the outcome of the referendum was effectively portrayed in timeless terms, as the immediate and decisive expression of the transcendent and immutable people, the People-as-One.[46]

However, as explained in more detail below, the implementation of the outcome of the referendum had to follow existing (and sometimes lengthy) constitutional rules and processes, which were often depicted by populist politicians and tabloids as obstacles or impediments to a seemingly clear political decision of the British electorate. There was also some sense of hesitation on the part of MPs, as illustrated by the internal strife within the Labour Party or the decision of the Liberal Democrats to oppose Brexit despite the outcome of the referendum.[47] Yet, it is precisely in that context of uncertainty, of apparent (or depicted) unresponsiveness by MPs to what was seen as a clear expression of the 'will of the people', that populism comes into play, notably with regard to discourse and action – what I have called in the previous chapter (as well as in the introduction to this chapter) the 'constitutional impatience' of populism.

First, as discussed above and in chapter one, many key actors amongst the ruling Conservative Party followed the ideal-typical populist discourse by repeatedly making references to the so-called 'will of the people', which is itself based on Carl Schmitt's conception of the people as unity,[48] when speaking about the outcome of the Brexit referendum.[49] From a temporal perspective, this characterisation of the Brexit vote as the pure and simple expression of the 'one and indivisible will of the people' illustrates populism's tendency to aggregate the revolutionary, mystical and eternal 'sovereign people', understood as the unified People-as-One, with transient, temporal and inherently ephemeral electoral majorities at a given point in time, thereby imbuing the latter with the characteristics of timeless unity, permanency and immutability.[50] Furthermore, from a spatial perspective, this populist

[45] See M Loughlin, *The Idea of Public Law* (Oxford, Oxford University Press, 2003) 83, discussed in more detail in ch 1 of this monograph. See also M Loughlin and S Tierney, 'The Shibboleth of Sovereignty' (2018) 81 *Modern Law Review*.

[46] See ch 1.

[47] See, eg, 'Brexit: MPs vote to reject no-deal Brexit' (*BBC*, 14 March 2019) www.bbc.co.uk/news/uk-politics-47562995.

[48] See ch 1.

[49] See, eg, T May, 'Theresa May's conference speech in full' (*The Telegraph*, 5 October 2016) www.telegraph.co.uk/news/2016/10/05/theresa-mays-conference-speech-in-full/ and ch 1 for other examples.

[50] See also ch 1.

discourse puts forward an artificially constructed and contested space in which the (central or 'federal') executive claims to speak on behalf of the entire UK, irrespective of devolution arrangements and of the outcome of the vote in those devolved countries, particularly Scotland and Northern Ireland.[51]

Second, many high-profile Conservative politicians took advantage of the widespread feeling of disenchantment amongst British voters vis-à-vis the institutions that govern them, particularly their feeling of spatial 'distance' between them and those who hold power, notably in Parliament. By promising to deliver Brexit – the outcome of a more active participation of the people in British politics – Conservatives like Boris Johnson appeared to be on the side of the people – against the 'disconnected' and 'detached' elite sitting in Parliament and in other (un)representative institutions – and to understand their aspirations. A good example of this rhetoric is the way in which Johnson, replacing May as Prime Minister in July 2019, expressed strong distrust of intermediaries such as Parliament, accusing MPs, for instance, of 'thwarting the will of the British people' over Brexit.[52] Of course, this was in a specific context – namely, after MPs had three times voted down a proposed withdrawal agreement and twice refused to dissolve Parliament. Nevertheless, this rhetoric and, in spatial terms, this new sense of apparent proximity between the public and their elected representatives could be criticised, at least from a liberal-constitutionalist perspective, as fictional or, perhaps, as only partial. In fact, for those in areas that predominantly voted to remain in the EU, such as in Scotland, for instance, this new 'proximity' arguably translated into an increased spatial distance between voters and their representatives.

Third, and in the same vein, populists amplified this feeling of alienation (and/or spatial distance) voters have against Parliament, notably by depicting the latter as an illegitimate and undemocratic impediment to the expression of the will of the people, with MPs being portrayed as slow-paced, disconnected '*ex post facto* yes or nay-sayers'.[53] This, in turn, contributed to the feeling of 'de-synchronization between democratic politics through parliamentary legislation' resulting in a 'state of affairs where citizens have lost faith in political

[51] See, eg, 'EU referendum: Results' (*BBC*, 2016) www.bbc.co.uk/news/politics/eu_referendum/results.

[52] For instance, Johnson said in the House of Commons, after failing a second attempt to trigger an early general election on 10 September 2019, that '[he] must warn members [of Parliament] that their behaviour in thwarting the will of the people is undermining respect for this House in the country'. HC Deb, vol 664, col 620 (9 September 2019). Other Conservative politicians, from former Prime Minister Theresa May to backbenchers, have also employed similar rhetoric. See, eg, 'Don't thwart the will of the people over Brexit – Sir Edward Leigh' (*BBC*, 12 June 2018) www.bbc.co.uk/news/av/uk-politics-44457827. Even after taking power with a comfortable parliamentary majority, Johnson maintained his difficult relationship with Parliament. See, eg, M Russell, 'Boris Johnson and parliament: an unhappy tale in 13 acts' (*The Constitution Unit Blog*, 1 September 2020) www.constitution-unit.com/2020/09/01/boris-johnson-and-parliament-an-unhappy-tale-in-13-acts.

[53] H Rosa, 'Airports Built on Shifting Grounds? Social Acceleration and the Temporal Dimension of Law' in L Corrias and L Francot (eds), *Temporal Boundaries of Law and Politics: Time Out of Joint* (Abingdon, Routledge, 2018) 83.

self-efficacy; for them, political institutions no longer respond to their needs and aspirations', as Harmut Rosa put it in a different context.[54] In fact, the way then-Prime Minister Johnson and other prominent Conservatives themselves fuelled disenchantment with the institutions of the representative system is reminiscent, at least to a certain extent, of the way Margaret Thatcher mobilised popular support against what she perceived and depicted as 'archaic institutions', such as the Civil Service and trade unions, while achieving a certain direct relationship with the electorate.[55]

Fourth, and perhaps more importantly for the purposes of this chapter, the populist impatience of the British executive was made apparent not only through its distrust of intermediaries such as Parliament, but also through its willingness to ignore or bypass the existing political processes and legal procedures. In the face of Parliament's apparent hesitation or 'unwillingness' to implement the outcome of the Brexit referendum and to trigger Article 50 of the Treaty on European Union (TEU), many high-profile Conservative members (including the Prime Minister) expressed their impatience, if not frustration, with Parliament, given the latter's reticence or disinclination to immediately and unreservedly initiate the formal process leading to the withdrawal of the UK from the EU.[56] One could argue, perhaps ironically, that although the referendum initially appeared to 'give power to the people', it did, instead, strengthen the executive against Parliament.[57] This possibility is discussed further later in this chapter.

Eager to implement the outcome of the 2016 Brexit vote, the UK executive thus decided to go down another route, that of the Royal Prerogative: ministers impatiently decided to immediately issue a formal notice of withdrawal – as required under Article 50 TEU[58] – through prerogative powers and, as such, without the prior approval of Parliament. Article 50 TEU leaves Member States full discretion as to the internal procedures leading to the notice of withdrawal. Yet, the decision to invoke the Royal Prerogative (without parliamentary approval) was significant because it was the only way, under UK domestic law, in which the UK Government could have triggered Article 50 TEU without obtaining prior parliamentary authority.

[54] ibid.

[55] In that regard, and on the way Thatcher contributed to the end of 'the era in which the political parties could be mediators between leaders and voters', see Bogdanor (n 23) 16–17. On Thatcher's populism, see also, generally, S Hall, *The Hard Road to Renewal: Thatcherism and the Crisis of the Left* (London, Verso, 1988).

[56] Interestingly, Johnson himself had voted, before he became Prime Minister, against Theresa May's Brexit deal on multiple occasions, thereby contributing to the very impasse he was criticising. See, eg, Russell (n 52).

[57] This was also apparent in the context of the Covid-19 pandemic, with the use of emergency measures, secondary legislation and the difficulty for Parliament to meet and exercise its scrutiny functions. See, eg, R Girard, 'Accountability, Populism and Expertise: The United Kingdom Government's Response to Covid-19' (2021) *Public Law*.

[58] Treaty on European Union, Consolidated Version [2008] OJ C115/13, art 50.

iii. The Miller (no 1) *Case: Institutional Stabilisation in Effect*

However, it is precisely against the backdrop of an impatient executive galvanised by the result of the 2016 Brexit referendum that the intervention of UK courts arguably slowed down the executive's pace of action and stabilised the system of constitutional governance. Indeed, the decision to trigger Article 50 TEU without parliamentary approval was challenged by Gina Miller, a pro-EU activist, and Deir dos Santos (the 'applicants'). After the Divisional Court of England and Wales ruled in favour of the applicants on 3 November 2016 in a decision[59] that sparked populist outrage,[60] the Secretary of State for Exiting the European Union appealed the judgment, and the matter was sent to the UK Supreme Court.

The Supreme Court ruled that the Royal Prerogative could not be used by ministers to trigger Article 50 TEU and that the prior authority of an Act of Parliament was required. Its reasoning was not based upon the soundness or desirability of the decision to withdraw from the EU, a 'political issue' that is a matter for ministers and Parliament to resolve;[61] rather, it was based upon its *effects* on the constitutional arrangements of the UK.[62] For the Court, the use of the Royal Prerogative to trigger Article 50 TEU raised legal issues pertaining to the constitutional arrangements of the UK, notably because they concerned

> (i) the extent of ministers' power to effect changes in domestic law through exercise of their prerogative powers at the international level, and (ii) the relationship between the UK government and Parliament on the one hand and the devolved legislatures and administrations of Scotland, Wales and Northern Ireland on the other.[63]

The Court ultimately ruled: 'We cannot accept that a major change to UK constitutional arrangements can be achieved by ministers alone; it must be effected in the only way that the UK constitution recognises, namely by Parliamentary legislation.'[64]

[59] *R (Miller) v The Secretary of State for Exiting the European Union* [2016] EWHC 2768.
[60] See section III of this ch, below.
[61] *R (Miller) v Secretary of State for Exiting the European Union* [2017] UKSC 5 [3].
[62] ibid [4].
[63] ibid.
[64] ibid [82]. It should be noted, however, that the Court's decision was accompanied with three powerful dissents, including one from Lord Reed, who wrote: 'Courts should not overlook the constitutional importance of ministerial accountability to Parliament. Ministerial decisions in the exercise of prerogative powers, of greater importance than leaving the EU, have been taken without any possibility of judicial control: examples include the declarations of war in 1914 and 1939. For a court to proceed on the basis that if a prerogative power is capable of being exercised arbitrarily or perversely, it must necessarily be subject to judicial control, is to base legal doctrine on an assumption which is foreign to our constitutional traditions. It is important for courts to understand that the legalisation of political issues is not always constitutionally appropriate, and may be fraught with risk, not least for the judiciary.' See ibid [240].

On that account, it could be said that the Court acted as an institutional stabiliser by both slowing down the populist acceleration of political time *and* ensuring that the mechanics of constitutional governance (including the constitutional decision-making process) are duly followed. It could indeed be argued, as Michael Freeden did, that the 'urgency of haste', that is to say, 'the fundamental preoccupation of populists with speed in implementing the "will of the people"' was in this case 'thwarted by the rule of law's insistence on the unavoidable "slowness" of due process and public scrutiny'.[65] Of course, following legal and institutional procedures does not, per se, necessarily slow down official actions. Nevertheless, this idea that institutions and intermediaries can 'impede', 'slow down' or even 'block' the immediate expression of the 'will of the people' is, as we have seen in the first two chapters of this monograph, an important feature of the ideal-typical populist discourse and imaginary.

In any event, it should be noted that the Supreme Court decision in *Miller (no 1)* did not, in effect, block or prevent the executive from launching the process of withdrawal from the EU, as Parliament ultimately voted on 1 February 2017 in support of a bill that gave the then Prime Minister, Theresa May, the power to invoke Article 50 TEU.[66] All the Court did, in that case, was slow down the executive's course of action and make sure that the proper (albeit seemingly slow and time-consuming) democratic procedures and processes were duly followed. One could therefore argue, as a commentator observed, that *Miller (no 1)* 'was about process, not politics'.[67] The Court thus played, I would argue, a democracy-enhancing role as an institutional stabiliser by re-establishing democratic channels and ensuring that the proper constitutional-institutional procedures, channels and processes are duly observed.

This is not to say that judges are necessarily conservative or reactionary,[68] nor that law is inherently (or should be) opposed to societal changes. The emphasis here is more procedural: the role of courts is to ensure that the constitutional decision-making process, which involves different institutions, has been followed – a process which by its very nature takes time. Indeed, this is, in my view, exactly what the Court did, not only in *Miller (no 1)*, but also, as argued in the next section below, in the *Miller (no 2)/Cherry* case a few years later.

[65] Freeden (n 21) 7–8.

[66] 'Brexit: MPs overwhelmingly back Article 50 bill' (*BBC*, 1 February 2017) www.bbc.co.uk/news/uk-politics-38833883 This, in and of itself, was 'an event without precedent', as MPs were required – due to the internal constraints of party politics – to 'vote for a policy which most of them oppose[d]'. V Bogdanor, 'On "Popular Sovereignty"' in Galligan (ed) (n 23) 39.

[67] R Murray, 'The Article 50 Legal Challenge: Clarifying the UK's Constitutional Requirements to Start Brexit' in Galligan (ed), (n 23) 102.

[68] For these views, part of a long mistrust towards the judiciary, see, eg, JAG Griffith, *The Politics of the Judiciary* (5th edn) (London, Fontana Press, 1997) and É Lambert, *Le gouvernement des juges et la lutte contre la législation sociale aux États-Unis : L'expérience américaine du contrôle judiciaire de la constitutionnalité des lois* (Paris, Marcel Giard, 1921).

B. The Prorogation of Parliament and the *Miller (no 2)/Cherry* Case

i. Executive Impatience and Prorogation

The impatience of populism – and its distrust of institutional mediators like Parliament – was also made apparent less than three years later, this time in the context of Prime Minister Johnson's attempt to prorogue Parliament in autumn 2019. In a nutshell, Parliament attempted to outlaw a no-deal Brexit, and the executive responded by proroguing Parliament – thereby putting an immediate end to parliamentary debates surrounding Brexit. However, it is worth discussing the context at more length.

On 25 November 2018, the then-Prime Minister, Theresa May, and her government had negotiated and concluded a Brexit withdrawal agreement with the EU. However, the withdrawal agreement was rejected three times by the House of Commons between January and March 2019.[69] Pursuant to section 13 of the European Union (Withdrawal) Act 2018, any withdrawal agreement reached by the government had to be approved by Parliament.[70] Theresa May resigned as leader of the Conservative Party on 7 April 2019, amid growing concerns regarding her ability to 'deliver Brexit', and on 24 July 2019, Boris Johnson replaced her as Prime Minister. He vowed to renegotiate the withdrawal agreement (and promised he was ready to make the UK leave the EU even without an agreement),[71] while highlighting on multiple occasions that he believed that the European Council would agree to changes to the withdrawal agreement only, and if only, there was a 'genuine risk' that the UK would leave the EU without such an agreement.[72] As a result of an extension to the notification period (previously sought and obtained by Theresa May) and of the governing legal framework (under both EU law and UK law),[73] the situation as of September 2019 was that the UK was going to leave the EU on 31 October 2019 whether or not there was a withdrawal agreement.[74] Increasingly concerned that leaving the EU without an agreement would be damaging to the UK economy, MPs voted on many occasions to reject a 'no-deal' Brexit.[75] In fact, they even passed legislation (commonly known as the Benn Act)

[69] *R (Miller) v The Prime Minister /Cherry v Advocate General for Scotland* [2019] UKSC 41 [12].

[70] European Union (Withdrawal) Act 2018 (c 16), s 13. See also *R (Miller) v The Prime Minister / Cherry v Advocate General for Scotland* [2019] UKSC 41 [11].

[71] See, eg, P Syrpis, 'Is Boris Johnson's Brexit posturing just a power play?' (*LSE Brexit Blog*, 31 July 2019) blogs.lse.ac.uk/brexit/2019/07/31/is-boris-johnsons-brexit-posturing-just-a-power-play.

[72] See, eg, ibid and *R (Miller) v The Prime Minister /Cherry v Advocate General for Scotland* [2019] UKSC 41, [14].

[73] Treaty on European Union, Consolidated Version [2008] OJ C115/13, art 50; European Union (Withdrawal) Act 2018 (c 16); European Union (Withdrawal) Act 2019 (c 16); European Union (Withdrawal) Act 2018 (Exit Day) (Amendment No 2) Regulations 2019 (SI 2019/859).

[74] Subject to the European Union (Withdrawal) (No 2) Act 2019 (c 26). See *R (Miller) v The Prime Minister /Cherry v Advocate General for Scotland* [2019] UKSC 41 [13], [22].

[75] See, eg, UK House of Commons, 'Amendment (a) to the motion on the UK's withdrawal from the European Union', Division 357: held on 13 March 2019 at 19:00 (312 Ayes; 308 Noes) votes.parliament.

that would outlaw such an exit on 31 October 2019 without an agreement, thereby forcing the Prime Minister to request an extension in the negotiations with the EU.[76] Yet, Johnson suggested that he would not comply with the latter Act, saying he would rather be 'dead in a ditch' than request an additional delay to Brexit negotiations.[77]

It is in that context of fierce tension between Parliament and an impatient executive that an Order in Council was made in late August 2019 ordering the prorogation of Parliament. Her Majesty the Queen, acting on the advice of the Prime Minister, gave her consent to a prorogation that would begin sometime between 9–12 September 2019 and end with the State Opening of Parliament on 14 October 2019. The prorogation ceremony took place on 10 September 2019. The government was seemingly convinced that the prorogation was legal. For instance, in a memorandum dated 15 August 2019 and prepared by the Director of Legislative Affairs in the Prime Minister's Office, the decision to prorogue was said to be not only perfectly legal, but also the most time-efficient decision, as it set the right balance between 'wash up' (that is to say, ensuring that the bills close to Royal Assent could obtain it) and 'not wasting time that could be used for new measures in a fresh session'.[78]

ii. The Miller (no 2)/Cherry *Ruling*

Yet, the UK Government's decision to use the Royal Prerogative (another prerogative power formally vested in the monarch and exercisable by them) to prorogue Parliament was quickly challenged, both in England and Wales and in Scotland. In London, the Divisional Court dismissed the claim on 11 September 2019 on the ground that the issue was 'inherently political in nature' and thus not justiciable in a court of law, but nevertheless allowed the case to come directly to the Supreme Court.[79] In Edinburgh, an application for an interim interdict to prevent prorogation was refused by Lord Doherty of the Outer House of the Court of Session on 30 August 2019[80] and, five days later, was also turned down on its merits by the same judge, on the ground that the issue was non-justiciable.[81] However, the decision was appealed, and, just a week later, three judges of the Inner House of the

uk/Votes/Commons/Division/626; UK House of Commons, 'Main motion, as amended by amendment (a) on the UK's withdrawal from the European Union', Division 359: held on 13 March 2019 at 19:33 (321 Ayes; 278 Noes) votes.parliament.uk/Votes/Commons/Division/628. See also, eg, 'Brexit: MPs vote to reject no-deal Brexit' (*BBC*) (n 47).

[76] European Union (Withdrawal) (No 2) Act 2019 (c 26), s 1(2). See also A Woodcock, 'Law to stop no-deal Brexit passed by Parliament' (*The Independent*, 6 September 2019) www.independent.co.uk/news/uk/politics/brexit-no-deal-bill-vote-house-lords-boris-johnson-law-parliament-latest-a9094741.html.

[77] ibid.

[78] *R (Miller) v The Prime Minister /Cherry v Advocate General for Scotland* [2019] UKSC 41 [17].

[79] *R (Miller) v The Prime Minister* [2019] EWHC 2381 (QB).

[80] *Cherry v Advocate General for Scotland* [2019] CSOH 68.

[81] *Cherry v Advocate General for Scotland* [2019] CSOH 70. See also *R (Miller) v The Prime Minister / Cherry v Advocate General for Scotland* [2019] UKSC 41 [24].

Court of Session allowed the appeal: they held that the matter was justiciable and, invoking considerations of time (and, indirectly, a response to the 'constitutional impatience' of the measure), ruled that 'circumstances demonstrate that the true reason for the prorogation [was] to reduce the time available for Parliamentary scrutiny of Brexit at a time when such scrutiny would appear to be a matter of considerable importance, given the issues at stake'.[82] The Court ruled that the prorogation was unlawful and, as a result, null and of no effect, and it gave permission to appeal to the Supreme Court.[83]

Following this ruling by the Court of Session – which also sparked populist outrage[84] – the matter was sent to the UK Supreme Court.[85] The Court rendered a unanimous decision: the 11 judges[86] who sat to hear the appeal ruled that the Prime Minister had exceeded his power to prorogue Parliament. The Court first acknowledged that the power to order the prorogation of Parliament is, indeed, a prerogative power recognised by the common law and exercised by the Crown – namely, by Her Majesty the Queen herself, acting on the advice of the Prime Minister.[87] However, the fact that Her Majesty is obliged by constitutional convention to accept that advice 'place[s] on the Prime Minister a constitutional responsibility, as the only person with power to do so, to have regard to all interests, including the interests of Parliament'.[88] In the same vein, the Court reiterated its role as a supervisory jurisdiction over the decisions of the executive, even those that 'have a political hue to them'.[89] Moreover, the fact that the Prime Minister is accountable to Parliament does not in and of itself mean that the judiciary has no legitimate role to play.[90] The Court added, finally and in the same vein, that deciding this case did not affect the separation of powers; on the contrary, by doing so, the court was 'giving effect' to that very separation of powers.[91]

[82] *Cherry v Advocate General for Scotland* [2019] CSIH 49 [53] (Opinion of Lord Carloway, the Lord President). See also [91] (Opinion of Lord Brodie); [117] and [123] (Opinion of Lord Drummond Young); and *R (Miller) v The Prime Minister /Cherry v Advocate General for Scotland* [2019] UKSC 41 [24].

[83] *R (Miller) v The Prime Minister /Cherry v Advocate General for Scotland* [2019] UKSC 41 [25].

[84] For example, on 12 September 2019, the *Daily Mail* published pages (in its printed edition) about the personal backgrounds of Scottish judges, noting that one was a '[m]inister's son with a passion for France' and another was a '[j]azz lover who said Brexit would be hard'. See, eg, T Connelly, 'A "jazz lover" and a "passion for France": Daily Mail mocked over weak attempt to undermine Scottish judges who ruled prorogation of parliament unlawful' (*Legal Cheek*, 12 September 2019) www.legalcheek.com/2019/09/a-jazz-lover-and-a-passion-for-france-daily-mail-mocked-over-weak-attempt-to-undermine-scottish-judges-who-ruled-prorogation-of-parliament-unlawful.

[85] *R (Miller) v The Prime Minister /Cherry v Advocate General for Scotland* [2019] UKSC 41 [25].

[86] Eleven judges of the Supreme Court sat to hear the appeal, only the second time in the Supreme Court's history that the maximum number of judges sat to hear the appeal, and the first time all 11 judges unanimously agreed. See, eg, J Rozenberg, *Enemies of the People? How Judges Shape Society* (Bristol, Bristol University Press, 2020) 73, 183.

[87] *R (Miller) v The Prime Minister /Cherry v Advocate General for Scotland* [2019] UKSC 41 [21].

[88] ibid.

[89] ibid [31]. See also [32].

[90] ibid [33].

[91] ibid [34].

With regard to the question on the applicable standard of review and the limits to the power of prorogation more specifically, the Court invoked the constitutional principles of parliamentary sovereignty and (democratic) accountability.[92] It invoked the famous 1611 *Case of Proclamations*[93] and ruled that 'a prerogative power is only effective to the extent that it is recognised by the common law'.[94] For the purposes of the case at hand, in what is perhaps the most important paragraph of the judgment, the Supreme Court held that the limit upon the power of prorogation is the following:

> a decision to prorogue Parliament [...] will be unlawful if the prorogation has the effect of frustrating or preventing, without reasonable justification, the ability of Parliament to carry out its constitutional functions as a legislature and as the body responsible for the supervision of the executive. In such a situation, the court will intervene if the effect is sufficiently serious to justify such an exceptional course.[95]

As for the applicable remedy, the Court made a declaration that Parliament had, in effect, not been prorogued. It allowed the respective Speakers of the House of Commons and of the House of Lords to take immediate steps to enable each House of Parliament to 'meet as soon as possible'.[96] And as a matter of fact, Parliament reconvened, at the speaker's request, the morning after the Supreme Court ruled that the prorogation of Parliament was unlawful.[97]

iii. The Supreme Court's 'Effects-Based Test' and the Re-establishment of the Empty Place of Power

Thus, in *Miller (no 2)/Cherry*, the Supreme Court once again acted, I would argue, as an institutional stabiliser. First, it contributed to slowing down the populist acceleration of political time by responding to the executive-led constitutional impatience. But it also played, I would add, a second, related role: it contributed to the (at least partial) re-establishment of deliberative-democratic channels and what Claude Lefort calls the 'empty place of power'.[98] As I have explained in more depth in chapter three, under a liberal-constitutionalist perspective, the populist focus on speed, spatial proximity and authenticity can sometimes transform into an attempt at taking over, filling or occupying the 'empty place of power', namely

[92] ibid [41–45], [46–47].

[93] *Case of Proclamations* [1610] EWHC KB J22; 77 ER 1352; 12 Co Rep 74: '[T]he King hath no prerogative, but that which the law of the land allows him'.

[94] *R (Miller) v The Prime Minister /Cherry v Advocate General for Scotland* [2019] UKSC 41 [49].

[95] ibid [50].

[96] ibid [70].

[97] R Mason and P Walker, 'MPs to return immediately in wake of supreme court ruling' (*The Guardian*, 24 September 2019) www.theguardian.com/politics/2019/sep/24/bercow-mps-return-urgent-supreme-court-ruling-suspension-parliament.

[98] C Lefort, *The Political Forms of Modern Society: Bureaucracy, Democracy, Totalitarianism* (Cambridge, Polity, 1986) 279. See also M Loughlin, 'The Constitutional Imagination' (2015) 78 *MLR* 1, 11. See also ch 3, s IV.

the specific constitutive gap between the ideal of popular sovereignty – that is, the view that political power emanates from the people and that the legitimacy of power is ultimately based upon them – on the one hand, and the distribution of power at any given point in time, on the other.[99]

Indeed, and as one commentator has noted, '[o]ne of the problems with the Brexit vote is the idea that the winner takes all, and appeals to *the* voice of the people – as though it has only one – are used to close down debate'.[100] In that sense, the reliance on – and depiction of – the Brexit vote as the single, immutable and permanent expression of the mystical and eternal 'sovereign people', combined with the somewhat impatient decision from the executive to bypass Parliament in triggering Article 50 TEU and, perhaps more importantly, the subsequent decision to prorogue Parliament, had arguably closed down the institutional-democratic spaces and channels. As a result of these actions, the executive had, in effect, prevented the further (post-referendum) engagement and participation of a wide range of citizens and actors who had different viewpoints. Perhaps ironically, populists – those who claim to 'give voice' to the people, to the unheard – had simultaneously silenced the voice of many others. They did so by invoking, as discussed at more length in Part I of this book, a sort of fictional substantial unity, unanimity and acclamation that eliminates democratic dilemmas and closes or puts an end to the 'perpetual conflict', 'indeterminacy' and 'unresolvability' inherent in both public law and democracy.[101] As alluded to in chapter three, the empty place of power implies 'the impossibility of representing democratic society as a body',[102] with one single will. This means that indeterminacy, social division, contestation, pluralism and heterogeneity are all constitutive features of democracy.[103] This, in turn, implies the necessity of erecting and protecting a multistage democratic process in which political power is not concentrated in the hands of one body (such as the executive, for example) representing the single will of the (homogeneous) people, but rather diffused and spread out across different institutions, spaces and channels, thereby allowing for various and perennial forms of questioning and contestation.

Yet, in this instance, the Supreme Court contributed, I would contend, to the re-establishment of not just the liberal-democratic temporality, but also its very own institutional-democratic spaces and channels, allowing for new forms of

[99] As discussed in more detail in ch 3.

[100] M Knights, 'Democracy Is About More Than Voting: Pre-Modern Petitioning and Its Implications for Today' in Galligan (ed) (n 23) 89–90 (emphasis in the original).

[101] See, in that regard, Jacco Bomhoff's discussion in J Bomhoff, 'Immanence and Irreconcilability: On the Character of Public Law as Political Jurisprudence' in M Wilkinson and M Dowdle (eds), *Questioning the Foundations of Public Law* (Oxford, Hart Publishing, 2018) 64, referring to M Loughlin, *Foundations of Public Law* (Oxford, Oxford University Press, 2010) 157. On the implications of populism (more particularly) in that regard, see D Prendergast, 'The Judicial Role in Protecting Democracy from Populism' (2019) 20 *German Law Journal* 248–250.

[102] A Arato and JL Cohen, *Populism and Civil Society: The Challenge to Constitutional Democracy* (Oxford, Oxford University Press, 2022) 116.

[103] ibid.

contestation and debate. The contested policy – in this case, the negotiation of an agreement with the EU – was sent back to Parliament 'for a new debate or further investigation, suggesting a re-articulation of political power'.[104] In this specific case, the Court did so by effectively creating what Tarunabh Khaitan has called an 'effects-based' (proportionality) test. The latter is defined as follows:

> Governmental action that has the effect of frustrating, preventing, or substantially undermining the ability of constitutional actors to discharge their constitutional powers, duties, or functions shall be unlawful, unless the government can show that such action was a proportionate means of achieving a legitimate objective.[105]

It is important to point out, however, as Kuo also does, that 'what the court is expected to do under the guidance of judicial deceleration is not to set aside the contested policy or law'.[106] On the contrary, the purpose of judicial deceleration is 'to make room for the learning function of constitutional democracy to play out and the rearticulation of politics by putting brakes on the populist feeling-driven decision'.[107] In both the *Miller (no 1)* and *Miller (no 2)/Cherry* judgments, the Supreme Court did not go as far as to second-guess the desirability, 'wisdom' or 'appropriateness' of the government's policy, nor of the outcome of the 2016 Brexit referendum itself. The Court, in a sense, was concerned with process rather than substance.[108] All it did, in the end, was slow down political time in the face of 'constitutional impatience' and populist pressures, stabilise the political-constitutional system, as well as 'restore the disrupted political temporality of constitutional governance'[109] through the re-establishment, notably, of constitutional-democratic channels and processes, particularly in the *Miller (no 2)/Cherry* case.

iv. Executive Impatience and Aggrandisement: A Crisis of Accountability?

In a sense, therefore, the approach taken by the judiciary in the context of prorogation was relatively similar to the context of *Miller (no 1)*, insofar as it counteracted, at least to a certain extent, the constitutional impatience of populism. In both cases, the executive had used the prerogative to circumvent Parliament and (or) prevent the latter from exercising its constitutional role. However, in the specific context of the 2019 prorogation of Parliament, the executive's plan was not simply to enable

[104] Kuo (n 9) 572 (fn 128). Kuo was referring to the *Miller (no 1)* Supreme Court judgment, but the same principle arguably equally applies to *Miller (no 2)/Cherry*.

[105] T Khaitan, 'The Supreme Court ruling: why the effects test could help save democracy (somewhat)' (*LSE Brexit Blog*, 24 September 2019) blogs.lse.ac.uk/brexit/2019/09/24/the-supreme-court-ruling-why-the-effects-test-could-help-save-democracy-somewhat.

[106] Kuo (n 9) 573–574.

[107] ibid.

[108] C Gearty, 'My Initial Thoughts on *Miller/Cherry*' (*Conor Gearty*, 25 September 2019) www.conorgearty.co.uk/2019/09/my-initial-thoughts-on-miller-cherry.

[109] Kuo (n 9) 571.

and accelerate the implementation of the 'will of the people' by bypassing existing institutions and procedures; there was also, arguably, a potential element of executive aggrandisement,[110] which raises important questions about the accountability of the executive.

In the UK executive's view, the decision to bypass (in *Miller (no 1)*) or to sideline (in *Miller (no 2)/Cherry*) Parliament was entirely justified. Because it claims to derive its legitimacy directly from the people,[111] the government, in its view, can under certain circumstances bypass the people's elected representatives, particularly when it sees it fit or urgent to achieve a certain policy outcome. Yet, as Lord Sumption has pointed out, '[s]ince the people have no institutional mechanism for holding governments to account, other than Parliament, the effect is that ministers are accountable to no one, except once in five years at general elections'.[112] This is precisely why accountability is fundamental in a constitutional democracy – and why the Supreme Court reiterated, in *Miller (no 2)*, the importance of making sure that 'the policies of the executive are subjected to consideration by the representatives of the electorate, the executive is required to report, explain and defend its actions, and citizens are protected from the arbitrary exercise of executive power'.[113]

Yet, what the Supreme Court did, especially in the *Miller (no 2)/Cherry* case, was not only confirm its ability to slow down the pace of executive action; it was also able to consolidate its role as a bulwark against executive aggrandisement. Indeed, for some, the *Miller (no 2)/Cherry* Supreme Court decision was a powerful assertion of judicial power and an illustration of the Court's willingness to embrace a more enhanced role in the UK constitutional order.[114] This willingness was evident in the following sentence of the judgment: in giving effect to judicially enforceable principles of law,

> the courts have the responsibility of upholding the values and principles of our constitution and making them effective. It is their particular responsibility to determine the legal limits of the powers conferred on each branch of government, and to decide whether any exercise of power has transgressed those limits.[115]

It is worth mentioning that more broadly, and beyond the specific factual circumstances of the two *Miller* cases, the rise of populism in the UK seems to be

[110] On this, see ch 5, section V.

[111] See, eg, Boris Johnson's claims to exclusive representation, sometimes depicting his government as 'the people's government'. For instance, and as mentioned earlier, during his election victory speech in December 2019, he said, flanked with 'The People's Government' signs in the background, that: 'You [the people of this country] voted for all these things, and it is now this government, the people's government, it is now our solemn duty to deliver on each and every one of those commitments.'

[112] J Sumption, 'Government by decree: Covid-19 and the Constitution' (Cambridge Freshfields Annual Law Lecture, 27 October 2020) resources.law.cam.ac.uk/privatelaw/Freshfields_Lecture_2020_Government_by_Decree.pdf, 2.

[113] *R (Miller) v The Prime Minister /Cherry v Advocate General for Scotland* [2019] UKSC 41 [39].

[114] Yvonne Tew describes this judicial 'strategy' as 'mini-maximalism'. See Y Tew, 'Strategic Judicial Empowerment' (2024) 72 *AJCL* 170, 219–221.

[115] Lady Hale in *R (Miller) v The Prime Minister /Cherry v Advocate General for Scotland* [2019] UKSC 41, [39].

accompanied by a certain reduction in various forms of scrutiny, including parliamentary scrutiny.[116] The latter tends to be viewed and depicted by populists as a sort of nuisance that unnecessarily and unjustifiably 'slows down' the political course of action. As Conor Gearty has put it, some recent political actors seem to view 'the law not as a core part of our constitutional system but as an unnecessary obstacle to the exercise of executive power'.[117] This becomes all the more evident in situations of emergency. As I have argued elsewhere,[118] the increased use of executive powers in situations of emergency like the Covid-19 pandemic has certainly made it more difficult for Parliament and other bodies, including the media, to perform their scrutiny functions. This is compounded by the fact that the UK Government has made extensive use of statutory instruments – the most common form of secondary (or delegated) legislation – including hundreds that were subject to the 'made negative procedure', which does not require prior parliamentary scrutiny.[119] As a result, some have argued that Parliament has been effectively sidelined.[120] The most striking use of secondary legislation is probably the Retained EU Law (Revocation and Reform) Act 2023[121] which, as Jeff King has explained, 'confers sweeping ministerial powers to revoke and replace EU law notwithstanding notorious accountability difficulties'[122] and which, at the time of writing, remains in force despite a July 2024 change in government.[123]

Of course, from a temporal perspective, it is essential that the executive be able to act quickly and flexibly, particularly in the face of immediate and serious threats. The Covid-19 health crisis provides a contemporary example. For instance, in the context of the review of the temporary provisions of the Coronavirus Act 2020[124] in September 2020, the then-Secretary of State for Health and Social Care, Matt Hancock, frequently referred to the need for the government to continue to have 'the powers at [their] disposal to respond quickly' to the progression of the virus; he also made reference to the importance of 'strik[ing] the right balance between

[116] As seen notably through the increased use of statutory instruments and Henry VIII clauses. See, eg, S Suteu, 'Democratic Constitutionalism under Attack: Peril & Promise of We The People' (UCL Lunch Hour Lectures, 8 June 2021) www.youtube.com/watch?v=3PDfXfNjHG8.

[117] C Gearty, 'In the Shallow End' (*London Review of Books*, 27 January 2022) www.lrb.co.uk/the-paper/v44/n02/conor-gearty/in-the-shallow-end.

[118] Girard (n 57).

[119] The government laid 582 coronavirus-related SIs before the UK Parliament between 27 January 2020 and 3 March 2022, including 417 subject to the 'made negative procedure', and a total of 1,957 SIs covering all subjects. See Hansard Society, 'Coronavirus Statutory Instruments Dashboard' (4 March 2022) www.hansardsociety.org.uk/publications/data/coronavirus-statutory-instruments-dashboard#total-coronavirus-sis.

[120] See, eg, M Russell and L James, 'MPs are right. Parliament has been sidelined' (*UCL Constitution Unit Blog*, 28 September 2020) www.constitution-unit.com/2020/09/28/mps-are-right-parliament-has-been-sidelined.

[121] Retained EU Law (Revocation and Reform) Act 2023 (c 28).

[122] J King, 'From Constitutional Crisis to Poisoned Chalice: A Letter from London' (*Verfassungsblog*, 28 June 2024) www.verfassungsblog.de/from-constitutional-crisis-to-poisoned-chalice.

[123] In fact, the new Labour Government does not appear to be very interested in a change of direction in that regard.

[124] Coronavirus Act 2020 (c 7).

acting at pace and proper scrutiny'.[125] However, the two are not necessarily contradictory. As Joelle Grogan and Nyasha Weinberg have pointed out,

> [e]ven where the protection of public health can justify action taken rapidly with more limited scrutiny by the legislature, there must be a robust and heightened commitment to the clear and transparent communication of the rationale for government action, substantiated with public debate and external engagement.[126]

This is an important requirement that the UK Government has, arguably, not always followed – prior to, during and after the Covid-19 crisis.

In short, the populist 'constitutional impatience' described in this chapter is arguably part of a broader project of executive aggrandisement and crisis of political accountability. This, of course, is not unique to the UK – a similar rise in the use of statutory instruments and (or) decrees accompanied by a decline in parliamentary activity and scrutiny has also been seen in other countries with populists in power, including Italy[127] and Türkiye,[128] amongst others. However, it is precisely in this context that the stabilising function of courts – or at least their ability to act as such – becomes all the more important, at least from a liberal-constitutionalist perspective.

III. The Limits of Institutional Stabilisation (in the UK Context)

What we have seen, so far, is that populists are impatient with liberal-democratic procedures – depicted by them as obstacles or impediments to the direct expression of the 'will of the people'. This often translates, as we have discussed, into a general 'executivisation' of political power, notably through an increased use of prerogative powers. Yet, courts have shown, at least in the UK context, that they can impede the populist acceleration of constitutional time and act as institutional stabilisers. While this chapter has thus far focused on the UK, there are many other recent examples of successful judicial interventions in slowing down (and in some cases stopping) populist constitutional impatience, democratic erosion and executive dominance. One may think, for example, of the May 2021 Kenyan High Court decision[129] establishing the 'basic structure' doctrine in

[125] HC Deb, vol 681, col 388 (30 September 2020).

[126] J Grogan and N Weinberg, 'Principles to Uphold the Rule of Law and Good Governance in Public Health Emergencies' (RECONNECT Europe – Policy Brief, August 2020) reconnect-europe.eu/wp-content/uploads/2020/08/RECONNECTPB_082020B.pdf 20.

[127] See, eg, C Fasone, 'Catalysing Marginalisation? The Effect of Populist Governments on the Legislative and Scrutiny Functions of the Italian Parliament' (2021) 74 *Parliamentary Affairs*.

[128] Especially in the period that followed the 2016 coup d'état attempt. See, eg, P Castillo-Ortiz, 'The Illiberal Abuse of Constitutional Courts in Europe' (2019) 15 *European Constitutional Law Review* 59.

[129] *Ndii and others v Attorney General and others* (2020) [2021 eKLR], Petition No E282 of 2020 (High Court of Kenya at Nairobi).

Kenya and ruling as unconstitutional the highly controversial Constitution of Kenya (Amendment) Bill 2020,[130] also known as the Building Bridges Initiative (Constitutional Amendment) Bill. This decision was confirmed in August 2021 by the Court of Appeal[131] and in March 2022 by the Supreme Court of Kenya (although the latter rejected by a 6-1 majority the claim that the basic structure doctrine applies in Kenya).[132] These decisions have been lauded by many and described by certain commentators as cementing 'the culture of rule of law and constitutionalism' and as a potential signal for the 'consolidation of constitutionalism and democracy in Africa'.[133]

That said, as the previous two chapters have shown, courts do not necessarily offer a panacea for 'constitutional impatience' – not even in established constitutional democracies like the UK. Their role and influence as institutional stabilisers are, in my view, dependent upon at least three main factors, namely: (1) the public (and political) reception of their judgments; (2) the (overwhelming) forces of politics; and (3) their institutional independence. Moreover, the more substantive virtues of judicial (or institutional) deceleration praised by Kuo – including its alleged contributions to democratic learning as part of the multistage process of constitutional-democratic governance[134] – are grounded in empirical claims that remain, ultimately, difficult to verify. These elements are discussed in the four following subsections.

A. The Public (and Political) Reception of Judgments

First, as is well known, the *Miller (no 1)* judgment sparked populist outrage in UK tabloids, with the *Daily Mail* going as far as to label the High Court judges who sided against the government as 'enemies of the people'.[135] In general, judges

[130] The Constitution of Kenya (Amendment) Bill 2020 (Kenya).

[131] *Independent Electoral and Boundaries Commission v Ndii and others* (2021), Civil Appeal No E291 of 2021 (Court of Appeal at Nairobi). See also R Albert, 'Constitutional Amendment and Dismemberment in Kenya' (*International Journal of Constitutional Law Blog*, 21 August 2021) www.iconnectblog.com/constitutional-amendment-and-dismemberment-in-kenya.

[132] *Attorney General and others v Ndii and others* (2022), SC Petition No 12 of 2021 (consolidated with petitions Nos 11 & 13 of 2021 (Supreme Court of Kenya).

[133] See, eg, G Imanyara, 'Decision cements rule of law and constitutionalism' (*Nation*, 15 May 2021) www.nation.africa/kenya/blogs-opinion/blogs/decision-cements-rule-of-law-and-constitutionalism-3400840; Y Roznai, 'The Basic Structure Doctrine arrives in Kenya: Winds of Change for Constitutionalism in Africa?' (*Verfassungsblog*, 19 May 2021) www.verfassungsblog.de/the-basic-structure-doctrine-arrives-in-kenya. See also, for a general account of the decision, BA Gebeye, 'Transformative Constitutionalism and the Basic Structure Doctrine: A New Account from Kenya' (*International Journal of Constitutional Law Blog*, 26 May 2021) www.iconnectblog.com/transformative-constitutionalism-and-the-basic-structure-doctrine-a-new-account-from-kenya.

[134] Kuo (n 9) 564.

[135] J Slack, 'Enemies of the people: Fury over "out of touch" judges who have "declared war on democracy" by defying 17.4m Brexit voters and who could trigger constitutional crisis' (*Daily Mail*, November 2016) www.dailymail.co.uk/news/article-3903436/Enemies-people-Fury-touch-judges-defied-17-4m-Brexit-voters-trigger-constitutional-crisis.html. Other newspapers also put critical headlines, like the *Daily Telegraph*'s 'The judges versus the people'. See P Dominiczak, C Hope and K McCann, 'Judges vs the people: Government ministers resigned to losing appeal against High

were depicted as 'out-of-touch' (and disconnected), following the populist, similarity-based identification between the rulers and the ruled discussed in more detail in chapter three.[136] This prompted some Conservative MPs to criticise 'unelected judges' and to call for 'power to the people!'[137] Interestingly (and perhaps tellingly), the government responded very weakly, if at all, to these attacks on the UK judiciary.[138] For example, the then-Lord Chancellor, Liz Truss (who later became Prime Minister), remained silent for several days with regard to these headlines and, when pressed, did not condemn the newspapers.[139]

Less than three years later, the *Miller (no 2)/Cherry* decision was also received with indirect personal attacks on judges, particularly against those of the Scottish Court of Session before the decision reached the Supreme Court.[140] One minister even raised questions about the perception of partiality of judges,[141] before the Lord Chancellor came to their defence.[142] In general, however, the reception of the judgment was divided: while it was met with dubious analyses of the Scottish judges' backgrounds by the *Daily Mail*, it was also received more favourably in Scottish newspapers – with the headline of *The Scotsman* depicting the Court of Session judges as 'Heroes of the People', as a nod to the *Daily Mail*'s headline 'Enemies of the People' three years earlier.[143] The reaction

Court ruling' (*The Telegraph*, 3 November 2016) www.telegraph.co.uk/news/2016/11/03/the-plot-to-stop-brexit-the-judges-versus-the-people. On the critical media responses to the case, and on the critique of the Lord Chancellor's response (or lack thereof) to the media, see P O'Brien, '"Enemies of the People": Judges, the Media and the Mythic Lord Chancellor' (2017) *Public Law* 135. It should be noted, also, that then-Prime Minister Theresa May responded very weakly to these attacks on the judiciary. See A Asthana and H Stewart, 'Theresa May defends newspapers over attacks on article 50 judges' (*The Guardian*, 6 November 2016) www.theguardian.com/politics/2016/nov/06/labour-will-not-block-article-50-jeremy-corbyn-allies-confirm.

[136] This sense of disconnection between the judiciary and other democratic bodies alludes to the spatiotemporal 'distance' described in ch 3. Yet, some, like Dimitrios Kyritsis, would probably argue that to ensure that they perform quality supervision, courts must enjoy a certain distance from the decision body it is reviewing (ie, Parliament, but also surely the executive). This idea is linked to the idea of judicial independence, discussed below. See D Kyritsis, 'Constitutional Review in Representative Democracy' (2012) 32 *OJLS* 1.

[137] See, eg, this tweet from former Conservative MP (later Secretary of State for Wales) David TC Davies: 'Unelected judges calling the shots. This is precisely why we voted out. Power to the people!' (*X/Twitter*, 3 November 2016).

[138] See N Lacey, 'Populism and the Rule of Law' (2019) 15 *Annual Review of Law and Social Science* 80.

[139] Rozenberg (n 86) 33.

[140] See, eg, D Wilcock and J Maidment, 'Senior Scottish judge who ruled Boris Johnson's proroguing of Parliament illegal once called Brexit "a very onerous task … of mammoth proportions"' (*Daily Mail*, 11 September 2019) www.dailymail.co.uk/news/article-7452951/the-Scottish-judges-handed-Boris-Johnson-massive-Brexit-headache.html.

[141] The minister in question, Kwasi Kwarteng, told the BBC: 'I think [judges] are impartial but I'm saying that many people, many leave voters […] are beginning to question the partiality of judges', as mentioned in Rozenberg (n 86) 43.

[142] The then-Lord Chancellor, Robert Buckland, said in a tweet: 'Our judges are renowned around the world for their excellence and impartiality and I have total confidence in their independence in every case', as mentioned in ibid.

[143] 'Brexit: Judges who ruled against Parliament's suspension are "Heroes of the People" – Scotsman leader comment' (*The Scotsman*, 12 September 2019) www.scotsman.com/news/opinion/columnists/brexit-judges-who-ruled-against-parliaments-suspension-are-heroes-people-scotsman-leader-comment-1407936.

to the Supreme Court's judgment was similarly polarised. In the media, Lady Hale was both praised and subject to personal abuse and *ad hominem* attacks, with a *Sun* columnist referring to her as a 'beady-eyed old nanny goat'.[144] In the academic sphere, the judgment was lauded by scholars such as Paul Craig,[145] Conor Gearty[146] and Thomas Poole – who described the ruling as 'the most significant judicial statement on the constitution in over 200 years'[147] – but also criticised in strong terms by others, including Martin Loughlin, who questioned the cogency of the judgment and denounced the Court for having 'convert[ed] political practices into constitutional practices, investing them with normative (and legal?) authority so as to assert the power to determine their meaning',[148] and John Finnis, who referred to the judgment as a 'well-intentioned but constitutionally unauthorised law making', a ruling that 'undermines the rule of law and constitutional settlement'.[149]

Perhaps more importantly, the *Miller (no 2)/Cherry* case – and in particular, the Supreme Court ruling – also led to (political) attacks against the institutional role and influence of courts. Jacob Rees-Mogg branded the decision a 'constitutional coup' and 'the most extraordinary overthrowing of the constitution' by the Supreme Court.[150] A Conservative MP, Desmond Swayne, even went as far as to call for the Supreme Court to be abolished entirely.[151] In a speech to the Bruges

[144] Q Letts, 'Judges blew their hallowed status with the Supreme Court ruling and will be fair game for public scrutiny' (*The Sun*, 25 September 2019) www.thesun.co.uk/news/9998887/judges-supreme-court-public-scrutiny, as mentioned in Rozenberg (n 86) 47.

[145] P Craig, 'The Supreme Court, Prorogation and Constitutional Principle' (2020) *Public Law* 248.

[146] Gearty (n 108).

[147] See, eg, T Poole, 'Understanding what makes "Miller & Cherry" the most significant judicial statement on the constitution in over 200 years" (*Prospect*, 25 September 2019) www.prospectmagazine.co.uk/politics/understanding-what-makes-miller-2-the-most-significant-judicial-statement-on-the-constitution-in-over-200-years.

[148] M Loughlin, 'A Note on Craig on Miller; Cherry' (2020) *Public Law* 278, 280. See also Loughlin's earlier critique of the Supreme Court decision, expressed in the form of a drafted judgment of a (fictitious) UK Constitutional Council in an (hypothetical) appeal against the Supreme Court's decision, in M Loughlin, 'The Case of Prorogation: The UK Constitutional Council's Ruling on Appeal from the Judgment of the Supreme Court' (*Policy Exchange*, 2019) www.policyexchange.org.uk/wp-content/uploads/2019/10/The-Case-of-Prorogation.pdf.

[149] J Finnis, 'Times Letters: Constitutional Implications of Judges' Ruling' (*The Times*, 26 September 2019) www.thetimes.co.uk/article/times-letters-constitutional-implications-of-judges-ruling-zzqb3pwwk as mentioned in Rozenberg (n 86) 47. See also J Finnis, 'The Unconstitutionality of the Supreme Court's Prorogation Judgment' (*Policy Exchange*, 2019) www.policyexchange.org.uk/wp-content/uploads/2019/10/The-unconstitutionality-of-the-Supreme-Courts-prorogation-judgment.pdf.

[150] See, eg, J Groves, '"Who runs this country?" Boris Johnson's allies blast "constitutional coup" after judges rule PM broke the law by suspending Parliament and he's forced to fly back from New York TODAY to face a furious resumed Commons' (*Daily Mail*, 24 September 2019) www.dailymail.co.uk/news/article-7500691/Boris-blasts-runs-Britain-PM-Johnsons-allies-declare-war-judiciary.html.

[151] Swayne said, in response to the *Miller (no 2)/Cherry* case that the Supreme Court 'well overstepped the mark' and that the Conservative manifesto for the 2019 general election 'should have a commitment to abolish the Supreme Court'. See '"This Parliament is a dead Parliament": Attorney general says MPs have no "moral right" to be in the Commons' (*ITV*, 25 September 2019) www.itv.com/news/2019-09-25/mps-return-to-westminster-after-bombshell-legal-ruling.

Group in September 2019, Martin Howe QC, the Chairman of Lawyers for Britain – a group of lawyers who supported the Secretary of State in the *Miller (no 1)* case – also criticised the Supreme Court judgment and called for the replacement of the Supreme Court with a 'newer low key and less activist court of final appeal'.[152] In November 2020, the then Lord Chancellor, Robert Buckland, suggested renaming the Supreme Court 'to downgrade its status'[153] as well as cutting the number of permanent justices on its bench.[154] Of course, none of these proposals came to fruition, but they illustrate a certain discomfort, among some in the political class,[155] with the idea of the judiciary acting as the final arbiter in politically-sensitive areas.

Finally, it is important to take into account the timescale, more specifically the fact that a judgment which may (or may not) be immediately well received by the public and (or) the political class might lead, over a longer period of time, to unforeseen consequences. To give an example, a court in a given jurisdiction could manage to block a certain piece of legislation or a policy today, but there is a possibility that such an action could lead to a subsequent backlash over a longer period of time, and vice versa. Simply put, the effects of a given judgment – even when initially seen as an instance of institutional stabilisation – can take a long time to become clear. For example, it is possible that the political backlash against the two *Miller* rulings may have led to a more conservative Supreme Court under Lord Reed's presidency, at least when it comes to public law.[156] More studies will therefore be needed to assess the long(er)-term effects of the two *Miller* cases as instances of institutional deceleration and stabilisation.

B. The Forces of Politics or Political Pressure

Second, and in relation to the previous point, the role and influence of courts as institutional stabilisers is also dependent on the (sometimes overwhelming) forces of politics, particularly in a context of democratic erosion and (or) intense political pressure.[157] As we have seen earlier in this monograph, in Hungary, Poland, Türkiye

[152] 'Martin Howe QC calls for a Restoration of the Constitution Bill' (*Lawyers for Britain*, 4 October 2019) lawyersforbritain.org/martin-howe-qc-calls-for-a-restoration-of-the-constitution-bill.

[153] 'Dominic Cummings and the unchained ministers' (*The Economist*, 21 November 2020) www.economist.com/britain/2020/11/19/dominic-cummings-and-the-unchained-ministers.

[154] E Malnick, 'Supreme Court to be overhauled to curtail its constitutional powers' (*The Telegraph*, 14 November 2020) www.telegraph.co.uk/politics/2020/11/14/britains-supreme-court-faces-overhaul-concerns-us-style-election.

[155] And, one may add on the above reference, among certain lawyers and (certain parts of) legal academia.

[156] For some empirical evidence that suggests this, see L Graham, 'The Reed Court by Numbers: How Shallow is the "Shallow End"?' (*UK Constitutional Law Blog*, 4 April 2022) www.ukconstitutionallaw.org/2022/04/04/lewis-graham-the-reed-court-by-numbers-how-shallow-is-the-shallow-end%EF%BF%BC%EF%BF%BC.

[157] See, eg, Y Roznai, 'Who Will Save the Redheads? Anti-Bully Theory of Judicial Review and Protection of Democracy' (2020) 29 *William & Mary Bill of Rights Journal*.

and Venezuela, for example, institutions have been overwhelmed by the concerted forces of politics.[158] Of course, the UK is not at the brink of descending into authoritarianism, 'abusive constitutionalism'[159] or 'autocratic legalism'.[160] Britain is a consolidated constitutional democracy and is likely to remain so. Despite the abovementioned attacks on the judiciary, we are yet to see more extreme incidents, such as judges being harassed or courts being stormed by protestors. Indeed, UK judges remain relatively popular and trusted, with a 2025 survey revealing that 78 per cent of Britons trust judges to tell the truth, compared to an abysmal 9 per cent who trust politicians.[161]

Nevertheless, it is hard to deny that the UK executive has in the past years put significant political pressure on the institutional role of the courts. For instance, amid the frustrations caused by Parliament's inability (or unwillingness) to pass the government's Brexit deal in the period leading up to the 2019 general election, the Conservative Party vowed, in its 2019 Election Manifesto, 'to look at the broader aspects of our constitution: the relationship between the Government, Parliament and the courts; the functioning of the Royal Prerogative; the role of the House of Lords; and access to justice for ordinary people'.[162] It also promised to 'set up a Constitution, Democracy & Rights Commission [to] examine these issues in depth, and come up with proposals to restore trust in our institutions and in how our democracy operates'.[163] Instead of these, however, the Conservative Government chose to conduct a series of smaller, independent reviews. These include the Independent Review of Administrative Law (IRAL, established in July 2020 to ensure that 'judicial review is not abused to conduct politics by another means or to create needless delays',[164] which submitted its report in January 2021 and has now been disbanded[165]), as well as the Independent Human Rights Act Review (IHRAR; launched in December 2020 and which submitted a full report in October 2021[166]). It also introduced in Parliament a Bill of Rights Bill, which would have repealed the Human Rights Act[167] and replaced it with a potentially weaker substitute, but was withdrawn in 2023.[168] In 2024, it entered into a fresh clash with courts with the passing of the Safety of Rwanda (Asylum and Immigration) Act 2024,[169] in direct response

[158] S Issacharoff, 'Democracy's Deficits' (2018) 85 *University of Chicago Law Review* 519.
[159] See D Landau, 'Abusive Constitutionalism' (2013) 47 *University of California Davis Law Review* 189.
[160] See KL Scheppele, 'Autocratic Legalism' (2018) 85 *University of Chicago Law Review* 545.
[161] 'Ipsos Veracity Index 2025' (*Ipsos*, 9 December 2025) www.ipsos.com/en-uk/ipsos-veracity-index-2025.
[162] The Conservative and Unionist Party, 'Manifesto 2019' 48.
[163] ibid.
[164] 'Independent Review of Administrative Law' (*Gov.uk*, 2021) www.gov.uk/government/groups/independent-review-of-administrative-law.
[165] ibid.
[166] 'Independent Human Rights Review' (*Gov.uk*, 2021) www.gov.uk/guidance/independent-human-rights-act-review.
[167] Human Rights Act 1998.
[168] Bill of Rights Bill.
[169] Safety of Rwanda (Asylum and Immigration) Act 2024 (c 8).

to a Supreme Court ruling according to which Rwanda is not a safe third country for the purposes of the removal of asylum seekers from the UK.[170] The Act also contained an ouster clause which prevented courts and tribunals from reviewing a decision under which Rwanda is not a safe country.[171]

While many of these efforts were interrupted by a change of government in July 2024, it is hard to see them as something other than part of a broader attempt to 'halt the current direction of constitutional travel and reinstate the executive at the centre of the Constitution'[172] – at the expense of judicial powers, one may add – efforts that could resume at any time, particularly in the event of a Reform UK or a new Conservative Government. The appointment of Suella Braverman as Attorney General, in February 2020, clearly hinted at the direction that the Conservative Government was very serious in its intentions to strengthen the executive against the judiciary. Indeed, just two weeks before her appointment, Braverman criticised the 'chronic and steady encroachment by the judges' and accused 'a small number of unelected, unaccountable judges' of having too much influence in the determination of wider public policy.[173] Claiming that British democracy cannot be said to be 'representative' anymore, Braverman added that 'Parliament's legitimacy is unrivalled and the reason why we must take back control, not just from the EU, but from the judiciary'.[174] Less than two years later, in a keynote speech delivered at the 2021 Public Law Project conference, then-Attorney General Braverman hinted in a similar direction, mentioning that judicial decisions such as the two *Miller* cases, but also *Adams*,[175] *Evans*,[176] *UNISON*[177] and *Privacy International*[178] 'have strained the principle of Parliamentary sovereignty and introduced uncertainty into the constitutional balance between Parliament, the Government and the Courts'.[179] Mentioning that judges are increasingly asked to 'decide essentially political matters on applications for judicial review', she went as far as to say that '[t]he legitimacy and reputation of [the UK] judiciary, which is inextricably linked to its political neutrality, is at stake'.[180] More recently, in August 2023,

[170] *R (AAA) v Secretary of State for the Home Department* [2023] UKSC 42.

[171] Safety of Rwanda (Asylum and Immigration) Act 2024, s 2(3). This Act was repealed in December 2025 with the enactment of the Border Security, Asylum and Immigration Act 2025 (c 31), s 40.

[172] Young, 'Back to the Future? UK Constitutional Reform in 2020' (*Verfassungsblog*, 19 December 2019) www.verfassungsblog.de/back-to-the-future.

[173] S Braverman, 'People we elect must take back control from people we don't. Who include the judges' (*Conservative Home*, 27 January 2020) www.conservativehome.com/platform/2020/01/suella-braverman-people-we-elect-must-take-back-control-from-people-we-dont-who-include-the-judges.html.

[174] ibid.

[175] *R v Adams (Northern Ireland)* [2020] UKSC 19.

[176] *R (Evans) v Attorney General* [2015] UKSC 21.

[177] *R (UNISON) v Lord Chancellor* [2017] UKSC 51.

[178] *R (Privacy International) v Investigatory Powers Tribunal* [2019] UKSC 22.

[179] Braverman (n 173).

[180] ibid.

Braverman – then Home Secretary – once again criticised the judiciary, both domestic and supranational, in what was a prelude to the Rwanda saga discussed above. Speaking in her personal capacity about the situation of asylum seekers in Britain, she said: 'If we are thwarted by the courts, or indeed by [the European Court of Human Rights in] Strasbourg, then we will have to do whatever it takes, ultimately, to ensure that we can stop the boats.'[181] While it remains too early to draw definitive and long-term conclusions on this apparent standoff between the judiciary and the executive, there are some early signs that the UK judiciary may have been at least partly responsive to these political claims (and questions on its legitimacy): in fact, two very government-friendly Supreme Court rulings rendered in 2021[182] appear to make up at least some of the ground 'conceded' in a few of the abovementioned cases such as the two *Miller* cases, *UNISON* and *Privacy International*.[183] One may also add the 2023 *Re Allister* case, in which the Supreme Court sided with the government's view of sovereignty against Jim Allister's claim to constitutional statutes, with the effect being that the Northern Ireland Protocol, a central part of the Brexit withdrawal, could become law.[184]

Despite the recent change of government, these issues are likely to persist, at least in the medium term. This is evident from actors such as former Prime Minister Liz Truss, who has blamed her downfall on the 'establishment' and who, in a February 2025 speech, blamed many of the country's issues on the 'deep state', the 'unelected bureaucrats' and the judiciary, before calling for a Trump-inspired British MAGA ('Make America Great Again') movement to turn the tides on the 'failing state' and its 'very powerful and unaccountable bureaucracy, quangocracy and judiciary'.[185]

Moreover, linked to this is the extent to which the relationship between the executive and courts is one of defiance. For example, in 2012 the UK Government repealed the Fixed-term Parliaments Act 2011[186] and revived the prerogative

[181] P Walker, M Weaver and D Taylor, 'Suella Braverman restates wish for UK to leave European court of human rights' (*The Guardian*, 28 August 2023) www.theguardian.com/politics/2023/aug/28/suella-braverman-restates-wish-for-uk-to-leave-european-court-of-human-rights.

[182] The first case is *R (SC) v Secretary of State for Work and Pensions* [2021] UKSC 26, in which the Supreme Court notably held that 'a low intensity of review is generally appropriate, other things being equal, in cases concerned with judgments of social and economic policy in the field of welfare benefits and pensions, so that the judgment of the executive or legislature will generally be respected *unless it is manifestly without reasonable foundation*' ([158], emphasis added). The second case is *Reference by the Attorney General and the Advocate General for Scotland – United Nations Convention on the Rights of the Child (Incorporation) (Scotland) Bill; Reference by the Attorney General and the Advocate General for Scotland – European Charter of Local Self-Government (Incorporation) (Scotland) Bill* [2021] UKSC 42, in which the Supreme Court held that some important provisions of these two bills fall outside the legislative competence of the Scottish Parliament ([80], [84] and [88–89]).

[183] See Gearty (n 117).

[184] *Re Allister and others* [2023] UKSC 5. I thank David Yuratich for raising this point.

[185] M Cooke, 'Britain needs a Trump-style MAGA movement to save it, Liz Truss claims' (*The Independent*, 20 February 2025) www.independent.co.uk/news/uk/politics/liz-truss-donald-trump-maga-cpac-b2701664.html.

[186] (c 14).

power to seek and obtain an early dissolution of Parliament.[187] Amongst the arguments raised by ministers in the foreword of the draft legislation were time- and speed-related arguments pertaining to 'efficiency' and 'effectiveness'. The aim, according to the foreword of the bill, was to 'enable Governments, within the life of a Parliament, to call a general election at the time of their choosing'.[188] For then-Ministers (and MPs) Michael Gove, Chloe Smith and Lord True, '[t]he long standing position is that dissolution is not reviewable by the Courts and judgement on the Government's actions in such matters should be left to the electorate at the polling booth or, in extremely exceptional circumstances, to the Sovereign'.[189] As such, the statute contains an ouster clause, which aims to 'make clear that the exercise of the prerogative powers to dissolve Parliament, and the extent of those powers is non-justiciable'.[190] As a result, the Act allows the Prime Minister to dissolve Parliament and declare a new election – at the date of his or her choosing – and without any checks by the courts, provided only that Parliament does not exceed its maximum term of five years.[191]

It remains to be seen what role courts will end up playing after this stand-off. Some, like Mark Elliott, have argued that notwithstanding these 'increasingly apparent and increasingly concerning' attempts by the executive to reduce the review powers of courts, the latter would nonetheless retain a certain 'vestige of judicial review', which could allow them to review (and potentially refuse to uphold) the ouster clause.[192] This would be in line with certain recent *dicta*, including that of Lord Carnwath, who wrote in the *Privacy International* case that 'it is ultimately for the courts, not the legislature, to determine the limits set by the rule of law to the power to exclude review'.[193] That said, regardless of the long-term outcome of this (potential) standoff, it is hard to deny that the current UK constitutional order has been under stress, with an 'increasing resistance within Government to both legal and political control',[194] as well as an increasing number of signs that civility and self-restraint between the government and the courts have been abandoned.[195]

[187] See Draft Fixed-term Parliaments Act 2011 (Repeal) Bill, particularly ss 1 and 2. This bill was later known as the Dissolution and Calling of Parliament Bill and has now received Royal assent as the Dissolution and Calling of Parliament Act 2022 (c 11).

[188] Draft Fixed-term Parliaments Act 2011 (Repeal) Bill, foreword.

[189] ibid.

[190] ibid. For the wording of this ouster clause, see Dissolution and Calling of Parliament Act 2022, s 3.

[191] ibid s 4. See also AL Young, 'The Draft Fixed-term Parliaments Act 2011 (*Repeal*) Bill: *Turning Back the Clock?*' (*UK Constitutional Law Association Blog*, 4 December 2020) www.ukconstitutionallaw.org/2020/12/04/alison-l-young-the-draft-fixed-term-parliaments-act-2011-repeal-bill-turning-back-the-clock.

[192] M Elliott, 'Repealing the Fixed-term Parliaments Act' (*Public Law for Everyone*, 2 December 2020) www.publiclawforeveryone.com/2020/12/02/repealing-the-fixed-term-parliaments-act.

[193] M Elliott, 'The UK constitution under pressure: A lost age of civility?' (*Public Law for Everyone*, 23 November 2020) www.publiclawforeveryone.com/2020/11/23/the-uk-constitution-under-pressure-a-lost-age-of-civility.

[194] Elliott (n 192).

[195] Elliott (n 193).

C. Institutional Independence

Third, and in relation to the previous points, the mid- and long-term capacity of UK courts to respond to constitutional impatience and stabilise the system of constitutional governance is contingent upon their institutional independence. Besieged or captured courts are obviously in a much more difficult position to act as institutional decelerators; on the contrary, they can become *de*stabilisers by transforming themselves into allies or even into instruments of legitimation for the populist regime, helping the latter to consolidate power while maintaining a façade of democracy, as the example of Ecuador (2007–2017), discussed in chapter five, illustrates. Türkiye (since 2010),[196] Hungary (since 2010)[197] and Poland (2015–2023)[198] also provide interesting examples. In other instances, such as in Robert Fico's Slovakia, apex courts – while not necessarily captured – have chosen to 'kneel' before the populist leader.[199] In the Philippines, courts were also excessively deferential to President Rodrigo Duterte and eventually became subservient to the executive despite the absence of any overt threat to curb the courts.[200]

Different elements can explain why the UK courts were able to counteract populist impatience and re-establish the more deliberative political tempo of constitutional governance (including parliamentary debates and scrutiny of executive action), while avoiding institutional capture. Of course, the UK is a consolidated constitutional democracy, with old and established democratic norms and institutions, as well as a tradition of institutional self-restraint. By contrast, and as Wojciech Sadurski explains, in countries with a more recent tradition of constitutionalism, '[t]he newness of institutions works against the resilience of the constitution because there is simply an insufficient reservoir of customs, conventions, established patterns of conduct, and collective memory as to the proper way of acting within these institutions'.[201] However, the venerableness of the UK's institutions does not, in and of itself, explain everything. For example, the UK Supreme Court is still a relatively recent institution: it was established in 2009 to replace the appellate jurisdiction of the House of Lords and to achieve a more complete

[196] See, eg, OO Varol, 'Stealth Authoritarianism in Turkey' in MA Graber, S Levinson and M Tushnet (eds), *Constitutional Democracy in Crisis?* (Oxford, Oxford University Press, 2018); N Christofis, 'Erdoğan's "New" Turkey' in N Christofis (ed), *Erdoğan's 'New' Turkey: Attempted Coup d'état and the Acceleration of Political Crisis* (Abingdon, Routledge, 2019) 99.

[197] See, eg, G Halmai, 'A Coup Against Constitutional Democracy: The Case of Hungary' in Graber, Levinson and Tushnet (eds) (n 196).

[198] See, eg, W Sadurski, *Poland's Constitutional Breakdown* (Oxford, Oxford University Press, 2019).

[199] See, eg, P Čuroš, 'The Slovak Constitutional Court has Kneeled before Robert Fico' (*IACL-AIDC Blog*, 24 October 2024) www.blog-iacl-aidc.org/2024-posts/2024/10/24/the-slovak-constitutional-court-has-kneeled-before-robert-fico, referring to Constitutional Court of Slovakia, Pl ÚS 3/2024-761.

[200] D Gatmaytan, 'The Case of the Philippine Judiciary – Guardian of Democracy or Enabler of Populism?' in S Hardt, AW Heringa and H-T Nguyen (eds), *Populism and Democracy* (The Hague, Eleven International Publishing, 2020).

[201] W Sadurski, *A Pandemic of Populists* (Cambridge, Cambridge University Press, 2022) 98.

separation between executive, legislative and judicial powers. It is, however and crucially, a resolutely independent institution. As we have seen in the previous chapter on Ecuador under Rafael Correa's presidency, a robust and durable judicial independence is an essential element for courts to be able to properly exercise – and to continue to exercise – their role as institutional stabilisers and safeguards against executive aggrandisement.

D. Courts as 'Democratic Educators'?

Lastly, some scholars have praised courts for their democracy-enhancing role. For them, courts have the power and ability to make policy making subject to further information, scrutiny, debate and deliberation in legislatures. As such, and as Christine Landfried has argued, courts can 'enhance the complexity of governance' and decision-making structures, which, in turn, 'is a resource for solving complex problems in liberal democracies of the twenty-first century'.[202] This function is tied to a further alleged role for courts, namely that of 'democratic educators'. For example, Alexander Bickel wrote in 1962 that the courts' 'insulation and the marvelous mystery of time gives [them] the capacity to appeal to men's better natures, to call forth their aspirations, which maybe have been forgotten in the moment's hue and cry'. He added: 'Hence it is that the courts, although they may somewhat dampen the people's and the legislature's efforts to educate themselves, are also a great and highly effective educational institution.'[203] Moreover, Irwin Stotzky argued a few decades ago that the process of constitutional adjudication in the US has established 'a tradition that ultimately protects individuals against the arbitrary action of government', notably by contributing to the creation of 'a moral consciousness in the citizenry through the process of rational discourse'.[204] Similarly, Joseph Goldstein opined that courts have 'an important part to play in widening the base of informed people', particularly in a context of democratic transition.[205] Some judges have also described themselves as 'educators', viewing the judiciary (especially a country's apex court) as a 'pedagogical institution'.[206] Other scholars, such as Tom Ginsburg, have praised courts for their 'informational' role, in the way they provide 'high-quality information to publics

[202] C Landfried, 'Introduction' in C Landfried (ed), *Judicial Power: How Constitutional Courts Affect Political Transformations* (Cambridge, Cambridge University Press, 2019) 5.

[203] AM Bickel, *The Least Dangerous Branch: Supreme Court at the Bar of Politics* (New Haven, Yale University Press, 1986 [1962]) 26.

[204] IP Stotzky, 'The Tradition of Constitutional Adjudication' in IP Stotzky (ed), *Transition to Democracy in Latin America: The Role of the Judiciary* (Boulder, Westview, 1993) 348–349.

[205] J Goldstein, 'The Opinion-Writing Function of the Judiciary of Latin American Governments in Transition to Democracy: *Martinez v. Provincia de Mendoza*' in Stotzky (ed) (n 204) 301.

[206] See, eg, A Barak. 'A Judge on Judging: The Role of a Supreme Court in a Democracy' (2002) 116 *Harvard Law Review* 19, 38: '[Judges] must educate the public about the law and the role of the judiciary. In this regard, a supreme court should function as a pedagogical institution whose judges are teachers participating, as Eugene Rostow puts it, "in a vital national seminar"'.

and elites', for example, through judgments that 'create common knowledge that a violation of the rules has occurred'.[207] Court rulings, according to Ginsburg, therefore 'provide information for other actors to coordinate on'.[208]

In a somewhat similar fashion, Kuo has argued that courts can exercise democracy-enhancing functions, notably through their contribution to 'democratic learning embedded in the multistage process of constitutional governance'.[209] This multistage process, Kuo suggests (drawing on Rosanvallon, Scheuerman and others), is anchored in a specific political temporality – namely, that of courts operating at a slow pace – which is in sharp contrast to the executive's high pace of action.[210] In that sense, and based on an understanding of democracy as a 'reflexive process of governance with the function of political learning',[211] courts can contribute to the regeneration of democratic education and articulated governance through their embedded slowness and their decelerating function, as well as their relative detachment from populist pressures.

While normatively appealing, this alleged contribution to democratic learning is nevertheless grounded in empirical claims that remain, ultimately, difficult to verify. More studies – notably empirical or socio-legal research – are needed to test and assess the true contribution of courts in that regard. Even the precise nature of the judicial contribution to parliamentary debates and deliberation remains relatively unclear. For instance, Kuo claims that through the judicial intervention following the post-Brexit vote, UK courts made a 'difference in the face of populist forces'[212] – notably by allowing subsequent parliamentary debate and scrutiny. This is in line with this chapter's argument that courts, in the two *Miller* cases, slowed down the populist course of action, stabilised the constitutional system of governance and contributed to the (at least temporary) re-establishment of the deliberative-democratic channels. This can be seen in the countless parliamentary debates on Brexit that followed the two court decisions. Nevertheless, the true extent to which courts have effectively contributed to democratic and political learning – and even deliberation and debate – remains unclear, particularly considering that the outcome of the Brexit referendum continued to be depicted, even after the two *Miller* cases, as the immediate, acute, decisive and unassailable expression of the transcendent and immutable People-as-One. One may add, furthermore, that the two *Miller* cases noticeably go out of their way to try and distinguish the legal questions from the political (Brexit) process itself, which points toward a potentially limited contribution of courts – as 'democratic educators' – to the

[207] T Ginsburg, 'The Jurisprudence of Anti-Erosion' (2018) 66 *Duke Law Review* 838–840.

[208] ibid 852.

[209] Kuo (n 9) 564.

[210] ibid 571. See also introductory ch.

[211] ibid 570 and K Olsen, 'Reflexive Democracy as Popular Sovereignty' in B de Bruin and CF Zurn (eds), *New Waves in Political Philosophy* (London, Palgrave Macmillan, 2009). On reflexive democracy, see also P Rosanvallon, *La Légitimité démocratique: Impartialité, réflexivité, proximité* (Paris, Seuil, 2008).

[212] Kuo (n 9) 572.

political process and debate.[213] Moreover, apex courts – at least in the UK context – often strive for unanimity where possible, in order to reduce the risk of sending mixed messages to the public.[214] However, the absence of dissenting opinions may, in some cases, deprive those on the opposing side of access to reasoned arguments that might otherwise inform ongoing debate.

In the same vein, the medium- to long-term 'effects' and 'effectiveness' of judicial deceleration or institutional stabilisation on democratic learning remain to be seen – particularly in a context in which very little scholarly attention has been paid to the effects (or consequences, or what Frederick Schauer described as the 'non-legal end-states') of laws, judicial decisions and legal doctrine.[215] The question of the relevant timescale of analysis also further complicates any search for 'effectiveness', with most analyses of the *Miller* cases focusing on the immediate aftermath of these decisions. These questions, intertwining frame and substance as they do, are currently not, in my view, sufficiently addressed in the existing literature.

IV. Conclusion

In the UK, as elsewhere, the rise of populism and its inherent 'constitutional impatience' have been accompanied by a certain 'executivisation' of political power, bolstered by a form of anti-institutionalism.[216] Indeed, the point of focus of politics in constitutional democracies, long conceived around legislative power, seems to be shifting towards executive power.[217] Populists in power view and depict core components of democratic governance – including slow-paced deliberative institutions – as illegitimate obstacles to the implementation of their electoral mandates and, as such, as barriers 'that are to be discredited, disregarded or otherwise overcome'.[218] Circumventing institutions like Parliament becomes fair game; in fact, any attempt by legislatures to prevent the executive from implementing by any means necessary what it deems to be the 'will of the people' is perceived and depicted by them as a usurpation of power. In contrast to slow-paced and seemingly inefficient legislatures and Parliaments, prerogative and other executive powers allow populists in power to act quickly and expediently[219] – and to avoid

[213] I thank David Yuratich for this point.

[214] See, eg, R Reed, 'Collective Judging in the UK Supreme Court' in B Häcker and W Ernest (eds), *Collective Judging in Comparative Perspective: Counting Votes and Weighing Opinions* (Cambridge, Intersentia, 2020). I thank David Yuratich for this reference.

[215] F Schauer, 'Comparative Constitutional Compliance: Notes Towards a Research Agenda' in M Adams and J Bomhoff (eds), *Practice and Theory in Comparative Law* (Cambridge, Cambridge University Press, 2012).

[216] See ch 3.

[217] Issacharoff (n 158) 498–504.

[218] Issacharoff in M Orey, 'The Undoing of Democracy?' (*NYU Law – The Magazine*, 11 September 2020) www.law.nyu.edu/news/ideas/undoing-democracy-richard-pildes-samuel-issacharoff.

[219] See, eg, A Young, 'Are Prerogative Powers Necessary in the Twenty-First Century?' in Galligan (ed) (n 23) 97.

'burdensome' and 'unnecessary' debate. Of course, populists in the UK act largely within the existing constitutional framework. Nevertheless, through their willingness to circumvent liberal-constitutionalist institutions on the basis of proximity, speed and efficiency, they show a clear tendency towards executive aggrandisement, thereby illustrating the interaction and interrelation between that propensity and what I have described earlier in this book as 'constitutional impatience'. As such, they are illustrative, I would argue, of a 'mixed' relationship between populism and constitutionalism, differing from both the more 'positive' relationship discussed in chapter four and the 'negative' one discussed in chapter five.

Yet, it is precisely in this context that courts can play, as Kuo has argued[220] – and indeed have played, in the context and circumstances described in this chapter – an essential function as institutional decelerators. As the scope of executive powers is reviewable by courts, at least in the UK, judges are well positioned to 'restrain the impulse to circumvent institutional constraints on consolidated power'.[221] However, in the context of pressures on institutional boundaries and formal divisions of governmental authority, the role of the courts goes beyond institutional defence, including parliamentary sovereignty, and the separation of powers. Courts can also have a further underexamined and underappreciated role: that of an institutional *stabiliser* in response to the constitutional impatience of populism and its inherent anti-institutionalism. In my view, courts can stabilise the constitutional decision-making process by ensuring that the institutional mechanics of the system of constitutional governance are followed; in so doing, they contribute to preventing this system from changing, failing or declining.

Indeed, the judicial responses to executive power grabs in the *Miller (no 1)* and *Miller (no 2)/Cherry* cases illustrate the above scenario: namely, that courts can, in certain circumstances, have a certain stabilising function by both slowing down the populist acceleration of political time (judicial deceleration) *and* ensuring that the institutional mechanics of constitutional governance (including the sometimes lengthy and time-consuming constitutional decision-making process) are duly followed (judicial stabilisation). In doing so, courts can restore (at least in part) what Scheuerman views as the traditional liberal-democratic temporal separation of powers[222] and act as a bulwark against populist constitutional impatience, notably in the face of the heightened use of prerogative powers by the executive. This is all part, at least in the UK, of a broader context of increasing assertions of authority by the courts, particularly against the executive use of prerogative powers.[223]

[220] Kuo (n 9).

[221] S Issacharoff, 'The Corruption of Popular Sovereignty' (2020) 18 *International Journal of Constitutional Law* 1115.

[222] Scheuerman (n 3) 29. See also introductory ch.

[223] This is not to say, however, that the two *Miller* cases mark a complete break from the past. Ever since the *Case of Proclamations* [1610] EHC KB J22, UK courts have intervened to clarify and sometimes limit the scope and use of prerogative powers. This case has been invoked and cited by UK courts in subsequent judgments in the following 400 years, from the famous *Dr Bonham's Case* [*Bonham v College of Physicians*] [1610] 8 Co Rep 107 to the two *Miller* cases discussed above.

Of course, courts are no more entitled to claim to speak on behalf of 'the people' and (or) the popular sovereign than the populist leader or other offices or institutions of the state.[224] Nevertheless, through their review function, courts can control the exercise of some executive powers, at least those that are 'justiciable' – that is to say, suitable for judicial review,[225] and ensure that the constitutional procedures have been properly followed. In doing so, I contend, they can stabilise the system of constitutional governance and decision-making by slowing down the populist tempo and ensuring that constitutional, democratic and institutional procedures are followed and respected. In fact, even the mere *possibility* that courts may intervene can suffice, in some instances, to decelerate the populist tempo and ensure that legislation and (or) executive action is compatible with a given constitutional framework.[226] Finally, these judicial responses also reveal that courts can contribute to the re-establishment of the empty place of power, through the safeguarding of institutional-democratic spaces and channels.

That said, courts are not necessarily a panacea for 'constitutional impatience', not even in the UK context. As the Constitution Committee of the House of Lords put it in a report on 'executive oversight and responsibility for the UK constitution' published in January 2025, '[t]he role of courts and political controls such as elections are not sufficient safeguards in and of themselves' against 'the risk of the erosion of constitutional norms'.[227] Moreover, the public reception of the two *Miller* cases, as well as political pledges to reassess 'the relationship between the Government, Parliament and the courts',[228] is a reminder that the longer-term effects of those cases remain to be seen, and that the courts' position in the UK constitutional order (particularly their relationship with the executive) remains fragile. Finally, the more substantive virtues of judicial (or institutional) deceleration praised by some – including its alleged contributions to democratic learning as part of the multistage process of constitutional-democratic governance – are grounded in empirical claims that are normatively appealing, but remain difficult to verify, particularly in the longer term.

[224] A Arato, 'Populism, Constitutional Courts, and Civil Society' in C Landfried (ed), *Judicial Power: How Constitutional Courts Affect Political Transformations* (Cambridge, Cambridge University Press, 2019) 331.

[225] Young (n 219) 99.

[226] See, eg, Roznai (n 157) 348–355.

[227] Select Committee on the Constitution, *Executive Oversight and Responsibility for the UK Constitution*' (HL Paper 72, 28 January 2025) [59].

[228] The Conservative and Unionist Party, 'Manifesto 2019' 48.

Conclusion

> Contraction in time, the disappearance of the territorial space, after that of the fortified city and armor, leads to a situation in which the notions of 'before' and 'after' designate only the future and the past in a form of war that causes the 'present' to disappear in the instantaneousness of decision.[1]

I. Recapitulation: Synthesis and Structure

A. Part I – *Understanding* Populism: Towards a Constitutional Theory of Populism

In recent years, many countries have witnessed the rise of populist politics, both in established and 'emerging' democracies. From a public law perspective, populists tend to criticise, amongst other things, the disconnection between ordinary citizens and the liberal-democratic institutions that are supposed to represent them. In their view, representative democracy is filled with slow, artificial, cumbersome and unnecessary legal-institutional procedures, rules and processes, which ultimately fail to give voice to the people, understood in collectivist and unitarist terms.[2] For these populists, political power has unjustly been taken away from the people and placed in the hands of spatially distant intermediaries, most notably elites, institutions and experts, which are often depicted as unaccountable.[3] The avowed aim of populism, therefore, is to be the 'authentic voice of democracy'[4] and to offer a direct and unmediated

[1] P Virilio, *Speed and Politics* (trans Mark Polizzotti) (Los Angeles, Semiotext(e), 2006 [1977]) 156–157.

[2] See chs 1, 2 and 3. See also, eg, L Corrias, 'Populism in a Constitutional Key: Constituent Power, Popular Sovereignty and Constitutional Identity' (2016) 12 *European Constitutional Law Review* 10; P Blokker, 'Populist Constitutionalism' in C de la Torre (ed), *Routledge Handbook of Global Populism* (Abingdon, Routledge, 2019), 113, 114, 122; N Urbinati, 'Political Theory of Populism' (2019) 22 *Annual Review of Political Science*; M-S Kuo, 'Against Instantaneous Democracy' (2019) 17 *International Journal of Constitutional Law* 557–558; N Walker, 'Populism and Constitutional Tension' (2019) 17 *International Journal of Constitutional Law* 519–520, 531.

[3] See, in particular, ch 4. See also, generally, Y Mounk, *The People vs. Democracy: Why Our Freedom Is in Danger and How to Save it* (Cambridge, Harvard University Press, 2018); J-W Müller, '"The People Must Be Extracted from Within the People": Reflections on Populism' (2014) 21 *Constellations* 486–487.

[4] C Lasch, *The Revolt of the Elites and the Betrayal of Democracy* (New York, Norton & Company, 1995) 106.

link with ordinary citizens, to provide a means to 'reenchant' democracy[5] and, ultimately, to restore the primacy of the people.[6] This is to be achieved, notably, through identity- and similarity-based appeals to authenticity,[7] but also through the exercise of the 'constituent power' of the people or nation and the use of majoritarian and plebiscitary instruments such as referendums.[8] As a result, the rise of contemporary populism has been accompanied by a shift of focus from the main, traditional institutions of constitutional democracy and modern democratic governance – including legislatures and political parties – to individual leaders and politicians, who claim to offer a better, faster and more direct link with the people.[9]

These institutional dynamics, as we have seen, do not operate in a vacuum; they take place in the context of what sociologists and social theorists have called 'social acceleration', referring mainly to various interrelated components of the social acceleration of contemporary life, including technological acceleration, social change or transformation and the heightened tempo of everyday life.[10] From a spatiotemporal perspective, populists take advantage of this social acceleration and the existing (spatio)temporal contours of liberal democracy in order to put forward an alternative conception of democratic representation and a constitutional project based on spatial proximity as well as temporal efficiency and rapidity. This alternative conception of representation – and the constitutional project it is associated with – has several spatiotemporal components of significant importance.

[5] P Blokker, 'Populism as a Constitutional Project' (2019) 17 *International Journal of Constitutional Law* 536.

[6] J-W Müller, 'Populism and Constitutionalism' in CR Kaltwasser, PO Espejo, P Taggart and P Ostiguy (eds), *The Oxford Handbook of Populism* (Oxford, Oxford University Press, 2017); AL Young, 'Populism and the UK Constitution' (2018) 71 *Current Legal Problems* 17, 35–36.

[7] See ch 3. See also, eg, M-S Kuo, 'Authenticity: The Ultimate Challenge in the Quest for Lasting Constitutional Legitimacy' (2021) 41 *Oxford Journal of Legal Studies*; C Fieschi, *Populocracy: The Tyranny of Authenticity and the Rise of Populism* (New York, Columbia University Press, 2019) 35–39, 157–160; Walker (n 2) 523, 527–528; Kuo (n 2) 558–559; M Valverde, *Chronotopes of Law: Jurisdiction, Scale and Governance* (Abingdon, Routledge, 2015); E Peruzzotti, 'El populismo como ejercicio de poder gubernamental y la amenaza de hibradación de la democracia liberal' (2018) 11 *Revista SAAP* 215–216; Corrias (n 2) 23–24; C de la Torre, *Populist Seduction in Latin America*, 2nd edn (Athens, Ohio University Press, 2010) xix, 10, 66, 109; F Panizza, 'Introduction: Populism and the Mirror of Democracy' in Francisco Panizza (ed), *Populism and the Mirror of Democracy* (London, Verso, 2005) 24–28.

[8] See, in particular, chs 1 and 2. See also, eg, Corrias (n 2) 10; J Scholtes, 'The Complacency of Legality: Constitutionalist Vulnerabilities to Populist Constituent Power' (2019) 20 *German Law Journal* 354; Blokker (n 5) 550; N Urbinati, 'Populism and the Majority Principle' in CR Kaltwasser et al (eds), *The Oxford Handbook of Populism* (Oxford, Oxford University Press, 2017) 585.

[9] See, eg, S Issacharoff, 'Democracy's Deficits' (2018) 85 *University of Chicago Law Review* 491; S Issacharoff, 'The Corruption of Popular Sovereignty' (2020) 18 *International Journal of Constitutional Law*.

[10] H Rosa, *Social Acceleration: A New Theory of Modernity* (New York, Columbia University Press, 2013); H Rosa, 'Social Acceleration: Ethical and Political Consequences of a Desynchronized High-Speed Society' (2003) 10 *Constellations*. See also WE Scheuerman, *Liberal Democracy and the Social Acceleration of Time* (Baltimore, Johns Hopkins University Press, 2004).

First, from the perspective of space, populism is based upon proximity, similarity and authenticity. Following the idea of a substantial identity between the rulers and the ruled, populists put forward a conception of democracy and a constitutional project that aims to remove means of mediation, from institutional mediators to mainstream media, thereby favouring fast-paced, immediate and direct communication (and indeed fusion) between *gouvernants* and *gouvernés*. Through their emphasis on the need for direct, authentic and immediate democratic means, they help reorganise and redraw the pre-existing spatiotemporal contours of liberal democracy. Second, from the perspective of time, populists want to do things faster: the temporal orientation of populist politics, discourses and imaginary is characterised by a sense of urgency and expeditiousness, which acts as a catalyst for social acceleration. Rejecting liberal-democratic forms of mediation, populists often put forward a 'politics of instantaneity', which focuses on means of direct democracy and the (re-)politicisation of liberal-democratic institutions, including courts, but also constitutions as well as other legal instruments. Their claim is that by redrawing the temporal contours of liberal democracy and circumventing the delays built into liberal democracy, the voice of the people can be directly and immediately heard.[11]

This focus on spatial proximity and temporal efficiency is not just theoretical; it also has important practical implications for public law and the institutions of constitutional democracy. Specifically, it often translates, from a legal-institutional perspective, into an increased use of executive (including prerogative) powers – as the most responsive and time-efficient branch of government, particularly compared to the seemingly slow, detached and unresponsive legislature. This 'executivisation' of power – or, at least, the increased use of executive powers – also has consequences for law itself, which appears increasingly 'in danger of becoming de-synchronised and anachronistic'[12] – in other words, in danger of becoming out-of-touch with the fast-paced and speed (and/or efficiency)-oriented political and sociological reality.

This emphasis on proximity and speed (and, to a certain extent, on politics rather than law) can, of course, be appealing at first blush. For instance, it could very well be seen as an effective way to 'reconnect' politicians and other power wielders with members of the public, the very same people they are meant to represent, and to reduce the distance (both metaphorical and physical) between themselves and the public. However, this emphasis on proximity and speed is driven and led by a form of what I have called in this monograph 'constitutional impatience'. By this, I refer mainly to the way in which some populists are impatient with institutions, procedures and intermediaries, perceived or depicted as 'thwarting the will of the people', and the way in which populists attempt to bypass

[11] See ch 3. See also, eg, Corrias (n 2) 12, 19.

[12] H Rosa, 'Airports Built on Shifting Grounds? Social Acceleration and the Temporal Dimension of Law' in L Corrias and L Francot (eds), *Temporal Boundaries of Law and Politics: Time Out of Joint* (Abingdon, Routledge, 2018) 85.

or circumvent them – to avoid delays and to reduce the distance between power wielders and the public. This drive for temporal efficiency and spatial proximity directly contribute to the reconfiguration of public law, as well as of its institutional and normative order. However, and from a more normative standpoint, this constitutional impatience runs the risk of transforming itself into a hegemonic system of simultaneity and occupation, which has the potential to ultimately affect or distort the constitutive elements of constitutional democracy in two main ways. First, through its emphasis on spatial proximity, immediacy and authenticity, populism not only shortens the distance between the rulers and the ruled; it can also shrink the public, discursive space between the state and the private sphere, possibly leading to a form of occupation. In the same vein, the emphasis on identity-based claims to authenticity can possibly lead to forms of expulsion or othering. Second, from a temporal perspective, the populist focus on instantaneity and decisionism is often done at the expense of reflexivity and deliberation. This space-time compression, as it were, runs the risk of distorting not just the (spatio)temporal contours of constitutional democracy, but also its constitutive features, including its important guardrails, ultimately collapsing what is worth protecting about the idea of constitutionalism.

B. Part II – *Responding* to Populism: Questioning the Role of the Judiciary against the 'Constitutional Impatience' of Populism

It is precisely in this context of social acceleration and, I argue, of populist-driven constitutional impatience, that the role of the courts comes into play. In the context of the growing literature on democratic decay, broadly speaking, several constitutional scholars have praised the judiciary for its ability, capacity (and, in some cases, duty) to perform democracy-enhancing functions, notably by constraining the executive and by acting as a bulwark against authoritarian and populist threats. In fact, some liberal-oriented scholars and actors have argued that it is precisely when populism thrives that the role of the judiciary becomes all the more important.[13] Contrary to the two political branches, it is argued, the legitimacy of judges stems from a 'complex constellation' that consists of professional expertise and institutional autonomy, amongst other elements.[14] Under the same reasoning, courts, as independent and expertocratic actors, have the ability to constrain the power of the political branches and to provide counter-majoritarian protection

[13] See, eg, A Arato, 'Populism and the Courts' (*Verfassungsblog*, 25 April 2017) www.verfassungsblog.de/populism-and-the-courts; W Sadurski, 'Judicial Review versus Populist Authoritarianism' 2025) 3 *Comparative Constitutional Studies*; S Baer, 'Challenges to Constitutionalism: The Role of Constitutional Courts', report for the Venice Commission (CDL-JU (2017)002, 30 July 2017).

[14] See, eg, JEK Murkens, 'Judicious Review: The Constitutional Practice of the UK Supreme Court' (2018) 77 *Cambridge Law Journal* 354. Murkens does not, however, make these claims in the context of populism per se.

against majoritarian politics. When representation fails, courts can also provide, it is said, a second democratic channel.[15] Moreover, the judiciary is said to be able to 'forestall [the] descent into executive command' and to 'provide a respite, frustrating political exclusions in the form of lustrations, ensuring the ability of dissident parties to operate, and most significantly, reinforcing a separation of powers to limit the executive'.[16]

Some scholars have built on the above to make more specific claims regarding the ability of courts to offer a constitutional-democratic response to contemporary populism. To give one example, Ming-Sung Kuo has contended that courts can play the role of 'judicial decelerators' vis-à-vis the 'instantaneous' conception of democracy put forward and defended by populists.[17] In short, in the growing liberal-constitutionalist literature on populism, courts are often said to have a key role to play in defending constitutionalism and liberal constitutional democracy more broadly.[18]

Yet, a closer look in this monograph – mainly through three case studies, including two from non-traditional and relatively understudied regions from the Global South and (or) 'periphery' and one from the so-called 'established democratic order'[19] – reveals a more nuanced picture – and, in a similar way, a more complicated relationship between populism and constitutionalism. It reveals, first, that courts can decelerate the populist impatience to promote and implement constitutional change, but they can do so to such an extent that it may sometimes, in fact, become a form of institutional obstruction – particularly in a context of 'transitional constitutionality', that is to say, the 'inevitable agenda of transition' from authoritarianism to constitutional democracy.[20] In such contexts, the judiciary – instead of securing democratic spaces, as strong and independent courts are often expected to do – can potentially as a constraint on political liberalisation[21] and might even become an 'authoritarian enclave'.[22] It is entirely possible, indeed, that the judiciary could eventually transform itself

[15] Arato (n 13). See also A Arato, 'Populism, Constitutional Courts, and Civil Society' in C Landfried (ed), *Judicial Power: How Constitutional Courts Affect Political Transformations* (Cambridge, Cambridge University Press, 2019).

[16] S Issacharoff, 'Safeguarding Democratic Institutions' (*Verfassungsblog*, 29 April 2017 www.verfassungsblog.de/safeguarding-democratic-institutions/).

[17] Kuo (n 2).

[18] See also, eg, Y Roznai, 'Who Will Save the Redheads? Anti-Bully Theory of Judicial Review and Protection of Democracy' (2020) 29 *William & Mary Bill of Rights Journal*; Arato, 'Populism, Constitutional Courts' (n 15) 338-339; D Prendergast, 'The Judicial Role in Protecting Democracy from Populism' (2019) 20 *German Law Journal*; T Ginsburg and AH Huq, *How to Save a Constitutional Democracy* (Chicago, University of Chicago Press, 2018) 186–191. See introductory ch for more details.

[19] S Issacharoff, *Democracy Unmoored: Populism and the Corruption of Popular Sovereignty* (Oxford, Oxford University Press, 2023) 7.

[20] See L Sólyom, 'The Role of Constitutional Courts in the Transition to Democracy: With Special Reference to Hungary' (2003) 18 *International Sociology* 137-ss and ch 4 of this monograph.

[21] AU Bali, 'The Perils of Judicial Independence: Constitutional Transition and the Turkish Example' (2012) 52 *Virginia Journal of International Law* 235, as cited in T Moustafa, 'Law and Courts in Authoritarian Regimes' (2014) 10 *Annual Review of Law and Social Science* 286.

[22] Moustafa (n 21) 286.

into the last rampart or bastion of an illegitimate *ancien régime* and (or) into a major hurdle in the transition from semi-authoritarianism to constitutional democracy. The case study on post-Velvet Revolution Armenia, discussed in chapter four, provides a ready example. This monograph also reveals, secondly, that courts can, in different circumstances, even contribute to the *acceleration* of the populist flow of time by becoming active agents of illiberalism[23] and (or) executive consolidation[24] at the service of an impatient and omnipotent executive. This was illustrated in chapter five, which focused on Ecuador during Rafael Correa's presidency.

That said, as we have also seen in chapter six (which focused on the UK in the aftermath of the Brexit vote), courts can, in the right circumstances, have a certain stabilising function by both slowing down the populist acceleration of political time *and* ensuring that the institutional mechanics of constitutional governance (including the sometimes lengthy and time-consuming constitutional decision-making processes) are duly followed. In doing so, courts can restore (at least in part) what Scheuerman views as the traditional liberal-democratic temporal separation of powers[25] and act as a bulwark against populist constitutional impatience, notably in the face of the heightened use of prerogative powers by the executive. To borrow an analysis mainly aimed at constitutional law (rather than courts per se), the judiciary – just like constitutional law itself – can, in some circumstances, act as a stable 'safeguard against the eroding pressure of high-speed dynamics'.[26] In other words, courts, like constitutional law, can guarantee 'that law-making follows stable, predictable patterns and pathways even in turbulent times, and thus [provide] long-term stability, calculability and predictability'.[27] Courts, it thus appears, can sometimes act as institutional decelerators and stabilisers in the face of the high velocity of social acceleration and what I have called the 'constitutional impatience' of contemporary populism. However, and as we have seen, the effects of institutional deceleration and stabilisation are subject to important contextual, political and institutional constraints. Moreover, the more substantive virtues of institutional (or judicial) deceleration – including its alleged contributions to democratic learning as part of the multistage process of constitutional-democratic governance[28] – are grounded in empirical claims that remain, ultimately, difficult to verify.

In light of the above, one may wonder if courts should probably be best seen not as heroic saviours of liberal constitutional democracy, but rather – and perhaps at most, under ideal conditions – as 'speed bumps'[29] which can 'slow or otherwise hinder

[23] See, eg, P Castillo-Ortiz, 'The Illiberal Abuse of Constitutional Courts in Europe' (2019) 15 *European Constitutional Law Review*.

[24] D Landau and R Dixon, 'Abusive Judicial Review: Courts Against Democracy' (2020) 53 *University of California, Davis Law Review*.

[25] Scheuerman (n 10) 29. See also introductory ch.

[26] Rosa (n 12) 84.

[27] ibid.

[28] Kuo (n 2) 564.

[29] The expression has also been used, notably, in T Ginsburg, AH Huq and M Versteeg, 'The Coming Demise of Liberal Constitutionalism' (2018) 65 *University of Chicago Law Review* 253 – referring to

efforts at democratic erosion'[30] or, in the words of this monograph, slow down the authoritarian populist-driven constitutional impatience. Indeed, independent courts can, in the right circumstances, exercise control over illegitimate attempts to consolidate (executive) power and to change or replace the constitution, for instance, through judicial instruments such as (judicial) review of executive action, or the unconstitutional constitutional amendment doctrine.[31] Nevertheless, their role and influence as institutional decelerators or stabilisers (or even as 'speed bumps') is contingent on a myriad of factors, including the public (and political) reception of their judgments, the (overwhelming) forces of politics as well as their institutional independence.

II. Key Findings of the Monograph

Three key findings thus emerge from this monograph. First, contemporary populism, while sharing a common 'core' in terms of ideal-typical discourses, comes with a wide range of practical applications, which are all illustrative of the differential impact of the tensions between populism and constitutionalism. The relationship between the two concepts is thus complex and context dependent. If the Ecuador case study indicates a largely negative relationship between populism and constitutionalism (chapter five) and the post-Brexit UK case study shows a rather mixed relationship (chapter six), the case study on post-Velvet Revolution Armenia points in the direction of a possible positive relationship between populism and constitutionalism and reveals the potential for a more 'democratic' or 'revolutionary' form of populism (chapter four). This, in turns, challenges assumptions about the institutional role of courts, as well as the relationship between populism and the judiciary. In instances such as the one described in chapter four, populist attacks on independent courts may even have a certain 'democratic' character, particularly when the said courts act as a constraint on political liberalisation by obstructing democratic reforms and (or) becoming a major hurdle in the transition from semi-authoritarianism to constitutional democracy. In such a scenario, judicial reforms to replace entrenched and partisan judges in apex courts can perhaps be justified, at least from a liberal-constitutionalist perspective. At the very least, this case study is an illustration that, to borrow Robert Howse's words, '[n]ot every move to change the judiciary is necessarily fully motivated by a demotic animus against civil liberties and the rule of law'.[32] Finally, and to go back

constitutional design in general (rather than courts more specifically). On courts as 'speed bumps', see, eg, B Bugarič, 'Can Law Protect Democracy? Legal Institutions as "Speed Bumps"' (2019) 11 *Hague Journal on the Rule of Law* 447, 449, 450; Roznai (n 18) 328, 341.

[30] Landau and Dixon (n 24) 1321.

[31] ibid 1320–1321. Good constitutional design can also play a similar role. See, eg, R Dixon and D Landau, 'Transnational Constitutionalism and a Limited Doctrine of Unconstitutional Constitutional Amendment' (2015) 13 *International Journal of Constitutional Law* 606, 613–614.

[32] R Howse, 'Epilogue: In Defense of Disruptive Democracy – A Critique of Anti-Populism' (2019) 17 *International Journal of Constitutional Law* 648.

to the analogy of populism as a (spatiotemporal) disruption, what this case study reveals is the possibility of a 'democratic-populist' disruption of the flow of time.

Second, the decelerating and stabilising function of the judiciary is arguably most appropriately conceptualised as lying on a continuum. On one end of the spectrum, courts can slow down constitutional impatience, thereby stabilising the system of constitutional governance – at least for a few weeks or months (as the UK Supreme Court did in the context of the two *Miller* cases, discussed in chapter six). On the other end of the spectrum, however, courts with strong ties to a former, semi-authoritarian regime can lead to a complete, long(er)-term judicial obstruction (as seen in chapter four in relation to the Constitutional Court of Armenia). In some cases, judicial capture can even lead to full-fledged acceleration of political time and constitutional impatience (as seen in chapter five in the context of the Ecuadorean Constitutional Court).

Third, and in the same vein, the ability of courts to act as institutional decelerators or stabilisers in this context of social acceleration and constitutional impatience is contingent upon a myriad of factors and conditions. While these factors and conditions will vary depending on the context, I suggest, based on the observations in this monograph, that at least three factors or conditions are likely to have an impact on the ability of courts to respond to populist impatience, whether as institutional decelerators or stabilisers (or perhaps even as 'speed bumps'). These three factors are: (a) institutional independence; (b) the stability of the constitutional framework and institutions; and (c) the existence of a *garantiste* constitutional culture.

Institutional (including judicial) independence is widely viewed as one of the cornerstones of a democracy.[33] However, it is a multi-faceted concept. Owen M Fiss distinguishes between three distinctive – albeit interrelated – notions of judicial independence. The first one, which he calls 'party detachment', requires judges to be independent from the parties in a particular controversy before a court, either by virtue of the fact that they are not related, in one way or another, to one or more of the parties in the controversy before the court, or be in any way under their influence or control.[34] It is of vital importance for judges, whether they are exercising private or public functions.[35] In the words of Paul W Kahn, even when judges are exercising private functions, that is to say when they adjudicate a controversy between two private parties, '[t]he judicial narrative imposes a public order on the private controversy'.[36] The second notion of independence, called 'individual autonomy', is concerned with power relationships between judges. It notably refers to the doctrine of *stare decisis* in common law systems, but also collegial control exercised by appellate

[33] See, eg, *R v Lippé*, [1991] 2 SCR 114 [139].

[34] OM Fiss, 'The Right Degree of Independence' in IP Stozky (ed), *Transition to Democracy in Latin America: The Role of the Judiciary* (Boulder, Westview, 1993) 55.

[35] PW Kahn, 'Independence and Responsibility in the Judicial Role' in Stozky (ed) (n 34) 75.

[36] ibid 76.

courts over lower courts. It also refers to the review and discipline of individual judges by judiciary councils.[37] The third notion of judicial independence, which Fiss calls 'political insularity', refers to the institutional independence of the judiciary vis-à-vis the other institutions of the state that, collectively, exercise the state's coercive power.[38]

This monograph is more concerned with the third notion of judicial independence, political insularity. This enables the judicial power to act as a check against the other branches of government or as a countervailing force within the larger system of government.[39] It also allows judges to enjoy a 'relative freedom from pressures of the moment',[40] which, in turn, enables them 'to take a more detached view' and to take 'difficult and unpopular decisions'.[41] In that sense, courts must be 'sufficiently independent not only from politics, but also from popular sentiment and populism'.[42]

However, institutional (including judicial) independence is not everything – and may not always be sufficient to resist constitutional impatience and prevent a government from falling into authoritarian populism. As we have seen in the case study focusing on Ecuador (but also, one may add, in other contemporary instances, including Poland under PiS[43] and Hungary under Fidesz[44]), even formally independent institutions – from courts to fourth-branch institutions like electoral commissions – can be captured from within. Once captured, these formally (and formerly) independent courts can transform into allies of a regime. Deploying legal tools and means[45] (or what could even be described as 'lawfare'), these captured institutions can help a regime maintain power by engaging in different legal processes, including, for example, what David Landau and Rosalind Dixon have called 'abusive judicial review'.[46]

Another key factor or condition, therefore, is the stability of the constitutional framework and its institutions. The case studies examined in this monograph reveal that courts are less likely to be able to exercise their role as institutional decelerators or stabilisers in a context of political, legal, institutional and constitutional instability. The case of Ecuador under the presidency of Rafael Correa, for example, illustrates that point. As discussed in more detail in chapter five, Correa

[37] Fiss (n 34) 55-56.

[38] Paul Kahn distinguishes between these different kinds of judicial independence in a similar way, but adds another one: judicial independence from particular political ideologies. See Kahn (n 35) 74.

[39] Fiss (n 34) 56.

[40] *R (Nicklinson) v Ministry of Justice* [2014] UKSC 38 [104].

[41] ibid.

[42] See Baer (n 13) 4. See also the discussion on penal populism in ch 2 of this book.

[43] See, eg, W Sadurski, *Poland's Constitutional Breakdown* (Oxford, Oxford University Press, 2019).

[44] See, eg, G Halmai, 'A Coup Against Constitutional Democracy: The Case of Hungary' in MA Graber, S Levinson and M Tushnet (eds), *Constitutional Democracy in Crisis?* (Oxford, Oxford University Press, 2018).

[45] See, eg, KL Scheppele, 'Autocratic Legalism' (2018) 85 *University of Chicago Law Review* 545.

[46] Landau and Dixon (n 24).

enacted a new constitution in 2008, one year after taking power, and created new institutions, including a new Constitutional Court. This constitutional *tabula rasa* was undoubtedly facilitated by the fact that Ecuador has had a long history of constitutional instability, with several elections and regime changes in the years that preceded Correa's access to power – and a (very) long history of short-lived constitutions.[47]

However, institutional independence *and* a stable constitutional framework and institutions are also not sufficient, in and of themselves, to ensure that courts can provide a meaningful response to constitutional impatience and other authoritarian threats to constitutional democracy. Political pressure, partial capture and (or) close judicial alignment with the executive branch can hamper the courts' ability to function as judicial decelerators or stabilisers. The recent US Supreme Court case of *Trump v CASA*,[48] rendered in June 2025, provides an example. In a blow to the judicial ability to 'slow down' populist impatience, the Supreme Court curtailed the federal district courts' power to issue nationwide injunctions that would temporarily prevent the government from enforcing federal policies, including those issued by executive order.[49]

Moreover, and as we have seen in chapter four on Armenia in the aftermath of the Velvet Revolution, a judiciary that is too close to a former regime is likely to lead to a system in which 'old' and 'entrenched' courts legitimise previous (semi-)authoritarian regimes, thereby hindering ongoing democratisation processes.[50] Indeed, constitutional courts with deep ties to a former regime can use their judicial review powers (either in their weak or strong forms) to actively undermine (rather than protect) liberal-democratic constitutionalism, notably by blocking democratic reforms and democratisation processes more broadly. In such instances, I contend, courts can be accurately described as institutional (or judicial) obstructors – rather than decelerators or stabilisers.

Linked to the above is a third factor or condition, namely the existence (or lack thereof) of a 'constitutional culture',[51] or perhaps what I would call – building on Giovanni Sartori – a *garantiste* constitutional culture. Sartori, in a famous article published in 1962, discussed the importance of the *garantiste* aspect of constitutions.[52] He here referred to constitutions abiding by the *telos* of constitutionalism, namely the idea of a constitution as 'fundamental law, or a fundamental set of principles, and a correlative institutional arrangement, which

[47] See ch 5.

[48] *Trump v CASA, Inc*, 606 US 831 (2025).

[49] The relevant executive order, in this case, is 'Protecting the Meaning and Value of American Citizenship' (Executive Order 14160, 29 January 2025) 90 Fed Reg 8449, which redefines birthright citizenship by restricting automatic citizenship for children born in the US only to certain limited categories of non-citizen parents. The Supreme Court, however, has not yet ruled on the merits.

[50] A Ohanyan, 'How Old Courts Derail New Democracies' (*Foreign Policy*, 14 August 2019) www.foreignpolicy.com/2019/08/14/how-old-courts-derail-new-democracies.

[51] See, eg, Halmai (n 44) 243.

[52] G Sartori, 'Constitutionalism: A Preliminary Discussion' (1962) 56 *American Political Science Review*.

would restrict arbitrary power and ensure a "limited government"'.[53] A *garantiste* constitution is in contrast to constitutions such as nominal or façade constitutions. The same analysis could be transposed, I contend, to the existence of (or lack thereof) a culture which rejects arbitrary power and which strives for, instead, the idea of a limited government – as opposed to a powerful and stable, but entrenched, authoritarian regime or dictatorship, for instance.[54]

When such a *garantiste* (or constitutionalist) culture is lacking, courts are, I suggest, less likely to have a democracy-enhancing role. They may well engage in a form of 'stabilisation', if the latter term is to be understood in its most basic and simplistic form – that is to say, as contributing to maintaining the existing regime and constitutional-legal system (with its institutions) in place. However, far from always being a form of democracy-enhancing institutional deceleration or stabilisation, the action of courts in certain instances can, as we have seen, transform into a form of institutional or judicial obstruction. This is particularly true in contexts of democratic transition and (or) in jurisdictions devoid of a long history of constitutionalism (and/or of a *garantiste* culture). The case of the Armenian judges impeding democratic reforms – and helping the previous power holders of the Republican Party regime who appointed them as judges – provides an example.

The focus in that regard (particularly in chapter four) has been on post-Velvet Revolution Armenia, but the analytical framework could be transformed to other jurisdictions and contexts. One of these is Ukraine, where the Constitutional Court ruled, in October 2020 that significant parts of the country's anti-corruption legislation, adopted in the period that followed the 2014 Euromaidan Revolution and the ousting of then-President Viktor Yanukovych, were unconstitutional.[55] In response to the Court's judgment, President Volodymyr Zelensky introduced a bill[56] that would have terminated the powers of all Constitutional Court judges and, later, suspended the Court's chairperson for two months, resulting in a political and legal crisis – and accusations of a power grab.[57] Facing pressure, Zelensky subsequently withdrew the bill and appealed to the Venice Commission, which, in December 2020, released two opinions highly critical of the Constitutional Court's judgment and expressing the Commission's support for a large-scale reform of the

[53] ibid 855.

[54] Irwin Stotzky calls this the necessity to 'internalize the importance and legitimacy of a constitutional system based on the rule of law [and the] universal standards of achievement and competition necessary to the proper functioning of a democracy'. See IP Stotzky, 'A Democratic Vision' in Stotzky (ed) (n 34) 396.

[55] Constitutional Court of Ukraine, Decision 13-r/2020 (27 October 2020). On the judicial reform in the aftermath of the Euromaidan, see M Popova and DJ Beers, 'No Revolution of Dignity for Ukraine's Judges: Judicial Reform after the Euromaidan' (2020) 28 *Demokratizatsiya* 113.

[56] Verkhovna Rada of Ukraine, Draft Law No 4288 'On the Restoration of Public Trust in Constitutional Justice' (29 October 2020).

[57] See, eg, Veronika Melkozerova, 'Ukraine sours on President Volodymyr Zelenskiy as challenges mount for former comedian' (*NBC News*, 22 November 2020) www.nbcnews.com/news/world/challenges-mount-ukraine-sours-comedian-turned-president-volodymyr-zelenskiy-n1248141.

country's apex court.[58] This, I contend, is another illustration of the long-lasting impact of judicial and institutional capture – and possibly of what I called 'judicial obstruction' in chapter four – at least in a post-authoritarian transitional context, even after semi-authoritarian (or hybrid) regimes have left power and have been replaced with more democratic ones.

III. Ramifications for Future Research

The above findings can, it is hoped, pave the way for new research in the field of comparative constitutional law, particularly on the longer-term 'effectiveness' (or lack thereof) of institutional deceleration and stabilisation. As discussed in chapter six, the medium- to long-term 'effects' and 'effectiveness' of judicial deceleration or institutional stabilisation remain to be seen – particularly in a context in which very little scholarly attention has been paid to the effects (or consequences – what Frederick Schauer has called the 'non-legal end-states') of laws, judicial decisions and legal doctrine in general.[59] It is hoped that this monograph will encourage legal scholars to pay more attention to these longer-term effects or consequences.

Furthermore, the legal, political and institutional context discussed in the case study on post-Velvet Revolution Armenia (chapter four) raises an important empirical question of broader relevance for constitutionalism, namely: after the fall of an authoritarian regime, is it preferable to preserve and maintain the existing counter-majoritarian institutions, such as constitutional and other apex courts, or to dismantle and (or) 'vet' them as remnants and agents of the former authoritarian regime?[60] This question is of interest to both policymakers and scholars; while policymakers may be ambivalent on this, academic circles tend to view the latter practices as 'illiberal', 'unconstitutional' and (or) 'undemocratic'. The case study in Armenia, in my view, is illustrative of a certain tension between institutional continuity and stability, on the one hand, and reckoning and accountability, on

[58] Venice Commission, *Urgent Joint Opinion of the Venice Commission and the Directorate General of Human Rights and Rule of Law (DGI) of the Council of Europe on the Legislative Situation regarding Anti-Corruption Mechanisms* (Opinion No 1012/2020, 11 December 2020) CDL-AD(2020)038; Venice Commission, *Urgent Opinion on the Reform of the Constitutional Court of Ukraine* (Opinion No 1012/2020, 11 December 2020) CDL-AD(2020)039. See also M Minakov and WE Pomeranz, 'Kennan Cable No 65: Constitutional Crisis in Ukraine: Looking for Solutions' (*Wilson Center, Kennan Institute*, March 2021) www.wilsoncenter.org/publication/kennan-cable-no-65-constitutional-crisis-ukraine-looking-solutions.

[59] F Schauer, 'Comparative Constitutional Compliance: Notes Towards a Research Agenda' in M Adams and J Bomhoff (eds), *Practice and Theory in Comparative Law* (Cambridge, Cambridge University Press, 2012).

[60] See, eg, A Mazmanyan, 'Constitutional Choices After a (Democratic) Revolution: Lessons from Armenia, and elsewhere' (paper presented at the 'Building Institutional Resilience' international workshop, Malyi Center, University of Chicago Law School, 26–27 September 2024; unpublished manuscript; on file with author).

the other. In this regard, and viewing Armenia's recent experience as submitting to mixed conclusions, Armen Mazmanyan suggests that 'inclusive institutions which provide room for the embattled "autocrats" to be engaged in the democratic game rather than creating incentives for them to mobilize and fight back might prove more resilient' than more aggressive tactics of marginalisation, vetting, exclusion and (or) removal.[61] For him, '[e]ngaging rather than marginalizing the former autocratic regime could be a smarter strategy especially in settings which prove fragile and prone to exogenous factors, such as war, international pressure and dependence on non-democratic powers',[62] although more comparative and empirical research is needed to prove this hypothesis.

Moreover, it is important to highlight once again, as mentioned in the introductory chapter, that the purpose of this monograph was not to provide an account of the origins or causes of contemporary populism, nor to provide a causal account of the sociocultural, economic and (or) institutional factors that explain why some jurisdictions mentioned in this monograph went in a certain direction and others went in another. There is still plenty of room in the academic literature for more work in that regard – including, possibly, empirical work – particularly in the social sciences. For instance, it would be interesting to conduct an in-depth empirical study to determine whether (and if so, how) different systems of government can affect the relationship between populism and constitutionalism. Indeed, based on the more positive example discussed in chapter four on post-Velvet Revolution Armenia – and, to a lesser extent, the rather mixed case study discussed in chapter six on post-Brexit UK – one may be inclined to think that parliamentary systems of government are more likely to generate (or offer the conditions for) a more positive relationship between populism and constitutionalism than their presidential (or semi-presidential) counterparts (as seen in chapter five on Ecuador, for example, but also in countries such as Türkiye, which transitioned from a parliamentary system to a presidential regime in 2017–2018).[63] In the same vein, a hypothesis could be made that courts in parliamentary systems are more likely to act as successful decelerators and (or) stabilisers than in presidential (or semi-presidential) regimes, although this, of course, remains to be tested empirically.

Similarly, while this book's focus in Part II was on the response of courts against populists in power (rather than in opposition), there is certainly room for more research regarding judicial roles – often under 'militant democracy' grounds – in *preventing* populists from gaining power in the first place. The extraordinary decision, by the Constitutional Court of Romania, to annul the December 2024 presidential elections[64] (due to suspected Russian interference on TikTok and

[61] ibid.

[62] ibid.

[63] Hungary and PiS-governed Poland would, however, provide important contemporary counterexamples. On this, see D Landau, 'Personalism and the Trajectories of Populist Constitutions' (2020) 16 *Annual Review of Law and Social Science* 305.

[64] Constitutional Court of Romania, *Ruling No 32 of 6 December 2024 on the Annulment of the Electoral Process for the Election of the President of Romania* (Official Gazette No 1231, 6 December 2024).

elsewhere), together with the subsequent disqualification in March 2025[65] of the populist frontrunner Călin Georgescu, have sparked controversy in the country.[66] While some have lauded the Court for the cancellation of the election (and the later disqualification of a far-right, pro-Russian candidate viewed as a threat to national security), others have criticised the decisions as 'undemocratic' – including members of Donald Trump's presidential administration, with Elon Musk accusing the Court of 'end[ing] democracy in Romania' and labelling the Court's chief justice as a 'tyrant'.[67] Beyond these sweeping claims, one may indeed criticise the rulings as setting a risky precedent, potentially elevating excluded candidates as 'martyrs', with long-term consequences that remain to be seen.[68]

Finally, it is worth acknowledging that many of the themes and events discussed in the monograph are still ongoing – and are moving fast. While the tectonic plates of contemporary populism keep shifting, I contend that several of the insights contained in this monograph transcend space and time. They are mainly used to illustrate some of the institutional dynamics and the different (potential) institutional (including judicial) responses to contemporary populism, but also to illustrate that populism comes in various shapes and forms – including, in some cases, more democratic forms that are often understudied or overlooked in the academic literature on populism. As we have seen, the three case studies in this monograph are illustrative of the differential impact of the tensions between populism and constitutionalism – showing that the relationship between the two concepts is complex and context-dependent. Similarly, in this monograph I have suggested preliminary lines for a potential distinction between more 'revolutionary' (or 'democratic') forms of populism, on the one hand, and more 'authoritarian' forms of the same phenomenon, on the other; as well as for a potential distinction between democracy-enhancing judicial deceleration (or institutional stabilisation), on the one hand, and anti-democratic judicial obstruction or acceleration, on the other. It is hoped that other scholars will explore these distinctions further, which could shed light on the contemporary populist phenomenon (or perhaps,

[65] The decision by the electoral commission was challenged by Georgescu, but was confirmed by the Constitutional Court on 11 March 2025 in *Ruling No 7 of 11 March on the Appeals filed against the Decision of the Central Electoral Bureau no 18D of 9 March 2025 concerning the rejection of the registration of Mr Călin Georgescu's independent candidacy for the 2025 Romanian Presidential elections, as well as the electoral symbol* (Official Gazette No 229, 14 March 2025). This ruling was grounded in an earlier – and equally controversial – Constitutional Court ruling that had confirmed the ban of another right-wing presidential candidate. See *Ruling No 2 of 5 October 2024 on the Challenge of the Registration of Mrs Diana Iovanovici-Şoşoacă's candidacy in the 2024 elections for President of Romania* (Official Gazette No 1050, 21 October 2024).

[66] See, eg, B Iancu, 'Romanian Militant Democracy and the Time Machine' (*Verfassungsblog*, 13 March 2025) www.verfassungsblog.de/romanian-militant-democracy-and-the-time-machine.

[67] J Henley, 'Romanian presidential hopeful Călin Georgescu faces criminal investigation' (*The Guardian*, 26 February 2025) www.theguardian.com/world/2025/feb/26/romanian-prosecutors-launch-investigation-into-far-right-politician-calin-georgescu.

[68] A similar analysis could potentially be made in relation to the recent disqualification of Marine Le Pen in France, discussed briefly in ch 3, although the circumstances are arguably different.

more accurately, contemporary populist *phenomena*), as well as on the various institutional (including judicial) responses to such phenomena.

In the same vein, the fact – as illustrated in this monograph – that courts behave and react to constitutional impatience in a myriad of ways depending on the context and jurisdiction highlights the potential need for a (new) theory of *when* apex courts will or will not succumb to political pressures. This monograph offers, it is hoped, preliminary avenues for reflection in that regard. Nevertheless, such a new theory, instead of being based upon a theory of populism (and/or a theory of courts), could perhaps be grounded on a theory of constitutionalism, one in which constitutional government is viewed and theorised as a system in which liberal-democratic institutions such as legislatures, electoral commissions, judicial selection commissions or disciplinary boards, among others, are all interconnected to one another in a web.[69] Thinking of constitutional government in these terms would potentially allow us to see more clearly how different configurations of political pressure can sometimes affect the system of constitutional governance in ways that are not always evident or visible from afar. Similarly, focusing on and (or) operating within such a theory of constitutionalism (rather than a theory of populism, for instance) would also allow us to see whether (and if so, to what extent) constitutional impatience can also be associated with other political actors and regimes that are authoritarian and (or) more openly and deliberately autocratic without necessarily being populist. As recent events have shown, such questions are likely to remain relevant in the years ahead – for better or worse.

[69] As we have seen in ch 5 in relation to Ecuador, but also recently in Hungary and Türkiye, executive actors abiding by the logic of 'constitutional impatience' often need assistance from other liberal-democratic institutions to subdue the courts and achieve their objectives.

BIBLIOGRAPHY

Abadjian, V, 'Pashinyan's Gambit or Armenia's Failed Revolution' (2020) 5 *Acta Via Serica* 121.

Abrahamian, L, and Gayane Shagoyan, G. 'Velvet Revolution, Armenian Style' (2018) 26 *Demokratizatsiya* 509.

Abts, K and Rummens, S, 'Populism versus Democracy' (2007) 55 *Political Studies* 405.

Ackerman, B, *Revolutionary Constitutions: Charismatic Leadership and the Rule of Law* (Cambridge, Harvard University Press, 2019).

Adamski, D, 'The Social Contract of Democratic Backsliding in the "New EU" Countries' (2019) 56 *Common Market Law Review* 623.

Aguilar, P, 'Judiciary Involvement in Authoritarian Repression and Transitional Justice: The Spanish Case in Comparative Perspective' (2013) 7 *International Journal of Transitional Justice* 245.

Albert, R, 'Constitutional Amendment and Dismemberment' (2018) 43 *Yale Journal of International Law* 1.

—— *Constitutional Amendments: Making, Breaking, and Changing Constitutions* (Oxford, Oxford University Press, 2019).

Algan, Y, Beasley, E, Cohen, D and Foucault, M, *Les origines du populisme : Enquête sur un schisme politique et social* (Paris, Seuil, 2019).

Alterio, AM, 'Reactive vs Structural Approach: A Public Law Response to Populism' (2019) 8 *Global Constitutionalism* 270.

Anastasiou, M, 'The Spatiotemporality of Nationalist Populism and the Production of Political Subjectivities' (2020) 13 *Subjectivity* 217.

Anselmi, M, *Populism: An Introduction* (Abingdon, Routledge, 2018).

Arat, Y, 'The Decline of Democracy in Turkey: Popular Support, Institutional Decay', unpublished manuscript, Princeton University, March 2015.

Arato, A, 'Political Theology and Populism' in C de la Torre (ed), *The Promise and Perils of Populism: Global Perspectives* (Lexington, University Press of Kentucky, 2014).

—— 'Populism, Constitutional Courts, and Civil Society' in C Landfried (ed), *Judicial Power: How Constitutional Courts Affect Political Transformations* (Cambridge, Cambridge University Press, 2019).

Arato, A and Cohen, JL, *Populism and Civil Society: The Challenge to Constitutional Democracy* (Oxford, Oxford University Press, 2022).

Arendt, H, *On Revolution* (New York, Viking, 1963).

—— *The Human Condition* (Chicago, University of Chicago Press, 1958).

Aslanidis, P,. 'Avoiding Bias in the Study of Populism' (2017) 2 *Chinese Political Science Review* 266.

—— 'Is Populism an Ideology? A Refutation and a New Perspective' (2016) 64 *Political Studies* 88.

Baer, S, 'The Rule of – and not by – Law. On the Need to Explain and Defend Constitutionalism Today' (2019) 71 *Current Legal Problems* 335.

Bajpai, A, '"Matters of the Heart": The Sentimental India Prime Minister on *All India Radio*' in C Kohl, B Christophe, H Liebau and A Saupe (eds), *The Politics of Authenticity and Populist Discourses: Media and Education in Brazil, India and Ukraine* (London, Palgrave McMillan, 2021).

Bakhtin, M, *The Dialogic Imagination: Four Essays* (Austin, University of Texas Press, 1981).

Bali, AU, 'The Perils of Judicial Independence: Constitutional Transition and the Turkish Example' (2012) 52 *Virginia Journal of International Law* 235.

Balkin, JM, 'Constitutional Crisis and Constitutional Rot' (2017) 77 *Maryland Law Review* 147.

—— 'Constitutional Rot' in Cass R Sunstein (ed), *Can It Happen Here? Authoritarianism in America* (New York, Dey St, 2018).
Barak, A, 'A Judge on Judging: The Role of a Supreme Court in a Democracy' (2002) 116 *Harvard Law Review* 19.
Barber, NW, 'Populist Leaders and Political Parties' (2019) 20 *German Law Journal* 129.
Barshack, L, 'Interpretation and the Legal Fabrication of Time' in S Ranchordás and Y Roznai (eds), *Time, Law, and Change: An Interdisciplinary Study* (Oxford, Hart Publishing, 2020).
—— 'Time and the Constitution' (2009) 7 *International Journal of Constitutional Law* 553.
Basabe-Serrano, S, 'Ecuador: Reforma constitucional, nuevos actores políticos y viejas prácticas partidistas' (2009) 29 *Revista de Ciencia Política* 381.
Becker, M, 'Correa, Indigenous Movements, and the Writing of a New Constitution in Ecuador' (2011) 38 *Latin American Perspectives* 47.
Bellamy, R, *Political Constitutionalism: A Republican Defence of the Constitutionality of Democracy* (Cambridge, Cambridge University Press, 2007).
—— 'Political Constitutionalism and Populism' (2023) 50 *Journal of Law and Society* S7.
Berlin, I, Hofstadter, R, McRae, D et al, 'To Define Populism' (1968) 3 *Government and Opposition* 137.
Berman, S, 'The Pipe Dream of Undemocratic Liberalism' (2017) 28 *Democracy* 29.
Bermeo, N, 'On Democratic Backsliding' (2016) 27 *Journal of Democracy* 5.
Betz, H-G, 'Conditions Favoring the Success and Failure of Radical Right-Wing Populist Parties in Contemporary Democracies' in Y Mény and Y Surel (eds), *Democracies and the Populist Challenge* (London, Palgrave MacMillan, 2002).
Bingham, LJ, 'The Rule of Law', Sixth David Williams Lecture, House of Lords (UK, 16 November 2006).
Blau, JL (ed), *Social Theories of Jacksonian Democracy: Representative Writings of the Period 1825–1850* (New York, Hafner, 1947).
Blokker, P, 'Introduction: Constitutional Challenges, Reform, and Acceleration' in P Blokker (ed), *Constitutional Acceleration within the European Union and Beyond* (Abingdon, Routledge, 2018).
—— 'Populism as a Constitutional Project' (2019) 17 *International Journal of Constitutional Law* 535.
—— 'Populist Constitutionalism' in C de la Torre (ed), *Routledge Handbook of Global Populism* (Abingdon, Routledge, 2019).
Bødker, H and Anderson, C, 'Populist Time: Mediating Immediacy and Delay in Liberal Democracy' (2019) 13 *International Journal of Communication* 5948.
Bogdanor, V, 'On "Popular Sovereignty"' in DJ Galligan (ed), *Constitution in Crisis: The New Putney Debates* (London, I.B. Tauris, 2017) 39.
Bogdanor, V, *Power and the People: A Guide to Constitutional Reform* (London, Victor Gollancz, 1997).
Bomhoff, J, 'Back to *The Bremen* (1972): Forum Selection and Worldmaking' (2018) LSE Law, Society and Economy Working Papers (6/2018).
—— 'Constitutionalism and Mobility: Expulsion and Escape among Partial Constitutional Orders' in J Bomhoff, D Dyzenhaus and T Poole (eds), *The Double Facing Constitution* (Cambridge, Cambridge University Press, 2020).
—— 'Immanence and Irreconcilability: On the Character of Public Law as Political Jurisprudence' in M Wilkinson and M Dowdle (eds), *Questioning the Foundations of Public Law* (Oxford, Hart Publishing, 2018).
Bottoms, AE, 'The Philosophy and Politics of Punishment and Sentencing' in C Clarkson and R Morgan (eds), *The Politics of Sentencing Reform* (Oxford, Clarendon Press, 1995).
Bourdieu, P, *Outline of a Theory of Practice* (trans R Nice) (Cambridge, Cambridge University Press, 1977).
Broers, L and Ohanyan, A (eds), *Armenia's Velvet Revolution: Authoritarian Decline and Civil Resistance in a Multipolar World* (London, I.B. Tauris, 2021).
Broers, L, 'Introduction: An Unlikely Transition?' in L Broers and A Ohanyan (eds), *Armenia's Velvet Revolution: Authoritarian Decline and Civil Resistance in a Multipolar World* (London, I.B. Tauris, 2021).
Brown Tindall, G (ed), *A Populist Reader, Selections from the Works of American Populist Leaders* (New York, Harper & Row, 1966).

Bugarič, B and Ginsburg, T, 'The Assault on Postcommunist Courts' (2016) 27 *Journal of Democracy* 69.

Bugarič, B, 'Can Law Protect Democracy? Legal Institutions as "Speed Bumps"' (2019) 11 *Hague Journal on the Rule of Law* 447.

—— 'Central Europe's Descent into Autocracy: A Constitutional Analysis of Authoritarian Populism' (2019) 17 *International Journal of Constitutional Law* 597.

—— 'Could Populism Be Good for Constitutional Democracy?' (2019) 15 *Annual Review of Law and Social Science* 41.

—— 'The Two Faces of Populism: Between Authoritarian and Democratic Populism' (2019) 20 *German Law Journal* 390.

Cahill, M, 'The Reign of Popular Sovereignty in Ireland: An Antidote to Populism?' in M Cahill, C Ó Cinnéide, S Ó Conaill and C O'Mahony (eds), *Constitutional Change and Popular Sovereignty: Populism, Politics and the Law in Ireland* (Abingdon, Routledge, 2021).

Canovan, M, 'Populism for Political Theorists?' (2004) 9 *Journal of Political Ideologies* 241.

—— *Populism* (London, Junction Books, 1981).

—— *The People* (Cambridge, Polity, 2005).

—— 'Trust the People! Populism and the Two Faces of Democracy' (1999) 47 *Political Studies* 1.

Carreira da Silva, F and Vieira, MB, 'Populism and the Politics of Redemption' (2018) 149 *Thesis Eleven* 10.

Castillo-Ortiz, P and Roznai, Y, 'The Democratic Self-Defence of Constitutional Courts' (2024) 18 *ICL Journal: Vienna Journal on International Constitutional Law* 1.

Castillo-Ortiz, P, 'The Illiberal Abuse of Constitutional Courts in Europe' (2019) 15 *European Constitutional Law Review* 48.

Castro-Montero, JL and van Dijck, G, 'Judicial Politics in Unconsolidated Democracies: An Empirical Analysis of the Ecuadorian Constitutional Court (2008–2016)' (2017) 38 *Justice System Journal* 380.

Christodoulidis, E, 'The Aporia of Sovereignty: On the Representation of the People in Constitutional Discourse' (2001) 12 *The King's College Law Journal* 111.

Christofis, N, 'Erdoğan's "New" Turkey' in N Christofis (ed), *Erdoğan's 'New' Turkey: Attempted Coup d'état and the Acceleration of Political Crisis* (Abingdon, Routledge, 2019).

Colliot-Thélène, C, 'Quel est le peuple du populisme?' in C Colliot-Thélène and F Guénard (eds), *Peuples et populisme* (Paris, Presses universitaires de France, 2014).

Colón-Ríos, J, *Weak Constitutionalism: Democratic Legitimacy and the Question of Constituent Power* (Abingdon, Routledge, 2012).

Conaghan, CM, 'Delegative Democracy Revisited: Ecuador Under Correa' (2016) 27 *Journal of Democracy* 109.

—— 'Ecuador: Correa's Plebiscitary Presidency' (2008) 19 *Journal of Democracy* 46.

Conaghan, CM and de la Torre, C, 'The Permanent Campaign of Rafael Correa: Making Ecuador's Plebiscitary Democracy' (2008) 13 *Press/Politics* 267.

Cooper, L, *Authoritarian Contagion: The Global Threat to Democracy* (Bristol, Bristol University Press, 2021).

Corrales, J, 'The Authoritarian Resurgence: Autocratic Legalism in Venezuela' (2015) 26 *Journal of Democracy* 37.

Corrias, L and Francot, L (eds), *Temporal Boundaries of Law and Politics: Time Out of Joint* (Abingdon, Routledge, 2018).

Corrias, L, 'Populism in a Constitutional Key: Constituent Power, Popular Sovereignty and Constitutional Identity' (2016) 12 *European Constitutional Law Review* 6.

Craig, P, 'The Supreme Court, Prorogation and Constitutional Principle' (2020) 2 *Public Law* 248.

Crick, B, *Democracy: A Very Short Introduction* (Oxford, Oxford University Press, 2002).

Dagger, R, 'Understanding the General Will' (1981) 34 *The Western Political Quarterly* 359.

Daly, E, 'Constitutionalism and Crisis Narratives in Post-Brexit Politics' (2020) 68 *Political Studies* 895.

Daly, TG, 'Democratic Decay: Conceptualising an Emerging Research Field' (2019) 11 *Hague Journal on the Rule of Law* 9.

—— 'The Alchemists: Courts as Democracy-Builders in Contemporary Thought' (2017) 6 *Global Constitutionalism* 101.

—— *The Alchemists: Questioning Our Faith in Courts as Democracy-Builders* (Cambridge, Cambridge University Press, 2017).
Dann, P, 'Southern Turn, Northern Implications: Rethinking the Meaning of Colonial Legacies for Comparative Constitutional Studies' (2023) 1 *Comparative Constitutional Studies* 174.
—— 'Temporality and Liberal Constitutionalism' in TA Börzel, J Gerschewski and M Zürn (eds), *The Liberal Script at the Beginning of the 21st Century* (Oxford, Oxford University Press, 2024).
Desrues, T and Gobe, E, 'Kais Saied's Governance: The Tunisian President's Drift from Inclusive Populist Constitutionalism to "Caesarism"' (2025) *Journal of North African Studies* (advance access).
de la Torre, C,. 'Global Populism: Histories, Trajectories, Problems and Challenges' in C de la Torre (ed), *Routledge Handbook of Global Populism* (Abingdon, Routledge, 2019).
—— 'Latin America's Authoritarian Drift: Technocratic Populism in Ecuador' (2013) 24 *Journal of Democracy* 33.
—— 'Latin America's Shifting Politics: Ecuador After Correa' (2018) 29 *Democracy* 77.
—— 'The People, Democracy, and Authoritarianism in Rafael Correa's Ecuador' (2014) 21(4) *Constellations* 457.
—— *Populist Seduction in Latin America*, 2nd edn (Athens, Ohio University Press, 2010).
de Malberg, C, *Considérations théoriques sur la question de la combinaison du référendum avec le parlementarisme* (Paris, Marcel Giard, 1931).
de Sá e Silva, F, 'From Car Wash to Bolsonaro: Law and Lawyers in Brazil's Illiberal Turn (2014–2018)' (2020) 47 *Journal of Law and Society* S90.
de Tocqueville, A, *De la Démocratie en Amérique*, vol 1 (Paris, M Lévy, 1864 [1835]).
de Wilde, M, 'Uncertain Futures and the Problem of Constraining Emergency Powers: Temporal Dimensions of Carl Schmitt's Theory of the State of Exception' in L Corrias and L Francot (eds), *Temporal Boundaries of Law and Politics: Time Out of Joint* (Abingdon, Routledge, 2018).
Debreczeni, J, *Arcmás* (Budapest, Noran-Libro Kiadó, 2009).
Deighton, A, 'Referendums for EU Politics?' in DJ Galligan (ed), *Constitution in Crisis: The New Putney Debates* (London, I.B. Tauris, 2017).
Delaney, EF, 'Brexit Optimism and British Constitutional Renewal' in MA Graber, S Levinson and M Tushnet (eds), *Constitutional Democracy in Crisis?* (Oxford, Oxford University Press, 2018).
Derrida, J, 'Declarations of Independence' in J Derrida and E Rosenberg (eds), *Negotiations: Interventions and Interviews, 1971–2001* (Redwood, Stanford University Press, 2001).
Dezalay, Y and Garth, BG, *Dealing in Virtue: International Commercial Arbitration and the Construction of a Transnational Legal Order* (Chicago, University of Chicago Press, 1996).
Dicey, AV, 'Ought the Referendum to Be Introduced into England?' (1890) 57 *Contemporary Review* 489.
—— *Introduction to the Law of the Constitution*, 8th edn (London, Macmillan, 1915 [1885]).
Diehl, P, 'Twisting Representation' in C de la Torre (ed), *Routledge Handbook of Global Populism* (Abingdon, Routledge, 2019).
Dixon, R and Landau, D, 'Transnational Constitutionalism and a Limited Doctrine of Unconstitutional Constitutional Amendment' (2015) 13 *International Journal of Constitutional Law* 606.
Dixon, R, 'Constitutional Rights as Bribes' (2018) 50 *Connecticut Law Review* 767.
—— *Responsive Judicial Review: Democracy and Disfunction in the Modern Age* (Oxford, Oxford University Press, 2023).
Dos Santos, JGB and Gallego, ES, 'Fighting Corruption, Dismantling Democracy: Antagonism, Communication and the Political Use of Lava Jato in Brazil' in S Botero, DM Brinks and EA Gonzalez-Ocantos (eds), *The Limits of Judicialization: From Progress to Backlash in Latin America* (Cambridge, Cambridge University Press, 2022).
Draï, R, 'Éloge de la patience juridique' in P Gérard, F Ost and M van de Kerchove (eds), *L'accélération du temps juridique* (Bruxelles, Presses universitaires Saint-Louis Bruxelles, 2000).
Driesen, DM, 'The Unitary Executive Theory in Comparative Context' (2021) 72 *Hastings Law Journal* 1.
Dupré, C, *The Age of Dignity: Human Rights and Constitutionalism in Europe* (Oxford, Hart Publishing, 2015).
Dworkin, R, *Law's Empire* (Cambridge, Harvard University Press, 1986).

Eatwell, R and Goodwin, M, *National Populism: The Revolt Against Liberal Democracy* (Elmwood, Pelican, 2018).

Eichengreen, B, *The Populist Temptation: Economic Grievance and Political Reaction in the Modern Era* (Oxford, Oxford University Press, 2018).

Fasone, C, 'Catalysing Marginalisation? The Effect of Populist Governments on the Legislative and Scrutiny Functions of the Italian Parliament' (2021) 74 *Parliamentary Affairs* 802.

Feldman, DL and Albasic, H. 'The Remarkable "Velvet Revolution": Armenia's Experiment Against Government Corruption' (2019) 21 *Public Integrity* 420.

Feldman, LC, 'Lockean Prerogative: Productive Tensions' in C Fatovic and BA Kleineman, *Extra-Legal Power and Legitimacy: Perspectives on Prerogative* (Oxford, Oxford University Press, 2013).

Fieschi, C, *Populocracy: The Tyranny of Authenticity and the Rise of Populism* (New York, Columbia University Press, 2019).

Finchelstein, F, 'Fascism and Populism' in C de la Torre (ed), *Routledge Handbook of Global Populism* (Abingdon, Routledge, 2019).

—— *From Fascism to Populism in History* (Oakland, University of California Press, 2019).

Fiss, OM, 'The Right Degree of Independence' in IP Stotzky (ed), *Transition to Democracy in Latin America: The Role of the Judiciary* (Boulder, Westview, 1993).

Fontana, D, 'Unbundling Populism' (2018) 65 *UCLA Law Review* 1482.

Francot, L, 'Suspended in Gaffa: Legal Slowness in the Acceleration of Society' in L Francot and L Corrias (eds), *Temporal Boundaries of Law and Politics: Time Out of Joint* (Abingdon, Routledge, 2018).

Frank, J, *Constituent Moments: Enacting the People in Postrevolutionary America* (Durham, Duke University Press, 2020).

Frank, T, *People Without Power: The War on Populism and the Fight for Democracy* (London, Scribe, 2020).

Freeden, M, 'After the Brexit Referendum: Revisiting Populism as an Ideology' (2017) 22 *Journal of Politicial Ideologies* 1.

—— 'Is Nationalism a Distinct Ideology?' (1998) 46 *Political Studies* 748.

Fukuyama, F, 'The End of History?' (1989) 16 *The National Interest* (Summer 1989).

Gachet, I, Grijalva, DF, Ponce, PA and Rodríguez, D, 'Vertical and Horizontal Inequality in Ecuador: The Lack of Sustainability' (2019) 145 *Social Indicators Research* 861.

Galligan, DJ, 'Introduction' in DJ Galligan (ed), *Constitution in Crisis: The New Putney Debates* (London, I.B. Tauris, 2017).

Galston, WA, *Anti-Pluralism: The Populist Threat to Liberal Democracy* (New Haven, Yale University Press, 2018).

Garapon, A, 'Judging the Past: Three Ways of Understanding Time' in L Corrias and L Francot (eds), *Temporal Boundaries of Law and Politics: Time Out of Joint* (Abingdon, Routledge, 2018).

Gardbaum, S, 'Are Strong Constitutional Courts Always a Good Thing for New Democracies?' (2015) 53 *Columbia Journal of Transnational Law* 285.

Gargarella, R, 'In Search of Democratic Justice – What Courts Should Not Do: Argentina, 1983–2002' in S Gloppen, R Gargarella and E Skaar (eds), *Democratization and the Judiciary: The Accountability Function of Courts in New Democracies* (London, Frank Cass, 2004).

Gatmaytan, D, 'The Case of the Philippine Judiciary – Guardian of Democracy or Enabler of Populism?' in S Hardt, AW Heringa and H-T Nguyen (eds), *Populism and Democracy* (The Hague, Eleven International Publishing, 2020).

Gerbaudo, P, 'Social Media and Populism: An Elective Affinity?' (2018) 40 *Media, Culture and Society* 745.

Giannoulopoulos, D and McDermott, Y (eds), *Judicial Independence Under Threat* (Oxford, Oxford University Press, 2022).

Ginsburg, T and Huq, AH, *How to Save a Constitutional Democracy* (Chicago, University of Chicago Press, 2018).

Ginsburg, T, Huq, AH and Versteeg, M. 'The Coming Demise of Liberal Constitutionalism?' (2018) 65 *University of Chicago Law Review* 239.

Ginsburg, T, *Judicial Review in New Democracies: Constitutional Courts in Asian Cases* (Cambridge, Cambridge University Press, 2003).
—— 'The Jurisprudence of Anti-Erosion' (2018) 66 *Duke Law Review* 823.
Girard, R, 'Accountability, Populism and Expertise: The United Kingdom Government's Response to Covid-19' (2021) *Public Law* 707.
—— 'Populism, "the People" and Popular Sovereignty' in M Cahill, C Ó Cinnéide, S Ó Conaill and C O'Mahony (eds), *Constitutional Change and Popular Sovereignty: Populism, Politics and the Law in Ireland* (Abingdon, Routledge, 2021).
—— 'Populism, Executive Power and "Constitutional Impatience": Courts as Institutional Stabilisers in the United Kingdom' (2022) 8 *Constitutional Studies* 35.
—— 'Réflexions sur la codification du droit des obligations au Québec' (2012) *Cahiers du PEQ* (student edition).
Goldstein, J, 'The Opinion-Writing Function of the Judiciary of Latin American Governments in Transition to Democracy: *Martinez v. Provincia de Mendoza*' in IP Stotzky (ed), *Transition to Democracy in Latin America: The Role of the Judiciary* (Boulder, Westview, 1993).
Grattan, L, 'Pierre Bourdieu and Populism: The Everyday Politics of Outrageous Resistance' (2012) 21 *The Good Society* 194.
—— *Populism's Power: Radical Grassroots Democracy in America* (Oxford, Oxford University Press, 2016).
Griffith, JAG, *The Politics of the Judiciary*, 5th edn (London, Fontana Press, 1997).
Grigoryan, A, 'Armenia's Path to Democratization by Recursive Mass Protests' (2019) 7 *Caucasus Survey* 157.
Grijalva, A, 'La consulta: Una violación infraganti de la Constitución' (2011), Repositorio Facultad Latinoamericana de Ciencias Sociales.
Guénard, F, 'Existe-t-il encore un peuple?' in C Colliot-Thélène and F Guénard (eds), *Peuples et populismes* (Paris, Presses universitaires de France, 2014).
Gyorfi, T, *Against the New Constitutionalism* (Cheltenham, Edward Elgar, 2016).
Habermas, J, 'Constitutional Democracy: A Paradoxical Union of Contradictory Principles?' (2001) 29 *Political Theory* 766.
—— 'Popular Sovereignty as Procedure' in J Habermas, *Between Facts and Norms: Contributions to a Discourse Theory of Law and Democracy* (trans W Rehg) (Cambridge, Polity, 1996).
Hailbronner, M, 'Introduction: Defending "Democratic Populism"?' (2019) 17 *International Journal of Constitutional Law* 681.
Hall, S, *The Hard Road to Renewal: Thatcherism and the Crisis of the Left* (London, Verso, 1988).
Halmai, G, 'A Coup Against Constitutional Democracy: The Case of Hungary' in MA Graber, S Levinson and M Tushnet (eds), *Constitutional Democracy in Crisis?* (Oxford, Oxford University Press, 2018).
Halmai, G, 'Is There Such Thing As "Populist Constitutionalism"? The Case of Hungary' (2018) 11 *Fudan Journal of Humanities and Social Sciences* 323.
—— 'Populism, Authoritarianism and Constitutionalism' (2019) 20 *German Law Journal* 296.
Hamilton, A [Publius]. 'Federalist No 70: The Executive Department Further Considered' (15 March 1788).
Hamilton, A, Jay J and Madison, J, *The Federalist: A Commentary on the Constitution of the United States* (London, T. Fisher Unwin, 1886 [1788]).
Harel, A and Kolt, N, 'Populist Rhetoric, False Mirroring, and the Courts' (2020) 18 *International Journal of Constitutional Law* 746.
Helmke, G, *Courts under Constraints: Judges, Generals, and Presidents in Argentina* (Cambridge, Cambridge University Press, 2012).
Hermet, G, *Les Populismes dans le monde: Une histoire sociologique – XIXe-XXe siècle* (Paris, Fayard, 2001).
Heydarian, RJ, 'Penal Populism in Emerging Markets: Human Rights and Democracy in the Age of Strongmen' in GL Neuman, *Human Rights in a Time of Populism: Challenges and Responses* (Cambridge, Cambridge University Press, 2020).

Hilbink, L, 'Judicial Populism: A Conceptual and Normative Inquiry' (2024) *Law & Social Inquiry* 1

Hira, A, *The Great Disruption: Understanding the Populist Forces Behind Trump, Brexit, and Le Pen* (Lausanne, Peter Lang, 2019).

Hirschl, R, 'The Question of Case Selection in Comparative Constitutional Law' (2005) 53 *American Journal of Comparative Law* 125.

Hirschl, R and Shachar, A, 'Spatial Statism' (2019) 17 *International Journal of Constitutional Law* 387.

Holmes, S, *Passions and Constraint: On the Theory of Liberal Democracy* (Chicago, University of Chicago Press, 1995).

Houle, C and Kenny, PD, 'The Political and Economic Consequences of Populist Rule in Latin America' (2018) 53 *Government and Opposition* 256.

Howse, R, 'Epilogue: In Defense of Disruptive Democracy – A Critique of Anti-Populism' (2019) 17 *International Journal of Constitutional Law* 641.

Hume, D, 'Essay IV: Of the First Principles of Government' in *Essays, Moral, Political and Literary (Part I)* (1777 [1741]).

Huntington, SP, *The Third Wave: Democratization in the Late Twentieth Century* (Norma, University of Oklahoma Press, 1991).

Huq, A, 'Democratic Erosion and the Courts: Comparative Perspectives' (2018) 93 *NYU Law Review* 21.

Huq, A and Ginsburg, T, 'Democracy without Democrats' (2020) 6 *Constitutional Studies* 165.

—— 'How to Lose a Constitutional Democracy' (2018) 65 *UCLA Law Review* 95.

Ionescu, G and Gellner, E (eds), *Populism: Its Meaning and National Characteristics* (London, Macmillan, 1969).

Ishkanian, A, 'Armenia's Unfinished Revolution' (2018) 117 *Current History* 271.

—— 'The Velvet Revolution in Armenia: How to Lose Power in Two Weeks' (2018) 26 *Demokratizatsiya* 465.

Issacharoff, S, 'Constitutional Courts and Democratic Hedging' (2011) 99 *Georgetown Law Journal* 961.

—— 'Democracy's Deficits' (2018) 85 *University of Chicago Law Review* 485.

—— *Democracy Unmoored: Populism and the Corruption of Popular Sovereignty* (Oxford, Oxford University Press, 2023).

—— 'The Corruption of Popular Sovereignty' (2020) 18 *International Journal of Constitutional Law* 1109.

—— *Fragile Democracies: Contested Power in the Era of Constitutional Courts* (Cambridge, Cambridge University Press, 2015).

Jackson, R, *Sovereignty: The Evolution of an Idea* (Cambridge, Polity, 2013).

Jacobsohn, GJ, *Constitutional Identity* (Cambridge, Harvard University Press, 2010).

Jansen, RS, 'Populist Mobilization: A New Theoretical Approach to Populism' (2011) 29 *Sociological Theory* 75.

Jaume, L, 'Le nom du peuple dans la révolution française et sa représentation politique' (2014) 57 *Cahiers du CEVIPOF* 43.

Johnson, (Alyn) J, 'The Case For a Canadian Nondelegation Doctrine' (2019) 52 *UBC Law Review* 817.

Johnson, DA, 'In Defense of Democratic Populism' in GL Neuman (ed), *Human Rights in a Time of Populism: Challenges and Responses* (Cambridge, Cambridge University Press, 2020).

Kahn, PW, 'Independence and Responsibility in the Judicial Role' in IP Stotzky (ed), *Transition to Democracy in Latin America: The Role of the Judiciary* (Boulder, Westview, 1993).

—— *The Cultural Study of Law: Reconstructing Legal Scholarship* (Chicago, University of Chicago Press, 1999).

Kantorowicz, EH, *The King's Two Bodies: A Study of in Medieval Political Theology* (Princeton, Princeton University Press, 1997 [1957]).

Katz, AS, 'Taming the Prince: Bringing Presidential Emergency Powers Under Law in Colombia' (2020) 18 *International Journal of Constitutional Law* 1201.

Kaufmann, E, *White Shift: Populism, Immigration, and the Future of White Majorities* (London, Penguin, 2019).

Kay, P, 'Is Representative Democracy Ripe for Review and Modification in Favour of More Direct Democracy?' in DJ Galligan (ed), *Constitution in Crisis: The New Putney Debates* (London, I.B. Tauris, 2017).
Kazin, M, *The Populist Persuasion: An American History* (Ithaca, Cornell University Press, 1998).
Keay, J, 'Making the "Velvet Revolution" Work' (2019) 33 *Global Finance* 144.
Kenny, M, 'Back to the Populist Future? Understanding Nostalgia in Contemporary Political Discourse' (2017) 22 *Journal of Political Ideologies* 256.
Khaitan, T, 'Executive Aggrandizement in Established Democracies: A Crisis of Liberal Democratic Constitutionalism' (2019) 17 *International Journal of Constitutional Law* 342.
—— 'Guarantor Institutions' 16 *Asian Journal of Comparative Law* S40.
—— 'Killing a Constitution with a Thousand Cuts: Executive Aggrandizement and Party-State Fusion in India' (2020) 14 *Law & Ethics of Human Rights* 49.
Knights, M, 'Democracy Is About More Than Voting: Pre-Modern Petitioning and Its Implications for Today' in DJ Galligan (ed), *Constitution in Crisis: The New Putney Debates* (London, I.B. Tauris, 2017).
Koch, CM, 'Varieties of Populism and the Challenges to Global Constitutionalism: Dangers, Promises and Implications' (2021) 10 *Global Constitutionalism* 400.
Kosař, D and Šipulová, K, 'Comparative Court-Packing' (2023) 21 *International Journal of Constitutional Law* 80.
Kramer, LD, *The People Themselves: Popular Constitutionalism and Judicial Review* (Oxford, Oxford University Press, 2004).
Kribbe, H, *The Strongmen: European Encounters with Sovereign Power* (Newcastle, Agenda, 2020).
Krygier, M, 'The Challenge of Institutionalisation: Post-Communist "Transitions", Populism, and the Rule of Law' (2019) 15 *European Constitutional Law Review* 544.
Kumm, M, 'The Best of Times and the Worst of Times' in P Dobner and M Loughlin (eds), *The Twilight of Constitutionalism?* (Oxford, Oxford University Press, 2010).
Kuo, M-S, 'Against Instantaneous Democracy' (2019) 17 *International Journal of Constitutional Law* 554.
—— 'Authenticity: The Ultimate Challenge in the Quest for Lasting Constitutional Legitimacy' (2021) 41 *Oxford Journal of Legal Studies* 265.
Kyritsis, D, 'Constitutional Review in Representative Democracy' (2012) 32 *Oxford Journal of Legal Studies* 1.
Lacey, N, *The Prisoners' Dilemma: Political Economy and Punishment in Contemporary Democracies* (Cambridge, Cambridge University Press, 2011).
—— 'Populism and the Rule of Law' (2019) 15 *Annual Review of Law and Social Science* 79.
Laclau, E, 'Populism: What's in a Name?' in F Panizza (ed), *Populism and the Mirror of Democracy* (London, Verso, 2005).
—— *On Populist Reason* (London, Verso, 2005).
Lambert, É, *Le gouvernement des juges et la lutte contre la législation sociale aux États-Unis : L'expérience américaine du contrôle judiciaire de la constitutionnalité des lois* (Paris, Marcel Giard, 1921).
Landau, D and Dixon, R, 'Abusive Judicial Review: Courts Against Democracy' (2020) 53 *University of California, Davis Law Review* 1313.
—— 'Tiered Constitutional Change' (2018) 86 *George Washington Law Review* 438.
Landau, D, 'A Dynamic Theory of Judicial Role' (2014) 55 *Boston College Law Review* 1501.
—— 'Abusive Constitutionalism' (2013) 47 *University of California Davis Law Review* 189.
—— 'Personalism and the Trajectories of Populist Constitutions' (2020) 16 *Annual Review of Law and Social Science* 293.
—— 'Populist Constitutions' (2018) 85 *University of Chicago Law Review* 521.
Landfried, C, 'Introduction' in C Landfried (ed), *Judicial Power: How Constitutional Courts Affect Political Transformations* (Cambridge, Cambridge University Press, 2019)
Langford, P, 'The Populist Disruption: Juridico-Political Reflections on Democracy, Law and Rights' (2018) 5 *Soft Power Revista euro-americana de teoría e historia de la política y del derecho* 79.

Lanskoy, M and E Suthers, E, 'Armenia's Velvet Revolution' (2019) 30 *Journal of Democracy* 85.
Lasch, C, *The Revolt of the Elites and the Betrayal of Democracy* (New York, Norton & Company 1995).
Latour, B, *The Making of Law: An Ethnography of the Conseil d'Etat* (trans M Brilman and A Pottage) (Cambridge, Polity, 2013).
Lazar, NC, 'Constitutional Preambles and the Uncertain Future' in L Corrias and L Francot (eds), *Temporal Boundaries of Law and Politics: Time Out of Joint* (Abingdon, Routledge, 2018).
—— *Out of Joint: Power, Crisis, and the Rhetoric of Time* (New Haven, Yale University Press, 2019).
Le Pen, J-M, 'Pour une vraie révolution française' (26 September 1985) *National Hebdo*.
Lefort, C, 'Le Pouvoir' in C Lefort, *Le Temps présent. Écrits (1945–2005)* (Paris, Belin, 2007 [2000]).
—— *Democracy and Political Theory* (Cambridge, Polity, 1988).
—— *The Political Forms of Modern Society: Bureaucracy, Democracy, Totalitarianism* (Cambridge, Polity, 1986).
Levitsky, S and Loxton, J, 'Populism and Competitive Authoritarianism in the Andes' (2013) 20 *Democratization* 107.
Levitsky, S and Way, L. *Competitive Authoritarianism: Hybrid Regimes After the Cold War* (Cambridge, Cambridge University Press, 2010).
Lindahl, H, 'Constituent Power and Reflexive Identity: Towards an Ontology of Collective Selfhood' in M Loughlin and N Walker (eds), *The Paradox of Constitutionalism: Constituent Power and Constitutional Form* (Oxford, Oxford University Press, 2008).
Lindseth, PL, 'The Paradox of Parliamentary Supremacy: Delegation, Democracy, and Dictatorship in Germany and France, 1920s-1950s' (2004) 113 *Yale Law Journal* 1341.
Locke, J, *Second Treatise of Government* in *Second Treatise of Government* and *A Letter Concerning Toleration* (Oxford University Press, 2016 [1689]).
Loughlin, M and Tierney, S. 'The Shibboleth of Sovereignty' (2018) 81 *Modern Law Review* 989.
Loughlin, M, 'A Note on Craig on Miller; Cherry' (2020) *Public Law* 278.
—— 'The Concept of Constituent Power' (2014) 13 *European Journal of Political Theory* 218.
—— 'The Constitutional Imagination' (2015) 78 *Modern Law Review* 1.
—— 'The Contemporary Crisis of Constitutional Democracy' (2019) 39 *Oxford Journal of Legal Studies* 435.
—— *Foundations of Public Law* (Oxford, Oxford University Press, 2010).
—— *The Idea of Public Law* (Oxford, Oxford University Press, 2003).
Loyseau, C, *Traicté des Seigneuries* (Paris, Abel l'Angelier, 1614).
Ludis, JB, *The Populist Explosion: How the Great Recession Transformed American and European Politics* (New York, Columbia Global Reports, 2016).
Machiavelli, N, *Discourses on Livy* (trans NH Thomson [1883]) (1532 [c. 1517]).
Maddox, G, 'A Note on the Meaning of "Constitution"' (1982) 76 *American Political Science Review* 805.
Madison, J [Publius], 'Federalist No 10: The Utility of the Union as a Safeguard Against Domestic Faction and Insurrection' (22 November 1787).
—— 'Federalist No 14: Objections to the Proposed Constitution from Extent of Territory Answered' (30 November 1787).
Mansbridge, J and Macedo, S, 'Populism and Democratic Theory' (2019) 15 *Annual Review of Law and Social Science* 59.
Marshall, G, 'The Constitution: Its Theory and Interpretation' in V Bogdanor (ed), *The British Constitution and the Twentieth Century* (Oxford, Oxford University Press, 2003).
Martínez Dalmau, R, 'Democratic Constitutionalism and Constitutional Innovation in Ecuador: The 2008 Constitution' (2016) 43 *Latin American Perspectives* 158.
Martinico, G, *Filtering Populist Claims to Fight Populism: The Italian Case in a Comparative Perspective* (Cambridge, Cambridge University Press, 2022).
Masala, A, 'Populism as the Crisis of Political Trust' in A Fabris (ed), *Trust: A Philosophical Approach* (Cham, Springer, 2020).
Mauss, M, *La Nation* (Paris, Presses universitaires de France, 1920).

Mazmanyan, A, 'Constitutional Choices After a (Democratic) Revolution: Lessons from Armenia, and elsewhere' (paper presented at the 'Building Institutional Resilience' international workshop, Malyi Center, University of Chicago Law School, 26-27 September 2024; unpublished manuscript; on file with author).

—— 'Judicialization of Politics: The Post-Soviet Way' (2015) 13 *International Journal of Constitutional Law* 200.

McIlwain, CH, *Constitutionalism: Ancient and Modern* (Ithaca, Cornell University Press, 1940).

—— *Constitutionalism: Ancient and Modern,* 2nd edN (Ithaca, Cornell University Press, 1958).

Mégret, F, 'Human Rights Populism' (2022) 13 *Humanity* 240.

Mélenchon, J-L, *L'Ère du peuple* (Paris, Pluriel, 2017).

—— *Qu'ils s'en aillent tous! Vite, la révolution citoyenne* (Paris, Flammarion, 2010).

Mény, Y and Surel, Y, *Par le peuple, pour le peuple : Le populisme et les démocraties* (Paris, Fayard, 2000).

—— 'The Constitutive Ambiguity of Populism' in Y Mény and Y Surel (eds), *Democracies and the Populist Challenge* (London, Palgrave MacMillan, 2002).

Merry, SE, 'Measuring the World: Indicators, Human Rights, and Global Governance' (2011) 52(Suppl 3) *Current Anthropology* S83.

Mészáros, G, 'Caught in an Authoritarian Trap of Its Own Making? Brazil's "Lava Jato" Anti-Corruption Investigation and the Politics of Prosecutorial Overreach' (2020) 47 *Journal of Law and Society* S54.

Michelet, J, *Le Peuple* (Flammarion, 1974 [1846]).

Mietzer, M, 'Movement Leaders, Oligarchs, Technocrats and Autocratic Mavericks: Populists in Contemporary Asia' in C de la Torre (ed), *Routledge Handbook of Global Populism* (Abingdon, Routledge, 2019).

Moffitt, B and Tormey, S, 'Rethinking Populism: Politics, Mediatisation and Political Style' (2014) 62 *Political Studies* 381.

Moffitt, B, *Populism* (Cambridge, Polity, 2020).

Montesquieu, *De l'Esprit des lois* (Paris, Barillot, 1748).

Morgan, ES, *Inventing the People: The Rise of Popular Sovereignty in England and America* (New York, Norton, 1989).

Mouffe, C, *For a Left Populism* (Verso, 2018).

—— 'The "End of Politics" and the Challenge of Right-Wing Populism' in F Panizza (ed), *Populism and the Mirror of Democracy* (London, Verso, 2005).

Mounk, Y, and Foa, RS, 'The Signs of Deconsolidation' (2017) 28 *Journal of Democracy* 5.

Mounk, Y, *The People vs. Democracy: Why Our Freedom Is in Danger and How to Save it* (Cambridge, Harvard University Press, 2018).

Moustafa, T, 'Law and Courts in Authoritarian Regimes' (2014) 10 *Annual Review of Law and Social Science* 281.

Mudde, C and Rovira Kaltwasser, C 'Exclusionary vs. Inclusionary Populism: Comparing Contemporary Europe and Latin America' (2013) 48 *Government and Opposition* 147.

—— 'Populism and (Liberal) Democracy: A Framework for Analysis' in C Mudde and C Rovira Kaltwasser (eds), *Populism in Europe and the Americas: Threat or Corrective for Democracy?* (Cambridge, Cambridge University Press, 2012).

—— *Populism: A Very Short Introduction* (Oxford, Oxford University Press, 2017).

Mudde, C, 'The Populist Zeitgeist' (2004) 39 *Government and Opposition* 541.

Müller, J-W, '"Enemies of the People": Populism's Threat to Independent Judiciaries' in D Giannoulopoulos and Y McDermott (eds), *Judicial Independence Under Threat* (Oxford, Oxford University Press, 2022).

—— 'Populism and Constitutionalism' in C Rovira Kaltwasser, P Ochoa Espejo, P Taggart and P Ostiguy (eds), *The Oxford Handbook of Populism* (Oxford, Oxford University Press, 2017).

—— '"The People Must Be Extracted from Within the People": Reflections on Populism' (2014) 21 *Constellations* 483.

—— *What is Populism?* (London, Penguin, 2017).

Murkens, JEK, 'Judicious Review: The Constitutional Practice of the UK Supreme Court' (2018) 77 *Cambridge Law Journal* 349.

—— *From Empire to Union: Conceptions of German Constitutional Law since 1871* (Oxford, Oxford University Press, 2013).
Murray, R, 'The Article 50 Legal Challenge: Clarifying the UK's Constitutional Requirements to Start Brexit' in DJ Galligan (ed), *Constitution in Crisis: The New Putney Debates* (London, I.B. Tauris, 2017).
Neuman, GL (ed), *Human Rights in a Time of Populism: Challenges and Responses* (Cambridge, Cambridge University Press, 2020).
Nikoghosyan, H and Ter-Matevosyan, V, 'From "Revolution" to War: Deciphering Armenia's Populist Foreign Policy-Making Process' (2023) 23 *Southeast European and Black Sea Studies* 207.
Norris, P and Inglehart, R, *Cultural Backlash: Trump, Brexit, and Authoritarian Populism* (Cambridge, Cambridge University Press, 2019).
Norton, P, 'Parliament: The Best of Times, the Worst of Times?' in Sir J Jowell and C O'Cinneide (eds), *The Changing Constitution*, 9th edn (Oxford, Oxford University Press, 2019).
O'Brien, P, '"Enemies of the People": Judges, the Media and the Mythic Lord Chancellor' (2017) *Public Law* 135.
O'Donnell, G, 'Delegative Democracy' (1994) 5 *Journal of Democracy* 55.
Oakeshott, M, *The Politics of Faith and the Politics of Scepticism* (New Haven, Yale University Press, 1996).
Ochoa Espejo, P, 'Power to Whom? The People between Procedure and Populism' in C de la Torre (ed), *The Promise and Perils of Populism: Global Perspectives* (Lexington, University Press of Kentucky, 2014).
Ohanyan, A, 'Velvet Is Not a Colour' in L Broers and A Ohanyan (eds), *Armenia's Velvet Revolution: Authoritarian Decline and Civil Resistance in a Multipolar World* (London, I.B. Tauris, 2021).
Olsen, K, 'Reflexive Democracy as Popular Sovereignty' in B de Bruin and CF Zurn (eds), *New Waves in Political Philosophy* (London, Palgrave Macmillan, 2009).
Ost, F, *Le Temps du droit* (Paris, Odile Jacob, 1999).
Ostiguy, P, 'Populism: A Socio-Cultural Approach' in C Rovira Kaltwasser, P Ochoa Espejo, P Taggart and P Ostiguy (eds), *The Oxford Handbook of Populism* (Oxford, Oxford University Press, 2017).
Paine, T, *The Rights of Man* (London, J.S. Jordan, 1791).
Panizza, F, 'Introduction: Populism and the Mirror of Democracy' in F Panizza (ed), *Populism and the Mirror of Democracy* (London, Verso, 2005).
—— 'What is Contested and What Is Not in the Debate About Populism', paper presented at the LSE Graduate Conference on Populism (3 November 2017) (unpublished manuscript; on file with author).
Pappas, TS, 'Modern Populism: Research Advances, Conceptual and Methodological Pitfalls, and the Minimal Definition' (2016) *Oxford Research Encyclopedia of Politics*.
Parker, RD, '"Here, the People Rule": A Constitutional Populist Manifesto' (1993) 27 *Valparaiso University Law Review* 531.
Partlett, W, 'Post-Soviet Constitution Making' in D Landau and H Lerner (eds), *Comparative Constitution Making* (Cheltenham, Edward Elgar, 2019).
Partlett, W, *The Post-Soviet as Post-Colonial: A New Paradigm for Understanding Constitutional Dynamics in the Former Soviet Empire* (Cheltenham, Edward Elgar, 2022).
Pech, L and Scheppele, KL, 'Illiberalism Within: Rule of Law Backsliding in the EU' (2017) 19 *Cambridge Yearbook of European Legal Studies* 3.
Pech, L, Wachiowiec, P and Mazur, D. 'Poland's Rule of Law Breakdown: A Five-Year Assessment of EU's (In)Action' (2021) 13 *Hague Journal on the Rule of Law* 1.
Perkins, F, *The Roosevelt I Knew* (London, Penguin, 1946).
Peruzzotti, E, 'El populismo como ejercicio de poder gubernamental y la amenaza de hibradación de la democracia liberal' (2018) 11 *Revista SAAP* 213.
Peters, BG and Pierre, J, 'A Typology of Populism: Understanding the Different Forms of Populism and Their Implications' (2020) 27 *Democratization* 928.
Pin, A, 'The Transnational Drivers of Populist Backlash in Europe: The Role of Courts' (2019) *German Law Journal* 225.

Pinelli, C, 'The Rise of Populism and the Malaise of Democracy' in S Garben, I Govaere and P Nemitz (eds), *Critical Reflections on Constitutional Democracy in the European Union* (Oxford, Hart Publishing, 2019).

—— "The Populist Challenge to Constitutional Democracy" (2011) 7 *European Constitutional Law Review* 5.

Pitkin, HF, *The Concept of Representation* (Berkeley, University of California Press, 1972).

Poole, T, 'Time and Timelessness in Constitutional Thought' (2020) 27 *Res Publica* 255.

Popova, M and Beers, DJ, 'No Revolution of Dignity for Ukraine's Judges: Judicial Reform after the Euromaidan' (2020) 28 *Demokratizatsiya* 113.

Portalis, J-M-É, *Discours préliminaire du premier projet de Code civil* (Confluences, 2004 [1801]).

Posner, EA and Vermeule, A, *The Executive Unbound: After the Madisonian Republic* (Oxford, Oxford University Press, 2010).

Prado, MM and De Assis Machado, MR, 'Using Criminal Law to Fight Corruption: The Potential, Risks, and Limitations of Operation Car Wash (*Lava Jato*)' (2022) 69 *The American Journal of Comparative Law* 834.

—— 'Turning Corruption Trials into Political Tools in the Name of Transparency: The Lava Jato Case' in S Botero, DM Brinks and EA Gonzalez-Ocantos (eds), *The Limits of Judicialization: From Progress to Backlash in Latin America* (Cambridge, Cambridge University Press, 2022).

Prandini, R, 'The Future of Societal Constitutionalism in the Age of Acceleration' (2013) 20 *Indiana Journal of Global Legal Studies* 731.

Pratt, J and Clark, M, 'Penal Populism in New Zealand' (2005) 7 *Punishment and Society* 303.

Pratt, J, *Penal Populism* (Abingdon, Routledge, 2007).

Prendergast, D, 'The Judicial Role in Protecting Democracy from Populism' (2019) 20 *German Law Journal* 245.

Preuß, UK, 'Judicial Power in Processes of Transformation' in C Landfried (ed), *Judicial Power: How Constitutional Courts Affect Political Transformations* (Cambridge, Cambridge University Press, 2019).

Přibáň, J, *Legal Symbolism: On Law, Time and European Identity* (Abingdon, Routledge, 2007).

Proudhon, P-J, *Solution du problème social* in P-J Proudhon, *Œuvres complètes* (Paris, Marcel Rivière, 1929 [1884]).

Ranchordás, S and Roznai, Y (eds), *Time, Law, and Change: An Interdisciplinary Study* (Oxford, Hart Publishing, 2020).

Rancière, J, *La Haine de la démocratie* (Paris, La Fabrique, 2005).

Rawls, J, *Political Liberalism* (New York, Columbia University Press, 1996).

Raz, J, 'The Rule of Law and its Virtue' in J Raz, *The Authority of Law: Essays on Law and Morality* (Oxford, Clarendon, 1979).

Reed, R, 'Collective Judging in the UK Supreme Court' in B Häcker and W Ernest (eds), *Collective Judging in Comparative Perspective: Counting Votes and Weighing Opinions* (Cambridge, Intersentia, 2020).

Reyes, O, 'Skinhead Conservatism: A Failed Populist Project' in F Panizza (ed), *Populism and the Mirror of Democracy* (London, Verso, 2005).

Roberts, JV, Stalans, LJ, Indermaur, D and Hough, M, 'Introduction' in JV Roberts et al (eds), *Penal Populism and Public Opinion: Lessons from Five Countries* (Oxford, Oxford University Press, 2003).

Rodrik, D, 'Populism and the Economics of Globalization' (2017) 1 *Journal of International Business Policy* 12.

Rosa, H, 'Airports Built on Shifting Grounds? Social Acceleration and the Temporal Dimension of Law' in L Corrias and L Francot (eds), *Temporal Boundaries of Law and Politics: Time Out of Joint* (Abingdon, Routledge, 2018).

—— 'Social Acceleration: Ethical and Political Consequences of a Desynchronized High-Speed Society' (2003) 10 *Constellations* 3.

—— 'The Speed of Global Flows and the Pace of Democratic Politics' (2005) 27 *New Political Science* 445.

—— *Social Acceleration: A New Theory of Modernity* (New York, Columbia University Press, 2013).

Rosanvallon, P, *Counter-Democracy: Politics in an Age of Distrust* (trans A Goldhammer) (Cambridge, Cambridge University Press, 2018).

—— *Democracy Past and Future* (New York, Columbia University Press, 2006).

—— *Democratic Legitimacy: Impartiality, Reflexivity, Proximity* (translated by Arthur Goldhammer) (Princeton, Princeton University Press, 2011).

—— *La Légitimité démocratique : Impartialité, réflexivité, proximité* (Paris, Seuil, 2008).

—— *Le Peuple introuvable : Histoire de la représentation démocratique en France* (Paris, Gallimard, 1998).

—— *Le Siècle du populisme : Histoire, théorie, critique* (Paris, Seuil, 2020).

—— *Penser le populisme* in C Colliot-Thélène and F Guénard (eds), *Peuples et populisme* (Paris, Presses universitaires de France, 2014) 27.

Rosenfeld, S, *Democracy and Truth* (Philadelphia, University of Pennsylvania Press, 2018).

Rousseau, J-J, 'The Social Contract' in V Gourevitch (ed), *Rousseau: The Social Contract and Other Later Political Writings* (Cambridge, Cambridge University Press 1997 [1762]).

—— *On the Social Contract, or Principles of Political Right* in J-J Rousseau (ed), *The Basic Political Writings* (Indianapolis, Hackett, 1986 [1762]).

Rouvillois, F, *Le gouvernement des juges : Histoire d'un mythe politique* (Paris, Desclée de Brouwer, 2023).

Roux, T, *The Politico-Legal Dynamics of Judicial Review: A Comparative Analysis* (Cambridge, Cambridge University Press, 2018).

Rovira Kaltwasser, C, Ochoa Espejo, P, Taggart, P and Ostiguy, P (eds), *The Oxford Handbook of Populism* (Oxford, Oxford University Press, 2017).

Rovira Kaltwasser, C, 'Explaining the Emergence of Populism' in C de la Torre (ed), *The Promise and Perils of Populism: Global Perspectives* (Lexington, University Press of Kentucky, 2014).

—— 'Populism vs Constitutionalism? Comparative Perspectives on Contemporary Western Europe, Latin America, and the United States' (2013) Policy Brief, *The Foundation for Law, Justice and Society*.

Rozenberg, J, *Enemies of the People? How Judges Shape Society* (Bristol, Bristol University Press, 2020).

Roznai, Y, 'Who Will Save the Redheads? Anti-Bully Theory of Judicial Review and Protection of Democracy' (2020) 29 *William & Mary Bill of Rights Journal* 327.

—— *Unconstitutional Constitutional Amendments: The Limits of Amendment Powers* (Oxford, Oxford University Press, 2017).

Rubinelli, L, 'Democracy, Parliamentarism and the Referendum, 1890-1940' in C Meckstroth and S Moyn (eds), *The Cambridge History of Democracy* (Cambridge, Cambridge University Press, forthcoming).

Russo, L, 'Social Media and Democracy' in DJ Galligan (ed), *Constitution in Crisis: The New Putney Debates* (London, I.B. Tauris, 2017).

Ryan, M, 'Red Tops, Populists and the Irresistible Rise of the Public Voice' (2004) 1 *Journal for Crime, Conflict and the Media* 1é

Sadurski, W, *A Pandemic of Populists* (Cambridge, Cambridge University Press, 2022).

—— 'Constitutional Crisis in Poland' in MA Graber, S Levinson and M Tushnet (eds), *Constitutional Democracy in Crisis?* (Oxford, Oxford University Press, 2018).

—— 'How Democracy Dies (in Poland): A Case Study of Anti-Constitutional Populist Backsliding' (2018) Sydney Law School Research Paper No 18/01.

—— 'Judicial Review Versus Populist Authoritarianism' (2025) 3 *Comparative Constitutional Studies* 81.

—— *Poland's Constitutional Breakdown* (Oxford, Oxford University Press, 2019).

Sartori, G, 'Constitutionalism: A Preliminary Discussion' (1962) 56 *American Political Science Review* 853.

Scharpf, FW, 'The Asymmetry of European Integration, or Why the EU Cannot Be a "Social Market Economy"' (2010) 8 *Socio-Economic Review* 211.

Schauer, F, 'Comparative Constitutional Compliance: Notes Towards a Research Agenda' in M Adams and J Bomhoff (eds), *Practice and Theory in Comparative Law* (Cambridge, Cambridge University Press, 2012).

Scheppele, KL, '"We Forgot About the Ditches": Russian Constitutional Impatience and the Challenge of Terrorism' (2005) 53 *Duke Law Review* 963.
—— 'Autocratic Legalism' (2018) 85 *University of Chicago Law Review* 545.
—— 'Democracy by Judiciary. Or Why Courts Can Be More Democratic than Parliaments' in A Czarnota, M Krygier and W Sadurski (eds), *Rethinking the Rule of Law After Communism* (Budapest, CEU Press, 2005).
—— 'The Party's Over' in MA Graber, S Levinson and M Tushnet (eds), *Constitutional Democracy in Crisis?* (Oxford, Oxford University Press, 2018).
Scheuerman, WE, 'Donald Trump meets Carl Schmitt' (2019) 45 *Philosophy and Social Criticism* 1170.
—— 'Motorized Legislation? Statutes in an Age of Speed' (2002) 88 *ARSP: Archiv für Rechts- und Sozialphilosophie / Archives for Philosophy of Law and Social Philosophy* 379.
—— *Liberal Democracy and the Social Acceleration of Time* (Baltimore, Johns Hopkins University Press, 2004).
Schmitt, C, 'The Liberal Rule of Law' in AJ Jacobson and B Schlink (eds), *Weimar: A Jurisprudence of Crisis* (Berkeley, University of California Press, 2000 [1928]).
—— 'The Plight of European Jurisprudence' (trans GL Ulmen) (1990 [1943/44]) 83 *Telos* 35.
—— 'Une étude de droit constitutionnel comparé : L'évolution récente du problème des délégations législatives' (trans P Roubier and H Mankiewicz) in *Introduction à l'étude du droit comparé : Recueil d'études en l'honneur d'Édouard Lambert* (Paris, Sirey: LGDJ, 1938 [1936]).
—— *Constitutional Theory* (trans J Seitzer) (Durham, Duke University Press, 2008 [1928]).
—— *Die Diktatur* (Berlin, Duncker & Humblot, 1994 [1921]).
—— *Political Theology: Four Chapters on the Concept of Sovereignty* (trans G Schwab) (Chicago, University of Chicago Press, 2006 [1922]).
—— *The Concept of the Political: Expanded Edition* (trans G Schwab) (Chicago, University of Chicago Press, 2007 [1932]).
—— *The Crisis of Parliamentary Democracy* (Cambridge, MIT Press, 2000 [1923]).
—— *Verfassunglehre* (Berlin, Duncker & Humblot, 1928).
—— *Volksentscheid und Volksbegehren: Ein Beitrag zur Auslegung der Weimarer Verfassung und zur Lehre von der unmittelbaren* (Berlin, Walter de Gruyter, 1927).
Scholtes, J, 'Abusing Constitutional Identity' (2021) 22 *German Law Journal* 534.
—— 'The Complacency of Legality: Constitutionalist Vulnerabilities to Populist Constituent Power' (2019) 20 *German Law Journal* 351.
Schumpeter, JA, *Capitalism, Socialism and Democracy* (Abingdon, Routledge, 2003 [1942]).
Sethi, A, 'Towards a Pluralistic Conception of Judicial Role' (2021) 90 *UMKC Law Review* 69.
Shachar, A, *The Shifting Border: Legal Cartographies of Migration and Mobility* (Manchester, Manchester University Press, 2020).
Shapiro, M, *Courts* (Chicago, University of Chicago Press, 1981).
Sieyès, EJ (Abbé), 'Sur le projet de décret pour l'établissement de l'instruction nationale' (1793) 5 *Journal d'instruction sociale* (6 July).
—— *Qu'est-ce que le Tiers État?* (Paris, Éditions du Boucher, 2002 [1789]) / (Presses universitaires de France, 1982 [1789]).
Silverman, G, '¡Che Milei! Argentina, the Far Right, and the Politics of anti-Peronism' (2024) 20 *IERES Occasional Papers.*
Sinpeng, A, Gueorguiev, D and Aries A Aruguay, AA, 'Strong Fans, Weak Campaigns: Social Media and Duterte in the 2016 Philippine Election' (2020) 20 *Journal of East Asian Studies* 353.
Skinner, S, 'Fault Lines in the Rule of Law' (2024) 20 *International Journal of Law in Context* 133.
—— 'Identifying Dangers to Democracy: Fascism, the Rule of Law and the Relevance of History' in D Giannoulopoulos and Y McDermott (eds), *Judicial Independence Under Threat* (Oxford, Oxford University Press, 2022).
Sólyom, L, 'The Role of Constitutional Courts in the Transition to Democracy: With Special Reference to Hungary' (2003) 18 *International Sociology* 133.
Sorabji, R, 'The Royal Prerogative, Referendums and the Outcomes of Brexit' in DJ Galligan (ed), *Constitution in Crisis: The New Putney Debates* (London, I.B. Tauris, 2017).

Stanley, B, 'The Thin Ideology of Populism' (2008) 13 *Journal of Political Ideologies* 95.
Stavrakakis, Y and Jäger, A, 'Accomplishments and Limitations of the "New" Mainstream in Contemporary Populism Studies' (2018) 21 *European Journal of Social Theory* 547.
Stotzky, IP, 'A Democratic Vision' in IP Stotzky (ed), *Transition to Democracy in Latin America: The Role of the Judiciary* (Boulder, Westview, 1993).
—— 'The Tradition of Constitutional Adjudication' in IP Stotzky, *Transition to Democracy in Latin America: The Role of the Judiciary* (Boulder, Westview, 1993).
Sunstein, CR (ed), *Can It Happen Here? Authoritarianism in America* (New York, Dey St, 2018).
Svensson, S, Molnar, A and Batory, A, '(e-)Participation and Propaganda: The Mix of Old and New Techology in Hungarian National Consultations' in T Randma-Liiv and V Lember (eds), *Engaging Citizens in Policy Making: e-Participation Practices in Europe* (Cheltenham, Edward Elgar, 2022).
Taguieff, P-A, *L'illusion populiste: Essai sur les démagogies de l'âge démocratique* (Paris, Flammarion, 2007).
Tarragoni, F, *L'esprit démocratique du populisme* (Paris, La Découverte, 2019).
Taş, H, 'The Chronopolitics of National Populism' [2020] *Identities* 1.
Tew, Y, 'Stealth Theocracy' (2018) 58 *Virginia Journal of International Law* 31.
—— 'Strategic Judicial Empowerment' (2024) 72 *AJCL* 170.
Thompson, DJ, 'Democracy in Time: Popular Sovereignty and Temporal Representation' (2005) 12 *Constellations* 245.
Touraine, A, *The Voice and the Eye: An Analysis of Social Movements* (trans A Duff) (Cambridge, Cambridge University Press, 1981).
Tushnet, M, and Bugarič, B, *Power to the People: Constitutionalism in the Age of Populism* (Oxford, Oxford University Press, 2022).
Tushnet, M, 'After the Heroes Have Left the Scene: Temporality in the Study of Constitutional Court Judges' in C Landfried (ed), *Judicial Power: How Constitutional Courts Affect Political Transformations* (Cambridge, Cambridge University Press, 2019).
—— 'Varieties of Populism' (2019) 20 *German Law Journal* 382.
—— *Taking Back the Constitution: Activist Judges and the Next Age of American Law* (New Haven, Yale University Press, 2020).
—— *Taking the Constitution Away from the Courts* (Princeton, Princeton University Press, 2000).
Urbinati, N, 'A Revolt Against Intermediary Bodies' (2015) 22 *Constellations* 477.
—— 'Antiestablishment and the Substitution of the Whole with One of its Parts' in C de la Torre (ed), *Routledge Handbook of Global Populism* (Abingdon, Routledge, 2019).
—— 'Democracy and Populism' (1998) 5 *Constellations* 110.
—— 'Political Theory of Populism' (2019) 22 *Annual Review of Political Science* 111.
—— 'Populism and the Majority Principle' in C Rovira Kaltwasser, P Ochoa Espejo, P Taggart and P Ostiguy (eds), *The Oxford Handbook of Populism* (Oxford, Oxford University Press, 2017).
—— *Democracy Disfigured: Opinion, Truth and the People* (Cambridge, Harvard University Press, 2014).
—— *Me, The People: How Populism Transforms Democracy* (Cambridge, Harvard University Press, 2019).
Urfalino, P, 'Un nouveau décisionnisme politique : La philosophie du populisme de gauche' (2019) 82 *Archives de philosophie : recherches et documentation* 291.
Vallet, É (ed), *Borders, Fences and Walls: State of Insecurity?* (Abingdon, Routledge, 2016).
Valverde, M, '"Time Thickens, Takes On Flesh": Spatiotemporal Dynamics in Law' in I Braverman, N Blomley, D Delaney and A Kedar (eds), *The Expanding Spaces of Law: A Timely Legal Geography* (Redwood, Stanford University Press, 2014).
—— 'Forms of Veridiction in Politics and Culture: Avowal in Today's Jargon of Authenticity' (2018) 11 *Behemoth* 96.
—— *Chronotopes of Law: Jurisdiction, Scale and Governance* (Abingdon, Routledge, 2015).
van Houtum, H and Naerssen, TV, 'Bordering, Ordering and Othering' (2002) 93 *Tijdschrift voor economische en sociale geografie* 125.
van Klink, B, 'Law at the Right Time: A Plea for Slow Law in Hasty Times' in L Corrias and L Francot (EDS), *Temporal Boundaries of Law and Politics: Time Out of Joint* (Abingdon, Routledge, 2018).

van der Tang, G and van Maarseveen, H, *Written Constitutions: A Computerized Comparative Study* (Dobbs Ferry, Oceana, 1978).
Varol, OO, 'Stealth Authoritarianism in Turkey' in MA Graber, S Levinson and M Tushnet (eds), *Constitutional Democracy in Crisis?* (Oxford, Oxford University Press, 2018).
—— 'Stealth Authoritarianism' (2015) 100 *Iowa Law Review* 1673.
Versteeg, M et al, 'The Law and Politics of Presidential Term Limit Evasion' (2020) 120 *Columbia Law Review* 173.
Vinx, L, 'Carl Schmitt on the Limits of Direct Democracy' (2021) 42 *History of Political Thought* 157.
Virilio, P, *Le Futurisme de l'instant : Stop-Eject* (Paris, Galilée, 2009).
—— *Speed and Politics* (trans Mark Polizzotti) (Los Angeles, Semiotext(e), 2006 [1977]).
Vitale, D, and Girard, R, 'Public Trust and the Populist Leader: A Theoretical Argument' (2022) 11 *Global Constitutionalism* 548.
Volcansek, ML, 'Judicialization of Politics or Politicization of Courts in New Democracies?' in C Landfried (ed), *Judicial Power: How Constitutional Courts Affect Political Transformations* (Cambridge, Cambridge University Press, 2019).
Volpp, L, 'Imaginings of Space in Immigration Law' (2012) 9 *Law, Culture & the Humanities* 456.
Waldron, J, 'Bicameralism and the Separation of Powers' in J Waldron (ed), *Political Political Theory: Essays on Institutions* (Cambridge, Harvard University Press, 2016).
—— 'Constitutionalism: A Skeptical View' in J Waldron (ed), *Political Political Theory: Essays on Institutions* (Cambridge, Harvard University Press, 2016).
—— 'Rule-of-Law Rights and Populist Impatience' in GL Neuman (ed), *Human Rights in a Time of Populism* (Cambridge, Cambridge University Press, 2020).
Walker, N, 'Out of Place and Out of Time: Law's Fading Co-ordinates' (2010) 14 *Edinburgh Law Review* 13.
—— 'Populism and Constitutional Tension' (2019) 17 *International Journal of Constitutional Law* 515.
Weale, A, *The Will of the People: A Modern Myth* (Cambridge, Polity, 2018).
Weyland, K, 'Clarifying a Contested Concept: Populism in the Study of Latin American Politics' (2001) 34 *Comparative Politics* 1.
—— 'Latin America's Authoritarian Drift: The Threat from the Populist Left' (2013) 24 *Journal of Democracy* 18.
Wistrich, AJ, 'The Evolving Temporality of Lawmaking' (2012) 44 *Connecticut Law Review* 737.
Wolkenstein, F, 'What is Democratic Backsliding?' (2022) 30 *Constellations* 261.
Yamunaque, P, Mabel, D, 'El error inexcusable y la independencia judicial interna' (2016) (unpublished Master's thesis, Universidad Andina Simón Bolivar).
Young, AL, 'Populism and the UK Constitution' (2018) 71 *Current Legal Problems* 17.
—— 'Are Prerogative Powers Necessary in the Twenty-First Century?' in DJ Galligan (ed), *Constitution in Crisis: The New Putney Debates* (London, I.B. Tauris, 2017).
Zakaria, F, 'The Rise of Illiberal Democracy' (1996) 76 *Foreign Affairs* 22.
—— *The Future of Freedom: Illiberal Democracy at Home and Abroad* (New York, Norton, 2007 [2004]).
Žižek, S, 'Against the Populist Temptation' (2006) 32 *Critical Inquiry* 551.
Zolyan, M, 'Thirty Years of Protest: How Armenia's Legacy of Political and Civic Protests Prepared the Velvet Revolution' in L Broers and A Ohanyan (eds), *Armenia's Velvet Revolution: Authoritarian Decline and Civil Resistance* (London, I.B. Tauris, 2021).
Zürn, M, 'How Non-Majoritarian Institutions Make Silent Majorities Vocal: A Popular Explanation of Authoritarian Populism' (2022) 20 *Perspectives on Politics* 788.

INDEX

accountability:
accountability of courts and judges, 83, 88, 151–52
executive aggrandisement, 230–33
political accountability, 98, 109, 210–11, 227–28, 230–33
Brexit, 230–33
politics over law, 74–75
reduced horizontal accountability, 126–27, 182
'unaccountable institutions', 66–67, 68, 94, 96, 100–1, 118–19, 259–60
American Revolutionary War (1775–1783), 62–63
anti-corruption measures, 86–87, 141, 146, 147, 149, 152, 161–62, 169–72, 173–74, 177, 258
anti-institutionalism, 14–15, 72, 99, 105–6, 115, 119–21, 130–32, 245–46
Arendt, Hannah, 176
Argentina, 1, 53, 106, 113, 159
Armenia (Velvet Revolution, 2018), 15–16, 173–78
background, 138–41
constitutional impatience, 141–42
opposition, in, 142–45
power, in, 145–47
democratisation, 169–73
forms of populism
authoritarian populism, 159–63, 165, 168
democracy-enhancing populism, 159–63, 168
revolutionary populism, 160–61, 164–65, 168
judicial deceleration, 156–59, 177–78
judicial reform, 147–54
Chairperson of the Constitutional Court, 154–56
see also Pashinyan, Nikol
authenticity and similarity, 29, 92–94, 123–25, 129, 133–34, 250–51
appeals to, 101–6, 248–49
empty place of power, 228–29
identity-based claims to authenticity, 101, 121–22, 134, 251
immediacy, 104, 106–10
populist conception of representation, 101–6
similarity-based claims to authenticity, 101, 143, 234–35, 249
authoritarian legalism, 204–6
authoritarian populism, 4, 11, 116, 159–63, 165, 168, 175–76, 209–10, 256
constitutional authoritarian populism, 157–59, 203

Babiš, Andrej, 1
'basic structure' doctrine, 233–34
Bardella, Jordan, 97,
Berlusconi, Silvio, 107, 113, 143
bias:
confirmation bias, 13
general will, relationship with, 110
selection bias, 13–14
Bolivia, 1, 14, 50, 53, 127, 179, 182, 194, 203
Bolsonaro, Jair, 87, 96–97, 108
Bourdieu, Pierre, 45, 122
Brazil, 86–87, 97, 108,
Brexit referendum (2016), 16, 212–14, 245–47
courts as democratic educators, 243–45
distrust of intermediaries, 222
empty place of power, 228–30
executive aggrandisement, 230–33
executive – judiciary relationship, 234–42
institutional independence, 242–43
judicial review, 238–39
Miller (no 1) case, 223–24
Miller (no 2)/Cherry case, 225–33
parliamentary sovereignty versus popular sovereignty, 219–20
political accountability, 230–33
prorogation of Parliament, 215, 225–26, 226–28
public reception of judgments, 234–37
Royal Prerogative, 212, 215, 222
separation of powers, 227, 242–43

sovereign people discourse, 220–21
spatial proximity of democratic representation, 220–22
Supreme Court rulings, 214–15, 223–33
temporal efficiency of democratic representation, 220
Bucaram, Abdalá, 101–2, 103
Bukele, Nayib, 103, 158, 203

Canada, 36, 37, 38, 103, 197
Carre de Malberg, Raymond, 70
Chávez, Hugo, 50, 53, 60, 102, 111, 175–76, 182
constituent power, 78
telepopulism, 107
checks and balances, 75, 83, 157–58, 168, 169, 184–85, 187, 199, 208–9
Colombia, 9–10, 106–7, 186
constituted power, 63, 77–78, 120
see also pouvoir constitué and *pouvoir constituant*
constituent power, 2, 45–46, 58, 63–64, 74, 75–77, 156, 202, 209–10, 249
constitutions under populism, 77–80
see also pouvoir constitué and *pouvoir constituant*
constitutional amendment, 9–10, 120–21, 124–25, 132, 138, 152–56, 157, 166–67, 195–96
constitutional authority, 79, 158–59
populism and popular constitutionalism compared, 80–84
Constitutional Courts:
Armenia
Chairperson of the Constitutional Court, 154–56
judicial reform, 147–54
Ecuador, 194–95
interim Constitutional Court, 195–98
state of exception in the judicial branch, 198–200
term limits, 200–4
constitutional impatience, 37, 250–51, 262
Brexit (UK), 214–15, 215–16, 220–21, 233–34, 242
empty place of power, 228–30
executive aggrandisement, 230–31, 233, 245–47
Correa (Ecuador), 179–80, 187–88, 194–95, 200, 208
judiciary deceleration role, 251–54, 255, 256–57
judiciary, weakening of, 187–88, 194–95, 200, 208
oversimplification of democracy, 129–33
simultaneity and occupation, 123–29
Pashinyan (Armenia), 141–47
spatial proximity and immediacy, 121
oversimplification, simultaneity and occupation, 123–29
representative democracy, 122–23
see also hegemonic occupation of the empty place of power
temporal instantaneity and decisionism, 121–22
constitutional interpretation, 20–21, 37, 79, 130–31, 149, 155, 194–95
constitutional replacement, 196–97
constitutional timelessness, 67, 72–74, 78
pouvoir constituant, 75–77
primacy of politics over law, 74–75
constitutionalism and populism, relationship between, 88–90
constraints:
checks and balances, 75, 83, 157–58, 168, 169, 184–85, 187, 199, 208–9
freedom from external constraints, 59–60, 77–78
power of the executive, 39, 75, 158–59, 194
Correa, Rafael, 5, 14, 16, 50, 179–80, 208–11
constitutional impatience, 179–80, 181, 187–88, 194–95, 200, 208
Citizen's Revolution, 181–85
legal symbolism, 187
spatial proximity of democratic representation, 185–86
temporal efficiency of democratic representation, 186–87
constituent power, 78
executive consolidation, 194–206
executive aggrandisement, 206–8
judicial capture, 187–93
telepopulism, 107
see also Ecuador
coronavirus:
emergency powers, 116, 168, 222, 232–33
corruption, *see* **anti-corruption measures**
Council of Europe:
European Commission for Democracy through Law, 149–50

counter-majoritarianism, 63–64, 88–89, 91, 180, 251–52, 259
courts:
accountability of courts and judges, 83, 88, 151–52
democracy-enhancing institutional decelerators, as, 4, 6–7, 8, 12, 27–28, 159, 216, 243–44, 251, 258, 261–62
democratic erosion, as barrier against, 10–11, 156–57, 260–62
perception of courts, 36–37, 38–39
UK's Brexit referendum, 16, 212–14, 245–47
courts as democratic educators, 243–45
Supreme Court Brexit rulings, 214–15, 223–33
courts as institutional stabilisers, 215–20, 233–41
Brexit referendum, 217, 218–19
political pressure, 237–41
referendums generally, 217–20
US Supreme Court
originalism, 36–37
weakening of, 1–4, 80–84
see also Constitutional Courts; judiciary
Covid-19, *see* **coronavirus**
cronyism, 127–28, 141
Czechia, 1

democratic degradation, 10, 86–87
democracy-enhancing institutional decelerators:
courts/judiciary as, 4, 6–7, 8, 12, 27–28, 159, 216, 243–44, 251, 258, 261–62
democracy-enhancing populism, 159–63, 168
Ecuador, 16
democratic backsliding, 4, 7–8, 10–11, 12, 20, 171, 206
democratic decline, 10–11, 13
democratic dysfunction, 7, 116–17
democratic erosion, 8, 10–11, 14–15, 20, 174, 203–4, 210, 233–34, 237–38, 253–54
democratic self-rule, 27, 65, 67, 77–78, 91
'democracy' concept, 24–25
Dicey, Albert V, 70, 217–18, 219–20
direct democracy, 110, 132–33, 145–46, 207, 219, 250
referendums, 67, 68–72, 127
dromology, 28
Duterte, Rodrigo, 53–54, 85–86, 104, 108, 131–32, 174, 242
Dworkin, Ronald, 36–37

Ecuador, 208–11
authoritarian legalism, 204–6
Citizen's Revolution (2007–2017), 16, 179–84
2008 Constitution, 184–85
constitutional amendment, 195–96
Constitutional Court, 194–95
interim Constitutional Court, 195–98
state of exception in the judicial branch, 198–200
term limits, 200–4
constitutional replacement, 196
control of judiciary, 187–88, 192–93
judicial discipline and sanctions, 190–92
judicial reform, 189–90
removal of judges, 188
replacement with regime-approved judges, 189
executive aggrandisement, 206–8
hyperpresidentialism, 184–85
judicial review, 204–6
legal symbolism, 187
partial reform, 196
Qualification of the Referendum Questions judgment, 195–98
revolutionary populism, 204–5
spatial proximity of democratic representation, 185–86
State of Exception in the Judicial Branch judgment, 198–200
temporal efficiency of democratic representation, 186–87
Term Limits judgment, 200–4
see also Correa, Rafael
emergency powers, 116–17, 212–13
Erdoğan, Recep Tayyip, 1, 49, 114, 210–11
constituent power, 78
empty place of power, 124–25
judicial/institutional capture, 192–93
seizing democratic spaces, 124–25
social media, 108
temporal references to Ottoman era, 111
El Salvador, 49, 86, 103, 158, 174, 203,
European Court of Human Rights (ECtHR), 149, 155–56, 167–68

executive aggrandisement, 7, 9–10, 17
  Brexit, 214, 245–47
    accountability, 230–33
  Ecuador, 178, 180, 210–11
    judicial capture, relationship with, 206–8
executive prerogative, 34, 115–19, 205, 212–13
executive, 34–36
executive – judiciary relationship, 234–42
'executivisation' of political power, 131, 190, 233–34, 245, 250
expeditious and responsive executives, 34–36, 250–51

Farage, Nigel, 49, 213
Fico, Robert, 1, 242
Fidesz, 1, 13, 78, 112, 175, 193, 256
France, 19, 20, 53, 58, 62, 69, 76, 97, 114, 122, 128, 261
France Insoumise, La, 53, 69, 114
Ford, Rob, 103
freedom from external constraints, 77–78
  see also constraints
Fujimori, Alberto, 16, 53
future-orientated executive, 111–12, 115–16
future-orientated judiciary, 36–37
future-orientated legislatures, 30–34, 35

Gaitán, Jorge Eliécer, 106
general will theory, 21, 48, 59–61, 99, 110
Georgescu, Călin, 260–261
Greece, 14, 23, 53, 142, 157, 160

Hamilton, Alexander, 31, 34–35, 105, 131
hegemonic occupation of the empty place of power, 123–24, 128–29
  Brexit, 228–30
  cronyism, 127–28
  plebiscitary instruments, use of, 127
  political space as highly dichotomised us – them, 125–26
  reduced horizontal accountability, 126–27
  seizing democratic spaces, 124–25
human rights, 38, 149–50, 238–39
Hungary, 1, 8, 9, 13–14, 15, 53–54, 55, 71, 78–79, 96, 112, 125, 127, 152, 175, 188, 192, 193, 194, 237, 242, 256, 262
hyperpresidentialism, 184–85, 193, 200, 210

ideal-typical populist discourse, 43–44, 64–65, 254–55
  'the People'
    ambiguity, 44–47
    otherness, 52–57
    the People as unity, 48–52
  'the People'/the nation as the ultimate (and only) holder of sovereignty, 57
    populist conception of sovereignty, 57–59
    general will theory, 59–61
    Rousseauian sovereignty, 59–61
    'the People' institutionalised as a sovereign, 61–64
identity-based claims to authenticity, 101, 121–22, 134, 251
identity-identification between rulers and ruled, 105–6, 123–24
illiberalism, 7, 12, 253
immediacy of popular sovereignty, 27, 39, 92–94, 115, 120, 251
  constitutional impatience, 121–22, 123, 131–33, 133–34
  Ecuador, 181, 209–10
  UK, 213–14
  unmediated and spontaneous populist use of social spaces (social media), 106–10
  see also constitutional patience; temporal efficiency of democratic representation
independence and impartiality of the judiciary, 37–38, 81, 88, 97–98, 255–56
  Armenia, 154–56, 158–59, 162, 164, 167, 171–73
    mass removal, 152–54
    undermining through vetting, 149–52
  Ecuador, 197, 242–43
  UK, 211, 218, 234, 238–39, 242–43, 254, 255–56, 257
India, 10, 49–50, 101–3, 107, 119–20, 210–11
individual autonomy, 255–56
inexcusable error doctrine, 190–91, 194, 208
institutional independence, *see* **independence and impartiality of the judiciary**
institutionalising 'the' People as sovereign, 61–64
interpretation, *see* **constitutional interpretation**

Ireland:
Constitution of Ireland, 66, 70
Israel, 1–2, 10, 12, 87–88, 96–97, 104
Italy, 1, 99, 105, 107, 233

Jackson, Andrew, 20
Johnson, Boris, 102–3, 213, 221–22
prorogation of Parliament, 225–26
judicial deceleration:
Armenia, 156–59, 177–78
constitutional impatience, 251–54, 255, 256–59
Ecuador, 179–80, 194–95
judicial review:
Brexit, 238–39
Ecuador, 204–6
judiciary, 36–37
Armenia
early retirement incentives, 152–53
forced removal of, 153–54
political control of, 147–68
removal of judges, 153–54
replacement with regime-approved judges, 154–56
Venice Commission, 149–50, 151, 152
vetting, 149–50
attacks on legitimacy of the judiciary, 97–98
bypassing of, 120
democracy-enhancing decelerators, as, 4, 6–7, 8, 12, 27–28, 159, 216, 243–44, 251, 258, 261–62
Ecuador, 187–88, 192–93
judicial discipline and sanctions, 190–92
judicial reform, 189–90
removal of judges, 188
replacement with regime-approved judges, 189
independence and a presumption of impartiality, 37–38, 81, 88, 97–98, 255–56
Armenia, 152–56, 158–59, 162, 164, 167, 171–73
Ecuador, 197, 242–43
mass removal, 152–54
UK, 211, 218, 234, 238–39, 242–43, 254, 255–56, 257
undermining through vetting, 149–52
perception of courts, 38–39
slowness of judicial procedures, 38–39
UK's Brexit referendum, 16, 212–14, 245–47
courts as democratic educators, 243–45
Supreme Court Brexit rulings, 214–15, 223–33
courts as institutional stabilisers, 215–20, 233–41
Brexit referendum, 217, 218–19
political pressure, 237–41
referendums generally, 217–20
US Supreme Court
originalism, 36–37
judicial supremacy, 11
populist criticism of, 80–81, 82–83

Kramer, Larry D, 11, 81–82

Law and Justice Party (Poland) (*Prawo i Sprawiedliwość*, PiS), 13, 193, 210, 260,
Le Pen, Jean-Marie, 69
Le Pen, Marine, 97
legal certainty, 149
legislatures:
future-orientated legislatures, 30–34, 35
separation of powers, 30–33
slowness of legislatures, 31–32
weakening of, 1–4, 119–20
legitimacy, 44, 47, 72, 76, 123, 228–29
democratic legitimacy, 36, 165, 180, 231, 239–40
legitimacy of courts, 88, 97–98, 251–52
Armenia, 147, 148–49, 151–52, 155
Ecuador, 198
UK, 218–19
'liberal constitutional democracy' concept, 24–25, 63
separation of powers, 29–30
executive, 34–36
judiciary, 36–39
legislatures, 30–33
Locke, John, 30–31, 34, 117, 131, 212–13

McCarthy, Joseph, 54
majoritarianism, 11, 63–64, 67, 69, 74, 83, 88–89, 91, 180, 249, 251–52, 259
Malaysia, 14
Marat, Jean-Paul, 20
Maréchal, Marion, 97
media, *see* **press and media**
mediation, institutional mediators and intermediary media:
removal/distrust of, 106–10
Brexit referendum, 222
Mélenchon, Jean-Luc, 69, 76, 113–14
Meloni, Giorgia, 1
Menem, Carlos, 16, 53

Milei, Javier, 1, 113
Mill, John Stuart, 131
***Miller (no 1)* case,** 223–24
***Miller (no 2)/Cherry* case,** 225–33
Modi, Narendra, 1, 49–50, 101, 107, 119–20
monism, 48–52
Montesquieu, 131–32
Morales, Evo, 14, 50, 53, 182, 194, 203
Musk, Elon, 80, 97, 261

Napoléon III, 20, 95, 128,
Narodnik movement, 19
nostalgic utopianism, 111–12

Ocasio-Cortez, Alexandria, 160
occupation, *see* **hegemonic occupation of the empty place of power**
omnipresent executives, 34, 36
one-partyism of US, 68–69
Orbán, Viktor, 1, 53–54, 71, 96–97
 borders, 125
 constituent power, 78
 nostalgic utopianism, 112
 political space as highly dichotomised us – them, 125–26
ordinary constitutional amendments, 195–96, 201
originalism, 36–37
'otherness', 52–57, 134, 251
 political space as highly dichotomised us – them, 121–22, 126, 129

partial reform, 196
Pashinyan, Nikol, 138–41
 constitutional impatience, 141–42
  opposition, in, 142–45
  leader, as, 145–47
 see also Armenia
past-orientated judiciaries, 36–39
penal populism, 60, 84–88, 189–90
Perón, Juan, 159, 174
Peru, 16, 53, 76, 161
Philippines, 14, 53–54, 85–86, 104, 108, 131–32, 174, 192, 242
plebiscitarianism, *see* **referendums**
Podemos, 23, 48, 53, 142
Poland, 8, 13, 14, 15, 74, 82, 97, 119, 125, 129, 152, 175, 176, 188, 192, 193, 194, 208, 210, 237, 242, 256, 260
'politics of faith', 89–90, 99
'populism' concept, 21–23
 popular constitutionalism compared, 80–84
populist authoritarianism, 7, 12, 253
populist punitiveness, 84–88
***populus legibus solutus est*,** 58, 64–65
***pouvoir constitué* and *pouvoir constituant*,** 67
 constituent power, 2, 45–46, 58, 63–64, 74, 75–77, 156, 202, 209–10, 249
 constituted power, 63, 77–78, 120
 constitutional timelessness, 75–77
 constitutions under populism, 77–80
press and media:
 public trust in media, 98–100
 social media and immediacy, 106–10
prorogation of Parliament, 215, 225–26, 226–28
Proudhon, Pierre-Joseph, 61–62
public trust in courts, 81, 88
public trust in media, 98–99

***Rassemblement National*,** 97
referendums, 67, 68–72, 127, 146
 politics of instantaneity, 115–21, 127
 UK's Brexit referendum, *see* Brexit referendum (2016)
 see also direct democracy
removal of judges:
 Armenia, 153–54
 Ecuador, 188
representation, 2–3, 123–25, 249
 proximity through identity and similarity, 101–6
 see also spatial proximity of democratic representation; temporal efficiency of democratic representation
restorative justice, 147
revolutionary populism, 160–61, 164–65, 168
rise of populism, 1–2, 12–13, 126–27, 231–32, 245–47
Romania, 97, 260–261,
Roosevelt, Franklin Delano, 106–107, 116, 119,
Rousseau, Jean-Jacques:
 Rousseauian sovereignty, 59–61
 volonté générale (general will theory), 59–61
Royal Prerogative, 212, 215, 222, 223, 226, 238
rule of law, 12, 24, 30–31, 36, 68, 74–75, 96–98, 116–17, 131–32, 146–47, 150, 170, 176–77, 201, 224, 234, 236, 241, 254–55

Saied, Kais, 78, 169
Saint-Just, 20
Salvini, Matteo, 97

Sanders, Bernie, 23, 160
Schmitt, Carl, 32–33
general will of 'the People', 59–60
Volksentscheide and *Volksbegehren*, 70–71
Second Nagorno-Karabakh War (2020), 169
separation of powers, 29–30, 82, 121–22, 251–52, 253
Armenia, 174
Ecuador, 199, 201
executive, 34–36
judiciary, 36–39
legislatures, 30–33
UK (Brexit), 227, 242–43, 246–47
similarity-based claims to authenticity, 101, 143, 234–35, 249
Slovakia, 1, 14, 242
slowness of legislatures, 31–32
social acceleration, 2–3, 27–30, 32–33, 35, 39, 92–94, 106, 120–22, 133, 212–14, 249–50, 251–54
social media, 103–4, 106–10, 118, 144
socio-cultural approach to populism, 103–4
'sovereign people' concept, 43–44
ambiguities, 44–47
general will concept, 59–61
institutionalising 'the People' as sovereign, 61–64
monism, 48–52
'otherness', 52–57
unity of 'the People', 48–52
ultimate (and only) holder of sovereignty, as, 57
populist conception of sovereignty, 57–59
Rousseauian sovereignty, 59–61
Schmittian sovereignty, 59–60
Spain, 23, 48, 53, 142
spatial proximity of democratic representation, 250–51
Armenia, 145
Ecuador, 185–86
immediacy of popular sovereignty, 67, 94, 104–5, 106–10
mediation, institutional mediators and intermediary media
removal of, 106–10
populist critique of liberal democratic elite, 94
physical distance, 94–95
symbolic distance, 95–100
populist reorganisation of space, 100–1
representation and proximity through identity and similarity, 101–6
social media and immediacy, 106–10
spatiotemporality of populism, 2–3, 25–27, 93
see also spatial proximity of democratic representation; temporal efficiency of democratic representation
***stare decisis* doctrine,** 255–56
state of exception, 116–17, 194–95, 198–200
Syriza, 14, 23, 53, 142, 157, 160

temporal efficiency of democratic representation, 110–11, 250–51
anti-institutionalism, 115
Armenia, 137, 141–47
collapse of populist temporal efficiency, 114–15
constitutional timelessness, 67, 72–74
pouvoir constituant, 75–77
primacy of politics over law, 74–75
Ecuador, 186–87
politics of instantaneity, 115–16
constitutional amendment, 120–21
executive prerogative, 116–19
judiciary, bypassing of, 120
legislative activity, 119–20
primacy of politics over law, 74–75
checks and balances, 75
democratic accountability, 75
populist rejection of liberal order, 74–75
urgency and expeditiousness, 111–13
third wave democracies, 8–9
transitional democracies, 11–12, 167–68
transitional justice, 147, 149–50, 156–57, 165, 175
Trump, Donald, 47, 49, 54, 68–69, 112–14, 257, 261
anti-institutionalism, 120
populist conception of representation, 102, 104
removal of judges, 80, 85–86
social media, 104, 108
state of emergency narrative, 117–20
travel ban, 125
truth, fluidity of, 83, 100, 103–4, 118–19, 123, 148, 238
Tsipras, Alexis, 23
Tunisia, 78, 169
Türkiye, 1, 8, 49, 54, 79, 108, 114, 124–125, 126, 192–193, 194, 206, 210, 233, 237, 244, 260, 262

Ukraine, 173, 258–59
ultimate (and only) holder of sovereignty, as, 57
populist conception of sovereignty, 57–59
Rousseauian sovereignty, 59–61
Schmittian sovereignty, 59–60
unconstitutional constitutional amendment, 253–54
United Kingdom:
courts as institutional stabilisers, 215–16, 233–37
Brexit referendum, 217, 218–19
political pressure, 237–41
referendums generally, 217–20
see also Brexit referendum (2016)
United States:
politics of faith, 99–100
Supreme Court's originalism, 36–37
Trump, 47, 49, 54, 68–69, 112–14, 257, 261
anti-institutionalism, 120
populist conception of representation, 102, 104
removal of judges, 80, 85–86
social media, 104, 108
state of emergency narrative, 117–20
travel ban, 125

unity of 'the People', 48–52
Uribe, Álvaro

Vance, JD, 54
Velasco Ibarra, Jose Maria, 102
Venezuela, 8, 50, 53, 76, 102, 127, 161, 175, 179, 182, 188, 191, 238,
volonté générale, 21, 48, 59–61, 99, 110

Waldron, Jeremy, 63, 131–32
Widodo, Joko, 103
Wilders, Geert, 97

Zelensky, Volodymyr, 258–59

www.ingramcontent.com/pod-product-compliance
Ingram Content Group UK Ltd.
Pitfield, Milton Keynes, MK11 3LW, UK
UKHW021120030526
470610UK00004B/151

9 781509 987542